Winston Churchill,
Myth and Reality

Winston Churchill, Myth and Reality

What He Actually Did and Said

RICHARD M. LANGWORTH

McFarland & Company, Inc., Publishers

Jefferson, North Carolina

To Hillsdale College,
pursuing truth and defending liberty since 1844
and
The Hillsdale College Churchill Project,
pursuing truth in Churchill studies since 2006

The present work is a reprint of the illustrated case bound edition of Winston Churchill, Myth and Reality: What He Actually Did and Said, first published in 2017 by McFarland.

Frontispiece: "Winston's Bag: He Hunts Lions and Brings Home Decayed Cats," cartoon by David Low in *The Star*, 21 January 1920. Low's mythical dead cats are Sidney Street (Chapter 7 herein), Antwerp (Chapter 11), Gallipoli (Chapter 12) and Russia (Chapter 17).

LIBRARY OF CONGRESS CATALOGUING-IN-PUBLICATION DATA

Names: Langworth, Richard M., author.
Title: Winston Churchill, myth and reality : what he actually did and said / Richard M. Langworth.
Description: Jefferson, North Carolina : McFarland & Company, 2017. | Includes bibliographical references and index.
Identifiers: LCCN 2017007625 | ISBN 9781476665832 (softcover : acid free paper) ∞
Subjects: LCSH: Churchill, Winston, 1874–1965. | Great Britain—Politics and government—20th century. | Prime ministers—Great Britain—Biography. | Statesmen—Great Britain—Biography. | Politicians—Great Britain—Biography.
Classification: LCC DA566.9.C5 L29 2017 | DDC 941.084092 [B] —dc23
LC record available at https://lccn.loc.gov/2017007625

BRITISH LIBRARY CATALOGUING DATA ARE AVAILABLE

ISBN (print) 978-1-4766-7460-5
ISBN (ebook) 978-1-4766-2878-3

Front cover: Winston Churchill (Library of Congress)

Printed in the United States of America

McFarland & Company, Inc., Publishers
Box 611, Jefferson, North Carolina 28640
www.mcfarlandpub.com

Table of Contents

Preface

The Challenge

Not a day passes when Winston Churchill, who proved himself indispensable when liberty hung in the balance, is not accused of something unfortunate, from alcoholism to xenophobia. Frequently there is no attempt to substantiate the charges. Lack of attribution, selective quotes cropped so as to advance preconceived notions, and repetitious canards are features of this busy industry.

A common approach is first to set up Churchill as the man who saved the West in 1940, when nobody else was available—then to tear him down with a familiar litany of charges: his supposed unconcern for other people; his penchant for chemical warfare; his enthusiasm for interning refugees; the rude things he said about Gandhi or Jews or votes for women; his disdain for the uncivilized, meaning people of color. According to two books, one recent, he was even responsible for the sinking of the *Titanic* and the *Lusitania*. On that electronic Speaker's Corner we know as the Internet, Churchill simmers in a gurgling, digital soup, his sins and errors stewing around him. Here is a morsel: he knew about Pearl Harbor before it happened and did not tell. Another: he plotted the 1929 Wall Street Crash!

The assault takes two forms, personal and political. The personal include charges that he was school dunce, a failure in his marriage, a warmonger, a narcissist who cared for no one but himself. Then there are the claims about his parents: Lord Randolph died of syphilis; Lady Randolph slept with 200 men, one of whom was the real father of Winston's brother Jack. Policy critiques range from what he did—military adventures like Antwerp and the Dardanelles—to what he didn't do—not bombing Auschwitz, not feeding occupied Europe, not stopping the Bengal famine.

Where some historians get their ideas about Churchill is beyond me. An academic active in the field recently stated that Sir Winston hated the Conservative Party. How could anyone get such an idea? Churchill served that party for most of his life, led it during his decisive and final years, and chose his successors. Someone said history doesn't repeat itself, historians just repeat each other—but this particular claim was new to me. All the more astonishing, it was uttered during a meeting of organizations devoted to Churchill's legacy.

The Lincoln and Churchill scholar Harry Jaffa identified a public appetite for books and articles "which denigrate the nobility or idealism" of the causes for which the Great Democracies have fought, and for which their progeny have died. "Politics as a vocation is today in bad repute. Young people are led to believe that to succeed in politics is to prove oneself a clever or lucky scoundrel. The detraction of the great has become a passion for those who cannot suffer greatness, and will not have it believed." This is owed to a skewed vision of the egalitarian principle, the theory that there are no great figures, we are all the same. "No regime can survive," Jaffa concluded, "that does not bind the affection of the citizens by the admiration of its heroes. The education of the young must be guided by the distinction between scoundrels, clever or otherwise, and people worthy of honor."[1]

The Goal

I look back to the birth of my Churchill interest—watching his state funeral on television in 1965—to realize that I have been more than fifty years "labouring in the vineyard," as Martin Gilbert described it. A good deal of that time was spent puncturing "myths, fables and things that go bump in the night." In writing this book, as Churchill wrote of 10 May 1940, "I thought I knew a good deal about it all, and I was sure I should not fail."[2]

I seek to refute, or at least challenge, the most frequent allegations against Winston Churchill, and by so doing, to demonstrate or to suggest what he really thought and did—about many subjects and issues still on our minds today.

I do not contend that Churchill was infallible. It diminishes him to treat him as super-human. In fifty years of political prominence there are many opportunities for error. In so long a span, mistakes were inevitable—sometimes big ones. On some subjects herein—such as Tonypandy, Ireland, the Dardanelles, India, the Second Front—accomplished scholars have persuasively catalogued Churchill's failings. I acknowledge these valid criticisms, while offering certain exculpatory facts which are not so well known.

Was Churchill a racist? In modern context some have argued that he was—yet there were striking episodes where he defied the racial attitudes of his class and time. Was he wrong about the Dardanelles? In one respect, certainly. He pressed too hard, without plenary authority—yet that tragedy, like Gallipoli afterward, was owed to many people and circumstances. On such subjects I have stated his case; the reader may decide how good it was.

Because he published fifteen million words, and left an archive of a million documents from liquor bills to state papers, Churchill is easy pickings for anyone determined to reveal his supposed feet of clay. Yet that same archive offers the full context. One has only to do one's homework. I have done it here. There is no missing context.

Things to Know

The first thing one learns, or should learn, about Churchill is that there is more to him than 1940—and much is worthy of attention. Martin Gilbert wrote: "As I open file after file of Churchill's archive, from his entry into Government in 1905 to his retirement in 1955, I am continually surprised by the truth of his assertions, the modernity of his thought, the originality of his mind, the constructiveness of his proposals, his humanity, and, most remarkable of all, his foresight."[3]

And what foresight. Churchill predicted mobile phones, jet and rocket travel, 24/7 news, social media, genetic engineering. A close observer of politics, he foresaw the dangers to democracy of its central rationale: the right of the people to set their own course. He warned of the potential for nuclear war fifteen years before Einstein wrote his famous letter to Roosevelt on the dire implications of splitting the atom. Churchill the so-called war enthusiast said of war: "What vile and utter folly and barbarism it all is."[4]

That was the "macro–Churchill," who thought deeply about the nature of humanity and its institutions. The "micro–Churchill" helped to solve hitherto unsolvable problems. In 1921, for example, he helped to negotiate the treaty that established Irish independence. Michael Collins, one of the Irish revolutionaries at those negotiations, declared: "Tell Winston we could never have done anything without him." In Cairo around the same time, Churchill helped draw the boundaries of today's Middle East—an act some say we should not thank him for. Yet the Cairo conference established a stable Jordan, which is there yet, and confirmed Britain's commitment to a Jewish national home. Also at Cairo, Churchill tried to create a Kurdish homeland, "to protect the Kurds from some future bully in Iraq." Perhaps that may be the next of his visions that comes to pass.

In the 1930s he fought and lost over India's independence, then told Gandhi to "use the powers that are offered, and make the thing a success." Decades earlier, Churchill had defended the Indian minority in South Africa. "I have got a good recollection of Mr. Churchill when he was in the Colonial Office," Gandhi said, "and somehow or other since then I have held the opinion that I can always rely on his sympathy and goodwill."[5] (An Indian colleague wrote me: "Gandhi *couldn't* have said that!" But he did.)

As a young reformer, Churchill campaigned for a "minimum standard" guaranteed by the state. But he feared socialism—"the philosophy of failure, the creed of ignorance, and the gospel of envy." He strove for measures to address the plight of the needy while not dislocating the system that provided the required wherewithal. We still argue over the proper balance in that system today. Since history never repeats itself, the policies Churchill adopted do not provide ready-made solutions today, wrote Paul Addison. "But Churchill's writings and speeches are full of reflections and philosophy that offer food for thought. It is rare to discover in the archives the reflections of a politician on the nature of man."[6]

Why after decades of criticism is his reputation undiminished? Because, I think, Winston Churchill *stood* for something: for certain critical human possibilities that are always worth bringing to the attention of thoughtful people. There will always be scoffers, Martin Gilbert said, who portray him as an anachronism, a grotesque. "In doing so, it is they who are the losers, for he was a man of quality: a good guide for our troubled present, and for the generations now reaching adulthood."[7]

Churchill fought and lost many battles in his life. He fought tyranny and he won. Yet it was not the significance of that victory, William Buckley said, "that causes the name of Churchill to make the blood run a little faster…. It is simply mistaken that battles are necessarily more important than the words that summon men to arms, or who remember the call to arms. The battle of Agincourt was long forgotten as a geopolitical event, but the words of Henry V, with Shakespeare to recall them, are imperishable in the mind, even as which side won the Battle of Gettysburg will dim from the memory of men and women who will never forget the words spoken about that battle by Abraham Lincoln. The genius of Churchill was his union of affinities of the heart and of the mind. The total fusion of animal and spiritual energy."[8]

Grateful Thanks

I am indebted to my wife Barbara, who gamely reads and vigorously criticizes every word I write, for her constant support in writing this book, which took almost twice as long as I told her it would. "I've already written half of it," I said glibly, not realizing that offhand opinions and one-liner responses to cranks are not the stuff of a serious book. I owe much to the Churchill scholars Paul Addison, Larry Arnn, Warren Kimball and Andrew Roberts, who read great wodges of the text and offered inarguable advice: revise, revise, revise! (As Churchill said when criticized for changing his opinion: "My views are a harmonious process which keeps them in relation to the current movements of events."[9])

The book would not be nearly as authoritative as it is without past conversations with people who really knew Sir Winston, and had the ability to explain him whenever I asked a question. First among these was Lady Soames, our dear friend Mary, replete with wisdom and balanced understanding of her father and his world. There were his grandson Winston, daughter-in-law Minnie, and nephew Peregrine; as well as Sir John Colville, Elizabeth Gilliatt, Ronald Golding, Grace Hamblin, Anthony Montague Browne and Elizabeth Nel. Those who did not know him personally but deeply influenced my thinking include William F. Buckley Jr., Alistair Cooke, Robert Hardy, Roy Jenkins, Jack Kemp, William Manchester, Christian Pol-Roger, Arthur M. Schlesinger Jr., Margaret Thatcher and Caspar Weinberger.

I thank also the historians Antoine Capet, David Dilks, Arthur Herman, Robert Rhodes James, David Lough, Douglas Russell, David Stafford and Manfred Weidhorn; the bibliographer Ronald I. Cohen; Allen Packwood and staff of the Churchill Archives Centre; Kyle Murnen and Soren Geiger of the Hillsdale College Churchill Project; and friends and colleagues who made themselves indispensible at critical moments: Paul Courtenay, Marcus Frost, Steve Goldfein, Parker Lee, Lewis Lehrman, Cyril Mazansky, Michael McMenamin, Suzanne Sigman, and Barry Singer.

No one can write about Churchill without reference to the godfather of Churchill Studies, Sir Martin Gilbert, whose continuing work on the longest biography in history it is our privilege at Hillsdale College to refract; and to Larry Arnn, Hillsdale's president, who determined to finish Martin's work no matter how long and hard the road might be: "To lift again the tattered flag" he "found lying on a stricken field."[10]

Part 1. Youth

1

"Chief leader of men"

The Myth:
Sir Winston Churchill Had Native American Ancestors

Churchill took great pride in his half–American ancestry, through his mother Lady Randolph Churchill, the former Jennie Jerome of New York. The Jeromes were deeprooted for generations in American soil, descended from Lt. Reuben Murray, who fought in Washington's army. This made Winston eligible for hereditary membership in the Society of the Cincinnati, which he proudly accepted in 1952. In his third speech to Congress the same year, he remarked that he was on both sides in "the war between us and we."[1]

But Churchill embellished his U.S. connection, repeating an old family legend that *native* American blood also ran in his veins. That canard has the honor of being the earliest, if not the most important, Churchill myth. It arose not from Churchill's own career, but in family stories long before he was born, prologue to scores of fables that surrounded Churchill in life.

In 1960, Sir Winston told one of his doctors that he was descended from a Seneca squaw. The Seneca were the farthest western branch of Iroquoian-speaking people; before the American Revolution they lived south of Lake Ontario, within the Six Nations or Iroquois League. Thus, in the opinion of some, "the quintessential Englishman was not only half–American but also one-sixty-fourth Native American."[2]

"Ba-ja-bar-son-dey"

On 2 November 1963, based largely on his family's claim, the National Congress of American Indians made Churchill a "Chief of the American Indians" giving him the name "Ba-ja-bar-son-dey," meaning "Great Leader of Men." Shortly afterward the NCAI sent him the full regalia of a North American chief which had apparently been worn in battle. It had belonged (ironically enough), to Chief White Man of the Brulé Sioux, part of the Lakota tribe in central South Dakota.[3]

"The tunic was decorated with the scalps of enemies killed in battle and the trousers, made of buffalo hide, were marked with bloodstains," wrote Roy Howells, part of Churchill's entourage. "The huge feathered war headdress was very heavy and decorated round the band with coloured beads."[4] An examination of the items, carefully preserved at Chartwell, discloses strands of attached black hair most likely from scalps, but only a few droplets of what may be blood: Chief White Man was evidently a dexterous scalper.

The prevailing family story was that Iroquois blood had been introduced into Churchill's family through his mother Jennie's maternal grandmother, Clarissa Willcox, who (like Jennie) had a pronounced dark complexion. It is quite possible, of course, that other children, confronted with Clarissa's visage, teased and even convinced her that she was part-native. However it started, the rumor had a life of its own. One broadly discredited biography of Jennie went so far as to suggest that Clarissa's mother, Anna Baker, "may have been raped by an Indian and that Clarissa Willcox may have been half-caste."[5]

Randolph Churchill who, like his sisters, accepted the Native American story, wrote in the Official Biography that Clarissa was "the grand-daughter of Eleazur Smith, of Dartmouth, Massachusetts, and Meribah (no maiden name recorded), who is believed to have been an Iroquois Indian."[6] This may have been the "Seneca squaw" his father mentioned.

Genealogical Facts

The Churchill genealogist Elizabeth Snell cut through all this two decades ago, revealing that Meribah was neither Clarissa Willcox's mother nor an Iroquois; she was the daughter of Benjamin and Sarah (Tompkins) Gifford, born in Dartmouth, Massachusetts, on 30 June 1722. Snell also identified Anna Baker's mother, and her background, thanks to an unearthed 1951 typescript on the descendants of the Baker family.[7]

Snell's evidence refuted not only Randolph Churchill's claim, but the entire family legend: Anna Baker, Snell wrote, was the daughter of colonial Americans, Joseph Baker and Experience Martin, who married in Swansea, Massachusetts, in 1760. Experience, named for her mother, was the daughter of Eleazer Martin (died 1749), and named as such in his will.

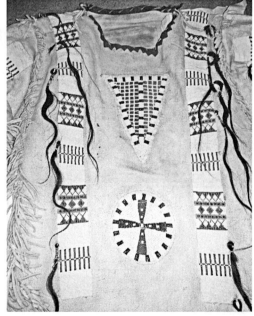

War bonnet and tunic presented by the National Congress of American Indians, the latter containing what Roy Howells supposed to be blood stains and strands of hair from human scalps (Chartwell, photographed by Nicole Day).

In 1861 the Bakers and other family members moved to Sackville, Nova Scotia, where Anna was born and lived until 1787; later the family returned to New England. "The ancestry of Joseph Baker," Snell wrote, "is well documented."[8] It is possible that the men of Anna's family were soldiers and Indian fighters at Fort Sackville at the time of her birth.

The Baker family returned to Massachusetts in 1787, where Anna Baker married David Willcox of Dartmouth. By 1791, Snell continues, the couple had moved to Palmyra, in northern New York,

> where Willcox purchased a 100-acre farm and also set up a blacksmith shop. The building believed to have been their dwelling was still in existence in 1970, when Anita Leslie, grand-niece of Jennie Jerome, visited Palmyra on a book promotion tour for her life of Lady Randolph Churchill. Anna Baker Willcox's daughter Clarissa was born 30 September 1796. David and Anna Willcox are buried together in Palmyra, where their headstones may still be seen. Anna's father, Joseph Baker, died 15 June 1796 and in his will named his daughter, "Anne Willcocks."[9]

As for the conjecture that Clarissa Willcox was the result of a rape by an Iroquois, Snell wrote: "There were no Iroquois in Nova Scotia, where Anna spent much of her young womanhood. While there were certainly Iroquois in upper New York state, where she moved as a 25-year-old wife and mother, her husband's will mentions their daughter 'Clarind Willcox' and her sisters, which in itself seems definitive."[10]

The Myth Continues

Which story is more believable? Was Clarissa an illegitimate half-Iroquois, whom the Willcoxes brought up as a daughter? Or should we accept, as Snell did, "the simple, forthright facts as recorded by her colonial family in their probate records"? The absence of proof does not make a story untrue; but it does not establish it, either.

Without any evidence we are left only with family stories, passed along through the generations. Clarissa ("Clara") Hall (1825–1895) married Leonard Jerome (1817–1891) in 1849. Jennie, born 1854, was the second of their four daughters. In 1874 she married Lord Randolph Churchill, and the rest is history—but not without continued claims of Iroquois ancestry.

All the "writing Leslies"—descendants of Jennie's sister Leonie—accepted the story. Shane Leslie wrote about it. Based only on family lore his daughter Anita, Winston's cousin, declared that Clara Jerome had for years "heard half-hushed rumors concerning her Indian blood … long before she understood the importance of a coat of arms, Clara knew herself to be a quarter Iroquois. a descendant of the tribe that for centuries had ruled the wooded hills around her home."[11]

The myth was passed along. Churchill's daughter, Lady Soames, certainly believed it, until confronted with the facts—as did her children: "I remember my daughter Emma, playing with her mates at Chartwell Farm," Lady Soames recalled. "Suddenly I heard her warn them not to misbehave: 'My Mama, you know, is part red Indian, and if we are naughty she will go on the war-path.'"[12] This vision was apparently enough to prevent any hijinks by Emma's youthful companions.

Churchill's son Randolph actually embroidered the story. Landing once in Johannesburg, Randolph was incensed by an immigration form asking him to state his race, an important matter in the time of Apartheid. "Damned cheek!," exclaimed the fiery Randolph, and he began writing furiously:

Race: human. But if, as I imagine is the case, the object of this enquiry is to determine whether I have coloured blood in my veins, I am most happy to be able to inform you that I do, indeed, so have. This is derived from one of my most revered ancestors, the Indian Princess Pocahontas, of whom you may not have heard, but who was married to a Jamestown settler named John Rolfe....[13]

Sir Winston's grandson Winston stuck to the tale, declaring: "For me, physical features speak louder than any entry in a register of births."[14] In the introduction to a collection of his grandfather's writings on America he wrote: "According to family tradition, Jennie's maternal grandmother, Clarisse Wilcox [sic], was half Iroquois."[15]

During grandson Winston's accompanying book tour, my wife and I drove him to old Plimouth Plantation, Massachusetts, where the *Mayflower* landed in 1620. There he encountered a Native American (or a staffer posing as one), whom he greeted by suggesting they might be related. In the car later I could help tweaking him: "Winston, you are as much Iroquois as my cat." He grinned and said, "It's my story and I'm sticking to it."[16]

The Native American story deserves pride of place in any catalogue of Churchill falsities, illustrating how, in their desire to embellish his saga, he or his relatives, and writers both admiring and critical, seized on legend unsupported by facts. Alas many tall tales that followed this one were less innocent, and some downright libelous. It is the purpose of this book to set the record straight.

2

Jennie's Indiscretions, Jack's Parentage

The Myth: One of Jennie's 200 Lovers Fathered Winston's Brother
---

The Irish novelist George Moore wrote that Jennie, Lady Randolph Churchill, had slept with 200 men. Assuming she did so, say, between ages 20 and 60, she averaged five per year, a ten-week average affair (if she had them one at a time with brief breaks between) which is a lot of lovers to maintain, given the state of Victorian and Edwardian locomotion.

However ridiculous, the claim stuck, and is regularly trotted out and even embellished on a medium poor Jennie never anticipated: the Internet. It occurs often because it's easy to rattle off, and prurient enough to raise a website's profile in Google Analytics—never mind whether it is even slightly feasible.

William Manchester called Moore's claim absurd. "She was far too fastidious for that, and only she would have known the figure anyhow. But though far from promiscuous, she had certainly led an active romantic life." Manchester did suggest certain lovers, starting with the indisputable love of her life, Karl, Eighth Prince Kinsky of Wchinitz and Tettau (1858–1919). Others included the American Congressman Bourke Cockran, who mentored her son Winston; and Albert Edward, Prince of Wales and later King Edward VII: "Jennie was one of those favored ladies who, invited to dinner by His Royal Highness, found that she was the only guest."[1]

Manchester's chief source was the writer Ralph Martin, who justified the claim of liaison with Edward by describing Lady Randolph's intellectual as well as physical allure: "Jennie had a significant and lasting influence on him because he respected her judgment…. She knew the level of his impatience and boredom, the danger point of his anger, and how to cope with them. In return, he was lavish in his gifts and in his open affection for her … after Randolph's death, the Prince's letters began to address Jennie as 'Ma chère Amie,' and they were signed 'Tout à Vous, Albert Edward' or simply 'A.E.'"[2]

Martin was speculating. While upperclass Edwardians were not strangers to affairs, they commonly addressed each other in terms of endearment—"My dear" was often said to each other by members of the same sex, so commonly still by Winston Churchill in World War II that staffers or generals would cock an eye at him when he said it. Martin's take, and that of A.J.P. Taylor, impressed Manchester enough that by his second Churchill volume, Jennie had become wanton:

> Those closest to [Winston] agree that he is undersexed; some suggest that the explanation lies in the promiscuity of his beautiful, wanton mother. The historian A.J.P. Taylor will reflect: "She moved from one man to another. And it's possible, I don't say this is the only explanation, that Churchill's really almost extreme chastity was a reaction to his mother's lack of it…. He once remarked: 'The reason I can write so much is that I don't waste my essence in bed.'"[3]

There is no comment in Churchill's writings concerning his mother's alleged promiscuity. When her third husband turned out to be a gentleman only three years older than Winston, her sons gloried in her happiness. The quotation about Winston's "essence" is found only in Manchester, and two subsequent books quoting him.[4] It might have referred to energy not sex: He was, after all, well known to spend active mornings in bed—reading the newspapers and dictating correspondence. It is reasonable to expect that such a singular remark would track to the contemporary observers who heard it—if it was ever said at all.

Since Jennie's love affairs are nowhere documented by her own diaries, or those of her supposed lovers, it is impossible to state how many there really were; but it would seem logical that the total was far below the estimates of George Moore, or wispy rumors unsupported by facts. The origin of those rumors more logically involves human nature. Jennie was beautiful, even into her sixties; she was also charming, intelligent, accomplished, a great diplomat, an effective behind-the-scenes politician (though she herself questioned the idea of women voting). Such attributes in a woman at that time often bred criticism, sometimes born of envy. The chatter stuck long enough to be revived by modern writers looking for a hook to hang a story on. As Richard Hough wrote:

> Rumours of promiscuity swirled around Jennie throughout her long, glittering social career. With her exceptional vivacity, she did attract many male friends and admirers, including the Prince of Wales, but according to close members of the family, Jennie did not find the sexual act particularly pleasurable, and most probably never went to bed with any of the 'lovers' gossip enjoyed ascribing to her.[5]

Jack Churchill's Paternity

Given the tales of Jennie's romances, it is unsurprising that someone would suggest one of her boys was not fathered by Lord Randolph Churchill. Winston was too obviously his father's son, so that dubious distinction fell to his brother, Major John Strange "Jack" Spencer-Churchill DSO TD (1880–1947)—although the idea became prominent only in 1969, nearly half a century after Jennie's death.

Jack was born in Dublin, where Lord Randolph was secretary to his father, the Seventh Duke of Marlborough, then Viceroy of Ireland. Like Winston, Jack was educated at Harrow. Both brothers married in 1908, Jack to the vivacious "Goonie," Lady Gwendoline Bertie, who bore him three children including Clarissa, later the Countess of Avon, wife of Anthony Eden.

In 1969, the same biographer who proclaimed that Jennie's supposed Iroquois blood was introduced through the rape of her great-grandmother added another titillating speculation. During her three years in Ireland, he wrote, one of Jennie's "favorite riding partners" was John Strange Jocelyn, later (1880) the Fourth Earl of Roden. Tall and handsome, "with flashing black eyes and curly black hair," Jocelyn had "a wild dash in him. [He was] the kind of man who could climb up the drainpipe to a bedroom window, and did." Jocelyn was said to be "barely fifty" (he was fifty-six), "in the prime of his vigour….

Jennie was again pregnant in the summer of 1879, and her second son was born in Dublin on February 4, 1880. She named him John Strange Spencer Churchill."[6]

British tabloids, even more scurrilous than the American, gleefully took up the story. Suddenly members of the Roden family and Jack Churchill's three children were receiving calls from reporters, asking what they thought of Lord Roden as their grandfather. Winston's cousin Anita Leslie, whose accounts of the Iroquois came from family legend, was in the midst of it: "The present Earl of Roden, who lives near us in Northern Ireland … was interrupted in the midst of giving his views on Ulster's troubles by a journalist who queried: 'And what is your opinion of old Lord Roden shinning up a drainpipe into Lady Randolph Churchill's bedroom?'"[7]

The Rodens and Churchills compared notes. "The results were hilarious," Leslie wrote. John Strange Joceyln was in fact a friend of the Viceroy, Jennie's father-in-law, and had a distinguished military career. A relative said that when Jocelyn was sixteen, he and his younger brother had indeed "shinned up a drainpipe—to avoid their angry parents. This episode had occurred some years before Jennie was born and no other climb has ever been recorded."

A review of Jocelyn's letters found no mention of Jennie, but disclosed that he was "of an unusually religious, even priggish, turn of mind, for when he visited Blenheim he criticised the atmosphere as 'frivolous and worldly.'" He was never Jennie's "riding partner." During those years "the elderly Colonel John Strange Jocelyn (married with a daughter Jennie's age) was living happily, if dully, in England. The wickedest record about him reveals that he sometimes backed horses and lost."[8]

The same month as Jack was born in Dublin, Jocelyn inherited the Earldom and arrived in Ireland to claim it. Jennie's second son was named after him "in order to please the old Marlborughs," Leslie wrote. "We all racked our brains to pick out more of these facts, but there really seemed no reason whatever to suppose that the beautiful Jennie should have preferred an old soldier of fifty-six to her lively twenty-eight-year-old husband—even if Roden had climbed a drainpipe some years before she was born!"[9]

Peregrine Churchill, Jack's younger son and Sir Winston's nephew, a determined guardian of family truth, was less inclined to hilarity. He took the offending author to court. That was before the routine use of DNA evidence, but Peregrine cited the family records, proving that Jocelyn was in England when Jack Churchill was conceived. "The result was conclusive," Peregrine recalled. "Several thousand copies of the book were destroyed and I obtained a signed agreement by the author never to publish that story again."[10]

One would think Peregrine's successful prosecution would have settled the matter, but the gossips were not mollified. If Jack's father wasn't John Strange Jocelyn, the tabloids murmured, what about the much younger Evelyn Boscawen, 7th Viscount Falmouth (1847–1918)?

Jennie's diaries were full of Boscawen, whom she called "The Star," who *was* in Ireland, serving as assistant military secretary to the Viceroy, when she was there. Jennie had even written to her mother that he had "the loveliest moustache." As late as 2007, another Jennie biographer asserted that he was Jack's father—citing only rumors, in this case from Jennie's sisters.[11] As to proof, there was none—no evidence in any diaries, no particular interest by "The Star" in his alleged son. Tellingly, while Boscawen is prominent in Jennie's published reminiscences, her genuine love, Count Kinsky, is mentioned only once.

Next in the sweepstakes was Lord Randolph's friend Lord Powerscourt, who lived in Dublin at the time and whose Christian names—wink wink, nudge nudge—were "John Strange." Again there is no evidence of an affair. "The biographers ready to risk brain-fever from surmises can have a field day," Anita Leslie concluded, "but the fact remains that although Jennie was a tremendous flirt and always had admirers in tow, there is no shred of evidence to lead one to suppose that she preferred 'Star' Falmouth or any other man to her attractive young husband during the years in Ireland."[12]

On to the Internet

The kerfuffle over Jack's parentage simmered for twenty years, only to erupt again in 1990 in a book review by Alistair Forbes, a Churchill family friend, of Richard Hough's *Winston and Clementine* (cited above). Forbes accused Hough of inconsistency, carelessness and hagiography. Based only on family conversations, he expressed astonishment at Hough's claim that Lady Randolph was not promiscuous, repeating the Jocelyn story and the canard that Lord Randolph Churchill died from syphilis (Chapter 4).

Peregrine Churchill demanded an apology from Forbes for his remarks on his father's parentage, and for suggesting that his grandmother, "then a young girl, was seduced by a man the same age as the Duke, her father-in-law." Hough retorted that Forbes "possesses in full the male conceit that beautiful women are incapable of friendship without sexual indulgence."[13] Forbes replied, stating that his information about Jocelyn had come from John Spencer Churchill, Peregrine's brother. But family members are as likely to repeat rumor or gossip as anybody else, perhaps more likely. Even more surprising, Forbes evidently had not considered the evidence that Jocelyn wasn't in Ireland when Jack was conceived.

By then, of course, the Internet was born, and to this day the diligent browser will uncover instance after instance of John Strange Jocelyn as the father of John Strange Spencer Churchill. After all, wasn't Jack named for him?

Confronted with these episodes from time to time, Peregrine Churchill (who bore a passing resemblance to his Uncle Winston) just snorted. "My father was blue-eyed and as a boy fair-haired, and looked like Winston," he said. I never contemplated a DNA test. Why re-prove what every reasonable person has already concluded?" The historian Robert Rhodes James added that Peregrine's sister, Clarissa "once told me that 'of course' her father was illegitimate, knowing full well that this was nonsense, but rather chic.... Her brother John was physically almost an exact replica of his Uncle Winston, and with an even more formidable capacity for alcohol; he lived to a much greater age than the modern Puritans deem possible, and was also a very good artist."[14]

3

The Menace of Education

The Myth: Young Winston Was a Schoolboy Dunce

Churchill's schoolboy failings have been greatly exaggerated, starting with Churchill himself in his autobiography. From the time he was handed a primer called *Reading Without Tears,* he claimed, he shed tears over the "menace" of education. While strongly supporting British "public" (private) schools, he added, "I do not want to go there again."[1]

His last comment is misleading. When Churchill wrote it he had already twice returned to speak at his old school, Harrow, joyfully and often in tears of remembrance. He would return there frequently from 1938 to 1962. Yet over half a century since he had left as a pupil, he was still declaiming on his failures. Receiving an honorary degree from the University of Miami in 1946, he professed mock surprise that he should be receiving so many honorary degrees when as a boy he was so bad at passing examinations.[2]

Churchill, an otherwise admiring scholar wrote, "was a pretty tough proposition for an organized system of education."[3] Yet he was by not nearly the dunce of popular mythology. If only subconsciously, he stressed his school failures to suggest how far he had come. Biographers have accepted his declarations all too innocently.

Before Harrow

From the start, young Winston was a problem learner. As a five-year-old in 1879, he started home-schooling under an apparition called "The Governess." Alarmed, he "took to the woods" (the garden of his residence). He was summarily extracted, and made to toil daily, not simply at words but, more shockingly, at numbers: "I thought it all very tiresome."[4]

His situation worsened in November 1882, when he was sent to St. George's School, Ascot. The head master was a 34-year-old tyrant named H.W. Sneyd-Kinnersley, who boasted two coats of arms for each side of his double-barreled name. Described by one alumnus as "an unconscious sodomite," he was known for flogging boys till they bled.

Breaking bad, Winston was told on arrival to learn the first declension of "mensa," Latin for "table." He memorized it, gabbled it off, then asked the head master about the vocative case: "Why 'O table?'" Sneyd-Kinnersley replied: "You would use that in addressing a table … in speaking to a table." *"But I never do!"* the astonished Winston replied.

"If you are impertinent, you will be punished, and punished, let me tell you, very severely."[5] And he was.

Winston hated St. George's passionately. (He vowed to return one day to wreak vengeance, and actually did in 1895, only to find that Sneyd-Kinnersley was nine years dead—a cause for celebration among his former charges.) The boy's health broke down, and on a visit home, his mother and nurse saw evidence of his beatings. He was removed to a smaller school at Brighton, where it was thought the sea air would do him good.

The Brighton school was run by two kindly sisters, Charlotte and Catherine Thomson. Here he was able to swim and ride, and soon recovered his health. He also found subjects he liked: history, poetry, literature. When he was only nine his father presented him with *Treasure Island,* which he devoured. The Misses Thomson objected, Churchill remembered, because he was "reading books beyond my years and yet at the bottom of the Form."[6] He was still hard to manage, and on 18 March 1888, when Charlotte Thomson escorted him to Harrow for the entrance exam, she did so with a sense of relief.

Examinations, Churchill wrote, were an "inhospitable region," a "great trial." The questions always seemed to be about what he did not know. He liked English and history, the examiners favored Latin and math: "I should have liked to be asked to say what I knew."[7] But was his experience very different from our own? I often had that feeling studying calculus and physics.

Entering Harrow

Although Churchill men usually attended Eton, his parents sent Winston to Harrow, the other leading public school, north of London, perched on a hill where the air was better, and in those days still in the country.[8] His autobiography famously recounts his dismal performance in the Latin entrance exam, which has been repeated ever since: all he produced on his sheet of paper was his name in block letters, the legend "[1]," an ink blot and several smudges. Harrow's head master, James Welldon, nevertheless admitted him, and critics ever since have asserted that Welldon acted in self-interest, not daring to deny a distinguished politician like Lord Randolph Churchill—which is quite wide of the mark. One explanation for his admission was "the consolatory thought that the off-spring of so distinguished a father could not fail somehow to make good."[9] Closer examination has shown that Welldon was "very much in admiration of Lord Randolph [and was] assured by Winston's teacher that he was capable of good work."[10]

After the exam, Charlotte Thomson explained to Lady Randolph that Winston had "suffered from severe nervous excitement," because he had never translated Latin into English—which was not true, since he had spent a year at Brighton translating Caesar and Virgil.[11] Significantly, Harrow historians have never found the offending Latin exam paper. Some say that in 1888, not even Lord Randolph's son could have been admitted to Harrow knowing no Latin. Also, though Churchill never mentioned them, the entry exam included other subjects, on which he presumably did better.

It is true that Welldon favored the boy, personally tutoring him and eventually admitting him to the Head Master's House. His esteem was reciprocated. Welldon, Churchill wrote, could see his potential: "I have always had the highest regard for him."[12] When they met in 1900, Welldon hoped he would soon see Winston in Parliament. He lived almost long enough to see Churchill as prime minister.

The boy was placed in the third (lowest) division of the fourth (bottom) form, where he remained for a year, when he transferred to the Army class, but never rose very high. Since the roster printed names alphabetically, "Spencer-Churchill" was only two from the last. The other two dropped out, and visitors looking for Lord Randolph's son would exclaim, "Why, he's last of all!" Biographers have given this more attention than it deserves. It does explain why, as a published author, he always used an alphabetically higher byline: Winston S. Churchill.

A.W. Simmons, a Harrow master who collected 19th century student histories, recorded the remembrances of Churchill's contemporaries: "Some people have thought that at that time he was stupid; but that is entirely a mistaken idea…. He had always a brilliant brain, but he would only work when he chose to and for the masters he approved of…. I formed the highest opinion of his abilities and never ceased to wonder why he did not rise higher."[13]

Winston had no learning disability, but he did have an "attitude." His first house

"At Harrow he took exception to everything…." As Mr. Davidson was leading Winston to his quarters the boy asked: "And what did you think of the House of Commons vote on the last military bill?" (Bernard Burns, Wikimedia Commons).

master was H.O.D. Davidson, who took him, wrote Robert Louis Taylor, "much as one might pick up a snake with a pair of tongs. What was Davidson's astonishment, as they proceeded to the boy's quarters, to hear Winston ask chattily, 'And what did you think of the House of Commons vote on the last military bill?'" The boy was then fourteen.

Taylor continued: "At Harrow he took exception to everything…. The boys looked upon masters as their natural enemies…. Every sort of classism was encouraged: the boys in the upper forms detested the boys in the lower forms [and] merry warfare reigned. The accommodations at both Harrow and Eton, and at most public schools, offered the usual comforts of the average Trappist monastery."[14]

His rule-breaking is not much mentioned in Churchill's autobiography, but it is part of the true picture. He was "quite incorrigible," a close observer wrote, "and had an unlimited vocabulary of 'back-chat,' which he produced with dauntless courage." Recorded but not confirmed was this exchange with a master: "Spencer-Churchill, I have very grave reason to be displeased with you." Winston: "And I, sir, have very grave reason to be displeased with you!" After a beating by a privileged upperclassman, he retorted, "I shall be a greater man than you!" He was given two extra whacks, but he was proven right.[15]

Against this negative testimony stands that of Wright Cooper, who ran a confectionary, the school's "tuck shop." Churchill, Cooper said, was

> an extraordinarily good boy … honest and generous in a day when robust appetites were not always accompanied by well-lined pockets. My family lived over the shop, and when Churchill was downstairs we all knew it. Boys always crowded round his table. He talked loudly and usually led the conversation. He knew, too, what he was talking about, and nothing came amiss to him. He was witty and critical and kept the other boys in roars of laughter. He was exceedingly popular and even the seniors sought his company. He was well behaved and had the ear of everyone. When his father or his mother came to see him, he used to book a table in the tuck shop, and that was a great occasion for him. He was extremely happy at Harrow and full of high spirits.[16]

Cooper's remarks are an interesting counter-opinion, but Churchill always did have a penchant for the working classes, and Cooper probably saw him at his best, especially when his parents visited.

Latin Siege to Latin Sage

How much Latin did Churchill really know? It is not a settled question. Peregrine Churchill was certain his uncle knew little or none. But Harrow historian Jim Golland noted that "in a number of terms [Churchill] was in the top half of the form in the Latin examinations." A schoolmate, Gerald Wollaston, thought "he was handicapped by his own idiosyncrasies, for he resolutely refused to absorb anything that did not interest him." Yet he was better at Latin than he let on.[17]

On exams he sometimes had illicit help. Churchill himself admitted that he exchanged English essays with a chum who did his Latin assignments—so obviously that Dr. Welldon noticed the dichotomy. Summoning the other boy, Welldon said how impressed he was with his essay, asking him to expand upon it. An embarrassed silence followed. Let off, his chum told Winston to play down his future assignments: "Write them more mediocre."[18]

Challenged by Latin, Churchill laid siege to the language. He studied a book of Latin quotations, committing them to memory. Three chapters of his first book, *The Story of the Malakand Field Force,* were distinguished by Latin quotes, aimed to convince readers of his classical erudition. After entering Parliament he deployed Latin in speeches, though was never sure about the grammar. At school Welldon had seemed "physically pained" by his mistakes; in the House of Commons, Prime Minister Asquith "used to have just the same sort of look on his face." But another prime minister, Stanley Baldwin, later quipped: "Mr. Churchill seldom speaks nowadays—and I rejoice to think of it—without a quotation from the Latin tongue."[19]

After World War I, arguing for generous treatment of defeated Germany, Churchill proclaimed, *"parcere subjectis et debellare superbo"* (spare the conquered and war down the proud). The Romans, he added, "have often forestalled many of my best ideas."[20] World War II came, and with it more Roman sayings. Robert Pilpel wrote of Churchill's "robust roast-beef-and-pewter phrases, rolling cadences, portentous Latinate locutions— alien yet eerily familiar, the echo of a racial memory."[21]

Approaching eighty he was still going strong. Warning the House that he was about to speak in Latin, he needled the opposition, hoping it would not baffle Labour Members schooled at less eminent institutions. He duly pronounced *"arma virumque cano,"* translating it as "arms and the men I sing." A Winchester-educated Labour Member asked: "Should it not be 'man,' the singular instead of the plural?" Churchill replied: "Little did I expect that I should receive assistance on a classical matter from such a quarter."[22] Geoffrey Fletcher wrote: "The days of 'O mensa' were long past."[23]

Flying Colors

Despite his Latin troubles, young Winston's success in other subjects refute the notion that he was backward. This was partly owed to the interest he took in history and English, and partly to skilled teachers. Aside from Welldon, Churchill recalled in 1940, there were three masters who really mattered to him—to which we, in retrospect, owe much.[24]

Charles Mayo taught Churchill math. "He convinced me," Churchill wrote, "that mathematics was not a hopeless bog of nonsense, and that there were meanings and rhythms behind the comical hieroglyphics." By then the boy was destined for Sandhurst, the Royal Military College. Fortunately, the entry examination did not require knowledge of what Churchill described as "a dragon called the 'Differential Calculus.'" In his first math exam he scored only 500 out of a possible 2500 marks. Mayo bore down, and on Winston's next try he made nearly 2000, the best of all candidates.[25]

Louis Moriarty headed Harrow's class for the army— the only place, his parents thought, for a boy lacking in academic prowess. Moriarty was Winston's tutor for five of his six terms there. They fenced together, and met to discuss essays and history; it was Moriarty who taught him to apply his growing love of English to the writing of essays.

Robert Somervell was the English master who taught Churchill the structure of "the ordinary British sentence." Somervell would break a sentence into its component parts: subject, verb and predicate; relative, conditional and conjunctive clauses. What Winston learned extended to his writing, and from here grew the mastery that ended with a Nobel Prize in Literature. "I am biased in favour of boys learning English," he later wrote. "I would let the clever ones learn Latin as an honour, and Greek as a treat. But the only thing I would whip them for is not knowing English."[26]

Churchill's writing at Harrow was celebrated but problematic. His first contributions to a periodical were six critical letters to *The Harrovian,* signed "De Profundis," "Junius, Junior" and "Truth…. Philistine Correspondent of *The Harrovian.*" The first critiqued the school library, others the inadequacies of the gymnasium. Flashing his Latin, the fifth was entitled: "*Magna Est Veritas, Sed Rara*" ("Truth Is, However, Rare").[27] His tutor Mayo had encouraged the first letter, but not the rest, to which the head master took exception. "If any more of the same sort appear," Welldon told the boy, "it might become my painful duty to swish you." The letters nevertheless showed that "Churchill's long training in the English language in the Fourth Form was bearing fruit, and give early evidence of his great gifts as a master of both the spoken and the written word."[28]

Prefiguring History

Churchill's most remarkable literary effort at Harrow was an 1889 essay, "The Engagement at La Marais," an imagined British invasion of Russia: 1500 words with maps and plans. Whenever I read this I am struck by Churchill's date for the engagement: 7 July 1914, within a month of the day when World War I engulfed Britain and Russia.

Military historian Douglas Russell wrote:

> Speaking Churchill's words, the narrator is of course the very brave hero. At one point he is taken prisoner by the enemy but cleverly manages to escape and return to the British lines. Later the narrator narrowly escapes death when an exploding shell lands on a spot where he had been standing moments before. Both episodes presage actual events in Churchill's own war service in later years. The story shows good skill at dramatic narrative and a fair knowledge of military organization, tactics and the language of command.[29]

Such remarkable productions at so early an age were abetted by Churchill's phenomenal memory—if not photographic, then close to it. He gained a Harrow prize by reciting 1200 lines of Macaulay's *Lays of Ancient Rome* without a mistake. He could quote whole scenes from Shakespeare plays, and did not hesitate to correct his masters when they misquoted the Bard. More than half a century later Richard Burton, playing Hamlet at the Old Vic, heard eruptions from the front row whenever he tried to shorten the play by skipping a few lines: Prime Minister Churchill was sitting there, mouthing the lines *sotto voce.*[30]

"Winston's Harrow career was second rate," Geoffrey Fletcher asserted:

> Apart from winning a prize for recital, becoming a competent fencer and a good swimmer, his scholastic ability was rudimentary: he was disinterested in many of the subjects taught…. It took him three attempts to enter Sandhurst, the final success owed to being coached by a "crammer." The army class at Harrow and at other public schools was for the "thick ones."[31]

Young Winston did not have a learning disability, nor was he obtuse. He simply studied hard only when the subject interested him. At Sandhurst, he had a better chance. Instead of Latin, French and math, he learned tactics, fortification, mapmaking, military law, drill, gymnastics and riding. His father, who so many writers say had given up on him, instructed a bookseller to send him any books he required. "So I ordered Hamley's *Operations of War*, Prince Kraft's *Letters on Infantry, Cavalry and Artillery,* Maine's *Infantry Fire Tactics* [and] histories dealing with the American Civil, Franco-German and Russo-Turkish wars…."[32] The backward student was forgotten; he was on his way.

4

What Killed Lord Randolph?

The Myth: Churchill's Father Died of Syphilis

Lord Randolph Churchill (1849–1895) was a younger son of the Seventh Duke of Marlborough. Not in line for the dukedom, he was not a peer ("Lord" was a courtesy title). Curiously, his son Winston might have become Duke (and likely with no House of Commons career) had Lord Randolph's elder brother died childless. Randolph chose to make his name in politics. For awhile he was good at it.

Elected to Parliament in 1874, the year of Winston's birth, he was a gadfly we might liken now to Ted Cruz or Bernie Sanders. In a series of brilliant speeches he attacked privilege and the old guard, alienating elements of both major parties. He dubbed his theme "Tory Democracy": liberal reforms to enlist Conservative support from the working classes, and opposition to excessive military spending. But privately he admitted it was "mainly opportunism."[1]

Popular with voters and the press, Lord Randolph rose rapidly, becoming Secretary of State for India in 1885. In 1886 Prime Minister Lord Salisbury made him Chancellor of the Exchequer and Leader of the House of Commons—where he largely spoke for the government, since Salisbury was in the House of Lords. In December he suddenly resigned in protest over the military budget, thinking he would be recalled and win his argument. But Salisbury had had enough. Asked later why he didn't bring Lord Randolph back he replied, "Have you ever heard of a man having a carbuncle on his neck wanting it to return?"[2]

After 1886 Lord Randolph's health progressively deteriorated and he "died by inches in public." By 1894, in his last speech in the Commons, he was almost incoherent. He died aged only forty-six in January 1895, mourned by a few loyal friends, and generally disliked by the political establishment.

This digression is necessary to understand the family atmosphere in which his sons grew up. His father's death convinced Winston that he too would die young, prompting him to take risks and rash acts for which critics would excoriate him. It also explains Winston's all too ready acceptance of the ugly rumor about Lord Randolph's fatal illness.

The Syphilis Rumor

Google "Lord Randolph Churchill" and "syphilis" and you'll get 20,000 hits, most of them blandly asserting that he died from the disease. While syphilis was not publicly named as his killer until 1924, it had been whispered among family and friends long before then. Sir Winston himself believed it. Late in life he told his private secretary, "You know my father died of locomotion ataxia, the child of syphilis."[3] Mary Soames reiterated the story in her 1982 photo-documentary,[4] though she revised her opinion after considering later evidence. Her forebears mostly believed it, and it is reasonable to suspect that family chatter spread the rumor. Mary's brother Randolph did also, but omitted mentioning it in the official biography.

Sir Winston, in his biography of his father, said Lord Randolph was "of a temper that gallops till it falls,"[5] and fall he did. As early as 1881 he suffered an attack of partial paralysis when he was almost unable to speak. That was the earliest year historians say he ceased sleeping with his wife (their son Jack was born in 1880), though Lord Rosebery put it at 1885.[6] For the next ten years he experienced periodic dizziness, palpitations, slurred speech, numbness of hands and feet, and temper tantrums.

Lord Randolph Churchill at the height of his career (Wikimedia Commons).

Sir Martin Gilbert, who succeeded Sir Winston's son as official biographer, considered the syphilis issue with his usual thoroughness. At the London launch of his book, *Churchill: A Life*, Gilbert said he had sent Lord Randolph's doctors' reports to a number of physicians, naming no names but asking them to identify the disease described. Their answer was always, "This patient is suffering from syphilis." Yet any well-read doctor might guess the person Gilbert was referring to. Sir Martin added that the theory was impossible to verify, and noted that Lord Randolph's doctors might have issued reports to back their diagnosis.[7]

There the matter rested until 1997, when Dr. John Mather, a dedicated researcher of Churchill's medical history, wrote a definitive paper casting serious doubt on the syphilis theory.[8] Lord Randolph's decline and his doctors' descriptions of it, Mather wrote, might indeed suggest "dementia paralytica in late or tertiary syphilis, which affects the brain and appears ten to twenty years after the primary infection." But this would likely have affected Lady Randolph and their sons, who were not. And, "if a diagnosis of advanced syphilis is to be accepted, there must have been an initial infection."[9]

"Initial Infection"

The syphilis theory had been public since 1924, when the Irish writer and publisher Frank Harris produced his salacious memoir *My Life and Loves*. Unremarkable by today's

"The Fourth Party," 1880, so-named for their attacks on their fellow Conservatives as well as the Liberals. Left to right: Lord Randolph Churchill, Arthur Balfour (later prime minister), Sir Henry Drummond-Wolff and Sir John Gorst (*Vanity Fair*).

standards, it chronicled the dawdling with prostitutes by Victorian and Edwardian swells, including Lord Randolph Churchill. Harris' claimed source was Louis Jennings, a political colleague of Lord Randolph who published a volume of Randolph's speeches.[10]

Jennings told Harris that Randolph had contracted syphilis as an Oxford undergraduate, where he woke up with an "ancient hag" after a night of carousing. She demanded payment; Randolph emptied his pockets, then "fled in livid terror." He was treated with disinfectant, but shortly after "a little, round, very red pimple appeared…." Dr. Mather's comment on this fanciful story is that the description suggests herpes not syphilis: "This is not the description of a primary chancre, a painless shallow ulcer. Also, the odds of contracting syphilis after one unprotected encounter are low, about 30 percent." Significantly, both Jennings and Harris had axes to grind. Jennings broke off when Lord Randolph attacked the Conservative Party in 1893; in the 1920s, Harris had fallen out with Winston, for whom he had been a literary agent.[11]

Shane Leslie, Lady Randolph's nephew and family chronicler, discounted the hag story but claimed Lord Randolph was infected by a "Blenheim housemaid" shortly after Winston's birth and "could no longer sleep with his wife." This allowed him to speculate on Jack Churchill's parentage (Chapter 2). His daughter Anita did not dispute Jack's parentage, but wrote that his father was infected by a French mistress in 1886.[12] All these theories rely on Lord Randolph being sexually promiscuous, but I can find little evidence of this in the literature.

Flawed Diagnosis

Citing the 19th century neurologist Dr. William Gowers and Lord Randolph's doctors, Robson Roose and Thomas Buzzard, Dr. Mather wrote that "there was a clear predisposition toward syphilis in their clinical diagnosis." Buzzard specialized in neurosyphilis, Mather continued: "It was his opinion that 95 percent of his patients had the disease."[13]

At the time, their preoccupation was understandable. "There was then no definitive blood test, no effective treatment, no sophisticated neurological testing, and no imaging techniques, such as CAT scans and MRIs," Mather wrote. "Syphilis has always been considered 'the great masquerader.' William Osler said, 'He who knows syphilis knows all of medicine.' Great care needs to be taken in concluding that a patient has syphilis, rather than another disease."[14]

There is no evidence of Dr. Roose actually identifying Lord Randolph's malady as syphilis. He used the term "general paralysis," which in those days suggested not only syphilis but nervous exhaustion: "Chronic inflammation of the brain attacks people of exhausted habits, brought on by excesses and irregular living," Roose wrote. "The only treatment is to try and combat the various morbid symptoms ... but, in two or three years, general paralysis is almost sure to occur." "Nervous exhaustion" is what Roose mentioned to the Prince of Wales, for example, when he asked about Lord Randolph's condition.[15]

There is also no evidence that Roose or Buzzard treated Lord Randolph with mercury or potassium iodide, the contemporary prescriptions for neurosyphilitic disease; had he taken them, Mather explained, their toxic effects, such as a distinctive grey pallor, would have been evident. Lord Randolph had always had a slight speech impediment, Mather noted, so it is difficult to connect this with syphilis affecting his brain:

> In the same sense, the muddled thoughts, memory lapses and confusion, all features of syphilis's dementia paralytica, were absent from Randolph's writings almost until his death. He wrote more lengthily, and his script became shaky, but it was never unintelligible. Until the last, when he was in a coma, his thoughts expressed in writing were rational; they include a cogent letter to Winston while on his world tour in August 1894.[16]

What Killed Lord Randolph?

If it wasn't syphilis, what did Lord Randolph die from? Historians willing to look beyond the canard were considering alternatives as early as 1977. Sir Robert Rhodes James wrote: "...there was no autopsy and, given the state of medical knowledge of brain conditions at the time, this verdict [of syphilis] is not fully convincing.... Among other real possibilities of the source of his decline and death is a brain tumor, a diagnosis which the limited available evidence strongly indicates could have been the cause."[17] That remarkably coincided with Mather's conclusion twenty years later. Mather offered several convincing theories to back this up. For example, Lord Randolph's speech problem—knowing what to say but being unable to say it—was

> strongly suggestive of a variety of epilepsy found in the deep parts of the brain, close to the speech area. The progressive march of the disease process strongly suggests an expanding lesion or mass. Consistent with his right handedness is the possibility that Lord Randolph developed a left side brain

tumor, for which no surgery was available. This would also be consistent with the circulation problems in his hands, which in turn would be related to his intermittent heart failure and arterial spasms from nicotine in cigarettes. Even Dr. Buzzard might have agreed when he wrote, "...intense pain in the head, when it is coupled with amaurosis (or prostration) is very suggestive of the presence of an intra-cranial tumor...."[18]

Sir Robert Rhodes James praised Mather's research:

> I never believed this [syphilis] canard. When I was researching my book, *Lord Randolph Churchill,* I discussed it with an eminent elderly specialist in the disease, who told me that, having looked at the symptoms, syphilis was the least likely of all the causes of his decline and death. He was certainly treated for it, by a physician who was on record as declaring all nervous diseases syphilitic, which of course we now know is nonsense. Dr. Mather's conclusion that the treatment only accelerated Lord Randolph's mental collapse and death seems to me to be fully justified. I am rather surprised that some of the Churchills told you they believed the story, although Randolph, ill-advised as usual, did. But the Churchills do like to tease.[19]

I consulted Dr. Mather over anything he may have learned since his 1997 essay. "The best advice I have received since, from a review of my medical report by an academic neurologist, is that Lord Randolph definitely had a progressive neuro-digenerative disease of the brain," he replied. "This does not rule out syphilis but allows for other diagnoses such as a brain tumor to be credible."[20]

It has been suggested that a brain tumor would not have taken so long to kill Lord Randolph. But Dr. Buzzard, the neurologist-syphilologist, was not consulted by Dr. Roose until 1893, Mather replied:

> There [are] over 100 different types of brain tumor with a wide range of severity and prognosis without treatment. The common lay view is that a brain tumor is a death sentence, but today we have surgery and other treatments not available in the 1890s, let alone the MRI and other powerful diagnostic tools. Lord Randolph could easily have had a relatively slow growing brain tumor that slowly but surely resulted in changes in his speech and balance.[21]

Among family members who rejected the syphilis theory from the outset was the late Peregrine Churchill, Sir Winston's nephew: "As a boy, Randolph suffered from glandular fever which weakened him permanently. As a man he smoked and drank too much. He was a flame of energy who burned out quickly. Instead of recuperating he drove himself harder, relying on medications like laudanum, belladonna and digitalis."[22] None of these medications were used to treat syphilis.

Peregrine was eleven in 1924, when Frank Harris' allegations surfaced in the press. His uncle had left the Liberal Party and was in the process of rejoining the Conservatives. "The Tories were incensed and attempted to blacken his name, calling him a drunkard and saying that he was infected with syphilis," Peregrine recalled. "At Summerfield Prep School, Oxford, I was confronted by a classmate who charged: 'My papa says all you Churchills have revolting diseases and are quite mad.'"[23]

5

Votes for Women

The Myth: Churchill Opposed Women's Suffrage.

In late 1999, *Time* magazine named Albert Einstein "Person of the Century." Fifty years earlier, when *Time* named Churchill "Man of the Half-Century," Einstein, whose life's work was then complete, had not even been considered. What happened to cause the great physicist to leapfrog the man who saved western civilization?

Time's explanation was that "perspectives change." After picturing Churchill in an ugly caricature next to Hitler and allowing him two lines of credit for 1940, *Time* labeled him "a romantic refugee from a previous era who ended up on the wrong side of history. He bulldoggedly [sic] opposed the women's-rights movement," etc., etc. Ironically, it was Einstein who warned us that "the world is more apt to be destroyed through bad politics than bad physics."[1]

The claim that Churchill opposed women's rights has hung around for decades. In 2002 Cdr. Holly Graf, second commanding officer of the USS *Winston S. Churchill*, criticized the ship's namesake because, she said, she deplored his attitude toward women. In 2012 a blogger for London's *Daily Telegraph* wrote: "His finest hours aside, Churchill was hardly a paragon of progressive thought. He believed that women shouldn't vote, telling the House of Commons that they are 'well represented by their fathers, brothers and husbands.'"[2]

Churchill never said those words, in or out of the Commons. He did write something similar in 1897, when he was 23: a note pasted into his copy of the 1874 *Annual Register*, where he was reviewing political issues to decide which side he would take. Parliament in 1897 had drafted a women's suffrage bill, though it was a token gesture. Most MPs knew that the government would not allow the bill to proceed, and even if it did, the House of Lords would reject it. Young Winston's opposition in 1897 was

> on the grounds that it is contrary to natural law and the practice of civilized states[;] that no necessity is shown[;] that only the most undesirable class of women are eager for the right[;] that those women who discharge their duty to the state viz marrying and giving birth to children are adequately represented by their husbands[;] that those who are unmarried can only claim a vote on the ground of property, which claim on democratic principles is inadmissible....[3]

It is certainly true that Churchill held that view at the age of twenty-three. It is equally true that as a politician (from 1900 on), he never campaigned against women's suffrage, and changed his youthful attitude quite early. Today, we would say he "evolved."

A suffragette protester alongside his car after Churchill won his seat at Dundee, Scotland, in 1908 (*Illustrated London News*).

In 1897, large numbers of women, if not still the majority, remained opposed to the female franchise. Although there was widespread sympathy for the idea, neither Churchill's father, Lord Randolph, nor his mother, Lady Randolph, had supported votes for women, wrote the historian Kevin Theakston, who considered young Winston's 1897 note the "conventional chauvinistic views" of a youthful Victorian.[4]

Lady Randolph, like most political wives of her time, was eager for her husband to succeed, and happy to compete with other wives through him. A strong partisan, she enjoyed canvassing for Randolph, and was amused by the experience. Once, at a factory, she asked the workers why they had received her in sullen silence. A spokesman said they "did not like being asked for their vote. 'But you have something I want,' I cried; 'how am I to get it if I do not ask for it?'" This struck them as quite reasonable, and when I left they cheered me."[5] I feel sure she wrote that with a smile.

In the 1870s and 1880s, government was far smaller and less involved in every aspect of people's lives. As government became more consequential to women, the suffrage movement gathered momentum. The National Union of Women's Suffrage Societies was founded in 1872, but its moderate tactics did not significantly shift national sentiments for thirty years. Even in the early 1900s, opposition was strong—in part through the violence of more militant organizations, led by the Emmeline Pankhurst's Women's Social and Political Union (WSPU).[6]

This was the milieu which confronted the young statesman. From his entry into Parliament in 1901, Churchill accepted the concept of votes for women. In 1904 he voted for a suffrage bill, which failed. But soon zealous protesters began to turn up at election rallies, and "his interest in women's suffrage, in spite of Mrs. Churchill's enthusiasm, wilted slightly under the attentions of its militant supporters."[7]

Clementine Churchill was indeed an "enthusiast." While she detested the tactics of militants, she strongly supported votes for women. As the debate reached its zenith she wrote humorously to *The Times,* ridiculing a long, pompous letter by an anti-suffragist: "…the question seems no longer to be 'Should women have votes?' but 'Ought women not to be abolished altogether? I have been so much impressed … that I have come to the conclusion that women should be put a stop to." Her letter was signed, "C.S.C. ('One of the Doomed')."[8] The anti-suffrage prime minister, H.H. Asquith, thought this "much the best thing" he had read on the subject.[9]

Support for suffrage grew after the 1906 election ushered in a Liberal government with a huge majority. Most suffragists were encouraged: the Liberals had run on reform, and some Liberal candidates had run on votes for women. Within the cabinet, however, opinion was divided: Churchill and Lloyd George favored the principle; other important figures, including Asquith, were adamantly hostile.[10]

Henpecked on the Hustings

Churchill's support cooled during the election campaign when he encountered the formidable WSPU leader Emmeline Pankhurst and her daughters, Christabel and Sylvia. At one of his rallies, Christabel and an ally interrupted so frequently that they were ejected, brought before a magistrate and fined. Churchill offered to pay their fines; they heatedly refused and spent a week in jail. Young Winston was not amused. "I am certainly not going to be henpecked into a position on which my mind is not fully prepared," he wrote later. Any more of this, he added, and he would not vote for suffrage in the next Parliament.[11]

Another suffragette harangued him during a speech a month later; Churchill offered five minutes at the end for any questions she wished to ask: she angrily declined and was ejected. He took questions anyway, expressing vexation. He had supported suffrage in 1904, he said, but was put off by the commotion and "utterly declined" to make any further commitments.

Suffragists were again hot on Churchill's trail in 1908, hounding him in his campaign to hold his seat in North West Manchester, which he lost; and then in Dundee, where he won. A year later in Bristol, he was attacked with a dogwhip by a militant named Theresa Garnett: "Take that in the name of the insulted women of England!" (When he was thrown out of office in the 1945 election Garnett, then elderly, announced that she was opening a suffragette museum, and asked him to return the whip.)[12]

By then it was clear that attacks were being directed on government ministers not because of their personal position but because of their prominence. The tactics employed by the WSPU are somewhat remindful of the present. Today as in 1909, certain audiences howl speakers off stages when they say anything deemed "offensive." In their defense, the suffragists' broad goal was to expand free speech, not to limit it.

It is hard to build from Churchill's statements and actions a figure opposed to women's rights—particularly when the same Churchill helped lay the foundations of the welfare state, with minimum wage legislation which covered many low-paid female workers, and illness and unemployment insurance. If Churchill now and then appeared "rather tepid" on suffrage, it was a human reaction to furious attacks from the side he thought he was on. "They make Winston very bitter," Lloyd George remarked chauvinistically: "His perorations, prepared with the utmost care, are completely wrecked and spoiled by squeaky voices calling out, 'Mr. Churchill! What about votes for women?'"[13]

"I am certainly not going to be henpecked…." Campaigning to retain his seat for Manchester North West, which he lost, April 1908 (Author's collection).

In July 1910 Churchill opposed a suffrage bill extending the vote to women on the same terms as men—who would be entitled to vote if they were "heads of household"—widows or women living alone. His reason was tactical: "Liberals feared that most of these would be propertied women inclined to vote Conservative," wrote Paul Addison. "And as Churchill pointed out, a prostitute would lose the vote on getting married, and regain it if she divorced." But Churchill's "democratic" case against this bill was "a convenient smokescreen for Liberals who were actually opposed to female suffrage."[14] Churchill, unfairly, was lumped in with them.

From his entry into Parliament, Churchill never wavered from his view that the sex disqualification was unwarranted in principle. But he would not vote for any bill likely to damage the electoral fortunes of his party, or not backed by a majority of electors.[15] He feared the Liberal government being brought down by what he called "petticoat politics." The right course, he said in 1911, was to hold two referenda: "first to the women to know if they want it; and then to the men to know if they will give it."[16] He was willing, he said, to abide by the result.

Women and the War

With the advent of World War I in 1914 domestic arguments, including women's suffrage and Irish Home Rule, were set aside. In 1918, with Churchill's support, Parliament passed the Representation of the People Act, enfranchising women over thirty who met minimum property qualifications. Churchill supported this reform, in part because of his observations of the role women had played in the war.

In Churchill's view, women had been the moral backbone of the country; their work had been vital. They might not have fought in the trenches, but they drove vehicles almost to the front lines, served in field hospitals, took men's places in war industries. A few served as spies and paid with their lives. That, Churchill wrote, enshrined for them "the vote which for so many years they had vainly sought to wrest from successive Governments by methods too often suggesting that they had not the civic sense to use the privilege rightly."[17] Clearly he still remembered being "henpecked."

It is true that Churchill expressed doubt in "one person/one vote" in the 1930s, when he wrote essays pondering the future of democracy. He once proposed that every householder—"by which I mean the man or woman who pays the rent and the rates of any dwelling in which more than two persons habitually reside"—should have *two* votes, since it was they who "had to face the real problems of life...."[18] Churchill was now speaking not of "man" but of "man and woman." Cynics might say that the majority of householders were men; but that would change, and the principle remained.

Again in World War II, Churchill was deeply moved by the efforts of British women. To his former private secretary, John Colville, he said: "When I think what women did in the war I feel sure they deserve to be treated equally." Colville recalled the "astonishment" when Churchill said he hoped that Churchill College, founded as a national memorial to him, would admit women on equal terms with men. "No college at Oxford or Cambridge had ever done any such thing," Colville wrote. "I asked him afterwards if this had been Clementine's idea. 'Yes,' he replied, 'and I support it.'"[19] He had, indeed, evolved from 1897.

In Sum

When Churchill entered politics in 1900, seven million men had the vote; when he died, thirty-six million men and women had it. Universal suffrage had arrived, wrote Kevin Theakston: "Yet far from it sweeping away, undermining or destabilizing the traditional institutions of the British state—which the pessimists had feared in the 19th century, and which Churchill himself was concerned about in the 1930s—mass democracy was accommodated and incorporated into the constitutional system of Parliament and monarchy he had long celebrated." In 1945, in praise of those institutions, Churchill cited "the will of the people expressed by free and fair election on the basis of universal suffrage."[20]

Contrary, then, to the imprecations of *Time,* the *Daily Telegraph,* Commander Graf, and others who have not done their homework, Churchill cannot be shown to have been against women's suffrage, or "women's rights" for that matter, at any time in the 20th century. He voted for suffrage as early as 1904. His hesitations in 1905–12 arose when militants tried to break up his speeches. He was against certain measures at certain times, for tactical reasons—unlike, say, Asquith, who opposed the very principle.

In 1910 Churchill opposed a franchise bill he feared might increase the Conservative vote at the expense of Liberals. In 1928, when Parliament extended the vote to all women over 21, he criticized it in cabinet, fearing that it would increase the Labour vote at the expense of Conservatives. While these may be considered petty objections, a century later some politicians resist immigration reforms they think will increase another party's vote. *Plus ça change, plus c'est la même chose.*

Churchill's support for women's rights was less ideological than his wife's, though she was certainly an influence. In part, too, it stemmed from political common sense. In 1945, for example, the Labour margin of victory was 19 percent among males but just 2 percent among females. "Papa supported votes for women," said his daughter, "when he realized how many women would vote for him."[21]

6

The Sinking of the *Titanic*

The Myth: Churchill Bears Heavy Responsibility for the Ship's Loss
---

In his 2012 book, *Who Sank the* Titanic?, British investigative journalist Robert Strange held Winston Churchill largely responsible for the 1912 disaster. This charge makes a nice bookend with the much older canard (Chapter 13) that Churchill conspired to sink the *Lusitania*.

On 10 April 1912, the world's largest passenger ship set out on her maiden voyage from Southampton, Cherbourg and Queenstown to New York. Four days later, RMS *Titanic* struck an iceberg and sank in under three hours, killing 1514 people. To his wife, Churchill reflected on the great traditions of the sea towards women and children, hoping that the story would mollify suffragettes (previous chapter) "who are so bitter in their sex antagonism." The tragedy, he added, proved "that in spite of all the inequalities and artificialities of our modern life," British civilization remained "absolutely democratic."[1]

Churchill was mistaken to believe the inequalities of the time did not matter: while 85 percent of first and second class women and children were saved, the figure was only 40 percent for women and children in steerage—not for lack of gallantry, but because strict class boundaries prevented many from getting to the boat deck in time, and because many lifeboats were not filled to capacity. Little could Churchill have anticipated that a century later, he would be singled out not as an aristocrat blind to class injustice, but as the chief architect of the *Titanic* disaster, by Strange, who spent three years researching documents in the National Archives.

Churchill at the Board of Trade

As president of the Board of Trade, Strange wrote, Churchill was responsible for marine safety when the *Titanic* was planned, designed and built—and was

fatally distracted by a combination of burning political ambition, wounded pride and the pursuit of his future wife Clementine…. From the start, he seems to have washed his hands of the Marine Division. Supervision of *Titanic*'s construction was passed to Francis Carruthers, a poorly-trained and underpaid Board of Trade engineer who failed to spot flaws in the ship's construction…. By the time the *Titanic* was finally launched, Churchill had achieved his aim of promotion to Home Secretary and thereby escaped public examination about his role in the *Titanic* debacle. [But] the ship was first pro-

RMS *Titanic* departing Southampton on 10 April 1912 (Wikimedia Commons).

posed, designed and had its keel laid down on his watch. It is inconceivable that the minister respon-sible for safety at sea would not have been fully briefed about the construction of what was to be the biggest ship afloat. And he was very aware of the lack of lifeboats. He had been warned again and again but failed to take action.[2]

Churchill was President of the Board of Trade from 12 April 1908 to 18 February 1910. RMS *Titanic*, and her sister ship *Olympic*, were conceived in mid–1907 and their plans drawn in late 1907 and early 1908. It is therefore incorrect to say that Churchill was in charge when the ships were proposed or designed.

Churchill *was* at the Board of Trade when the final plans were approved (July 1908) and the hulls laid down (December 1908, March 1909). But *Titanic* complied with all Board of Trade regulations. Her lifeboat capacity (1178) actually exceeded the legal requirement (990).[3] And if Francis Carruthers, the engineer assigned, "failed to spot flaws" in the ship's construction, how was it possible for Churchill to spot them?

What about the "fatal distraction" of Churchill's "burning ambition, wounded pride and pursuit of his future wife"? He was offered the Board of Trade in April 1908. He lost the then-mandatory re-election for new ministers in Manchester, but secured a new seat for Dundee in May. His "pursuit" of Clementine was nearing its successful end by July. All these prideful accomplishments were *before* the *Titanic* plans were submitted to the Board of Trade.

Devils in the Details

Earlier researchers have suggested that weaknesses in *Titanic*'s steel plates and rivets contributed to her rapid sinking.[4] This begs the question of how the *Olympic* managed an illustrious twenty-four-year career, including troop transport during World War I and several collisions, earning the nickname "Old Reliable," with faulty rivets and weak plates. True, *Olympic* was refitted with a double hull after the *Titanic* disaster. Yet oil tankers up to five times her tonnage, and 100 feet or more longer, remained single-hulled until the *Exxon Valdez* episode in 1989. To blame Churchill for design weaknesses suggests that the president of the Board of Trade should also have been an engineer.

Neither was it Churchill's responsibility personally to review ship plans. His duty was on a higher level. He saw his role "as responsible for the direct defence of Free Trade," and fostering "the commercial interests of our country, within the limits of state intervention."[5] It is certainly true that he found those tasks more interesting than rivets and steel plate, which he quite properly assigned to the Marine Division.

Strange contended that Churchill was warned about the ship's insufficient lifeboats yet failed to take action; and that he should have known (somehow) that corners were being cut (maybe) in *Titanic*'s construction. Her lifeboat capacity was indeed vastly short of her total passengers and crew. But this had been the lifeboat situation for twenty years before Churchill arrived. Queried about lifeboats in Parliament before the sinking,

Last lifeboat launched from *Titanic* **was a collapsible, with canvas sides, here photographed by a passenger on the rescuing ship** *Carpathia,* **the morning after the sinking (National Archives).**

Churchill had replied: "I am advised that it would not be practicable" for liners to carry boats for all."[6] This is no different from what his predecessors had been saying on the advice of their experts.

Strange argued that lifeboat quotas were purposely kept low by greedy ship-owners who "never wanted to pay for boats or for the men who could launch them."[7] He shows how Thomas Ismay, owner of the White Star Line, "cooked" the minutes of an 1888 committee on lifeboats to delete references to lifesaving "appliances" for all aboard. "In fairness to Ismay," he adds, the committee "probably never imagined" their regulations would still be in force two decades later."

Yet by 1908 the same greedy ship-owners were building elaborate watertight compartments controlled from the bridge, which cost a lot more than lifeboats, and which, they thought, would keep a liner afloat in any conceivable situation. (They would have, if *Titanic* had hit the iceberg at virtually any other angle.) Churchill, we are expected to believe, should have divined that the ship's watertight compartments were not high enough, that slicing her hull open for 200 feet in a glancing blow would cause them to overflow, one into another, until she sank. That is asking a lot of a minister taking the advice of experts.

As for not wanting to pay for enough men to launch lifeboats, *Titanic* carried 900 crew—which proved more than enough to launch every boat hanging from the davits, and then some (two collapsibles were lashed to the boat deck). And, anticipating an increase in lifeboat requirements, the builders had provided davits for double the number of boats, enough for everyone on board.

The fact that many lifeboats left the ship short of capacity, saving nearly 500 fewer lives than they might have, is something even Churchill could not foresee: at first, passengers hung back, preferring the apparent safety of the ship to small boats on the open sea; later, officers sent boats away unfilled, believing they might buckle on the way down, not knowing they had been tested with full loads.

There are many besides Churchill in Mr. Strange's indictment—captain, crew, shipowners, politicians, builders, steel suppliers, riveters, inspectors. He does make a powerful case that White Star, in its haste to build *Titanic* and her sisters, may have accepted poor quality steel and/or rivets. But he admits this theory is "controversial" and can only say with certainty that "the steel of 1912 was less resistant to stress than the steel of today."

But Churchill remained in his crosshairs: "...it is hard to believe that the politician in charge of the Marine Division could not have been aware of the ship's construction" Really? "It would have been odd," he adds, "if Churchill hadn't talked to Lord Pirrie" of Harland & Wolff, *Titanic*'s builders." Why? Well, they were close enough to be "the main speakers at a Belfast rally in favour of Home Rule."[8] Which proves what, exactly?

There are many thoughtful books on the *Titanic* and her construction, on the outmoded lifeboat rules, and the actions of her captain, crew, owners and builders, which all had a part in the tragedy. But none including this one have proved that Churchill bears "a heavy burden of responsibility" for the loss.

7

The Unpleasantness on Sidney Street

The Myth: Churchill Interfered with Police and Fire-Fighters

Winston Churchill was Home Secretary from February 1910 to October 1911. The only member of Asquith's cabinet to have experienced four wars on three continents, he was characteristically intrigued whenever bullets whistled in anger. Imagine his sense of opportunity when bullets began to whistle in the heart of London, jolting him from his safe civilian post as Secretary of State for the Home Department, and coaxing him once again to present during an armed fray.

In early January 1911, a group of criminals from London's East end barricaded themselves in a house at 100 Sidney Street, resisting the police with deadly fire from Mausers. Churchill duly showed up on the scene, where he was photographed, later to be maligned in Parliament and the press for interfering with professionals and exposing himself to danger. The "folly of Sidney Street," a minor incident, was hung around his neck for years, and in a few quarters it still hangs.

Criminal Elements

Donald Rumbelow, a City of London policeman who wrote the most complete account,[1] said the burglars were Latvian refugees, who had fled Latvia after a revolt was suppressed by Czarist forces in 1905. Large numbers of people from Russia had claimed asylum and were admitted to Britain in those days. In a sense prefiguring the activity of certain refugees today, a small minority practiced revolutionary activities, funding themselves through crime.

Among their leaders was Peter Piaktow, nicknamed "Peter the Painter," whom Churchill later described as "one of those wild beasts" who would dominate the Bolshevik tyranny in Russia.[2] But Piaktow's subsequent history is unknown, and Churchill may have been referring to Jacob Peters, his cohort. Peters later emerged as part of the Cheka, Lenin's secret police, only to be liquidated during Stalin's purges of the 1930s.[3] Rumbelow also named Jacob Fogel, William or Joseph Sokolow, Fritz Svaars, George Gardstein, Nina Vassilleva, Luba Milstein and Max Smoller. It is worth mentioning that contrary to many reports, not all the gang were Latvians. In fact, only Svaars and Peters are Latvian names.

In 1909, the gang assaulted a messenger carrying wages for a Tottenham rubber

The Battle of Sidney Street, 1911, with Home Secretary Churchill (first top hat on the left) in the war zone (Author's Collection).

factory; police caught them after a six-mile pursuit in which two people were killed and twenty-seven injured, but most of the assailants escaped. In December 1910, they made plans to rob the safe of a jeweler's shop in Houndsditch by renting an adjacent building and tunneling through. On December 16th, a neighbor heard the noise and summoned the police. In the ensuing gun battle, three unarmed constables were shot, along with several burglars. "Peter the Painter," with one or two companions and a hired locksmith, made good their escape.

The murders of the policemen sparked outrage throughout London, along with anti-immigrant fervor. East Enders protested, "'o let 'em in?" referring to the Liberal government's lenient immigration policies. As Home Secretary, Churchill was particularly sensitive to this.

The Crisis

On New Year's Day, 1911, an informant told police the criminals were hiding at 100 Sidney Street, and by the early morning of 3 January, constables had cordoned off the block. The gang's weapons proved superior to the few guns of the police, who normally weren't armed in those days. The police asked for troops from the Tower of London. Their call reached the Home Secretary in his morning bath.

Dripping wet, Churchill hurried to the telephone and granted permission to use whatever force was necessary. A company of Scots Guards was dispatched. Dressing hastily, Churchill went to the Home Office for more news, but found little. He decided to see the action for himself. "I thought it my duty," he wrote, but admitted also "a strong sense of curiosity which perhaps it would have been well to keep in check."[4]

The Home Secretary, distinguished in top hat and Astrakhan-collar overcoat, duly arrived at Sidney Street, where large crowds had gathered behind the police cordon. The gunfire was intense, the attackers firing endless rounds into the upper floors, the gang firing back. Churchill began to realize that his presence might prove embarrassing, and possibly cause confusion among those giving the orders. But, transfixed by the battle, he held his place.

While trying to keep out of the command structure, Churchill could not resist offering ideas. He suggested they summon artillery batteries, then storm the house from different directions. Then perhaps they could advance up the stairs behind a steel shield. The police actually went in search of a shield in nearby foundries.

Such tactics proved unnecessary when smoke began drifting from the upper windows, quickly engulfing the top floor. The fire spread downwards, driving the gunmen before it. Here Churchill played his only operative role.

The fire brigade arrived, treating the blaze as it would any other, expecting to rush past the police cordon and extinguish the fire. The police stopped them, and an argument broke out. Churchill made himself known, telling the fire brigade to stand down, lest they be injured in the exchange of bullets. He did ask them to remain on scene, to put out any fire spreading to adjacent buildings.

As 100 Sidney Street was consumed, gunshots from inside slackened. The police and soldiers, training their weapons on the front door, expected the gang to charge out for a final showdown. But no one emerged. The fire brigade was allowed to extinguish the flames, and in the ashes police found the charred bodies of two burglars. Jacob Peters was eventually arrested, but a bungling prosecution saw him released, and he eventually returned to Russia. Of Peter the Painter there was no sign; he and his remaining companions had disappeared.

Repercussions

Churchill was quickly attacked for playing a personal role in the episode. In the House of Commons, former Prime Minister Arthur Balfour said: "We are concerned to observe photographs in the illustrated newspapers of the Home Secretary in the danger-zone. I understand what the photographer was doing, but why the Home Secretary?"

Churchill later called Balfour's comment "not altogether unjust."[5] It is reasonable to suggest that Churchill had no more business at the scene of the siege than he did at the D-Day landings—and apposite to remember that he was dissuaded from joining the D-Day forces only by King George VI, and only at the last minute. Nevertheless, he had not interfered with police directing the action; his only involvement was to dissuade the fire brigade from risking their own lives.

It was a typical piece of Churchillian chutzpah, and he was roundly criticized as a grandstander in search of publicity. This does not seem to be his immediate impulse. He was, after all, only a decade removed from his years as war correspondent. His real weakness was that he found the attraction of guns ablaze in London too fascinating to resist.

Suggesting that his action was more impulsive than conniving was the scene back in Whitehall, when he returned to his office to face his irate civil servant, Charles Masterman. "What the hell have you been doing now, Winston?" said Masterman, bursting into his office. "Now Charlie," said Churchill, with his inimitable lisp. "Don't be croth. It was such fun."[6] "It must have been irresistible," wrote A.L. Rowse, "to serve such a Minister, who had the heart of a boy."[7] Yet one can imagine many 35-year-old men behaving similarly.

The less forgiving had a field day over Churchill's impetuosity, and Sidney Street followed him around. Twelve years later he was criticizing the government, saying, "… they have not succeeded in handling a single public question with success." A voice in the crowd cracked: "They succeeded at the battle of Sidney Street, didn't they?" Jovially, Churchill deflected the parry: "We have always been wondering where Peter the Painter got to."[8]

In the longer view, his friend Violet Bonham-Carter, daughter of Prime Minister Asquith, offers the keenest appraisal:

> Many Liberals were disturbed, not for the first or last time, by his zest for planning and directing military operations, by his tendency to over-dramatize a situation and himself and to use a steam-hammer to crack a nut … their charge of dramatizing events was not unfair but the motives they ascribed to him were, in my view, wholly misconceived. It was not the pursuit of limelight nor the lure of blood and thunder which had drawn him to the Siege of Sidney Street…. A deeper impulse was at work to which we find a clue in his own words. "After all," he once wrote regretfully, "a man's life must be nailed to a cross either of thought or action." But though he admitted this necessity he never accepted it. The realm of thought alone has always seemed to him to be an insufficient kingdom, cramping and cold. Where his imagination led, his body needs must follow.[9]

The "Siege of Sidney Street" has interesting parallels in our own day of contemporary terrorism, wrote Christopher Harmon. "There are familiar patterns: the international operatives, robbery to finance terrorism, female as well as male terrorists, the murder of police, the role of police in suppression of terrorist cells, the challenges for civic officials of 'incident management.'"[10]

8

"The sullen feet of marching men in Tonypandy"

The Myth: Churchill Sent Troops to Crush and Kill Welsh Strikers

For more than a century it has been part of socialist demonology that Churchill, as Home Secretary in 1910–11, sent troops against striking coalminers in the Rhondda Valley, Wales. In an otherwise generous tribute following Churchill's death in 1965, Labour Prime Minister Harold Wilson found it necessary to remind Parliament of Sidney Street (Chapter 7), Gallipoli (Chapter 12), and "the sullen feet of marching men in Tonypandy."[1]

And for half a century Churchill's defenders, beginning with his son, insisted the striker stories were fabrications. Randolph Churchill wrote that his father's conduct had been "grotesquely distorted…. Socialist propagandists have sought to make martyrs of the miners of Tonypandy comparable to those of Tolpuddle in 1834. Tonypandy in reality is only distinguished from the other Welsh villages involved because of the high degree of looting in which the miners indulged; but a lie once started can seldom be overtaken."[2] Randolph left the impression that his father had forbidden the dispatch of troops.

Out of this has grown a considerable muddle, so let us start by correcting the record: Churchill *did* send troops to scenes of strikes and rioting in Wales on a few occasions; in 1911 their presence at one location resulted in two to four fatalities.

Now, as the traffic judge used to allow me to do in my leaded-foot days as a teenage driver, I shall plead on Churchill's behalf: "Guilty with an explanation."

Tonypandy, Wales, November 1910

The miners' strike in the Rhondda Valley grew out of disputes over wage differentials for working hard and soft seams and the demand for more safety inspections—death rates in mines had reached the highest since statistics had been compiled. Up to 30,000 miners struck, and some rioted. Local authorities appealed for troops. On 6 November William Abraham, a Member of Parliament and president of the South Wales Miners federation, arrived at the Home Office to plead with Churchill not to send troops.

Convinced, Churchill met with Secretary of State for War Richard Haldane, and together they resolved to dispatch police constables, but no troops. Churchill said the use of soldiers was inappropriate in a civil disorder. He also promised the strikers an immediate Board of Trade inquiry, and sent them a message:

Their best friends here are greatly distressed at the trouble which has broken out and will do their best to help them get fair treatment…. But rioting must cease at once so that the enquiry shall not be prejudicial and to prevent the credit of the Rhondda Valley being impaired. Confiding in the good sense of the Cambrian workmen we are holding back the soldiers for the present and sending police instead.[3]

The Conservative press attacked. *The Times* said that the Liberal Home Secretary "hardly seems to understand that an acute crisis has arisen which needs decisive handling. The rosewater of conciliation is all very well in its place, but its place is not in face of a wild mob drunk with the desire of destruction. Men's lives are in danger, not to mention the poor horses…."[4]

The Liberal press defended Churchill, praising his restraint. "The brave course was also the wise one," wrote the *Manchester Guardian*. "One can imagine what would have happened if the soldiers instead of the policemen had come on the rioters while they were pillaging. Bayonets would have been used instead of truncheons … and instead of a score of cases for the hospital there might have been as many for the mortuary."[5]

But the decision to withhold troops was short-lived. Rioting did not end, and spread to the town of Tonypandy, where one man was fatally injured and sixty-three shops were vandalized. The officer commanding the Southern Command dispatched 400 standby soldiers, but on 8 November Churchill ordered that "in no case should soldiers come in direct contact with rioters unless and until action had been taken by the police." If police were overpowered, troops could be deployed, but even then a number of police should remain, "to emphasise the fact that the armed forces act merely as the support of the civil power."[6]

"By preventing bloodshed," Paul Addison wrote, "Churchill also prevented a debacle for Liberalism." Writing to Lloyd George the following spring, Churchill attempted to follow-up his November promise to address grievances. The government, he said, should institute stronger safety regulations and inspections, financing the expense with a sur-charge on mineowners' royalties. His hopes were thwarted, Addison continued: "The soldiers did not kill anybody, but they remained in the Rhondda until October 1911 and as David Smith observes, their presence 'ensured that the miners' demands would be utterly rejected.'"[7]

Llanelli, Wales, August 1911

Nine months later, a national railway strike broke out when rail operators refused to recognize the unions as negotiators. Troops were sent to numerous scenes of distur-bances around the country. Throughout this strike, troops had orders to stand by and act only if public security was endangered. Mostly the troops acted with caution, and when they did fire, they usually aimed over the heads of crowds.

Lloyd George settled the rail strike by convincing the railways to recognize union negotiators. But in Llanelli, Wales—two days, ironically, after the strike had ended—the only fatalities from the use of troops occurred. A train was held up by rioters and the engine driver knocked senseless. Soldiers attempted to clear the track but looting began, and they fired into the crowd, killing two to four rioters (accounts vary).

With the strike over, the troops were withdrawn. On August 20th King George V telegraphed Churchill: "Glad the troops are to be sent back to their districts at once: this will reassure the public. Much regret unfortunate incident at Llanelli. Feel convinced that prompt measures taken by you prevented loss of life in different parts of the country."[8]

It is possible to conclude that Churchill had been unwise to send troops to take control of the rail network, though he was not of course directly responsible for the shootings. "For all the criticism that came Churchill's way from the Labour members of Parliament for his attitude to the use of troops during this strike," wrote Randolph Churchill, "there is little doubt that the King's telegram represented public opinion at the time. But Labour was not to forget...."[9] The myths of Tonypandy were revived by Labour during the General Strike of 1926, and the events there and at Llanelli have repeatedly been confused over the years.

Police officers blocking a street during the Tonypandy riots of 1910 (Wikimedia Commons).

"Guilty with an explanation"

There was another reason why anxiety ran high during the 1911 rail strike. A few weeks earlier, the Germans had sent a gunboat to Agadir, French Morocco. Britain was France's ally, and rumors of war with Germany were rife. David Lloyd George, insisting that the Agadir Crisis was a threat to peace, declared that the Germans "would not hesitate to use the paralysis into which the country was falling in order to attack Britain." Paul Addison recorded the public mood:

> The unprecedented challenge of a simultaneous national stoppage by all four railway unions convinced respectable opinion that the world was about to be turned upside down.... Churchill's own apprehensions were connected, apparently with fear of subversion in Germany.... He was also informed by Guy Granet, the general manager of the Midland Railways, of allegations that labour leaders were receiving payments from a German agent.... Conservatives applauded him for taking decisive action. But there were loud protests from the Labour party and left-wing Liberals, who accused him of imposing the army on local authorities against their will, and introducing troops into peaceful and law-abiding districts.[10]

In handling the rail strike, Ted Morgan wrote, what Churchill's critics could not see "was the number of saved, and the number of tragedies averted. In their drunken frenzy, the Llanelli rioters had wrought more havoc and shed more blood and produced more serious injury than all the fifty thousand soldiers all over the country."[11]

After the deaths at Llanelli, Churchill was roundly condemned and the *Manchester Guardian* turned against him. Keir Hardie, founder of the Labour Party, accused Churchill and Prime Minister H.H. Asquith of "deliberately sending soldiers to shoot and kill strikers." That charge has endured for a century; yet Churchill in August 1911 had told the

House of Commons: "There can be no question of the military forces of the crown intervening in a labour dispute."[12]

Why then were military forces used at Llanelli? Defending himself to William Royle, organizer of the Manchester Liberal Party, Churchill explained: "The progress of a democratic country is bound up with the maintenance of order. The working classes would be almost the only sufferers from an outbreak of riot & a general strike if it c[oul]d be effective would fall upon them & their families with its fullest severity."

Churchill told Royle, as he had Lloyd George, that the miners' wages were far too low. The rise in the cost of living, he wrote, made it necessary that wages be raised: "I believe the Government is now strong enough to secure an improvement in social conditions without failing in its primary duties."[13]

Old Men Remember

The old slanders of Tonypandy were still circulating in the general election of 1950. Speaking at Cardiff, Churchill told his Welsh audience that he had sent police to Tonypandy, with the sole object of preventing bloodshed. He was much criticized, he added, for his "so-called weakness…. But I carried my point." The police had met the strikers "not with rifles and bayonets, but with their rolled-up mackintoshes. Thus all bloodshed, except perhaps some from the nose, was averted and all loss of life prevented."[14] This was inaccurate, but it does not alter Churchill's judicious instincts and actions, or his wish to address strikers' grievances.

The myth lived on. Two years after Churchill's death an Oxford undergraduate, discussing Sir Winston's career with his tutor, asserted confidently that "Churchill had ordered tanks to be used against the miners at Tonypandy. His tutor commented that this showed remarkable farsightedness on Churchill's part, as the tank had not yet been invented."[15]

Vindication of a sort did appear via the BBC, which interviewed surviving strikers fifty-five years after Tonypandy. Among them was W.H. (Will) Mainwaring, at the time one of the youngest militants in the South Wales coalfields, subsequently co-author of a famous pamphlet, *The Miners' Next Step*. All those many years later, this ardent Labour Party activist still spoke with pride of his championing of the miners and his record as a protestor. On Churchill's actions Mainwaring was unequivocal:

> We never thought that Winston Churchill had exceeded his natural responsibility as Home Secretary. The military that came into the area did not commit one single act that allows the slightest resentment by the strikers. On the contrary, we regarded the military as having come in the form of friends to modify the otherwise ruthless attitude of the police forces.[16]

Over a century later, when the actions of police forces are questioned, when the National Guard is sometimes deployed during riotous protests in which local residents are the main victims, Churchill's experience is worthy of study. And his magnanimity is worthy of reflection.

9

Ireland: "We could never have done anything without him"

The Myth: Churchill Opposed Irish Self-Rule

The Irish, a people conversant with the heroes and villains of history, admire William Gladstone, the 19th century Liberal prime minister whose career foundered over his early support for Irish Home Rule. Fewer Irish recall the later Liberal government, led by H.H. Asquith, which steadily advanced Home Rule until interrupted by World War I—or the Liberal-led coalition government which pushed through the Irish Treaty, leading to Ireland's independence. Churchill is unfairly regarded by many as an steadfast foe of Irish self-determination. Yet he was a member of both those governments, fought hard for compromise, strongly supported Home Rule before the war, and the Irish Treaty afterward.

Why the confusion? It's an emotion-laden subject, for one thing. But Irish misunderstanding of Churchill reminds me of a proverb quoted by Cordell Hull, President Roosevelt's Secretary of State during World War II: "A lie will gallop halfway round the world before the truth has time to pull its breeches on."[1]

It is important to distinguish between the prewar and postwar concepts. Home Rule did not mean independence. It was rejected by Catholic Ireland in the 1918 general election in favor of the Sinn Fein ("Ourselves alone") party. The British government was opposed to full independence and would never have granted it without the guerrilla warfare waged by the Irish Republican Army between 1919 and 1921. Irish independence was not Churchill's preference—but he was among the first to recognize that Britain could not continue to rule by force, and to accept negotiations with Sinn Fein that led to the Irish Treaty.

"Ulster will fight, and Ulster will be right"

Churchill's negative reputation among the Irish began with his father, Lord Randolph Churchill, who was at the peak of his career in 1886, when a dramatic shift in power occurred in Britain. That was the year Gladstone's Liberals split over the prime minister's support of Irish Home Rule. They were defeated by Randolph's Conservatives, led by Lord Salisbury. With the exception of one brief period in the 1890s, the Liberals remained out of office for twenty years.

Lord Randolph, Paul Addison explained, "played a brilliant and unscrupulous part in manipulating the Irish question for the benefit of the Conservative Party. In 1886 he played the 'Orange Card' when he travelled to Belfast and whipped up Protestant fervour with a ringing declaration in favour of rebellion: 'Ulster will fight, and Ulster will be right.' For this and other services he was rewarded, in July 1886, by his appointment as Chancellor of the Exchequer and Leader of the House."[2] It was the beginning of his brief, spectacular ascendancy. (See Chapter 4.)

Lord Randolph's son, though he sympathized with unionist Ulster, took a different line. From 1910 to 1914, Winston Churchill tried to appease both the northern and southern Irish and, to his misfortune, appeased neither. In the aftermath of the Great War, he and others forged the delicate compromise which led to the Irish Treaty. Northern Ireland was not a party to the Treaty negotiations, though Churchill did mediate between North and South afterward, when they were on the brink of war. In the end, the North had to be content with assurances that they would never be coerced into a united Ireland.

In 1938, much to Churchill's displeasure, the Chamberlain government abandoned its access to the Treaty Ports—Berehaven, Queenstown (modern Cobh) and Lough Swilly. Then, when World War II started, Ireland proclaimed neutrality. As Chamberlain's First Lord of the Admiralty in 1939, Churchill pressed unsuccessfully to reoccupy those ports, and as prime minister he had very rough language for Irish Taoiseach Éamon de Valera. Yet Churchill never violated Ireland's status, and Ireland did afford Britain unofficial support in various ways.

Churchill Embraces Home Rule

As on votes for women, Churchill's first views on Home Rule were reactionary. In 1897, he wrote his mother that he would "never consent" to it; that Liberal support for it was the one reason he would not enter Parliament as a Liberal.[3] In 1904, six weeks before he officially left the Conservatives, he stated privately to a Liberal official that an Irish Parliament would be "dangerous and impracticable."[4] But on 31 May 1904 he crossed the floor to take his seat with the Liberals, and his attitude began to change.

Ireland's quarrel, Churchill declared that month, stemmed more from economic factors than religious differences: "If Ireland were more prosperous she would be more loyal, and if more loyal more free." In 1905 he expressed regret that moderate opinion did not outweigh "passionate advocacy." Ireland, he said, posed "one of the most difficult, as it was one of the most attractive" questions before the politicians.[5]

Ever the optimist, Churchill could not see why reason should not prevail, as it had in South Africa, where he had helped draft a generous settlement with the Boers within the British Empire. But the Conservatives remained negative, and encouraged Ulster's Protestant majority to fight and be right.

Churchill countered by offering two compromises: (1) Home Rule for the south, with Ulster temporarily excluded; (2) a federal Britain with regional parliaments for England, Scotland and Wales as well as Ireland, and an imperial Parliament for national affairs. The latter was "typically Churchillian in its radicalism but it won few prominent supporters," wrote Jeremy Havardi. Some Conservatives "unconstitutionally approached the King, urging him to dissolve Parliament rather than accede to Home Rule."[6] As the debate built, Churchill found himself deploring "bigotry and intolerance," demanding that a "fair effort" be made at a settlement. Never, he said, had "so little been asked" and "so many people asked for it."[7]

As in many things, Churchill was ahead of his time. Today, regional parliaments are *de rigueur* in Wales, Scotland and Northern Ireland, though England is still without one. A century ago, there was no chance of such a solution. Asquith's government offered a measure of Home Rule including Ulster—a proposal to which Ulster Protestants responded by threatening armed resistance should the government attempt to impose it. In March 1914, officers at the Curragh Camp in County Kildare threatened to resign rather than inflict Home Rule on the populace, and Churchill was accused by the Tories of masterminding a "pogrom" against Ulster. The Home Rule bill was passed, but postponed. Except for the outbreak of World War I, civil war might have risen from what Churchill called "the mists and squalls of Ireland."[8]

The Black and Tans

His sense of logic—and his faith in British imperialism—at first prevented Churchill from grasping the emotions involved. To him the problem was "largely technical in nature," as Paul Cantor noted: There was "no underlying reason why the Irish and the British should be in conflict; on the contrary, they have much in common (including a language!) and above all congruent economic and political interests. What stands in the way of their realizing these common interests is history—the long, painful, and sad history of British rule in Ireland."[9]

Submerged by World War I, the Irish quarrel was not forgotten. In 1916 the "Easter Rising" proclaimed a republic. Though quickly put down, it was the most serious revolt in over a century. With the Armistice and general election of 1918, the issue came roaring back. Sinn Fein became the dominant political party, winning 76 of Ireland's 105 seats in Parliament. Demanding independence, they set up an Irish parliament, the Dail. The Irish Volunteers, later the Irish Republican Army, began a guerrilla war. Prime Minister Lloyd George dissolved the Dail and set about quelling the rebellion by force.

In January 1919, Winston Churchill became Secretary of State for War. As such, according to legend, he created the "Black and Tans," a temporary constabulary, so named for their uniforms. Most members were English, some Irish. Their methods of suppression were so violent that they provoked a lasting anger against Churchill which still exists today.

In fact, as Paul Addison has written, Churchill "seems to have played no part in the initial [1919] decision to recruit them." It was not until January 1920 "that he realized the state of chaos in Ireland." But Churchill was "less than candid" in his defense of the constabulary, who sometimes, in an excess of zeal and the press of events, carried out reprisals and murders against innocent people. "Realizing that their activities were getting out of hand, Churchill swung round to the view that it would be better to pursue a policy of official reprisals in order to avoid 'excesses.'"[10]

Addison adds an observation that we should always bear in mind about Churchill, noting "his lifelong tendency to seek victory as the prelude to a magnanimous settlement with the defeated party.... He was quite prepared to go much further with concessions ... but he was not prepared to make these concessions at a time when they would be claimed as a victory for the Sinn Feiners."[11]

Churchill did not personally create the Black and Tans. But he defended them despite atrocities that exceeded their remit. Against that, he must also be credited with a leading role in forging Ireland's independence.

Peace at Last

In 1922, Churchill played a key part in engineering a peace that would last nearly fifty years. The story of the Irish Treaty has been recounted by numerous biographers. It was Churchill, most prominently, who brought the warring parties together: not only the British government and Irish revolutionaries, but, after the Treaty was forged, Michael Collins and Ulster Prime Minister Sir James Craig.

By June 1921 the situation was acute. Civil war was in the air, and the Cabinet concluded there must be negotiations. Churchill pointed out that continued strife would alienate the United States, always a factor in his thoughts.[12] A truce was signed in July, and an Anglo-Irish conference scheduled for October. Churchill was one of the British delegates. The Irish delegation was headed by Arthur Griffiths, a writer and scholar who scarcely said a word; and Michael Collins, president of the Republican Brotherhood and Adjutant General of the IRA.

Doggedly, as the weeks crawled by, Churchill pursued the prize. He and Collins were much alike, Manchester wrote,

> fearless, charismatic, fiercely patriotic, ready to sacrifice everything for principle. Both had cherubic features but bulldog expressions, and they shared a ready wit…. Their friendship grew; after a day of exhausting deliberations, Winston would take his recent enemy home and sit up late, talking, arguing, drinking, even singing. Another time he slyly produced a thumbnail appraisal of himself which Collins had written: "Will sacrifice all for political gain…. Inclined to be bombastic. Full of ex-officer jingo or similar outlook. Don't actually trust him." There was a moment of silence; then both men burst into laughter. Collins trusted him now, but it was Churchillian charm which kept them together.[13]

At one strained moment, when Collins complained that the British had put a price on his head, Churchill showed him his framed copy of the Boer wanted poster for the escaped desperado, Churchill, in 1899: "At any rate it was a good price—£5000," he said. "Look at me—£25 dead or alive. How would you like that?" Collins read the poster and broke out laughing. Feelings eased. They had established the basis of a common understanding.

Michael Collins signed the Irish Treaty, and with it, he predicted, his death warrant. He was too right—gunned down by an assassin in August 1922. His last message to Churchill, sent through a friend under stress of a presentiment of the end, was: "Tell Winston we could never have done anything without him."[14]

With the Treaty signed, Churchill engineered a meeting between Collins and Ulster Prime Minister Sir James Craig. "They both glowered magnificently," wrote Churchill, who "slipped away" on some pretext and let them have at it: "What these two Irishmen, separated by such gulfs of religion, sentiment, and conduct, said to each other I cannot tell." Hours passed: "mutton chops, etc., were tactfully introduced about one o'clock." Around 4pm "the Private Secretary reported signs of movement."[15]

Miraculously, the two fearful enemies agreed to help each other: to consult when disputes arose, to stand united against violence. It was not totally successful: within a week each was making violent speeches to their supporters, and with this disappointment Churchill set out to defend the Irish Treaty before a divided Parliament.

Undaunted, Churchill said that the Treaty offered something for all sides. The twenty-six southern counties would form, not a republic but a "Free State" within the Empire. Its officials would swear allegiance to the crown. The Royal Navy could patrol the coast and keep the Treaty Ports. The Dail would control Irish affairs. The six counties of Northern Ireland would not be coerced to join, and remained, as they do to this day, part of the United Kingdom.

Churchill had once insisted the Irish problem was technical not emotional. Now he emotionally appealed to his colleagues not to harken to the diehards, in words that we might apply to similar quarrels today:

> These absolutely sincere, consistent, unswerving gentlemen, faithful in all circumstances to their implacable quarrels, seek to mount their respective national war horses, in person or by proxy, and to drive at full tilt at one another, shattering and splintering down the lists, to the indescribable misery of the common people....[16]

Parliament ratified the Irish Treaty, and on 7 January 1922, the Dail did likewise. Collins and Griffiths headed a provisional government. The strife wasn't over: de Valera rejected the Treaty's subordination of Ireland to the Crown, which for Churchill and Lloyd George was key to the settlement. This led to civil war in Ireland and, although defeated in the short run, de Valera and anti–Treaty party prevailed politically in the 1930s and 1940s.

The Irish Free State had a brief life. Oddly enough, de Valera drew back from declaring Ireland a republic and retained a symbolic role for the King in external affairs. Ireland continued to be recognized by Britain as a member of the Commonwealth, though it behaved like an independent republic, and finally declared itself such in 1948.

By then, of course, matters had long passed out of Churchill's hands.

Public relief over passage of the Irish Treaty in 1922 was manifest, Churchill wrote. The British and most Irish felt they were "awaking from a nightmare. The whole Empire rejoiced, and foreign countries smiled approvingly, if sardonically."[17] One supposes there are still sardonic smiles over the part Churchill played. But the facts tell the story: Churchill had proven himself, if not a loving friend of Ireland, at least an ally in her quest for peace and freedom.

Plus Ça Change, Plus C'est la Même Chose

Reading Churchill's *The Aftermath*," wrote Paul Addison, "I'm struck by the admiration Churchill expresses for the Irish of all kinds and his high hopes of the Irish Free State, later dashed of course. He must have detested de Valera for undoing the Free State, in which he clearly took a paternal pride."[18]

This is an astute observation. Ireland excited Churchill's passion, but mostly in a positive way, for he always respected Irish patriotism and heroism. In World War II Paddy Finucane, one of many Irishmen who volunteered to fight for Britain, destroyed thirty-two German aircraft before being shot down over France. "If ever I feel a bitter feeling rising in me in my heart about the Irish," he said in 1948, "the hands of heroes like Finucane seem to stretch out to soothe it away."[19]

In the end, his magnanimity overcame his regrets. In "The Dream," his imaginary conversation with the ghost of his father after World War II, Churchill penned a wistful coda to his long experience with Ireland.

"What happened to Ireland?," Lord Randolph asks. "Did they get Home Rule?"

"The South got it," Winston replies, "but Ulster stayed with us."

"Are the South a republic?"

"No one knows what they are. They are neither in nor out of the Empire. But they are much more friendly to us than they used to be. They have built up a cultured Roman Catholic system in the South. There has been no anarchy or confusion. They are getting more happy and prosperous. The bitter past is fading."[20]

10

"All his war paint"

On 4 August 1914, with Britain about to declare war on Germany, Prime Minister H.H. Asquith wrote to his lady friend: "Winston, who has got on all his war-paint, is longing for a sea-fight in the early hours of the morning to result in the sinking of the *Goeben*. The whole thing fills me with sadness."[1]

A week earlier Churchill had written to his wife: "Everything tends towards catastrophe & collapse. I am interested, geared-up & happy...."[2]

Those two quotations, and others carefully pruned, have been repeated by scores of critics including some respected historians who argue that in 1914, Churchill was dead-set for war, urging no compromise with Germany, determined to engage the Royal Navy, and withal to plunge Europe into chaos.

Almost every critic quotes only the above part of his message to his wife. The rest of it casts him in an entirely different light: "...Is it not horrible to be built like that?" he continued. "The preparations have a hideous fascination for me. I pray to God to forgive me for such fearful moods of levity. Yet I would do my best for peace, and nothing would induce me wrongfully to strike the blow."[3]

Asquith's "war paint" remark is often used to suggest that as head of the Navy, Churchill was somehow wrong to prosecute the war vigorously once it had begun, while the poor prime minister could only stand by helplessly. Sir Martin Gilbert, in his methodical way, explained why Churchill wanted action at that point. The new German battle-cruiser *Goeben*, larger and better armed than her predecessors, was loose in the Mediterranean, a threat to French transports shuttling troops from Africa. Churchill wanted her sunk. He also understood that acts of war could not be taken before the British ultimatum [for Germany to withdraw from Belgium] expired.

Immediately on his return to the Admiralty on 4 August, Churchill telegraphed a caution to the navy: "The British ultimatum to Germany will expire at midnight GMT 4th August. No acts of war should be committed before that hour, at which time the telegram to commence hostilities against Germany will be despatched from Admiralty."[4]

Churchill as Warmonger

Feverish assertions about Churchill spoiling for the fight have mainly been the realm of radical revisionists, most of whose books were not taken seriously, at least by serious people.[5] More recently, however, similar statements appeared by respected historians, including Sir Max Hastings.

Hastings' book, *Catastrophe 1914,* is a rich and suspenseful account of how and why World War I happened. It documents each fateful step, each wrong assumption and bad decision by Europe's leaders, interleaved with the experiences of ordinary Europeans. It begins with the murder of Archduke Franz Ferdinand on 28 June 1914, and ends in December, with touching scenes of the "Christmas Truce," as opposing soldiers sing hymns and exchange gifts before resuming battle the day after. I read it with appreciation, and recommend it to anyone—while profoundly disagreeing with its portrait of Winston Churchill.

Catastrophe 1914 uses both quotes noted at the head of this chapter, and others, to label Churchill as strident for war. Throughout the fatal summer of 1914, Churchill is depicted as "bent upon belligerence even before the issue of [Germany marching through] Belgium emerged."[6] On 29 July, Hastings states, "Churchill suggested, absurdly, that participation [in the war] need not cost much: 'Together we can carry a wide social policy…. The naval war will be cheap.'"[7]

"Absurdly" is a word that can be applied only in hindsight. The naval war *was* cheap—comparatively. As late as August 1914, it was by no means certain that Britain would send its paltry army to fight in Europe. Britain was a "sea animal," said Churchill, who visualized Britain fighting a "naval war." The French and Russian armies, it was then thought, would face Germany and Austria-Hungary in two fronts on the ground.

That things didn't work out that way is well-known in retrospect. Churchill had contemplated the possible need for ground forces in a private 1911 memorandum; yet publicly he opposed conscription ("the draft") before the war. The British government's view at the advent of war is documented by Hastings: "The 1913 Army Estimates made no mention whatsoever of a possible British ground role in a European conflict."[8] In *Catastrophe 1914,* three pages after Churchill's "absurd" suggestion of a naval war, we read of General Sir John French (who would later command the British Expeditionary Force) being summoned to Downing Street on 3 August. French was told "there was still no question of Britain sending an army to the continent."[9]

On 3 August, Britain warned Germany to stay out of Belgium. (Germany's refusal to do so was the proximate cause of Britain declaring war.) "Because such vestigial delusions persisted in government," Hastings writes, "no minister would authorise immediate dispatch of an army to the continent." They may well have been vestigial delusions, but as late as 3 August, as the book states, nobody in the government had proposed otherwise. Why then was Churchill's idea of Britain fighting a naval war absurd? It is only absurd based on what we know now: Belgium and France were invaded, France asked for help on the ground, and help was duly sent—ultimately from America as well as Britain in a worldwide conflagration.

It is surprising to find so many partial, out-of-context Churchill quotes in so scholarly a book. For example, in the run-up to war we are told: "Churchill adopted a shamelessly cynical view … 'if war was inevitable this was by far the most favourable opportunity and the only one that would bring France, Russia and ourselves together….'"[10]

"The Grand International: Mr. Churchill: 'What price German Navy?' Admiral Tirpitz: 'Give you 8 to 5.' Mr. Churchill: 'I want 2 to 1.' Admiral Tirpitz: 'Well, I'll make it 16 to 10.' Mr. Churchill: 'Right, I'll take you'" (Leonard Ravenhill in *Punch*, 19 *February* 1913).

That remark (not footnoted) is *not* from 1914. It is from a 1925 letter from Churchill to Lord Beaverbrook, commenting on a draft of Beaverbrook's war memoirs—and Hastings omits what followed: "...But I should not like that put in a way that would suggest I wished for war and was glad when the decisive steps were taken. I was only glad that they were taken in circumstances so favourable."[11] Deleting this part of Churchill's words casts him in a very different position than the one he actually took. From it we can incidentally see that Churchill, even as early as 1925, anticipated that his views would be distorted.

Catastrophe 1914 correctly states: "It is unlikely that any course of action adopted by Asquith's government could have averted a European war in 1914"[12] But it does not make clear that Churchill, uniquely among his colleagues, offered concrete ideas by which war might be *avoided*. He should get some credit for them: a "Naval Holiday" with Germany (1913–14), and a last-ditch "conference of sovereigns" to settle the quarrel and prevent hostilities (1914).

Churchill's "Naval Holiday"

As First Lord of the Admiralty, it was Churchill's duty to maintain the "Two-Power Standard": a Royal Navy powerful enough to defeat the next two strongest naval powers combined. From the early 1900s, one of these was Germany. Berlin made no secret of striving to build a fleet to rival Britain's—a plan likely to catch British attention.

Between 1908 and 1912, Germany built seventeen battleships and armored cruisers to Britain's twenty-nine, a serious challenge to the Two-Power Standard. Churchill knew that such a fleet, so close to British home waters, posed a first-strike capability—an "ever-present danger."[13] True to his instinct for technical, practical solutions to political problems, Churchill set out to stop the naval race.

On three separate occasions before the war, he proposed that Britain and Germany take a "Naval Holiday," freezing shipbuilding to ease tensions.[14] Why, he asked a constituent, should war between Britain and Germany be inevitable? "I do not believe in the theory of inevitable wars." Instead he looked forward to "the peaceful development of European politics [through] the blessed intercourse of trade and commerce...."[15] Churchill was quite specific. Early in 1912 he told Parliament that if, in 1913, Germany would scrap plans for three new capital ships, Britain would cancel plans for five: a "perfectly plain and simple plan" to abate what he called a "keen and costly naval rivalry."[16]

German leaders viewed Churchill's plan seriously, but not with much enthusiasm.

While the German ambassador to Britain, Prince Lichnowsky, at first warmed to the idea, it was greeted with flabbergasted disdain by Kaiser Wilhelm and his naval chief, Admiral von Tirpitz. The latter had his own turf to defend, of course. But the Kaiser backed him, taking it as an affront that any English politician should say what was best for Germany. The German chancellor, Theobald von Bethmann Hollweg, was opposed to increased military spending, but he too fell in line. Churchill, he said, "really seems to be a firebrand past praying for."[17]

Characteristically devoted to pursuing ideas he believed right, whatever the odds against them, Churchill would not take "no" for an answer. In March 1913, speaking on the 1914 naval budget, he offered to drop plans for four new battleships if Germany cancelled or delayed two—surely no disadvantage to Germany's relative position. After all, he said, "nobody builds 'Dreadnoughts' for fun."[18]

Realizing that a formal answer to this was now necessary, Bethmann Hollweg waffled, saying no official proposal had yet been received from Britain. In fact Germany had no intention of considering the idea: "We are on our guard!" said the Kaiser. "If England only intends to extend her hand to us under the condition that we must limit our fleet, that is an unbounded impudence which contains in it a bad insult to the German people and their Emperor." The influential newspaper *Deutsche Tagerzeitung* suggested that "Mr. Churchill should take a holiday from making speeches."[19]

The historian John Maurer noted the negative influence of internal German politics on Churchill's plan: "Arms control, Tirpitz feared, might give an opening to domestic political enemies [like Bethmann Hollweg] who opposed his program of battleship building…. Another consideration was economic: a Naval Holiday might dislocate the German shipbuilding industry, bringing about an increase in unemployment and social unrest."[20]

Churchill thought he saw one last opening in spring 1914, when Berlin invited a squadron of British battleships to visit Kiel for the annual naval regatta. Mutual friends worked to get Churchill invited. The Germans even allocated a mooring for the Admiralty yacht *Enchantress,* on which Churchill would presumably arrive. But the invitation was half-hearted. The First Lord would probably show up with his "Sea Lords and his beautiful and charming wife," Lichnowsky warned in May. "Churchill is an exceedingly crafty fox and is sure to try to spring some proposal or other on us."

Lichnowsky considered the visit acceptable, so long as the Germans were ready for foxy proposals, but Kaiser Wilhelm did not. Churchill, he said, was always showing up uninvited at German events—pointing to 1909, when Churchill had attended German army maneuvers (at his invitation, in fact). When it likewise became obvious that Britain's foreign secretary Sir Edward Grey disapproved of Churchill meddling in foreign affairs, Churchill decided not visit Kiel. (It was at Kiel on 28 June 1914 where Wilhelm, apprised of the murder of Archduke Franz Ferdinand at Sarajevo, ominously quitted the festivities.)

Churchill's behavior over the Naval Holiday proposal was entirely in character, and characteristically unlikely to win favor with his colleagues, let alone the Germans. Tirpitz and Wilhelm were bent on building up their fleet. But Churchill's efforts to foster an agreement that would stop the arms race and discourage war were admirable—and hardly those of a jingo bent on war at all costs.

Churchill's "Kingly Conference"

Another aspect of Churchill's character was his faith in personal diplomacy, as we have seen over the Irish problem (Chapter 9), and would see again with Roosevelt and Stalin in World War II (Chapter 26). It was in evidence during the drift toward war in 1914: his little-known proposal for conference of heads of state (including, it seems, French President Poincaré), a last-ditch effort to save the peace.

Although ready to meet personally with his German counterpart over shipbuilding, Churchill realized by July that the deteriorating situation demanded a meeting between the heads of state themselves. This was not unprecedented; Kaiser Wilhelm had proposed a peace conference after the Sarajevo assassinations, and private messages were being exchanged between the Kaiser and Czar Nicholas in the days before war was declared. But other than the official biography, there is little on Churchill's proposal in the literature. There is no reference in Churchill's *The World Crisis,* the biographies by Manchester, Jenkins and Birkenhead, or the critical works by Rose, Charmley and Hastings. Ted Morgan mentions it, but assigns the wrong date.[21]

Churchill first proposed the "kingly conference" to the cabinet on Monday, July 27. Asquith failed to mention it in his report to King George V (the only written record of cabinets in those days). Professor David Dilks suggested that Asquith might have told his lady friend, Venetia Stanley, but if so, it is not in their published letters. He did write ungenerously (28 July): "Winston on the other hand is all for this way of escape [war] from Irish troubles, and when things looked rather better last night, he exclaimed moodily that it looked after all as if we were in for a 'bloody peace.'"[22] No one can say what Churchill meant by "a bloody peace." He could very well have referred to averting war for the time being while Germany remained aggressive in Europe.

Asquith frequently put the least charitable spin on Churchill's actions—but why had things looked "rather better" on the 27th? The reason may have been the "kingly conference." In an accompanying footnote, the editors of the Asquith-Stanley letters write: "Lichnowsky told Grey on the afternoon of 27 July that the 'German government accept in principle mediation between Austria and Russia by the four powers, reserving, of course, their right as an ally to help Austria if attacked. France and Italy also accepted the conference proposal."[23]

In the event, Churchill's hope was dashed. On the evening of 27 July the British ambassador in Berlin telegraphed: "[German] Secretary of State for Foreign Affairs says that conference you suggest would practically amount to a court of arbitration and could not, in his opinion, be called together except at the request of Austria and Russia." This reversal "seems to have resulted from [German Chancellor] Bethmann Hollweg's belief, which the Kaiser did not share, that Russia would not intervene to save Serbia if this were known to risk war with Germany."[24]

That was the end of the "kingly" initiative, although Churchill, the man supposedly wearing the war paint, was still chafing at this lost opportunity. The rest of his 28 July letter to his wife, quoted at the beginning of this chapter, illustrates Churchill's continued desire for peace. Referring to "the wave of madness" which had "swept the mind of Christendom," he wrote: "I wondered whether those stupid Kings and Emperors could not assemble together and revivify kingship by saving the nations from hell but we all drift on in a kind of dull cataleptic trance. As if it was somebody else's operation!"[25]

History is judged too easily in hindsight. The scholar Manfred Weidhorn has suggested that if Hitler had been assassinated in 1938 he would have gone down as the restorer of German greatness; if he had died in 1941, the inevitable result of his policies in 1942–45 would have left loyal Nazis pining, "Ach, if only der Fuehrer were still alive."[26]

Had Churchill been killed on the Western Front, where he went to fight in 1916, we would probably still have these skewed views of his attitude toward war in 1914, spread about by everyone from pot-stirrers to seasoned historians. In fact, Churchill strove longer and harder than any member of the Asquith cabinet to create proposals by which war might be prevented.

11

The Defense of Antwerp

The Myth: Churchill's Actions Were Rash and Irresponsible

Churchill's role in the defense of Antwerp, in October 1914, has long been a feature of his "characteristically piratical" adventures. Max Hastings called it "a shocking folly by a minister who abused his powers and betrayed his responsibilities. It is astonishing that [his] cabinet colleagues so readily forgave him for a lapse of judgment that would have destroyed most men's careers."[1]

As the Germans closed in around Antwerp, Hastings wrote, Churchill "assembled a hotchpotch of Royal Marines and surplus naval personnel … his own private army." Then he "abandoned his post at the Admiralty" and "had himself appointed Britain's plenipotentiary to the beleaguered fortress."[2]

The Royal Naval Division

Before the war, Churchill had opposed conscription ("the draft"); soon after it started, he became convinced that more men would be needed for victory. As head of the navy, he considered what contribution the Admiralty could make. Upon the declaration of the war, there was a surplus of some 20–30,000 Royal Navy reservists not needed aboard ships. Churchill proposed that some of these be organized into one marine and two naval brigades for operation on land.[3] With the addition of two naval brigades—and with cabinet approval—the Royal Naval Division was organized on August 16th. "Its men regarded Churchill as their patron," Martin Gilbert wrote. "Later, in action, when things went well they called themselves 'Churchill's Pets.' When things went badly they were known as 'Churchill's Innocent Victims.'"[4]

The Royal Naval Division was approved by the Secretary of State for War, Lord Kitchener, and Churchill was besieged by political associates to make places for their relatives. The Conservative leader Andrew Bonar Law wrote on behalf of his two nephews; ironically, Bonar Law and others like him would later be among Churchill's leading critics.

The RND first saw action at Ostend, where two battalions of marines were landed temporarily to secure the city during the allied retreat. It is quite true, as later critics said, that naval personnel were not ideal for shore operations. But Kitchener never visualized the RND as first-line troops, rather as an auxiliary force to be landed and used temporarily when regular troops were unavailable.

Britain's Decision to Defend Antwerp

Churchill's "piratical adventure" to support Antwerp's defense was actually that of the unanimous British cabinet. As Churchill had predicted,[5] the Germans had made rapid advances in the opening weeks of the war. They secured Brussels, the capital, and by the end of September 1914 were threatening Antwerp, one of Belgium's last lines of defense. The Belgians informed their allies that Antwerp would have to surrender by 3 October. The British government said: not so fast.

Lord Kitchener—backed by the cabinet—emphasized the importance of holding Antwerp as long as possible, while transferring troop and equipment transportation to safer ports farther south on the Channel coast. Meanwhile, Antwerp would pose a barrier to the enemy's line of advance. Kitchener said that if the Germans reached Calais, they might be able to launch an invasion of Britain. Churchill supported him, since one of the Admiralty's prime duties was to keep the Channel ports open for movements of troops and materiel. The cabinet agreed that "the more troops [the Germans] would be forced to divert to the siege … the more coastline would remain in Allied hands."[6]

Foreign Minister Lord Grey, who saw a moral as well as military imperative to aid "brave little Belgium," told the Belgians that the allies believed a "further effort" should be made at Antwerp, and that Britain would send troops. Pending their arrival, Kitchener, at Churchill's suggestion, decided to send the RND marine brigade, which was already in Dunkirk, returning from its Ostend engagement. Meanwhile the French government, in emergency session at Bordeaux, promised to send two territorial (reserve) divisions, complete with artillery and cavalry, "with the shortest delay possible." The French also promised to launch an offensive toward Lille that would pressure the Germans from another direction. Some questioned the effectiveness of territorials in a fight for the city—yet reservists were the same kind of troops the Germans were using, albeit in substantial numbers (60,000).[7]

Kitchener wished to deploy regular army troops at Antwerp, but he needed information on the situation, which appeared vague at best. His eye fell upon Churchill, who on 2 October was en route to Dunkirk to evaluate the marine brigade and consult with the British commander, Sir John French. Kitchener stopped Churchill's train and returned it to London, where they met, along with Lord Grey and the First Sea Lord, Prince Louis of Battenberg. They agreed to re-route Churchill to Antwerp, where he might report the exact situation. Churchill did not, therefore, "have himself appointed."

Neither is it true that Churchill "abandoned his post." He left Battenberg in charge at the Admiralty, under direction of Prime Minister Asquith, before he set off. Asquith and Kitchener anxiously awaited Churchill's report, Asquith with gusto: "I don't know how fluent he is in French, but if he was able to do himself justice in a foreign tongue, the Belges will have listened to a discourse the like of which they have never heard before."[8]

Rrieg und Sieg.

Antwerpen, die Königin der Schelde.

GENERAL v BESELER

E. Sturtevant

Rings sant Dein Reich in Scherben
Vorm deutschen Schwerte hin,
Dann galt es erst zu werben
Um Dich, o Königin.

Nun nahm der deutsche Freier
Im Sturm Dich in Besitz.
Das war eine Hochzeitsfeier
Mit Donner und mit Blitz!

U.M.

German patriotic postcard celebrating the taking of Antwerp, "The Queen of the Scheldt," by General Hans Hartwig von Beseler, 1914. Drawing by E. Sturtevant (Wikimedia Commons).

"Churchill's Private Army"

Nor did Churchill favor or authorize the "hotchpotch collections of naval personnel," including recruits, that showed up at Antwerp. Kitchener had planned to send a "substantial" Antwerp relief force under the command of Sir Henry Rawlinson to take over the defense. They could not be sent immediately, so Kitchener accepted Churchill's suggestion of the marine brigade, supplemented by two naval brigades from the Royal Naval Division: Churchill's so-called "private army."

Asquith knew the truth. He had explained to the King that in the present emergency, there were no other troops available to support Antwerp's defense. Asquith also knew that

> on October 4, in his telegram to Kitchener, Churchill had explicitly requested the Naval Brigades to be sent, "*minus recruits*"; all subsequent arrangements for the despatch of the brigades had been made at the Admiralty by Prince Louis…. The recruits could easily have been held back had Prince Louis or Asquith desired. When, on October 5, Churchill found that the brigades had come *with* their recruits, and were about to be exposed to the full weight of a German assault, he had given immediate orders for them to take up a less exposed, defensive position[9] [emphasis added].

These facts were not made public at the time. Clearly, they have engendered the venomous accounts of Churchill's actions.

Churchill arrived in Antwerp at mid-day on 3 October, wearing the uniform of an Elder Brother of Trinity House (Britain's lighthouse service), distinguished by a naval cap with badge and pea jacket. A Belgian officer asked what this get-up signified. Churchill replied, in his lame French: *"Moi, je suis un frère aîné de la Trinité."* The astonished Belgian exclaimed: *"Mon dieu! La Trinité?"*[10] He had misunderstood Churchill to have proclaimed himself divine—a story that would not be lost on critics who believed Churchill thought of himself in that way!

An eye-witness described the scene as Churchill drove out to inspect the defenses:

> It was a chilly day and he [had changed into] a long black overcoat with broad astrakhan collar and his usual black top hat, and swung his silver-topped walking stick. In his customary manner, he completely ignored the enemy fire from howitzers, rifles and machine guns and astonished the Belgian troops by taking complete charge of the situation, criticizing the siting of guns and trenches and emphasizing his points by waving his stick or thumping the ground with it. He then climbed back into his car, waiting impatiently to be driven to the next section of the front line. Later, when the reinforcing Royal Marines arrived and were settled in, Winston came along to inspect them, dressed suitably for this more maritime occasion: "enveloped in a cloak, and on his head wore a yachtsman's cap," observed an accompanying journalist. "He was tranquilly smoking a large cigar and looking at the progress of the battle under a rain of shrapnel, which I can only call fearful."[11]

The Outcome

By 5 October neither French territorials, nor British troops, nor the designated on-scene commander, General Rawlinson, had shown up. There was no leader at all, save Churchill. In what seemed to him an emergency, but with an impulse for which he was later ridiculed, Churchill cabled Asquith his willingness to resign from the Admiralty to conduct the defense of the city. Instead of an unsordid sacrifice, this was greeted by Asquith as a piece of glory-seeking. The prime minister, who should have had Churchill's back, remarked privately: "Winston is an ex-Lieutenant of Hussars, and would if his proposal had been accepted, have been in command of two distinguished Major Generals, not to mention Brigadiers, Colonels etc: while the Navy were only contributing its little brigades."[12]

Lieutenant of Hussars he may have been, but among Asquith's cabinet, Churchill had had more first-line military experience than anyone else, and had thought more about the business than any of his colleagues. Asquith didn't bother to add, Martin Gilbert noted, "that those 'little brigades,' whose role he minimized, were in fact the only British forces at that moment available for immediate despatch to Antwerp, and that one of them, the marine brigade, constituted at the time the only British force engaged in the city's defence."[13]

To Churchill's face, Asquith was charm itself. He needed him. The First Lord was required at home, the PM assured him. When would he return? The answer proved to be: when Rawlinson got to Antwerp. The general finally showed up late on the 6th, having taken three times as long to arrive as Churchill had. Ironically, Rawlinson left Antwerp shortly after Churchill, having decided further defense was futile.

In the absence of promised French or British reinforcements, "hotchpotch" British defenders, under the command of Major-General Archibald Paris, were ordered by Churchill to continue the defense for as long as possible and to be ready to cross to the west bank rather than participate in a surrender. General Paris conducted a gallant defense for three more days. Antwerp formally surrendered on 10 October.[14]

The Reaction

The First Lord returned home believing he had significantly slowed the German advance and prevented the enemy from turning the Allies' flank. Instead of a welcome, he faced a witch hunt. Typical was the editorial by H.A. Gwynne of the *Morning Post,* ironically a newspaper that had once lauded his contributions as a war correspondent. The government, Gwynne wrote, needed

> to keep a tight hand upon their impulsive colleague [and] see that no more mischief of the sort is done…. The attempt to relieve Antwerp by a small force of Marines and Naval Volunteers was a costly blunder, for which Mr. W. Churchill must be held responsible…. Is it not true that the energies of Mr. W. Churchill have been directed upon this eccentric expedition, and that he has been using the resources of the Admiralty as if he were personally responsible for the naval operations? It is not right or proper that Mr. Churchill should use his position as Civil Lord to press his tactical and strategical fancies upon unwilling experts…. We suggest to Mr. Churchill's colleagues that they should, quite firmly and definitely, tell the First Lord that on no account are the military and naval operations to be conducted or directed by him.[15]

But facts are stubborn things, and the facts say otherwise. In no case did Churchill advance "strategical fancies upon unwilling experts." In no case did he deploy troops without approval of the responsible minister, Lord Kitchener. The object was not the "relief" of Antwerp. The object was to delay and harass the enemy, forestalling a greater disaster.

The Royal Naval Division brigades were closest and easiest to transport, and acquitted themselves well, with only fifty-seven deaths out of 8000. Kitchener and Rawlinson (in a foretaste of Gallipoli) had dawdled and failed to deliver. The French (in a foretaste of 1940) had failed utterly. It was Asquith and the Admiralty, with Kitchener's approval, who had sent recruits, which Churchill had specified not be used.

The Reality

As a government minister, Churchill could not reply to all this, and he received no public defense from Asquith or Kitchener. The truth was declared, belatedly, by the King of the Belgians. In a letter to General Paris in March 1918, which he later dictated as a memorandum, King Albert wrote:

> You are wrong in considering the Royal Naval Division Expedition as a forlorn hope. In my opinion it rendered great service to us and those who deprecate it simply do not understand the history of the War in its early days. Only one man of all your people had the prevision of what the loss of Antwerp would entail and that man was Mr. Churchill….
>
> Delaying an enemy is often of far greater service than the defeat of the enemy, and in the case of Antwerp the delay the Royal Naval Division caused to the enemy was of inestimable service to us. These three days allowed the French and British Armies to move North West. Otherwise our whole army might have been captured and the Northern French Ports secured by the enemy. Moreover, the advent of the Royal Naval Division inspired our troops, and owing to your arrival, and holding out for three days, great quantities of supplies were enabled to be destroyed. You kept a large army employed, and I repeat the Royal Naval Division rendered a service we shall never forget.[16]

12

"What about the Dardanelles?"

The Myth: Churchill Was Architect
of the Dardanelles and Gallipoli Debacles

The failed attempts in 1915 to "force" (sail through) the Dardanelles to Constantinople, and subsequently to occupy the Gallipoli Peninsula in European Turkey, are tales of military and political failure at the highest level. They offer timeless examples of the hypocrisy, skewed logic, idle gossip, wishful thinking and blind inertia that often assail governments at war. Alas, many historical accounts, almost to the present day, fix most of the blame on First Lord of the Admiralty Winston Churchill.

A century removed, an observer may wonder why Prime Minister H.H. Asquith wasn't forced out of office sooner. Here was a nation, the superpower of its day, fighting for survival. Yet at critical meetings of the government, Asquith rarely opened his mouth—for almost two crucial months he didn't even hold a war council. Privately, he spoke like any gossip to his lady friend Venetia Stanley. Most of what we know about his opinions at that time we know through their letters.

In cabinet, Asquith encouraged Churchill; behind his back he doubted and disparaged him. Nor was Lloyd George above criticizing the friend he had mentored. The First Lord was also second-guessed by one of his civil commissioners, Sir Francis Hopwood, who went so far as to carry slander to the King's private secretary. Churchill's First Sea Lord, Admiral Fisher, military head of the navy, owed his position to Churchill, threatened to resign every time he failed to get his way, and ultimately did so, abandoning his post. Above all stood Lord Kitchener, the Minister of War, enthusiastic for the operation but unwilling to commit the necessary troops at critical junctures: vain, unyielding, with an absolute veto over the decisions of the prime minister himself. Under such circumstances, it is difficult to see how any operation so dependent on timing and Army-Navy cooperation could have succeeded.

Origins

It is widely believed that Churchill proposed the Dardanelles expedition in December 1914, as a way to get round the static slaughter in Europe's trenches. While this is true in the abstract, the plan was not hatched overnight in one man's sudden vision of heroic

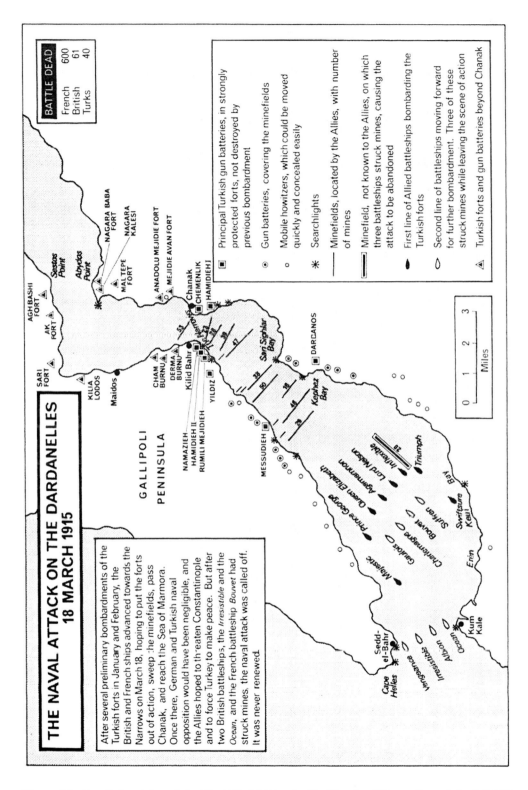

THE NAVAL ATTACK ON THE DARDANELLES
18 MARCH 1915

After several preliminary bombardments of the Turkish forts in January and February, the British and French ships advanced towards the Narrows on March 18, hoping to put the forts out of action, sweep the minefields, pass Chanak, and reach the Sea of Marmora. Once there, German and Turkish naval opposition would have been negligible, and the Allies hoped to threaten Constantinople and to force Turkey to make peace. But after two British battleships, the *Irresistable* and the *Ocean*, and the French battleship *Bouvet* had struck mines, the naval attack was called off. It was never renewed.

BATTLE DEAD	
French	600
British	61
Turks	40

■ Principal Turkish gun batteries, in strongly protected forts, not destroyed by previous bombardment

⊙ Gun batteries, covering the minefields

○ Mobile howitzers, which could be moved quickly and concealed easily

✳ Searchlights

▬ Minefields, located by the Allies, with number of mines

▬ Minefield, not known to the Allies, on which three battleships struck mines, causing the attack to be abandoned

🔻 First line of Allied battleships bombarding the Turkish forts

◊ Second line of battleships moving forward for further bombardment. Three of these struck mines while leaving the scene of action

◭ Turkish forts and gun batteries beyond Chanak

GALLIPOLI PENINSULA

NAGARA BABA FORT
NAGARA KALESI
SESTOS POINT
ABYDOS POINT
MAL TEPE FORT
ANADOLU MEJIDIE FORT
MEJIDIE AVAN FORT
AGH BASHI FORT
AK FORT
SARI FORT
KILIA LODOS
Maidos
CHAM BURNU
DERMA BURNU
Kilid Bahr
Chanak
CHEMENLIK
HAMIDIEH I
NAMAZIEH
HAMIDIEH II
RUMILI MEJIDIEH
YILDIZ
MESSUDIEH
DARDANOS
San Sighar Bay
Kephez Bay
Triumph
Lord Nelson
Agamemnon
Queen Elizabeth
Prince George
Bouvet
Suffren
Swiftsure
Gaulois
Charlemagne
Majestic
Erin Keui Bay
Kum Kale
Ocean
Albion
Irresistible
Vengeance
Sedd-el-Bahr
Cape Helles

Miles
0 1 2 3

(From *The Routledge Atlas of the First World War*, by Sir Martin Gilbert, Copyright © 1970), Dorset Press, 1970, third edition 2008, reproduced by permission of Taylor & Francis Books UK and www.martingilbert.com.)

excess. Actually, Churchill and others were contemplating an attack on Germany and Austria-Hungary from the south a month after the start of World War I, before trench warfare had settled in.

When it began to look like Turkey would join the Central Powers, making Greece a likely British ally, Churchill thought the Royal Navy might support Greek action against Turkey. On 4 September 1914 he cabled Rear Admiral Mark Kerr, on loan to the Greeks to command their Navy, authorizing him to voice this thought to the Athens government. The Admiralty, he told Kerr, would supplement the Greek fleet "to any extent and with any class of vessel circumstances may render necessary. The right and obvious method of attacking Turkey is to strike immediately at the heart." Churchill envisioned the Greeks occupying the Gallipoli Peninsula and an Anglo-Greek fleet forcing the Dardanelles, linking with the Russian Black Sea fleet and dominating the region.[1]

If Greece did not enter the war, or was "paralysed" by a Turkish or Bulgarian attack, Churchill offered an alternative to Foreign Secretary Sir Edward Grey: the use of Russian troops against European Turkey. He made no mention of *British* troops, saying, "No other military operations are necessary." The price to be paid might be heavy, he wrote, but such an enterprise would mean "no more war with Turkey."[2]

With British military concerns fixed firmly on the Western Front, no action was taken on Churchill's ideas. Then, at the end of September, the Turks mined the Dardanelles, cutting off the Russians from an ice-free link to their allies. "British military supplies could no longer reach Russia except by the hazardous northern route to Archangel," Martin Gilbert wrote. "Russian wheat, on which the Tsarist exchequer depended for so much of its overseas income—and arms purchases—could no longer be exported to its world markets."[3]

On October 28, Turkey entered the war alongside the Central Powers, and two days later began shelling Russian Black Sea ports. The British cabinet worried over the effect on Russia, and whether the Turks might also attack Egypt. Asquith wrote to Venetia Stanley: "Few things would give me greater pleasure than to see the Turkish Empire finally disappear from Europe." He added the wish that "Constantinople either become Russian (which I think is its proper destiny) or if that is impossible neutralised and become a free port."[4] These are certainly examples of vapid imaginings.

With the approval of his First Sea Lord, Admiral Fisher, Churchill ordered the Mediterranean commander Admiral Carden, "without risking any ships," to bombard the forts at the Dardanelles entrance, at a safe distance from Turkish guns: "…retirements should be made before fire from the forts becomes effective. Ships guns should outrange older guns mounted in the forts."[5]

Carden did so on 3 November, proving that the forts were vulnerable to naval bombardment—a concept previously doubted by many. No allied ships were damaged; one shell hit the magazine of a fort at Sedd-el-Bahr (Gallipoli side of the straits) which blew up with the loss of almost all its artillery. It was never repaired—nor did the Turks improve other Dardanelles defenses, which remained short of guns, mines and ammunition.[6]

Genesis of the Naval Attack

The successful shelling of 3 November changed many opinions. "Like most other people," Churchill wrote, "I had held the opinion that the days of forcing the Dardanelles were over." Now Carden had demonstrated otherwise—as did "fortresses throughout Europe … collapsing after a few days' attack by field armies without a regular siege." Admirals Jackson and Oliver of Admiralty War Group concurred.[7]

As Churchill later told the Dardanelles commissioners, the impression was that the allies were up against a less than first-class power. Small British forces easily took the Ottoman port of Basra (now in Iraq) on 7 November; a month later they captured Kurna, where the Tigris met the Euphrates. In December the Mediterranean port of Alexandretta (now Iskerenderun) surrendered under the guns of a single British cruiser, HMS *Doris*. The Turks actually assisted in demolishing its defenses. It seemed, Churchill testified, that "we were not dealing with a thoroughly efficient military power, and that it was quite possible that we could get into parley with them."[8] Characteristically, Churchill was always looking for a chance to talk.

On 3 January 1915 Churchill, with Fisher's approval, asked Carden if he thought the Dardanelles straits could be forced "by the use of ships alone," having in mind a fleet of older British battleships superfluous to needs of the Grand Fleet in home waters. Churchill added: *"Importance of results would justify severe loss"* (emphasis added).

Carden replied that while he did not think the Dardanelles could be "rushed," they might be "forced by extended operations with a large number of ships." Stephen Roskill, a critical naval historian, wrote that Carden was "actually a second-rate officer who found himself unexpectedly in a sea command instead of in charge of Malta dockyard."[9] But Carden was the man at the scene; one only wishes Churchill was blessed with such clear contemporary vision as Admiral Roskill in hindsight.

The historian Alan Moorehead summarized:

> Up to this point, nobody, either in the Admiralty or at the War Office, had reached any definite conclusions…. But here for the first time was something positive: the Admiral on the spot believed that he might get through the straits, and by a method that had not been broached before: that of a slow progress instead of a rush, a calculated shelling of the forts one by one…. Churchill telegraphed again to Carden: "Your view is agreed with by high authorities here. Please telegraph in detail what you think could be done by extended operations, what force would be needed, and how you consider it should be used."[10]

It is important to remember that Churchill's top military commander, First Sea Lord Admiral Fisher, was at this time still strongly behind the enterprise. He even proposed to supplement Churchill's older naval vessels with HMS *Queen Elizabeth,* the navy's latest battleship and the first to mount 15-inch guns. Since she was about to leave for the Mediterranean to test her guns, Fisher suggested "…why shouldn't she use her practice shots on the Dardanelles etc and the possibilities flowing from it."[11]

Admiral Carden said he would need twelve battleships, three battle-cruisers, three light cruisers, a flotilla leader, sixteen destroyers, six submarines, eight seaplanes, twelve minesweepers and twenty other craft. Excepting *Queen Elizabeth,* the ships would be older, surplus vessels of pre–*Dreadnought* design (before 1908). HMS *Majestic* dated back to 1895. These ships were still fit to fight because Churchill had devoted some of his prewar budget to maintaining them. They were available because elements of the German High Seas Fleet beyond German home waters had been eliminated at the Battle of the Falkland Islands, six weeks earlier.

Carden proposed to start by bombarding the forts long-range and then, preceded by minesweepers, to sail into the straits, demolishing shore batteries as he found them. He proposed a feint at Gallipoli (something Churchill had mentioned on November

25)—a bombardment, but no landings. Emerging into the Sea of Marmara, Carden would keep the straits open by patrols in his wake. Weather and morale of the enemy were variables, he said, but he "might do it all in a month about."

The British War Council met on 13 January, every one of them enthusiastic. "The idea caught on at once," the cabinet secretary Maurice Hankey wrote. They "turned eagerly from the dreary vista of a 'slogging match' on the Western Front to brighter prospects, as they seemed, in the Mediterranean. The Navy, in whom everyone had implicit confidence, and whose opportunities so far had been few and far between, was to come into the front line."[12] Prime Minister Asquith himself drew up the fateful minute, and the War Council signed on to a man. Nobody seemed to notice one curious addition. The Admiralty, Asquith wrote, should "prepare for a naval expedition in February to bombard and take the Gallipoli Peninsula with Constantinople as its objective."[13]

How do you "take" a peninsula without troops? Did Asquith mean for them then to march on Constantinople? In the general euphoria, no one questioned this. All eyes were on sailing through the straits. A fleet this size, appearing off Constantinople, would surely cow the enemy. Turkey would surrender.

Churchill alone, at that meeting, held out for an alternate: attacking the north German coast. Kitchener said there were no troops for that—he was always short of troops, except to be slaughtered in Flanders—and Churchill dropped it. Yet Kitchener said nothing about "taking" Gallipoli. Of the naval enterprise he was fully supportive. Fisher did not demur.

The War Council went on to consider bonus visions: a naval attack up the Danube, a landing at Salonika, and sending a fleet up the Adriatic. One member, Colonial Secretary Lewis Harcourt, went so far as to circulate a paper he entitled "The Spoils": the end of the Ottoman Empire, expansion of the British Empire as far as Palestine.[14] None of these naively optimistic visions belonged to Winston Churchill.

The Naval Attack

Churchill's hopes for Greek or Russian troop support had not materialized. Seeming to understand that they could not "take" Gallipoli without soldiers, he asked the war cabinet whether there should military as well as naval action. Again Kitchener insisted that no troops were needed. Churchill asked for his dissent to be recorded. The cabinet agreed to go ahead with a purely naval attack.

Matters quickly deteriorated, Martin Gilbert wrote: "When, a few days later, Kitchener showed no interest in providing air support, in the shape of the army's fledgling Flying Corps, Churchill stepped in with the even smaller, but keen, Naval Air Service, which he had helped to establish as an independent air fighting force." Years later Gilbert found and interviewed one of those pilots. He was "indignantly sure as many other survivors of the campaign that if only Churchill had been allowed to continue, victory might have come."[15]

The powerful Anglo-French naval force began bombarding the outer forts of the Dardanelles on 19 February 1915. True to Churchill's expectations, those forts were silenced and the entrance cleared of mines in less than a week. Marines landed to destroy the guns at Kum Kale (Asiatic north coast) and Sedd el Bahr (Gallipoli), while ships' guns trained further in toward Kephez. Some Turkish batteries were mobile; they evaded the fleet's guns and fired at British minesweepers—a motley assortment manned by civilians (definitely a mistake by the Admiralty). On 4 March, Carden assured Churchill his force would arrive off Constantinople in as little as two weeks.[16]

Shortly after this optimistic forecast, Carden fell ill, and resigned on the 15th. He was replaced by Admiral John de Robeck, whom Churchill described as "a good seaman and a fine disciplinarian." Even Stephen Roskill admits he "certainly was an improvement."[17]

De Robeck launched the "forcing" attack on the 18 March, and for awhile it was looking good: eighteen battleships, with cruiser and destroyer support and minesweepers in the van, advanced to midway through the narrowest part of the straits, barely a mile wide. By 2pm, according to the Turkish General Staff, "all telephone wires were cut, all communications with the forts were interrupted, some of the guns had been knocked out … in consequence the artillery fire of the defence had slackened considerably."[18]

Then misfortune struck. The French battleship *Bouvet* hit a mine and sank. Three of the older British battleships were damaged by mines, and two sank; 650 sailors perished. Other vessels were damaged, and the civilian minesweeper crews were terrified. Admiral de Robeck, believing he could not sustain further losses, issued a general recall. Churchill was furious. In his original query to Carden he had emphasized: "Importance of results would justify severe loss." Angrily he denounced the commander as "Admiral de Row-back." Commodore Roger Keyes, commanding *Queen Elizabeth,* was certain they

HMS *Irresistible* abandoned and sinking after the naval attack of 18 March 1915 (Wikimedia Commons).

were capable of passing through the narrows and into the Marmara[19]; but Fisher backed de Robeck and the fleet was withdrawn—never, in the end, to return.

Debacle

Churchill never gave up his belief that the Dardanelles could have been forced by a renewed attack. But Asquith and the cabinet blinked. There was no appetite to renew the naval attack without a major assault to hold and control adjacent land—which Asquith had designated as an objective but without committing troops. For another two months, Churchill strove to bolster the naval forces, hoping they would be called upon again, but he could not overrule his naval advisors or the admiral on the spot. Attention shifted to a plan for which he was not responsible: a military assault on Gallipoli itself.

Landings began at the end of April, ultimately to gain little beyond a foothold. In view of the disproportionate numbers often bandied about, the nationality of those brave soldiers needs enumeration. There were over 450,000 British (including Indians and Newfoundlanders), 80,000 French, 50,000 Australians and 14,000 to 17,000 New Zealanders. The Turks mustered 315,000. Casualties and losses were horrific: 250,000 among the Allies, a similar number of Turks.[20]

General Ian Hamilton, commanding the allied assault, pleaded in vain for Kitchener to send better artillery and better trained, regular troops. With the Admiralty sidelined, Churchill could play no more than a support role on Gallipoli. He certainly did so, hoping for another opportunity to sail through the straits. So many died unnecessarily that he has come in for the greatest share of blame, especially in Australia. It is hard to understand this, since Churchill played no role in directing the landing and had, since the previous September, cast around for ways to avoid using British and Empire troops.

While Churchill as naval head gave the order, he was not the sole author and advocate of the naval attack. It had a long genesis, dating back almost to the opening of the war, and was approved by high-level authorities up to Asquith and Kitchener. Lord Fisher, at first all for the expedition, became increasingly hostile, and finally resigned in mid–May 1915. That cost Churchill his position as First Lord of the Admiralty. From a political viewpoint he should have resigned after the naval attack failed in March. A lesser man would have, but resignation wasn't in his makeup. It is valid to fault Churchill for failing to carry his First Sea Lord with him in advocating a renewed naval attack.

Churchill's anguished, handwritten letters to Asquith "poured out his inner feelings with intensity, holding back nothing, and risking the derision of the Prime Minister." But the opposition Conservatives now demanded a coalition government with the First Lord's head as its price. This became obvious when Asquith callously asked Churchill: "And what are we to do for you?"[21]

From the end of May to 12 November 1915, Churchill held a meaningless sinecure, Chancellor of the Duchy of Lancaster, whose only task was appointment of rural judges. Unable to play any role in the ongoing fiasco, he resigned in November to join his regiment on the Western Front. "Like a sea-beast fished up from the depths, or a diver too suddenly hoisted," he wrote, "my veins threatened to burst from the fall in pressure. I had great anxiety and no means of relieving it; I had vehement convictions and small power to give effect to them…. I was forced to remain a spectator of the tragedy, placed cruelly in a front seat."[22] His wife had a more poignant remembrance: "When he left the

Admiralty he thought he was finished…. I thought he would never get over the Dardanelles; I thought he would die of grief."[23]

Retrospective

Clement Attlee, who fought at Gallipoli and later headed the 1945 Labour government, said the Dardanelles operation was "the only imaginative concept of the war."[24] Historians have long debated his view. Jeffery Wallin, one of the few authors to take Churchill's side, argued that the concept was strategically sound and would have worked; that at the time de Robeck broke off his attack, the Turkish forts were almost out of ammunition.[25] Critics countered that the Turkish mobile batteries made up for the loss of fixed cannon, citing their efficiency against the minesweepers—but still others question how much ammunition even the mobile batteries had left. The minesweepers assigned were insufficient and should not have been crewed by civilians. That detail mistake was the Admiralty's, thus ultimately Churchill's.

A further question which has never been answered is: what would have been the effect of the Allied fleet appearing, with guns trained, off Constantinople? Would Turkey have surrendered, as the British thought? "…few analysts, then or now, with the benefit of long hindsight, commit themselves to that assurance," wrote Christopher Harmon. "Lord Kitchener, in charge of the War Office, and Churchill, in charge of the Royal Navy, both said at various times that ships alone could suffice. But at other times, each thought otherwise."[26]

The record suggests that the immediate failures of the Dardanelles and Gallipoli were due to gross errors by the commanders. De Roebeck was wrong to break off the attack with fourteen of his eighteen battleships intact and some about to pass through the narrows. Hamilton was faulted for landing troops with uncertain objectives. Professor Harmon summarizes:

> Churchill correctly understood the futility of further offensives in the West until some new approach or technology could be ready. He was also correct to want to devote the somewhat inactive Royal Navy and certain Army divisions to this Dardanelles operation; and with or without troops, he wanted to commit many ships. But Kitchener, who offered, then withheld, then provided too late, the 29th Division from Egypt, made a shambles of Admiralty plans to transport the unit, and eliminated any chance of sufficient manpower to sweep away the Turks…. He should have seen that nothing was more important than that this new expedition not fail, not embarrass the Allies, and not waste precious lives of trained men.[27]

Lessons Learned—or To Be Learned

In 1917 a commission of inquiry into the Dardanelles and Gallipoli operations issued its preliminary report. While stating that Churchill had been "carried away by his sanguine temperament and his firm belief in the success of the operation which he advocated," its main criticism was of Asquith, for the lack of war council meetings between 19 March and 14 May, and for "the atmosphere of vagueness and want of precision which seems to have characterised the proceedings of the War Council."[28]

Kitchener, the commissioners concluded, "did not sufficiently avail himself of the services of his General Staff, with the result that more work was undertaken by him than was possible for one man to do, and confusion and want of efficiency resulted."[29] Perhaps Kitchener might not have escaped so lightly, but he had become a martyr, drowning on the way to Russia in June 1916.

What a story! A prime minister unwilling to be prime; a war minister reluctant to make war; backbiting among colleagues; idle babble to outsiders and the press; daily changes of tune; dreaming about the spoils of war; unwillingness to hear those who understood the real needs.... It doesn't sound so far removed from the criticism now thrown at Western governments who have inherited the mistakes of a generation, and are expected to mend them overnight.

Many have asked what Churchill regarded as the worst mistake of his life. Look no farther. "I was ruined for the time being in 1915 over the Dardanelles, and a supreme enterprise was cast away, through my trying to carry out a major and cardinal operation of war from a subordinate position," he wrote. "Men are ill-advised to try such ventures. This lesson had sunk into my nature."[30]

He never made that mistake again. When World War II found him at the pinnacle, he appointed himself Minister of Defence, ensuring that he would direct no operations from a "subordinate position." He asked pointed questions over detailed operations, even exercises, demanding detailed answers before granting his approval.[31] But the record shows that in 1915, in naval attack at the Dardanelles, he did all he could to assure success.

13

Losing the *Lusi*

The Myth: Churchill Wanted Her Sunk
to Get the Americans into World War I

A 2002 article on the *Lusitania* sinking, by the late John Updike, is remindful of what Churchill said during one of his early military skirmishes. He was shot at without result:

> To what extent was Winston Churchill, First Lord of the Admiralty, distracted from his duties in the U-boat war by his cherished, though ill-advised, campaign to seize the Dardanelles? He was off in Paris concluding an agreement on the use of the Italian Navy in the Mediterranean when the *Lusitania* sank.

Numerous historians (and the previous chapter) conclude that the Dardanelles campaign was not so much ill-advised as ill-managed. But having fallen down on that subject, to paraphrase Churchill, Mr. Updike hastily picked himself up and hurried on as if nothing had happened:

> Churchill's commitment to the safety of noncombatant shipping was less than keen: three months before the sinking he wrote to the President of the Board of Trade that it was "most important to attract neutral shipping to our shores in the hope especially of embroiling the U.S. with Germany.... For our part, we want the traffic—the more the better; if some of it gets into trouble, better still."[1]

As so often the case with revisionist accounts, this is a selective quotation. Pray consider the parts Mr. Updike omitted.

First, the sentence replaced by ellipses: "The German formal announcement of indiscriminate submarining has been made to the United States to produce a deterrent effect on traffic."

Second, the rest of Churchill's letter: "Therefore do please furbish up at once your insurance offer to neutrals trading with us after February 18th. The more that come, the greater our safety and the German embarrassment. Please act promptly so that the announcement may synchronize with our impending policy."[2]

What is the reality of the inference by Updike, and others anxious to accuse Churchill of sinking the *Lusitania* and drowning 1,400 people? (1) Churchill's main concern was to counter the "deterrent effect" of Germany's threat to sink cargo vessels. (2) RMS *Lusitania* was *not* "noncombatant shipping." She a passenger liner, not a cargo steamer. (3) Churchill wanted Runciman to "furbish up" Britain's offer to insure cargos of neutral nations trading with Britain—a confident response to Germany's declaration that they were now fair game for U-boats.

So what are we left with? At worst, we have an indiscreet remark in a private letter—testifying mainly to Churchill's curious determination to win wars—a letter Mr. Updike wouldn't even know of, had Churchill not kept every scrap of paper he wrote, now the property of the nation. Yet "indiscreet" may be too negative a description. Britain needed trade, in war and peace, but especially in war. Churchill was prepared to share in the cost of losses to that trade. Britain did not sink the ships. She sank the ships that were sinking the ships.

At the crux of the Dardanelles-Gallipoli crisis, the torpedoing of the Royal Mail Ship *Lusitania* on 7 May 1915 was a trifling matter. Yet for eighty years, rumors swirled that she was deliberately sacrificed by the British, chiefly Churchill, in the hope of bringing the United States into World War I. More recently, critics charged that the Admiralty purposely contrived to steer the ship into harm's way.

The complaint against Churchill reached critical mass in Colin Simpson's *The Lusitania* (1972), which had high sales, was selected by four book clubs, and was excerpted in the *Reader's Digest* and *Life*. Simpson's statements have been frequently repeated, especially since the arrival of the Internet. As recently as 2014, a book on Franklin Roosevelt, *The Mantle of Command,* casually alleged that Winston Churchill had a role in the loss of the "ill-fated American liner."[3] Scholarly testimony to the truth has been published, but lacking glitz and pathos, it tends to be ignored.[4] Yet the replies to many of Simpson's charges were decades old before his book, when the controversy over *Lusitania* erupted.[5]

Artist Norman Wilkinson dramatically captures the rapid sinking of RMS *Lusitania* on 7 May 1915 (*Illustrated London News*).

The *Lusitania* was British, not American, operated by the Cunard Line, commanded by Captain William Turner RNR. Inbound from New York, she was torpedoed by the German submarine *U-20* eleven miles off the Old Head of Kinsale, Ireland. She experienced two explosions, the second one violent, and sank in only eighteen minutes; 1409 people lost their lives, including 128 Americans.

An Armed Cruiser Used for Troops and Munitions?

After the sinking, the German government referred to its prior warnings to travelers to avoid the vessels of Germany's enemies. Such ships were liable to be sunk, the Germans declared, particularly if they were armed. Simpson, in describing the sighting of the liner by *U-20,* claims its Captain, Walther Schwieger, was given this description: "either the *Lusitania* or the *Mauretania* [her identical sister], both armed cruisers used for trooping."[6]

If that was really how the Germans saw her, it is inaccurate. The *Lusitania* (built in 1908 with possible wartime use in mind) did have twelve emplacements for small, six-inch guns. But no guns were fitted; if they had been, she certainly would have been an "armed cruiser." The Germans and others had examined her in New York; had they found mounted guns they would have demanded she be interred. They never did, and 109 witnesses at the subsequent British and American inquiries agreed that they saw no sign of guns.[7] Also, no troops were aboard.

If the guns weren't mounted, Simpson argued, they were certainly on board, not explaining what use they would be unmounted. M.R. Dow, a reviewer with family connections to Cunard and the ship, confounded even that argument: "Simpson must have seen a German propaganda poster showing the *Lusitania* with guns popping out all over." Historian Thomas Bailey wrote that a German reservist who claimed to have seen guns mounted "confessed [to] perjury and was imprisoned."[8]

"Another claim, that the ship had been modified in order to carry a huge cargo of guncotton, the detonation of which blew the bottom out, is also pure fantasy," wrote Dow. "The amount of explosive claimed by Simpson actually amounts to what was a very high percentage of explosives delivered to the Western Front."[9] The actual manifest included 173 tons of rifle cartridges and unarmed shrapnel shells, not much in a 32,000-ton ship. They were "not considered capable of causing a large detonation. American law apparently forbade only munitions which were considered a hazard to the safety of the passengers."[10]

Witnesses did confirm two explosions, the first caused by the German torpedo, the second of unknown but conspiratorial interest. The *Lusitania* was "loaded" with munitions, goes the story; these caused the second explosion, which did most of the damage. More recent scholarship suggests it was more likely caused by sea water coming in contact with the ship's boilers after the torpedo hit.[11]

The Germans' best argument that *Lusitania* was a ship of war was an order by the British Admiralty for merchant vessels to ram U-boats, but this was not their main line of defense. Speed, not ramming, was her main advantage. At her flank speed of 28 knots, *Lusitania* was three times as fast as a submerged U-boat, and nearly twice as fast as one on the surface.

Sailing into Danger

Professor Harry Jaffa, who placed most of the blame on Captain Turner, described the *Lusitania*'s voyage as "one of great incompetence. Not only was her steam reduced; her crew was also. The best men had been taken by the Royal Navy, and the lifeboat drills were listless and slovenly. Moreover, the lifeboats—and in particular the davits by which they had to be lowered—were virtually unworkable from the moment the ship began to list. But the greatest of all the failures was the captain's, since he navigated almost exactly as he would have done in peacetime." Turner, Jaffa explained, had slowed down after striking the Irish coast so as to arrive with the tide at Merseyside.

Not all of Simpson's charges were new. Political opponents anxious to discredit Churchill's warnings about Germany in the 1930s circulated talk that he had purposely endangered *Lusitania*. "This view was widely held by the Germans," wrote Bailey, "and was even [at the time] communicated to Ambassador Gerard by the Kaiser. No evidence has ever been presented to support the theory."[12]

In 1972, the charge was more pointed. *Lusitania* had been issued with "sailing orders," Simpson wrote, which instructed Captain Turner to rendezvous with a naval escort, the cruiser HMS *Juno,* off southwest Ireland—putting her on a direct course for areas known to be infested with U-boats. Confusingly, Sir Courtenay Bennett, the British Consul-General in New York, was later quoted by Simpson saying no such orders were issued.[13] Captain Turner never referred to them, and Churchill, when questioned in the House of Commons after the sinking, said no orders were issued.

It would have made no sense, Churchill said: The navy did not have the resources to escort more than a handful of the hundreds of merchantmen. Exceptions were sometimes made, but not for ships like *Lusitania*. Even later, with the convoy system in place, fast passenger liners were not convoyed. "In a channel, where she could not maneuver, the *Lusitania* might well have needed an escort of destroyers or other high-speed, short-range auxiliary craft," Jaffa wrote. "But why she should need one forty miles west of Fastnet is something it was incumbent upon Mr. Simpson to explain."[14]

The second allegation against Churchill is a meeting said to have occurred on 5 May 1915 in the Admiralty map room, between Churchill, First Sea Lord Admiral Fisher, Chief of Naval War Staff Admiral Oliver, Director of Naval Intelligence Captain Hall, and Commander Kenworthy of Naval Intelligence. On the map were markers denoting the *U-20* (apparently the British knew exactly where she was), *Juno* and *Lusitania,* "closing Fastnet at upwards of twenty knots."

Simpson wrote: "Admiral Oliver drew to Churchill's attention the fact that the *Juno* was unsuitable for exposure to submarine attack without escort, and suggested that elements of the destroyer flotilla from Milford Haven should be sent forthwith to her assistance." He also wrote, "the Admiralty War Diary stops short, perhaps understandably, as it was here the decision was made that was to be the direct cause of the disaster…. Shortly after noon on May 5 the Admiralty signaled *Juno* to abandon her escort mission and return to Queenstown…. The *Lusitania* was not informed that she was now alone."[15]

The "Admiralty War Diary" mentioned in this melodramatic paragraph appears nowhere else in Simpson's book, not even the bibliography. No historian has found it. Professor Jaffa concluded that it was mix of accurate records and sheer supposition: "However much the ebullient Churchill interested himself in naval operations, it was not his primary task to make operational decisions"—particularly in the presence of Fisher, with whom Churchill was then "quarreling bitterly over the Dardanelles."[16] (Fisher resigned ten days later; see previous chapter.)

The only eyewitness Simpson offered was Commander Joseph Kenworthy, later Baron Strabolgi, a Liberal turned Labourite and prominent pacifist.[17] In his 1927 book, *The Freedom of the Seas*, he said *Lusitania* "was sent at considerably reduced speed into an area where a U-boat was known to be waiting and with her escorts withdrawn."[18] The only part of this that is credible is the last three words. HMS *Juno* (laid down 1898) made no sense as an escort. Her top speed was 19.5 knots, well below *Lusitania*'s. It might be argued that Turner with his "sailing orders" slowed to rendezvous with *Juno*, having not been "informed" he was "now alone." But Turner, who survived, never confirmed this.

Summary

Except for Kenworthy's account, which was backed by no other evidence, there is no proof, even circumstantial, of a conspiracy to sink the *Lusitania*. The chief cause of her loss was Captain Turner's decision, after sighting the Irish coast, to proceed northward at reduced speed to "make the tide" at Merseyside, as he would have in peacetime. At his normal cruising speed, chances of a successful torpedo attack would have been greatly reduced. Alternatively, since he had the time, he could have headed out to deeper waters, maintaining speed and further reducing the danger. There was no advantage and every danger in slowing down.

It might be argued that Churchill and Fisher should have accepted Admiral Oliver's undocumented recommendation to escort the liner with destroyers. But as a recent *Lusitania* historian, David Ramsay, noted: "...the Dardanelles operation entailed the diversion from home waters of destroyers—the one class of ship in which the Royal Navy had a negligible superiority over the Germans. Commenting on the loss of the *Lusitania*.... Admiral Duff wrote: 'Indirectly the Dardanelles operation contributed; the [destroyers] that should be guarding merchant shipping are being used there.'"[19] Ramsay, writing in 2004, confirmed the findings of Bailey and Jaffa, adding: "I quote from historians Stephen Roskill and David Stafford, who are at one in rejecting any conspiracy, by Churchill or anyone else."[20]

14

America and World War I

It is amusing to consider that Churchill is accused both of conspiring to get the Americans into the First World War (previous chapter), and insisting they should have stayed out. Of course, this is from different sets of critics—I think.

Google these words and you will find multiple citations attributing them to Churchill:

> America should have minded her own business and stayed out of the World War. If you hadn't entered the war the Allies would have made peace with Germany in the Spring of 1917. Had we made peace then there would have been no collapse in Russia followed by Communism, no breakdown in Italy followed by Fascism, and Germany would not have signed the Versailles Treaty, which has enthroned Nazism in Germany. If America had stayed out of the war, all these "isms" wouldn't today be sweeping the continent of Europe and breaking down parliamentary government—and if England had made peace early in 1917, it would have saved over one million British, French, American, and other lives.[1]

Churchill acknowledged that in 1914 the United States had good reasons for staying out of the war.[2] But on America's entry in 1917 he was unequivocal. The "moral consequence" of American involvement was "the deciding cause in the conflict...."[3] Without the U.S., he added, the war would have ended in negotiated peace, "or, in other words, a German victory."[4] A German victory was never something Churchill favored. Nor did he advocate Britain (he would not have said "England") making peace in 1917.

Griffin and the Enquirer

Churchill's supposed belief that America should have kept out of the war had its origins in William S. Griffin (1898–1949), a protégé of William Randolph Hearst, who in 1926 founded the *New York Enquirer*, a Sunday afternoon broadsheet designed as a platform for ideas which Hearst might adopt in his own papers.[5] Hearst and Griffin were isolationists who opposed American involvement. In the 1930s Griffin frequently demanded that Britain pay her World War I debts to America. Of Irish heritage, he often spoke in Ireland on trade, *Time* reported: "Occasionally Publisher Griffin starts a movement to draft William Griffin for mayor (1937) or senator (1938)."[6]

Griffin was also critical of Hitler, and won awards from Jewish organizations for

74

promoting Christian-Jewish amity. Although Roosevelt had asked him to second his nomination for President in 1932, Griffin remained fiercely isolationist, and by the late Thirties was leading the Keep America Out of War Committee. But he considered it "an honor" when his paper was banned in Germany in 1940, and he was on the enemies list of the German-American Bund.[7]

In 1942, with America at war again, a grand jury indicted Griffin for sedition, though the charges were later dropped.[8] "For a number of years before Pearl Harbor," a New York newspaper commented, Griffin had "used the 'no danger' line…. [He] constantly praised the utterances of Ham Fish and worked closely with Prescott Dennett."[9] Griffin died in 1949; the *Enquirer*'s circulation was down to 17,000 when it was sold in 1952 to Generoso Pope, Jr., who turned it into the supermarket tabloid it remains to this day.[10]

The Churchill-Griffin Interview

Griffin was in London in the summer of 1936, when, he claimed, he received a "telegram" from Churchill (which he never produced), asking him to "come to see me."[11] The Churchill Archives indicate that Griffin not Churchill requested the meeting. When Churchill asked his private office to check, his secretaries reported that Griffin had made several phone calls seeking an appointment, describing himself as "a friend of the President and the Ambassador here [Robert Bingham], and an admirer of yours." Griffin said he had "no axe to grind," nor did he wish "to speak of anything particularly."[12] The meeting took place in Churchill's flat at 11 Morpeth Mansions at 5 p.m. on 5 August 1936.

Griffin *did* have an axe to grind and *did* wish to speak of something particularly: the British war debt. Churchill agreed Britain owed America the money, Griffin wrote later, but insisted that Britain should "deduct fifty percent of the cost of all the shot and shell she fired at the Germans from the time America declared war in the Spring of 1917 until she actually put troops in the front lines a year later," an estimated $4.9 billion, plus interest. Griffin claimed he demurred, saying, "if we hadn't entered the war England would have lost," and that "England would probably be ruled from Berlin."[13]

Churchill, according to Griffin, retorted "that there was no one in England happier over [America's] decision to enter than he was but he could see now that our entry had been a great mistake," followed by the remark at the top of this chapter. Then Churchill added: "You may want to stay out of [the next war], but … you will find yourselves fighting shoulder to shoulder with us."[14]

Churchill then offered an article "containing all of the statements he had made to me that day" for $500 ($8000 in today's money) provided Griffin would publish nine more articles at the same price "I said I could not see my way clear to buy ten articles but that I would be glad to buy one," Griffin wrote. "Mr. Churchill was not willing to agree to this stipulation."[15]

Ever living "from mouth to hand,"[16] Churchill frequently proposed articles to publishers; he certainly wished to syndicate his foreign affairs column for the *Evening Standard* in America. But it was Churchill's startling assertions that the U.S. should have "minded its own business" and that U.S. entry was "a mistake," that Griffin would publish in his newspaper that same month. There is no evidence that Churchill knew of their publication. But as he would learn three years later, the matter was merely dormant.

Hoisted on Someone's Petard

As war clouds gathered in the summer of 1939, Churchill's alleged remark was raised by a powerful isolationist, Senator Robert Rice Reynolds (D., N.C.) who said he had the story from Griffin. Insisting he had said no such thing, Churchill engaged an attorney, William N. Stokes, Jr., of Houston, who protested to Reynolds: "Mr. Churchill's distinguished career in public life as well as his outstanding contributions as an historian have led me to believe that in future years he will be recognized as one of the great men of our generation. Certainly he has analyzed Great Britain's position in the world of nations much more accurately than those who have guided his nation's destinies during the past decade."[17] Stokes sent Reynolds a photostat of Churchill's written denial, which does not survive. "I had hoped he would insert it in the *Congressional Record*," Stokes wrote. Given Reynolds' point of view, this was a forlorn hope.[18]

Churchill's next embarrassment was an August 26th German radio broadcast quoting his alleged remarks to Griffin. The next day the *New York Times* asked him to confirm. Churchill pronounced the story "a vicious lie."[19] Queried by the *Philadelphia Evening Bulletin*, Churchill called Griffin a liar and (inaccurately) denied having heard of him. The September 1939 issue of *The Catholic Worker* reprinted Churchill's alleged 1936 statement.[20]

That'll Cost You

Griffin responded with a $1 million libel suit, asking New York courts to attach Churchill's earnings from his New York publishers against the settlement.[21] The *Enquirer's* October 9 issue headlined the lawsuit,[22] Griffin claiming that his account of their 1936 conversation had been published at the time without Churchill's objection, and that he had testified to Churchill's alleged statement before the Senate Naval Affairs Committee.[23]

Churchill responded that while Griffin "may" have called on him in 1936, he had "no recollection" of their meeting. But he was adamant "that I never said anything which remotely resembles in substance or form the passage [Griffin claims]. These views are entirely contrary to all the views I hold and have frequently expressed." He would have ignored Griffin's story, he added, "if his account had not been the exact opposite of the truth, and a palpable travesty and distortion of anything I have ever said or thought."[24]

Based on his secretaries' confirmation of their meeting, Churchill then corrected himself: "No doubt he came to see me on suggestion of some friend of mine that his papers could syndicate in States my fortnightly articles, whereupon private and casual conversation followed. No thought of an interview." He added a marginal note: "Can deny on oath."[25] If the libel was Churchill's denial of meeting Griffin (rather than calling him a liar), it seems odd that the lawsuit continued after Churchill's admission.

The case dragged on. In January 1940 the *Enquirer* fanned the flames, reporting, "Churchill tries to defeat justice."[26] Churchill, by now part of the British government, asked that the Foreign Office investigate his antagonist, suggesting (without apparent foundation), "There is no doubt in my mind that Griffin is set on by German agents, which would fully explain his malignity against this country."[27]

Griffin, though a witness in the suit, did not hesitate to comment publicly. In the

February 1941 *Scribner's Commentator,* which had republished the alleged Churchill remarks the previous November, he penned a detailed version of his story, saying Churchill had sought *him,* not the other way round. Churchill's remarks had been published at the time "in a large number of newspapers," he continued, omitting to mention that he himself had circulated them.

For Griffin to say Churchill never denied his allegations is like saying that if someone doesn't protest a false statement, it must be true. Churchill had been denying the alleged quotation since he first heard about it July 1939. He admitted to having met with Griffin.[28] The editorial stance of *Scribner's Commentator* was itself called into question in 1942, when it shut down over allegations of bribe-taking from Japanese interests, in return for publishing propaganda promoting United States isolationism.[29]

His lawyers suggested Churchill not contest the lawsuit, certain that any damages would be minimal. But the pugnacious prime minister wanted to fight it out, and the British Treasury agreed to help meet his legal expenses on the grounds that Griffin was politically motivated. After Griffin was indicted, Churchill wrote the British Ambassador in Washington, Lord Halifax: "He has now been arrested for aiding the enemy, but that is no reason why his suit against me should not be carried forward or dismissed."[30]

On 22 October 1942 Churchill had his wish: the judge dismissed Griffin's lawsuit, apparently because Griffin had not appeared in court. Suffering from the effects of a heart attack, he was still under indictment, and under house arrest in his hospital.[31]

The Resurrection and the Life

Griffin's Churchill quotation was revived in a 1956 book by J.F.C. Fuller, who in the 1930s had been a member of the British Union of Fascists and Nordic League. Fuller had been Hitler's guest at his Berlin birthday parade in April 1939. In 1999 the story surfaced again, quoted from Fuller's book by *The Spectator* editor Frank Johnson. While Johnson made no comment as to the quote's veracity, Fuller had been more careful, writing that it was "alleged."[32] The quote can be found in several places today on the World Wide Web.

Churchill's denials, all his published writings, and his determination to contest Griffin's lawsuit in the midst of a desperate war, powerfully support his contention that he never believed America should have stayed out of World War I. Griffin's lifetime isolationism is ample motive, but putting the kindest light on it, he may have misinterpreted some offhand remark in their private conversation and believed what he wished.

Bodyguard of Truths

Some parts of the supposed Churchill quote *do* sound authentic: being happy that America entered the war, being certain the U.S. would be "shoulder to shoulder" with Britain in the next one. It's an old journalistic tactic (to make an antiphrasis of a famous Churchill aphorism): a lie should always be surrounded with a bodyguard of truths.

American isolationists were prominent in the 1930s. Churchill himself had few nice things to say about American demands for payment of the British war debt. It annoyed him that the U.S. should wish to receive payment for "shot and shell" fired at the enemy

American doughboys dug in on the Western Front, World War I (Wikimedia Commons).

by British soldiers risking their lives. He believed that the war debt carousel—Germany paid France, France Britain, Britain America, and America Germany—helped no one. *But nowhere in his war debt critiques* did he say that America should have kept out of the war.[33]

We may visualize Churchill voicing such thoughts as conjecture or an alternate scenario, which he sometimes did out of amusement or curiosity, among family or friends. Harder to accept is his declaring this his settled view. Churchill was an open book. If he ever really felt that America should have "minded her own business"—that American intervention led to Nazism, Communism and Fascism—there would be examples in his archive, from which nothing is censored. There is not a single one.

"History with its flickering lamp…"

One event does not follow another; history is too complicated for that. Individuals and peoples make choices. Nazism was *not* the inevitable consequence of World War I, except insofar as any defeated nation hopes for a strong leader. Far more crucial, as Churchill explained, was the harsh peace of Versailles and Germany's postwar depression.[34] A weakened Kaiser in postwar Germany would have given in to Hitler as easily as the more respected Hindenburg. The exiled Kaiser held his nose at Hitler's pogroms but was equally anti–Semitic, and congratulated Hitler on his 1940 victories. But Hitler held Wilhelm in contempt, having concluded he didn't need him.[35] Nor would a 1917 German victory have forestalled Italian Fascism or Russian Communism in the Twenties.

It wasn't just that politically Churchill *had* to deny the Griffin quote in 1939; he would have denied it in 1936—and before. From 1934, Churchill was striving for collective security against Hitler, his anxious gaze resting first on France, then on Russia, then on America. Why would he at *any* time in the Thirties have said words which would only encourage American isolation?

Griffin himself cast the final doubt on his own credibility when he claimed Churchill also said: "You may want to stay out of [the next war], but … you will find yourselves fighting shoulder to shoulder with us." Quite a switch by the British leader who had preferred earlier that America mind its own business. But that, at least, is one sentiment of Churchill's we can accept as genuine.

15

Chemical Warfare

The Myth: Churchill Favored the Use of Poison Gas

The uproar over use of chemical weapons in Syria led the world's media to Winston Churchill. Reports circulated to the effect that, after all, Britain and Churchill were no different from Syria and its warlords: that Churchill favored and/or used "poison gas" from World War I through World War II, notably on the Indians and Bolsheviks in 1919 and the Iraqis in the 1920s. What's more, he wanted to "drench" German cities with gas in 1943.

In developing a story on all this, the BBC asked me about "Winston Churchill's advocacy of poison gas, specifically in Russia and in World War II." Was this something I might wish to discuss? Well, yes—before it all got out of hand. (It did anyway.)

"Uncivilised tribes" vs. Welfare of Troops

At the Second Battle of Ypres in April 1915, the horrors of German poison gas broke upon a shocked world. Outraged, the Allies retaliated in kind, although British manufacture of poison gas—chlorine, and later phosgene—was only a small fraction of that produced by the French and Germans. Though the killing capacity of those gasses was limited to only 4 percent of combat casualties, the revulsion over their insidious effects and the suffering they caused was widespread.[1]

After World War I, with Churchill at the War Office, Britain was faced with the question of using gas against rebel tribesmen in Northwest India and in Mesopotamia, now Iraq. It was never proposed to use chlorine or phosgene, but Churchill confused the matter when he used the words "poisoned gas" in a departmental minute in 1919.

It was "sheer affectation," he wrote, "to lacerate a man with the poisonous fragment of a bursting shell and to boggle at making his eyes water by means of lachrymatory gas." His next sentence is widely quoted today: "I am strongly in favour of using poisoned gas against uncivilised tribes." The sentence after that is usually omitted: "The moral effect should be so good that the loss of life should be reduced to a minimum."[2]

Ten days after that minute, Churchill addressed the India Office's reluctance to use non-lethal gas against rebellious tribesmen: "Gas is a more merciful weapon than high explosive shell, and compels an enemy to accept a decision with less loss of life than any other agency of war. The moral effect is also very great. There can be no conceivable reason why it should not be resorted to. We have definitely taken the position of maintaining gas as a weapon in future warfare, and it is only ignorance on the part of the Indian military authorities which interposes any obstacle."[3]

Churchill went on to cite what he saw as the greater good, which in his view made tear gas acceptable: the welfare of soldiers. In all the accounts of his supposed enthusiasm for "poison gas," I have never seen this portion of his minute cited with the rest:

> Having regard to the fact that [the India Office] are retaining all our men, even those who are most entitled to demobilisation, we cannot in any circumstances acquiesce in the non-utilisation of any weapons which are available to procure a speedy termination of the disorder which prevails on the frontier. If it is fair war for an Afghan to shoot down a British soldier behind a rock and cut him in pieces as he lies wounded on the ground, why is it not fair for a British artilleryman to fire a shell which makes the said native sneeze? It is really too silly.[4]

Those words are always absent from quotes alleging Churchill's penchant for chemical warfare. They testify that Churchill was thinking more broadly, and more humanely, than others: He was thinking of sparing serving soldiers, most of them not volunteers, from ugly deaths by barbarous methods.

The issue of gas came up again after Britain had occupied Mesopotamia, formerly in the old Ottoman Empire, and was trying to restore order and establish a state, later Iraq—"nation building," we might call it today. Incidentally, he was not primarily concerned with securing more oil, which Britain had obtained from other sources. Churchill usually considered "Messpot," as he called it, a huge waste of money.

Rather than "boots on the ground," to use a modern phrase, Churchill saw it safer and cheaper to use the Royal Air Force. This, he explained to Air Marshal Trenchard, might require "the provision of some kind of asphyxiating bombs calculated to cause disablement of some kind but not death…."[5] A year later Churchill urged Trenchard to continue "experimental work on gas bombs, especially mustard gas, which would inflict punishment upon recalcitrant natives without inflicting grave injury upon them."[6]

It is true that mustard gas is much worse than tear gas. It causes itching, skin irritation, and large, putrid blisters. If a victim's eyes are exposed they become sore. A victim can contract conjunctivitis, where the eyelids swell, resulting in temporary blindness. But Churchill was correct that mustard gas was not often lethal. Of 165,000 British mustard gas casualties on the Western Front in World War I, only 3000 or 2.5 percent were deaths. Chlorine, first used by the Germans, in its later "perfected" stage, killed nearly 20 percent.[7] In the event, neither tear gas nor mustard gas was used in India or Iraq.

Gassing the Russians

The strongest case for Churchill as poison gas advocate involves Russia, and was made by Giles Milton in *The Guardian* on 1 September 2013. Milton wrote that in 1919, scientists at the government lab in Porton, Wiltshire, developed the top secret "M Device," an exploding shell containing highly toxic chemical diphenylaminechloroarsine. The man in charge of its development Major General Charles Foulkes, called it "the most effective chemical weapon ever devised."

Tests, Milton wrote, "suggested that it was indeed a terrible new weapon." Uncontrollable vomiting, coughing up blood and instant, crippling fatigue were the most common reactions. The overall head of chemical warfare production, Sir Keith Price, was convinced its use would lead to the rapid collapse of the Bolshevik regime: "If you got home only once with the gas you would find no more Bolshies this side of Vologda."[8]

Milton continued:

> ... a staggering 50,000 M Devices were shipped to Russia: British aerial attacks using them began on 27 August 1919.... Bolshevik soldiers were seen fleeing in panic as the green chemical gas drifted towards them. Those caught in the cloud vomited blood, then collapsed unconscious. The attacks continued throughout September on many Bolshevik-held villages.... But the weapons proved less effective than Churchill had hoped, partly because of the damp autumn weather. By September, the attacks were halted then stopped.[9]

If Churchill planned, or even countenanced, dropping a lethal gas weapon on Russian villages, even for three days, he is certainly culpable, assuming he understood its horrific nature. It would be the only case where he advocated such use on civil populations, rather than on the battlefield. But no appearance of "M Device" can be found in the published or online Churchill Papers, and the only contemporary correspondence between Churchill and Keith Price consists of queries about munitions in 1917–18. And the link provided by *The Guardian* to the test site at Porton, Wiltshire states that it was active between 1939 and 1989—twenty years after the alleged tests of the M Device.

I respectfully asked Milton for the sources of his statements, and had no response. I am not sure why I should have had to ask. One would expect that a writer making such serious charges would offer sources. No matter: my BBC correspondent put me onto his source: Simon Jones, in a 1999 article which Milton paraphrased, but in my judgment quite misconstrued.[10] According to Jones, Foulkes did consider the M Device and DM gas effective, and Price was convinced it would eliminate any "Bolshies" who came in contact with it. Likewise, Churchill *did* order General Ironside, in command at Archangel, to make "fullest use" of the new weapon—for the same reason he always cited with regard to gas: "Bolsheviks have been using gas shells against Allied troops...." (Jones explains that the Bolsheviks were using German shells recovered on the battlefield.)[11]

Nowhere, however, does Jones state that anyone thought the M Device "would lead to the rapid collapse of the Bolshevik state." Neither Jones, nor Milton paraphrasing Jones, said anything about deaths or civilian casualties. If they occurred, they could not have been many. In a September attack on Chunova, for example, "ten Bolsheviks were affected." Opposing British troops were advised that in the event of accidentally inhaling DM, "cigarette smoking would give relief."[12]

Reading Jones, DM comes off as an ugly, disgusting, but generally non-lethal advance on tear gas. Reading Milton, it sounds almost like Zyklon-B, the gas of choice at Auschwitz and the other killing factories of World War II. Milton's *Guardian* article then transitions on to the subject of India, as if the same gas were proposed there. But Sir Charles Foulkes was next posted to India, where he "investigated and rejected proposals to use gas against the fiercely independent North West Frontier tribes who guarded the main strategic routes into Afghanistan."[13]

It is possible to believe Churchill would countenance use of the M Device in Russia, which he regarded as a struggle against barbarians. Yet a document in the Churchill Archives, at the time of the Allied intervention in Russia, suggests that his views here were no different than over India and Iraq:

> Because an enemy who has perpetrated every conceivable barbarity is at present unable, through his ignorance, to manufacture poisoned gas, is that any reason why our troops should be prevented from

taking full advantage of their weapons? The use of these gas shell[s] having become universal during the great war, I consider that we are fully entitled to use them against anyone pending the general review of the laws of war which no doubt will follow the Peace Conference.[14]

There is nothing here suggesting a Churchill penchant for using gas against civilian populations. Indeed Churchill qualified his recommendation: "pending the general review of the laws of war."

World War II and Beyond

Churchill's chemical weapons philosophy leading up to the Second World War remained along the lines he had expressed about India and Iraq, as illustrated by a comment to the House of Commons on 13 May 1932: "Nothing could be more repugnant to our feelings than the use of poison gas, but there is no logic at all behind the argument that it is quite proper in war to lay a man low with high-explosive shell, fragments of which inflict poisonous and festering wounds, and altogether immoral to give him a burn with corrosive gas or make him cough and sneeze or otherwise suffer through his respiratory organs." Churchill added that Britain's attitude had "always been to abhor the employment of poison gas," which was only kept in British arsenals so as not to put Britain "at a hopeless disadvantage if, by any chance, it were used against us by other people."[15]

Gas was not used by the Germans or Allies in World War II. Churchill, all evidence suggests, was content with that stand-off, and even declared against the first use of chemical weapons in 1942. He was always prepared to use them ruthlessly if they were first used by the enemy. The possibility first arose in February 1943, when it was feared that the Germans might use gas against the Russians in their counter-attack on the Donets Basin. The Prime Minister immediately minuted the Chiefs of Staff Committee that if this happened,

> … my declaration of last year of course stands. We shall retaliate by drenching the German cities with gas on the largest possible scale. We must expect their counter-measures. Is everything in readiness for this contingency both ways? It is quite possible that another warning like I gave last year might check them off at the last minute, but we must be ready to strike and make good any threat we utter with the utmost promptitude and severity.[16]

The out-of-context quote one often encounters here is "drenching the German cities with gas on the largest possible scale." It is clear, however, that Churchill's minute was a response, not an order. The Vice Chiefs of Staff reported back: "we are prepared offensively and defensively for gas warfare and are in a position to retaliate by air on a very large scale."[17]

Sir Martin Gilbert stated that the Prime Minister was talking about mustard gas (already described above) "from which nearly everyone recovers." Even then he would use it, he continued, only "it was life or death for us" or if it would "shorten the war by a year.… It is absurd to consider morality on this topic, when everybody used it in the last war without a word of complaint from the moralists or the Church. On the other hand, in the last war the bombing of open cities was regarded as forbidden. Now everybody does it as a matter of course."[18]

It would be several weeks or even months, Churchill added, "before I shall ask you to drench Germany with poison gas." In the meantime he wanted the matter studied, he wrote, "in cold blood by sensible people, and not by that particular set of psalm-singing uninformed defeatists which one runs across, now here, now there." Again the military replied that they were ready, although they "doubted whether gas, of the essentially non-lethal kind envisaged by Churchill, could have a decisive effect, and no gas raids were made."[19]

In view of the celerity with which critics attack Churchill over chemical warfare, it is proper to mention Sir Martin's next paragraph—a poignant reminder of who the real killers were, and the difference between "us" and "them": "News had just reached London of the mass murder in specially-designed gas chambers of more than two and a half million Jews at Auschwitz, which had hitherto been identified only as a slave-labour camp."[20]

Myth and Reality

If anyone still believes that Churchill was an enthusiast of lethal gas, they will have to come up with better evidence than we have seen so far—and some acceptable response to the many instances where, faced with its possible use, Churchill chose not to use it. Truly, they thought on rather higher moral planes we have seen recently in places like Syria.

We need also to consider attitudes at the time: what mattered the most. After the Bolshevik Revolution and the Russian exit from World War I, this same Winston Churchill advocated sending a "commissar" (as he put it) to Lenin, who would offer—in exchange for Russia reentering the war—that Britain would guarantee the Bolshevik revolution. Sir Martin Gilbert said that he first revealed this in a lecture in Moscow to academic and military audiences which were transfixed at the revelation.[21]

Clearly, while Churchill never advocated the first use of lethal gas, his main goal in both world wars was victory: "Victory at all costs," as he put it in 1940, "Victory in spite of all terror." To that end he would consider almost anything. Describing the outbreak of the Great War in 1914 he wrote sadly that almost everything in mankind's arsenal would be used: tanks, smoke, torpedo-seaplanes, directional wireless, cryptography, mine fenders, monitors, torpedo-proof ships: "all were being actively driven forward or developed. Poison gas alone we had put aside—but not, as has been shown, from want of comprehension."[22]

I have always been impressed with the words of his daughter Lady Soames: "My father would have done almost anything to win the war, and I daresay he had to do some pretty rough things. But they didn't unman him."[23]

16

"Taking more out of alcohol"

The Myth: Churchill Was an Alcoholic

"The potentially darker side of Churchill's use of alcohol has been presented, but only in caustic and irresponsible fashion," wrote the historian Warren Kimball.

> Neither accusation, nor the argument that Churchill watered and nursed his drinks, are persuasive to this writer, but such is the fate of iconoclasm. All that said, there is no credible testimony of Churchill being drunk, in the falling down, non-compos mentis sense, while he was prime minister, whatever the occasional reports of slurred words. Perhaps, as C.P. Snow quipped, Churchill was no alcoholic, because "no alcoholic could drink that much."[1]

Churchill certainly had the capacity for high intake without effect, and was fond of fanning his reputation as a serious drinker. "I had been brought up and trained to have the utmost contempt for people who got drunk," he wrote in his autobiography—"except on very exceptional occasions and a few anniversaries...."[2] There is on record only one "exceptional occasion" when he was clearly intoxicated.

He did seem to think it was a sign of manly vigor to suggest that he could really "put it away." A favorite tableau was acted out many times with the help of his scientific advisor, Professor Frederick Lindemann. "Prof!" Churchill would command in a restaurant or dining room: "Pray calculate the amount of wine, champagne and spirits I have consumed in my life and indicate how high they would reach in this room." Aware of the script, Lindemann would pretend to calculate with his slide rule and then say sadly, "I'm afraid not more than a few inches, Winston." And Churchill would reply: "How much to do, how little time remains!"[3]

The Alcohol Menu

David Lough's *No More Champagne*, a learned treatise on Churchill's finances, proved irresistible to writers anxious to document Churchill's failings. Lough wrote that Churchill spent an average of £1160 per year (£100,000 today) between 1908 and 1914. A reviewer noticed that this would be nearly a quarter of his annual salary as a cabinet minister, and found that this was actually the total for eight years. The tab was much higher by 1936 (Lough £920, the reviewer £515).[4] Although these are still impressive liquor bills, one has to consider that Churchill entertained, fed and watered people in large numbers. In the business of politics, it was part of his overhead.

Consider Churchill's established habits. His hour's nap each afternoon enabled him to work and dictate into the wee hours of the morning. He would wake at eight a.m., peruse the papers and his correspondence in bed, with an ample breakfast occasionally accompanied by a glass of hock—a white wine from the Rhine—which he also sometimes drank at lunch. Very occasionally, especially when guests were present, he took a small glass of sherry, though he really didn't like fortified wines. He made an exception for port if stilton were present, cracking the Biblical injunction, "What therefore God hath joined together, let not man put asunder."[5]

His dinner standard was champagne, which critics claimed he drank by the bucket. "In fact," recalled Christian Pol-Roger, of the famous champagne house Churchill favored, "he often ordered imperial pints"—a bottle of twenty ounces, but not overwhelming when consumed in the course of a two-hour lunch interrupted by frequent conversation. He would finish with brandy.[6] Ralph Mansfield, his spirits merchant in the 1950s, investigated the Chartwell wine cellar in 1954 and pronounced it a "shambles," except for the vintage Pol Roger, Hine Brandy and Johnny Walker scotch.[7]

A.L. Rowse, the Oxford historian, wrote of a visit to Chartwell in 1955 which serves to illustrate a typical Churchill luncheon. It was, he said,

> rather burdensome for a teetotaler—I didn't dare to be one, alone with Churchill. There had been Bristol Cream before lunch, a very good hock during lunch. When it came to cheese, I drew the line at port—port, at lunch! "What? No port? Then you must have some brandy." (I can't bear brandy.) "What? No brandy? Then you must have some liqueur with your coffee. Have some Cointreau: it's very soothing." I had some Cointreau: it was *very* soothing. Slightly sozzled, I tottered upstairs after him to the big study next to his bedroom—over the fireplace a large landscape of Blenheim—and we devoted ourselves to history.[8]

Remarkably, Rowse said, Churchill was perfectly able to get back to work after this impressive intake, a fraction of which had almost put the non-drinking Rowse under the table. But Churchill liked to inflict alcoholic rigors on teetotalers—Professor Lindemann was always obliged to take two ccs of brandy after dinner at Chartwell. Sure of its medicinal benefits, Churchill declared that he had "taken more out of alcohol than alcohol has taken out of me."[9]

Not even royalty escaped the rigors of Churchill's routine. In February 1945, after the Yalta Conference, he paid a visit to King Ibn Saud at the Fayoum Oasis in Egypt. His daughter Sarah, making arrangements for the luncheon, was informed that neither smoking nor alcohol were allowed in the Royal presence. This matter was characteristically confronted head on:

> Winston informed the interpreter that if it was the religion of His Majesty to deprive himself of smoking and alcohol he must point out that his rule of life prescribed as an absolutely sacred rite, the smoking of cigars and the drinking of alcohol before, after, and, if need be, during all meals and in the intervals between them. The King graciously accepted the position, and his own cup bearer even offered the Prime Minister a glass of water from the sacred well of Mecca—"the most delicious that I have ever tasted," said Winston—which, for him, was going quite a long way.[10]

Churchill later described the King's reaction as "complete surrender." Ibn Saud even ordered that his guest be given what Churchill described as a very nasty cocktail."[11] It turned out to be an aphrodisiac.

Part of Churchill's secret was that he drank most heavily during meals. Meals were long affairs, giving him ample time to hold forth at length, and the alcohol time to dilute. He reacted quite furiously to any suggestion that he was drunk. One night, tired after a long session of the House of Commons, he was toddling out of the Chamber when he met the formidable Labour MP Bessie Braddock: "Winston, you are drunk," she exclaimed, "and what's more, you are disgustingly drunk." Churchill's daughter was certain his retort never happened, until an eye-witness, his bodyguard at the time, confirmed it. "Bessie, my dear," her father retorted, "you are ugly, and what's more you are disgustingly ugly, but tomorrow I shall be sober and you shall still be disgustingly ugly." Pedants might say this was an admission of intoxication; but Churchill had not been drinking, and had just picked up a line stored in his capacious memory.[12]

No member of Churchill's family ever saw him drunk. But after many years, an eye-witness turned up to one occasion when he would not have passed a breathalyzer test. Danny Mander was a bodyguard at the 1943 Teheran conference with Roosevelt and Stalin. After a long night of vodka toasts with the Russians, Mander said, "He was still walking, just…. I put my arm within his to hold him steady…. [Churchill and Eden] were yet able to walk home in true British fashion after a heavy night, talking loudly but not singing, and living to fight another day." Churchill himself disparaged "silly tales" of those Russian drinking bouts, writing: "I had been well brought up."[13]

"Scotch-flavoured mouthwash"

The fact that Churchill kept a glass of whisky and water by his side for most of the working day is the chief source of the myth that he constantly swilled scotch. A private secretary, John Colville, quickly learned that his whisky intake was not what it appeared. "Winston's whisky was very much a whisky and soda," Colville later told Martin Gilbert. "It was really a mouthwash. He used to get frightfully cross if it was too strong."[14]

The story of what his daughter Mary called "The Papa Cocktail" (a smidgen of Johnnie Walker covering the bottom of a tumbler, filled with water and sipped throughout the morning), is confirmed by so many observers that it could hardly be untrue. But the oft-quoted tale that Churchill first used whisky in tropical climes because they had to add it to make water drinkable cannot be traced to anything he wrote or said.

In fact, Churchill acquired the habit with the Malakand Field Force in 1897. Faced with terrific heat he had never before experienced, he had nothing to drink but tepid water, or water with lime-juice or whisky. "Grasping the larger hope," he had within five days "completely overcome my repugnance to the taste of whisky." The smoky taste which so many find repugnant in scotch developed an appeal. From then on, he wrote, "although I have always practised true temperance, I have never shrunk when occasion warranted it from the main basic standing refreshment of the white officer in the East."[15]

There was "always some alcohol in his bloodstream," insisted William Manchester. Indeed, Churchill took pains to see he was supplied, even in "dry" countries. Dr. Otto Pickhardt, who attended him after he was knocked down by a car New York in 1931, issued a medical note which Barry Singer says "instantly entered the annals of Prohibition." Churchill's convalescence, the doctor wrote, "necessitates the use of alcoholic spirits especially at mealtimes. The quantity is naturally indefinite but the minimum requirement would be 250 cubic centimeters [slightly more than eight ounces]."[16]

There are of course many such reports, but they all draw the same conclusion, that throughout the day, Churchill was judicious drinker. Robert Rhodes James quoted a close friend: "He never drank the sort of quantities of alcohol frequently ascribed to him at the time, though indeed he drank somewhat more than the average…. He would have about three really mild whiskies and sodas—sometimes brandy and soda—as a thirst quencher during the day. Not before 11 a.m., one at tea-time, and one before going to bed, perhaps one other during the evening…. W. was usually most careful never to absorb a lot of mixed drinks." Another friend emphasized "the mathematical exactness of the amount Churchill drank daily, and the times at which he drank. He has also stressed the fact that Churchill hardly ever mixed his drinks."[17]

If he was not an alcoholic, was Churchill "alcohol-dependent"? It is hard to judge because of his habit of allowing people to think he had a bottomless capacity. If he were truly dependent, it seems he would have had a hard time winning a £600 bet with Lord Rothermere that he could abstain from brandy or undiluted spirits in 1936, which apparently he did.[18] This might have been easier than it sounds. He never drank scotch neat, and sometimes remarked to those who did, "You are not likely to live a long life if you take it like that"—or words to that effect.

The Ultimate Tipple

If there was anything Churchill truly loved, it was France's most famous wine. "I could not live without champagne," he exclaimed. "In victory I deserve it. In defeat I need it." A glass of champagne imparts exhilaration, braces the nerves and stirs the imagination. A bottle, he warned, "produces the opposite effect. Excess causes a comatose insensibility." Like war, he added, champagne was best appreciated by sipping.[19]

Readers of these pages probably don't have to be told that his favorite brand was Pol Roger, for which orders of his date back to the early 1900s. Kay Halle, a family friend, remembered a vision familiar to many Chartwell guests:

> Mr. Churchill sat at the head of his table in Renaissance splendor in an open-throated silk shirt, a velvet smoking jacket and slippers with "WSC" threaded in gold on the toes. In front of him stood a bottle of Pol Roger. Later in World War II Madame Pol-Roger is said to have allocated the remaining output of that particular year for his use in gratitude for the liberation of France. After the war, he was to name one of his race horses Pol Roger.[20]

His favorite vintage after the war was the '47, which the Pol-Roger family reserved for him. I hosted a visit by a Churchill tour party to Epernay in the 1990s, where a party of Churchillians enjoyed some of that very vintage, uncorked in their honor—a heady, old-style champagne whose nose filled the air.

Mythical Miscellany

Rumors of Churchill as an alcoholic will likely continue, because he fanned the image so well. As early as 1930 he told Robert Boothby: "I find alcohol a great support in life. Sir Alexander Walker, who keeps me supplied with your national brew, told me that a friend of his, who died the other day, drank a bottle of whisky a day for the last ten years of his life. He was 85!"[21] This was a good laugh, but not a serious prescription. He neither wanted alcohol nor needed it, Churchill insisted in the 1940s, "but I should think it pretty hazardous to interfere with the ineradicable habit of a lifetime."[22]

His justly admired still life painting, "Bottlescape," dominated by a huge bottle that

"Drunken Weltanschauung," a wartime German cartoon: "Churchill tries to find luck in drink, but the bottle distorts the view" (*Der Stürmer*, Nuremberg, 26 February 1942).

looks like a magnum, is offered by some critics as proof of his heavy consumption. This is a stretch. His nephew Peregrine told the writer that Chartwell had to be scoured to come up with all the bottles in that picture: "A friend had given him a huge bottle of brandy one Christmas, and he sent us children around the house, commanding us: "Fetch me associate and fraternal bottles to form a bodyguard to this majestic container.""[23]

During Sir Martin Gilbert's 1980s BBC television series on Churchill, *The Times* referred to Gilbert's interview with Sir Ian Jacob of Churchill's wartime Defense Staff, who had mentioned the boss's "huge intake of alcohol." This made the usual headlines and rounds of the press, but again the tall tale was punctured by an authority. Sending Sir Martin this cutting, wartime private secretary John Peck wrote:

> To me *The Times* notice gave a completely mistaken picture, based on a misunderstanding of Ian Jacob's statement that "he always had a bottle of champagne for lunch." I have already been challenged on this and I have said (i) Ian Jacob hardly ever had lunch with Winston so he could only have been quoting hearsay; (ii) even if Churchill had had champagne for lunch every day he would never have got through an entire bottle, and even if he had a glass or two by himself, I fear that Sawyers the butler would have ensured that none was wasted.[24]

The "bottle," incidentally, was the aforementioned "Imperial pint."

If none of this convinces the reader of Churchill's more or less normality with respect to a good drink, steadily supplied in moderation, consider whether alcohol helped or hindered. This should be evident by his performance. People complained to Lincoln that General Grant drank too much. Lincoln allegedly replied: "Find out what he is drinking and send all my generals a case."[25]

17

The Bolshevik Menace

The Myth: Churchill Was a Consistent Foe of Communism

Bolshevism and Communism received Churchill's most withering denunciations, but the picture of Churchill as an unswerving anti-communist is inaccurate, a fact that will not appeal to modern politicians who hold him as such—but there it is.

The October 1917 revolution that brought Lenin to power unleashed a cornucopia of Churchillian invective. In March 1918 he referred to the Bolsheviks as "vampires."[1] In May he declared: "Bolshevism is not a policy; it is a disease … it is not a creed; it is a pestilence."[2] Weeks later he referred to Lenin's followers as "a league of the failures, the criminals, the unfit, the mutinous, the morbid, the deranged, and the distraught in every land…."[3] In November he said that Lenin had been sent to Russia "in the same way that you might send a phial containing a culture of typhoid or cholera…."[4] Over the decades, his attitude seemed consistent. In 1954, reflecting on the two devastating World Wars, he declared that had he been properly supported in 1919, "we might have strangled Bolshevism in its cradle, but everybody turned up their hands and said, 'How shocking!'"[5]

Some people were shocked at some of his remarks immediately after World War II. The Soviets, after all, had been an intrinsic part in the coalition which defeated Hitler. In 1949, when Churchill suggested that strangling them at birth would have been "an untold blessing to the human race," a Labour MP interrupted: "If that had happened we should have lost the 1939–45 war." Churchill retorted, "No, it would have *prevented* the last war."[6] He was visualizing the outcome if Hitler had been opposed by the West and a non-communist Russia, of the kind he had tried with little success to see into existence after World War I.

Minister of War

With the irony for which he was renowned, Prime Minister David Lloyd George made Churchill Secretary of State for War in January 1919, two months after the Great War had ended. Churchill immediately found a way to be controversial, becoming involved in the debate over Western aid to the so-called White Russians, Kolchak, Deniken and Wrangel, who were fighting the "Reds" of Lenin and Trotsky.

Alexander Kolchak, a naval admiral, had established a provisional anti-communist government in Siberia, and for eighteen months was internationally recognized as the leader of Russia. Former Czarist generals Anton Denikin and Pyotr Wrangel headed anti–Bolshevik armies in south Russia. Denikin nearly captured Moscow in the summer of 1919, but Lenin allied himself with the anarchists, who attacked Denikin's lines of supply, forcing his retreat. Lenin then eliminated his anarchist partners.[7] Kolchak, whom the communists executed in 1920, is widely regarded as an autocrat who refused to contemplate autonomy for ethnic minorities or to cooperate with socialist non–Bolsheviks. His chief of staff insisted that he and his allies were "patriots with a deep love for their country and worked for its salvation without any regard for self-advancement … for a National Assembly, chosen by the people."[8]

Whatever their faults or virtues, Churchill took Kolchak and company at their word, and endorsed British aid. But despite the widespread belief that Churchill wished to have "boots on the ground," Britain sent only 600 troops to Archangel, and a few hundred to Vladivostok—a fraction of the 13,000 Americans, 23,000 Greeks, and thousands sent by other countries.[9] When in 1919 he called for defeating "the foul baboonery of Bolshevism," Churchill was proposing not a British army, but the dispatch of arms, munitions, and technical services. Indeed his main goal as War Minister was to demobilize the vast World War I army. It was "malicious," he insisted, to suggest that the wartime draft be prolonged "because of the enterprises we have on foot in Russia."[10]

Churchill as Pro-Bolshevik

But the statesman with such strong anti-communist credentials was less consistent than he seemed. Churchill's initial quarrel with the Bolsheviks stemmed from their March 1918 treaty with Germany, five months after they came to power, taking Russia out of the war. Always fixed on victory, Churchill the next month made a startling proposal. Why not send a "commissar" to Moscow—he suggested Theodore Roosevelt, who was then in Paris—and, in exchange for Lenin rejoining the war against Germany, the Allies would find a way of "safeguarding the permanent fruits of the Revolution." After all, Churchill told Lloyd George, Lenin and Trotsky were "fighting with ropes round their necks…. Show them any real chance of consolidating their power, of getting some kind of protection against the vengeance of a counter-revolution, and they would be non-human not to embrace it."[11] Sir Martin Gilbert, who had not uncovered this evidence when he wrote the corresponding volume of the official biography, was at first astonished at this discovery, but concluded that it was characteristic of Churchill's determination to seek victory at all costs. (For Soviet reactios, see page 147.)

Churchill's radical notion proved rather *too* radical for his colleagues, not to mention Lenin, who based much of his appeal to the masses on his promise to take Russia out of the war. Thus, within a year, Churchill had concluded that the Bolsheviks actually were non-human, after all. After the war his condemnations became ideological, as he called for aid to the Whites. Describing, in 1920, the Bolsheviks as a "vile group of cosmopolitan fanatics," he declared: "the policy I will always advocate is the overthrow and destruction of that criminal regime."[12]

A greater deviation from his usual line came in World War II, and the years leading up to it. Churchill's demands for an Anglo-French-Soviet alliance in the 1930s, and the "Grand Alliance" of the 1940s, are well known. He was conscious, of course, that by so arguing he was making an astonishing volte-face. He justified it by declaring that Hitler's Germany was the greater danger. In June 1941, when Hitler invaded Russia, making the USSR Britain's ally, he would crack famously: "If Hitler invaded Hell I would at least make a favourable reference to the Devil in the House of Commons."[13]

From the time Hitler occupied on the Rhineland, in March 1936, Churchill strove for Anglo-Soviet cooperation. The historian Donald Cameron Watt wrote: "He fell into the clutches of Ivan Maisky,[14] Soviet ambassador to London." Maisky was clever and worldly, practised in English ways, spoke perfect English, a smooth cultivator of British leaders. But "fell into the clutches" is wide of the mark. Given Churchill's loathing for Communism, it seemed quite a departure to court Stalin's ambassador. Yet Churchill could also add and subtract, and Britain needed help.

Speaking in November 1936, after criticizing Soviet involvement in the Spanish Civil War, Churchill described "another Russia, which only wishes to be left alone in peace." When Maisky complained about his remarks over Spain, Churchill referred him to the latter part of that speech, "the collective security part."[15] He had fought with all his strength against Communism, he said later, but the greatest threat to the British Empire was Nazism, "with its doctrine of world domination by Berlin."[16]

When Hitler occupied Austria in early 1938, Moscow proposed extending the Franco-Soviet pact to Britain, recreating in effect the Triple Entente that had declared war on Germany in 1914. Churchill's arguments to accept this offer fell on skeptical ears of Prime Minister Neville Chamberlain, who took no action, frustrating Churchill and Maisky. By autumn, with Hitler threatening Czechoslovakia, Chamberlain and the French met Hitler at Munich in hope of preserving peace; but no Soviet representative was invited. London's few contacts with the Russians, Maisky wrote, did not feature "a single case of consultation with the Soviet Government." There is no doubt that Churchill shared Maisky's sentiment. Harold Nicolson recorded: "Winston says (and we all agree) that the fundamental mistake the PM has made is his refusal to take Russia into his confidence."[17]

A year later, Poland was Hitler's target and Churchill was making another plea for a Soviet British understanding. Harold Nicolson vividly recalled an episode outside the Commons on 3 April:

> I am seized upon by Winston and taken down to the lower smoking room with Maisky and Lloyd George. Winston adopts the direct method of attack. "Now look here Mr. Ambassador, if we are to make a success of this new policy we require the help of Russia. Now I don't care for your system and I never have, but the Poles and the Romanians like it even less. Although they might be prepared at a pinch to let you in, they would certainly want some assurances that you would eventually get out. Can you give us such assurances?"[18]

Maisky's answer is not recorded. But assurances or not, no cooperation was offered by the Chamberlain government to Moscow. In August Stalin, seizing the only solid offer he had, concluded a non-aggression pact with Hitler. Poland was invaded, and World War II had begun.

After the onset of the war Churchill continued to hope Russia would eventually make common cause with the West. "Indeed, even Churchill's magnificently combative speech on the BBC on the day of [Hitler's attack on Russia] was balanced in such a way that he did not appear as an enthusiastic convert of Communism," wrote Antoine Capet: "He was careful not to use the word 'Bolshevik' and its derivatives, now only part of the vocabulary of Hitler and the various quisling régimes in Occupied Europe, but to speak of Russia"[19]:

At four o'clock this morning Hitler attacked and invaded Russia…. No one has been a more consistent opponent of Communism than I have for the last twenty-five years. I will unsay no word that I have spoken about it. But all this fades away before the spectacle which is now unfolding.[20]

The record of Churchill's wartime relations with the communist tyrant he and Roosevelt nicknamed "Uncle Joe" is the subject of vast scholarly study. Replete with doubts, mistrust and worries over the likely behavior of Russia after the war, it nevertheless constitutes the closest collaboration between three highly disparate allies in modern history. Throughout the war, Churchill maintained his prewar deviation from his earlier anticommunist line, as he fought what he saw as the greater evil of Nazism.

After Hitler was defeated, Churchill began warning of a Russian-dominated Eastern Europe. He was roundly reviled by the Western media for turning on a former ally—only to be reviled in turn by conservatives when, in the early Fifties, he sought a "settlement" of the Cold War with Stalin's successors—with whom, he considered, there might be an opportunity for productive negotiations.

"One may approve or denounce Churchill's eminently pragmatic position towards the various forms of the extreme Right and extreme Left," wrote Professor Capet. "But one cannot deny his remarkable consistency if one accepts that his constant overriding aim was the preservation of 'bourgeois' liberties—the key, in his eyes, to the survival of civilisation."[21]

Churchill was eternally an optimist. He had hoped that wartime collaboration between the "Big Three" would lead to a generation of peace. That it didn't happen is not at issue here. The point is simply that Churchill was not the implacable anti–Communist he is so frequently (and fondly) portrayed by politicians, scholars and the media.

18

Trial by Jewry

The Myth: Churchill Was an Enemy of the Jews and Zionism

Churchill has long been accused of being a closet anti–Semite, no friend of Jews in general and an enemy of Zionism. The accusations sometimes come from Jews, who collectively tend to admire him. But quoting Churchill out of context has become a hobby among those determined to find among his fifteen million words exactly what they expect to find, instead of what he actually believed.

Two examples, among many, will serve to expose the myth that Churchill was anything but a "righteous Gentile": His early statements about Marxism, in which he is said to have claimed that Jews were largely behind that movement; and his outrage over the assassination of Lord Moyne by Zionist extremists in 1944, which some say proves he turned against Zionism. A fair appraisal of each suggests that Churchill's critics have failed to make their case.

"Zionism versus Bolshevism"

On the basis of something he wrote after World War I, Churchill is frequently accused of equating Jews with Marxists. According to carefully selected quotations from that article, he is seen to argue that Jews were part of a "world-wide conspiracy for the overthrow of civilization and the reconstitution of society on the basis of arrested development."[1]

This isolated quotation comes up in books and articles, even by respected writers. It is derived from Churchill's February 1920 newspaper article, "Zionism versus Bolshevism." There Churchill made the not-very-controversial statement that many leading Bolsheviks were Jews. He also offered a reason: "The adherents of this sinister confederacy are mostly men reared up among the unhappy populations of countries where Jews are persecuted on account of their race. Most, if not all, of them have forsaken the faith of their forefathers, and divorced from their minds all spiritual hopes of the next world."[2] This is interpreted to infer that *all* Jews were Bolsheviks, and thus, as Churchill is supposed to have written, "enemies of civilization." (Actually that phrase does not appear in his 1920 article.)

Churchill begins with words less often quoted. The Jews, he writes, are "beyond all question the most formidable and the most remarkable race which has ever appeared in the world. He cites three main lines of "political conception" in which Jews are prominent. In two—contributions to their countries in war and peace, and progenitors of liberal and progressive thought—Jews have been "helpful and hopeful citizens." He cites British Jewish soldiers, some who rose to high command, others who won the Victoria Cross. But in a third area of politics, Jews have been "absolutely destructive." Prominent among Jewish Bolsheviks, he continues, are Leon Trotsky (Russia), Bela Kun (Hungary), Rosa Luxemburg (Germany) and Emma Goldman (United States). In the Soviet pantheon, with the exception of Lenin, "the majority of the leading figures are Jews."[3]

In "Zionism vs. Bolshevism," Churchill prefigures his later indictment of Nazi Germany, writing that nothing is more wrong than denying an individual the right to be judged on personal merits rather than race or origin. If a Briton says, "I am an Englishman practising the Jewish faith," he expresses "a worthy conception, and useful in the highest degree."[4] This part of Churchill's essay is rarely quoted. Nearly half a century later, Martin Luther King, Jr., would echo his sentiment, dreaming of a day when people would be judged only by the content of their character.[5]

Critics also refer to the Sidney Street siege of 1911 (Chapter 7), claiming that "the Jews of London's East End" who barricaded themselves against the police were cast by Churchill as "Bolsheviks and alien extremists."[6] Could they not have been all three? Yet there is scant evidence that the Sidney Street criminals were portrayed as Jews at the time. Churchill, the government and press referred to them as "anarchists," "Latvians" and "Russians." Speculations of Jewish ethnicity were absent.

Partial quotations taken out of context distort what Churchill was saying. One may not seriously use his article, "Zionism versus Bolshevism," to accuse Churchill of anti–Semitism. Writers need to go to the source, and get it right. Jews might wish that the misinformed, uneducated, simple-minded bigots were right, and that they truly had the power, wealth and control ascribed to them. Then indeed they would be a force to reckon with.

Terrorists by Any Other Stripe

Zionism was established as a political entity by Theodor Herzl in 1897, and later led by Chaim Weizmann. Its aim was to reestablish a Jewish nation in that part of Palestine which was the ancient homeland of the Jews. In "Zionism vs. Bolshevism," Churchill wrote that if "there should be created in our own lifetime by the banks of the Jordan a Jewish State … an event would have occurred in the history of the world which would, from every point of view, be beneficial."[7]

His critics dispute Churchill's consistency on the subject. "He was no stranger to the latent anti–Semitism of his generation and class," wrote the Israeli professor Eli Shealtiel: "…he lost interest in Zionism after his close friend Lord Moyne was assassinated by Jewish Lehi (Stern Gang) extremists in Cairo in November 1944."[8]

Churchill was not an uncritical friend of Jews. Outraged when Moyne was killed, Churchill asked the Colonial Secretary, Oliver Stanley, to impress upon Zionist leader Chaim Weizmann "that it was incumbent on the Jewish Agency to do all in their power to suppress these terrorist activities." In Parliament he added: "If our dreams for Zionism are to end in the smoke of assassins' pistols, and our labours for its future to produce

only a new set of gangsters worthy of Nazi Germany, many like myself will have to recon-
sider the position we have maintained so consistently and so long in the past."[9]

A Steady Friend Since 1904

Churchill's righteous condemnation of the killing of Lord Moyne is no indication
of his broader views. He supported Zionism at least from the time he represented the
heavily Jewish constituency of Oldham, a suburb of Manchester, in 1904. On 30 May of
that year he wrote a widely publicized letter to Nathan Laski, leader of the Jewish community, opposing the Aliens Bill—an attempt to curb the influx of Jewish refugees from
pogroms in Russia. Churchill emphasized Britain's tradition of asylum for refugees, and

**Churchill (left) with Lawrence and Abdullah (right, later first King of Jordan) at Jewish set-
tlements, Jerusalem, 1921. Churchill had no trouble selling the concept of a Jewish homeland
to such moderate Arabists, but never contemplated the reaction of the more reactionary elements (Library of Congress).**

how few aliens there really were at the time. Listening to the bill's proponents, he remarked, one would think "we were being overrun by the swarming invasion and 'ousted' from our island."[10] The Aliens Bill was roundly defeated.

In November 1917, British Foreign Secretary Arthur Balfour wrote Lord Rothschild, a leader of the British Jewish community:

> His Majesty's government view with favour the establishment in Palestine of a national home for the Jewish people, and will use their best endeavours to facilitate the achievement of this object, it being clearly understood that nothing shall be done which may prejudice the civil and religious rights of existing non–Jewish communities in Palestine, or the rights and political status enjoyed by Jews in any other country.[11]

As Colonial Secretary in 1921 Churchill backed the Balfour Declaration, promoting a Jewish homeland in Palestine (which, remember, was 6/7ths Arab, consisting of modern Jordan as well as modern Israel). In the ensuing debate, some in Parliament attempted to renege on the Declaration, with warnings that sound eerily familiar. The House of Lords voted against the Balfour Declaration 60 to 29, declaring that the Palestine Mandate was unacceptable as being "opposed to the sentiments and wishes of the great majority of the people of Palestine." Lord Sydenham said: "Palestinians would never have objected to the establishment of more colonies of well-selected Jews; but, instead of that, we have dumped down 25,000 promiscuous people on the shores of Palestine.... What we have done is ... to start a running sore in the East, and no one can tell how far that sore will extend."[12]

In a bravura performance in the Commons on 4 July 1922, Churchill hurled the earlier words of the doubters back at them to turn back the House of Lords vote against the Balfour Declaration: "Lord Sydenham said, 'I earnestly hope that one result of the War will be to free Palestine from the withering blight of Turkish rule, and to render it available as the national home of the Jewish people, who can restore its ancient prosperity.'"[13] Any visitor to Palestine, Churchill continued, could hardly miss how fertile fields and gardens had been converted from the desert, to the benefit of Arabs and Jews alike.

It was, Paul Johnson wrote, "one of his greatest speeches, which swung Members of Parliament round into giving the Jews their chance." The House of Commons voted 292–35 in favor of the Palestine policy, reversing the House of Lords. Johnson considered that speech a watershed: "Without Churchill it is very unlikely that Israel would ever have come into existence."[14]

As Colonial Secretary, Churchill had refused King Ibn Saud's demand to stop Jewish immigration. In 1922 he proposed a compromise, allowing immigration to be based on Palestine's economic capacity. As a result, 400,000 Jews escaped from Europe before World War II. In the 1930s he opposed Hitler's pogroms and, unsuccessfully, a British government 1939 Palestine White Paper again attempting to halt immigration. In 1941 Churchill exempted Palestine from the Atlantic Charter, explaining to Roosevelt that the Arabs would claim a majority and block Jewish immigration. In 1943 he offered sanctuary in Gibraltar to hundreds of Jews being held in Spanish detention camps.

Churchill's speeches from 1948 to 1955 were replete with pro–Israel sentiments. The close affection of Jewish friends, from Ernest Cassel to Bernard Baruch, attended him all his life. On his 75th birthday Churchill received a message from David Ben-Gurion, Israel's first prime minister: "Your words and your deeds are indelibly engraved in the annals of humanity. Happy the people that has produced such a son."[15]

"History with its flickering lamp stumbles along the trail of the past," Churchill said, "trying to reconstruct its scenes, to revive its echoes, and kindle with pale gleams the passion of former days."[16] To reconstruct a scene, one must consider the wider context— and the wider context is dispositive. In 2015, the Simon Wiesenthal Center and Museum of Tolerance in New York posthumously honored Churchill "for his everlasting love and affection for the Jewish people…. Over 600 people watched with an awe that transcends generations and signaled gratitude to a family that bore much criticism, heartache and professional consequence for its steadfast support of our people and our national home."[17]

19

The Trouble with Mr. Gandhi

The Myth: Churchill Was a Racist
Who Opposed Freedom for India

In May 1940, as Hitler was absorbing most of Western Europe and Britain was turning to Churchill, Mohandas Gandhi wrote a friend: "I do not consider Hitler to be as bad as he is depicted. He is showing an ability that is amazing and seems to be gaining his victories without much bloodshed."[1]

"May 1940 was certainly a late date for a respected world leader to be writing such a thing," wrote Larry Arnn.[2] Months earlier, in Czechoslovakia and Poland, Hitler's *Einsatzgruppen* and *Schutzstaffel* had begun their deadly work, as they soon would in the Low Countries and France, rounding up and deporting *untermenschen* for slave labor or extermination, because of their race or political views or nationality. Perhaps Mr. Gandhi was unaware of this. He was not alone.

Let us consider Churchill and his troubles with Gandhi. Churchill was an opponent of the Government of India Act, initiated in 1931. A step toward independence, it was the actual basis of constitutional law after the subcontinent was partitioned into India and Pakistan in 1947. The Act provided a large measure of autonomy to the provinces, and a federation of India and the "princely states"—those regions with their own rulers. Gandhi supported the India Act. But "Churchill's views on this matter are not today well-known," Arnn wrote. "His opinion was that the people of India were entitled to self-government."[3]

Churchill's Case

How could Churchill believe Indians were entitled to self-government while opposing the India Act? The problem, for Churchill, lay in the concept of India as "the home of a strongly coherent, united race. India was nearly as large as Europe, he said. It was "no more a political personality than Europe." It contained scores of sects, races and religions, many in a state of antagonism. "In short, India is a geographical term. It is no more a united nation than the Equator."[4] Churchill argued that Gandhi's Congress Party, clamoring to rule in the 1930s, constituted a small, elite minority, with racist and exclusionary views toward many, particularly Muslims and the 60 million Hindu "Untouchables," the lowest level of the caste system.

Until that problem could be resolved, Churchill asserted, Britain carried a responsibility.

Most of India's then-350 million people, only a few million literate, depended on the British-Indian civil service, which had "no personal interests of their own"—impartial, as he saw it, between the races and classes. Without their involvement—in defense, administration, medicine, hygiene, judiciary, transportation, irrigation, public works and famine prevention—Churchill predicted that "India will fall back into the barbarism and privations of the Middle Ages."[5]

That was Churchill's case against the 1935 India Act. Gandhi's case for it was that the problems Churchill described could never be solved from London. Resolving their difficulties was the price Indians must pay for independence and dignity, and well worth paying. "A Tory in 1776 might have reasonably argued that Britain's holding on to the American colonies would spare them the fate of undergoing either balkanization or a brutal civil war," wrote Manfred Weidhorn, "and he would have been correct. Yet how many Americans wish to undo the Revolution for that reason?"[6]

Proving Churchill's contention that a unified state was not feasible, independence in 1947 brought a civil war that killed hundreds of thousands, perhaps millions, and divided the subcontinent between India and Pakistan. In 1971, East Pakistan seceded to become Bangladesh. Over the years, Sikhs in Kashmir sporadically erupted for independence. In 1947, asked by a Swedish journalist how he felt about India achieving freedom, Gandhi said sadly: "Madame, you may write in your paper that India has never followed my way."[7] Two years later, he was murdered by Hindus who opposed his policy of fairness toward Pakistanis and Indian Muslims.

Churchill vs. Gandhi

Because they were ranged on opposite poles, Churchill and Gandhi have long been regarded as implacable enemies. Like everyone, Gandhi had his dark sides, but Churchill has more often been cast as the villain, his attitudes based on racism and a limited understanding based on the long-ago India of his youth. Churchill's party leader, Stanley Baldwin, wrote Weidhorn

> has much to answer for at the bar of history, but in this matter he was right. While Churchill carried on about how the facts were against Indian independence, Baldwin likewise urged people to face up to the truth. The principle fact "today," he concluded, was that "the unchanging East has changed." With that one nugget, the usually pedestrian Baldwin shoots the usually eloquent Churchill, with his romantic, Victorian, imperial rhetoric, right out of the water.[8]

Churchill's speeches nursed Baldwin's image of him as a hopeless diehard. At the height of the debate Churchill called Gandhi "a seditious Middle Temple lawyer, now posing as a fakir of a type well-known in the East, striding half-naked up the steps of the Vice-regal palace … to parley on equal terms with the representative of the King-Emperor."[9] Gandhi was "surrounded by a circle of wealthy men, who see at their fingertips the acquisition of the resources of an Empire on cheaper terms than were ever yet offered in the world."[10]

Incongruously, Churchill's strident language drew no rejoinder from Gandhi—who was not above harshly criticizing Britain and the British. To understand why, we must look deeply into their relationship. Surprising to many, it went back a long way, and was not as uniformly antagonistic as it is made out.

Churchill and Gandhi met personally on 28 November 1906, when the 37-year-old Gandhi was in London and Churchill, 32, was assistant secretary of state at the Colonial Office. Both were veterans of the Boer War in South Africa; they had nearly crossed paths at the Battle of Spion Kop. Gandhi and a Muslim colleague had come to plead the case of Indians in the Transvaal. The legislature there had passed the "Black Act," requiring Asians to register and be fingerprinted "as if they belonged to a barbarous race."[11] (The cynical will note that Gandhi was not pleading the case of blacks, who also fell under this rule; a more generous interpretation is that he was practicing "the art of the possible.")

Churchill was in a tricky spot. He had just unveiled the Transvaal constitution, which had eased tensions with the ruling Boers by providing local (white) control. Yet he was impressed by Gandhi's "marshalling of the facts," and promised to do what he could. As Gandhi returned to South Africa, Churchill stated that the British government would not assent to the Black Act. Gandhi's joy was short-lived. In 1907 the government reneged. Britain could not grant local control to the Transvaal, they said, and then nullify its laws, however repugnant, without jeopardizing the delicate peace. Let the Transvaal "shoulder the burden" of offending British opinion with its racist acts, Churchill said. "Why should we?"[12]

Britain's naked act of imperial self-interest convinced Gandhi that for Indians, British justice was a chimera. "The old ways of doing things, with petitions and respectful delegations, had failed," wrote Arthur Herman. Gandhi realized there must be a new political movement: "passive resistance, or, as he preferred to call it, *satagraha*. It would have a dramatic impact not only on India and South Africa but on the civil rights movement in the United States and on every other group that would later invoke the term 'civil disobedience.'"[13]

Mohandas Gandhi in South Africa in 1909, shortly after he met and was impressed by Winston Churchill; their encounter was recalled by Gandhi at the height of the India Bill controversy (Wikimedia).

Mutual Magnanimity

Oddly, however, Gandhi never blamed Churchill for the British reversal. His views may have been tempered by reading what Churchill said about Amritsar, the 1919 massacre of Indians by a British general who fired into an unarmed crowd. In the House of Commons, Churchill denounced British "frightfulness," demanding punishment of those responsible. "What I mean by frightfulness," Churchill had said, "is the inflicting of great slaughter or massacre upon a particular crowd of people…. Frightfulness is not a remedy known to the British pharmacopoeia…."[14]

In mid–1935, after the Government of India Act had passed, Churchill surrendered gracefully, quoting Lord Salisbury: "It is the duty of every Englishman, and of every English party to accept a political defeat cordially, and to lend their best endeavours to secure the success, or to neutralise the evil, of the principles to which they have been forced to succumb."[15] His magnanimity extended to the man chiefly responsible for defeating him. On 25 August he invited Ghanshyam Das Birla, one of Gandhi's chief lieutenants, for an afternoon at Chartwell, including a two-hour lunch.

The meeting, Birla reported to Gandhi, was "one of my most pleasant experiences." Far from a "fire eater," he found Churchill "a most remarkable man…. As eloquent in private talk as he is in public speech…. He did 75 percent of the talking, the other 25 percent was divided between myself and Mrs. Churchill. I only occasionally interrupted by correcting him and putting a question or two but I enjoyed the conversation. It was never boring."[16] (Birla corrected Churchill's youthful impression that most rural villages were isolated from larger towns and not accessible by motorcar.) Birla continued:

> He asked what Mr. Gandhi was doing. He was immensely interested and said "Mr. Gandhi has gone very high in my esteem since he stood up for the untouchables. I do not like the Bill but it is now on the Statute Book…. So make it a success." I said, "What is your test of success?" He said, "My test is improvement in the lot of the masses, morally as well as materially. I do not care whether you are more or less loyal to Great Britain. I do not mind about education, but give the masses more butter. I stand for butter…. Reduce the number of cows but improve their breed. Make every tiller of the soil his own landlord. Provide a good bull for every village."

Churchill ended with a direct message: "Tell Mr. Gandhi to use the powers that are offered and make the thing a success. I did not meet Mr. Gandhi when he was in England [in 1931]. It was then rather awkward." Alluding to possible war, he added:

> I have got real fears about the future. India, I feel, is a burden on us. We have to maintain an army and for the sake of India we have to maintain Singapore and Near East strength. If India could look after herself we would be delighted…. I would be only too delighted if the Reforms are a success. I have all along felt that there are fifty Indias. But you have got the things now; make it a success and if you do I will advocate your getting much more.[17]

Birla's letter of thanks included a memory from 1906. Gandhi, he wrote, "was very much interested to hear specially of my interview with you and remarked, 'I have got a good recollection of Mr. Churchill when he was in the Colonial Office and somehow or other since then I have held the opinion that I can always rely on his sympathy and good-will.'"[18] Given Churchill's reversals back in 1906, this was a remarkably generous statement; clearly Gandhi was looking deeper than mere policy disagreements.

The Birla episode suggests incidentally that Churchill was not much of a racist, as he is often accused of being. By the standards of that time, a racist would not have expressed such concern for the wellbeing of brown people (or invited one to lunch). Two decades later Churchill would strike up a friendship with Nehru, whom would call "the light of Asia."[19] Of course, he and Nehru were Harrow Old Boys, and Churchill always had a soft spot for his old school.

It is true that Churchill could say reprehensible things in the heat of the moment. His oft-quoted remark, "I hate Indians," in response to disputatious bureaucracy in Delhi in mid–World War II, was dismissed jovially by William F. Buckley, Jr.: "I have no doubt that the famous gleam came to his eyes when he said this, with mischievous glee—an offense, in modern convention, of genocidal magnitude."[20]

Churchill was not a hater. His early books are filled with accounts of the bravery and steadfastness of Indian troops, particularly Sikhs, whom he ardently admired. Churchill did share the Victorian conviction of his era that white Westerners were the most advanced peoples. But that belief was tempered by a fundamental sense of fairness that led him to sympathize with the plight of non-whites. Unlike most of his contemporaries, Churchill thought deeply on the nature of man and society. It is rare to see that in a politician.

Last Words

When World War II broke out in 1939, Gandhi first offered "nonviolent moral support" to Britain, but even this lukewarm endorsement was anathema to the Congress Party, so Gandhi declared that India would not participate in a war for freedom while freedom was denied India itself. This culminated in the "Quit India" policy, which caused him and Congress leaders to be arrested in 1942. Imprisoned for two years, Gandhi suffered the death of his wife and contracted malaria; he was released a month before D-Day on health grounds, but also because the British feared he would die an imprisoned martyr. In July 1944 Gandhi wrote personally to the Prime Minister:

> You are reported to have a desire to crush the simple "Naked Fakir" as you are said to have described me. I have been long trying to be a Fakir and that naked—a more difficult task. I therefore regard the expression as a compliment, however unintended. I approach you then as such and ask you to trust and use me for the sake of your people and mine and through them those of the world.[21]

"This strange, jocular note was classic Gandhi," wrote Arthur Herman. "It was his effort to reach out to Churchill in the aftermath of their epic battle." But Churchill never received it. Gandhi found out, tried to resend it, and released it to the press a year later, but by then it was non-sequitur: Churchill's party had been turned out in the general election, and he was no longer prime minister.[22]

Churchill loved to repeat the old Boer expression, "all will come right." In India, to a large extent, it has. Today India is the world's largest democracy: imperfect, as they all are, but seeking in the main to respond to the will of its citizens. We praise Gandhi, Larry Arnn wrote,

> because he did not wish the death or suffering of anyone, Muslim or Jew, Hindu or Christian. That is greatly to his credit. Churchill was a different sort of man with different principles. He, like Gandhi, wished the good of the people of India and of every nation and every faith. But he was prepared to raise an army in defense of right and justice. He was prepared to fight for freedom and to give his life in that cause if necessary. And he possessed that prudence which could see into the future and predict destruction before it came.[23]

Conclusion

Every time you realize how badly the media mangles something you know about, you wonder how well they are reporting everything else.

The 2014 announcement that a statue of Gandhi would be placed in Parliament Square near that of Winston Churchill unleashed a barrage of ignorance. Would Churchill wish to share space with his "onetime nemesis"?

The Associated Press quoted Churchill's famous "half-naked fakir" crack (inaccurately), and said he called Gandhi a "middling lawyer." (The term was "Middle Temple lawyer," something else entirely.)[24] The *Wall Street Journal* worried that Parliament Square also included a statue of Jan Smuts, "a prime minister of South Africa in the early 20th century who favored segregation." Actually, Smuts was voted out of office when he advocated relaxing segregation. And, like Churchill, he had Gandhi's respect.[25]

Churchill did have a tic about an Indian independence movement led by the Brahmin class. But his statements to Gandhi, via Birla, suggest a better understanding of contemporary India than his critics acknowledge. And Gandhi's statements about him suggest a perceptive understanding of Churchill, despite the vast gulf between them in the early 1930s.

For a man so often described as a racist and imperialist, Churchill had broad principles in common with Gandhi. Both viewed a break-up of the subcontinent with regret and sadness. Both feared religious extremism, Hindu or Muslim. Both believed in the peaceful settlement of boundary disputes. Both strove for liberty. Such precepts, more widely held, would be welcome today. In Parliament Square, Churchill stands well with Gandhi. And Smuts.

20

Mussolini, Lawgiver and Jackal

The Myth: Churchill Admired and Offered Peace to Mussolini

The art of the out-of-context quote is practiced wonderfully over Churchill's supposed opinions of Benito Mussolini, "Il Duce," the Italian fascist dictator. With careful editing, one can almost cast Churchill as an ardent *Fascisti*. Indeed those two words were once used by Churchill to the Italians, whose "renowned Chief," with his "Roman genius," was pronounced "the greatest lawgiver among living men."[1]

By themselves, the words sound damning, knowing what we do of Mussolini's true nature—but the indictment gets worse. "Before the war, Churchill offered Il Duce a deal," wrote Clive Irving in 2015. "After the war, British intelligence tried to destroy their correspondence.... When Churchill became prime minister in May 1940 he tried, in a series of letters, to dissuade Mussolini from joining the Axis powers. He was ignored."[2] This assertion mixes a little that is true with much that is trite; the problem is that what's true is trite, and what's not trite is not true.

Early Encounters

One of Churchill's responsibilities as Chancellor of the Exchequer (1925–29) was recouping what he could of foreign war debt. Italy owed Britain £592 million (£30 billion today). In 1926–27, with its Finance Minister Count Giuseppe Volpi, Churchill agreed to defer payments until 1930, then to accept installments through 1988. Needless to say, the debt was never paid. Mussolini sent "the warmest expressions of gratitude" and offered him a decoration, which he wisely refused.[3] (Imagine if *that* was among Churchill's medals.)

In Rome in January 1927, Churchill had two brief meetings with Mussolini. At a press conference afterward, Churchill told journalists:

> I could not help being charmed, like so many other people have been, by his gentle and simple bearing and by his calm, detached poise in spite of so many burdens. If I had been an Italian, I am sure that I should have been whole-heartedly with you from start to finish in your triumphant struggle against the bestial appetites and passions of Leninism.[4]

That remark, redolent of his usual courtliness to foreign hosts—often cropped after the word "finish"—damns Churchill as a fascist in the eyes of some. Yet it is clear that he was talking about Italy, not Britain. One tends to say polite things about a nation's leader when he has promised to pay your country a lot of money. As the context shows, what Churchill approved of was Italy not falling to Bolshevism—which in 1927 he feared more than anything. "…in the conflict between Fascism and Bolshevism," he wrote, "there was no doubt where my sympathies and convictions lay."[5]

The advent of Hitler made Churchill think of Rome as a potential ally. Hitler's ideas of a greater German Reich, encompassing Austria and, no doubt, Trieste, would not be in Italy's interest, Churchill reasoned. On 17 February 1933, a fortnight after Hitler had come to power, Churchill gave an impassioned speech to the Anti-Socialist and Anti-Communist Union. Contemptuously reacting to a recent motion by the Oxford Union—"That this House refuses in any circumstances to fight for King and Country"—Churchill contrasted Germany's "clear-eyed youth," demanding to be drafted into the army, and Italy's "ardent *Fascisti*, her renowned Chief and stern sense of national duty.… One can almost feel the curl of contempt upon the lips of the manhood of all these peoples when they read this message sent out by Oxford University in the name of young England."

But Churchill went on to reject fascism for Britain. The "greatest lawgiver among living men," and his fascist government, was "not a sign-post which would direct us here."[6]

The diplomatic tightrope became harder to navigate in 1935, when Mussolini, on a flimsy pretext, invaded and occupied Ethiopia (Abyssinia). Speaking on 26 September, Churchill said Britain would support the League of Nations in applying sanctions and an arms embargo on Italy. Later he told Parliament that though the conflict was "a very small matter," the League was "fighting for all our lives."[7]

With his gaze fixed on Germany, Churchill was never more than lukewarm about challenging Mussolini. In his war memoirs he dissembled: "I would never have encouraged Britain to make a breach with him about Abyssinia or roused the League of Nations against him unless we were prepared to go to war in the last extreme."[8] Britain was not prepared to go to war, and Churchill knew it. In May 1937 he contemplated a Mediterranean pact "for mutual protection of further aggression" by Hitler, hoping Mussolini could be persuaded to join.[9] By then, however, the breach was complete, and Mussolini would never forgive Britain's support of sanctions.

Trying to Keep Italy on Side

Was Churchill's attitude over Mussolini's invasion of Ethiopia inconsistency or realism? Italy's aggression, unlike Hitler's, was directed far from pivotal Europe. The peril to Europe also caused Churchill to consider Germany more dangerous than Russia, a judgment for which he was later criticized by anti-communists. Behind the scenes he courted both Rome and Moscow, often at the same time. In early 1939, when Churchill was courting Soviet Ambassador Maisky with proposals of collective security against Hitler, Maisky said that "Russia will not come in to any coalition which includes Italy and that they will have no confidence in France or ourselves if we start flirting with Italy and opening negotiations with Mussolini." Churchill shot back "that the main enemy is Germany and that it is always a mistake to allow one's enemies to acquire even unreliable allies."[10]

On 16 May 1940, as France was reeling before the Germans, Churchill, now prime minister, became more loquacious than ever toward the Italian dictator. Recalling their cordial meetings in 1927 he wrote his first and only letter to Mussolini, imploring him "to stop a river of blood" from flowing between Britain and Italy. "I have never been the enemy of Italian greatness," Churchill declared, again referring to "the Italian lawgiver." He was not writing in a "spirit of weakness," Churchill added, although of course he was, as Mussolini was aware. Il Duce's answer came two days later:

> Without going back very far in time, I remind you of the initiative taken in 1935 by your Government to organise at Geneva sanctions against Italy, engaged in securing for herself a small space in the African sun without causing the slightest injury to your interests and territories or those of others. I remind you also of the real and actual state of servitude in which Italy finds herself in her own sea ... the same sense of honor and of respect for engagements assumed in the Italian-German Treaty guides Italian policy today and tomorrow in the face of any event whatsoever."[11]

On 10 June, Italy declared war on France and Britain. Ironically, Mussolini was the first major wartime figure to fall. On 25 July 1943, the Fascist Grand Council repudiated their leader of two decades. "The keystone of the Fascist arch has crumbled," Churchill told the House of Commons. By then, of course, Mussolini had long gone from "lawgiver" to "whipped jackal" in the Churchill lexicon.[12]

"La Pista Inglese"

Was Churchill impressed by the Mussolini of the twenties and thirties? Quite possibly. A lot of people were, although a realist might conclude that Churchill said what he did mindful of British national interests. Churchill redacted little from his archives, where researchers can pore over a million documents to pursue obscure theories. One such theory the Churchill Archives cannot prove involves the so-called Churchill-Mussolini "peace" correspondence, which has long been rumored to exist—somewhere.

The existence of three incriminating letters from Churchill to Mussolini, with offers of support provided Italy left the Axis, were rumored at least since 1954, when Giovanni Guareschi published the purported texts in his magazine *Candido*. Guareschi was later prosecuted and imprisoned for publishing forged letters by Alcide De Gasperi, postwar head of the Italian government. The Churchill letters were also alluded to by Renzo De Felice, official historian of Fascism and biographer of Mussolini, who died in 1996, his evidence unpublished. In 1985 the most persuasive conspiracist, Arrigo Petacco, reproduced copies of the three letters (two dated 1940, one 1945). Ignoring their stilted English, even the casual would find it difficult to believe they are genuine. The Italian historian Patrizio Giangreco reviewed them in 2010, proving them obvious fakes.[13]

The Churchill Archives hold only one Churchill letter to Mussolini—that of 16 May 1940—and Mussolini's negative reply two days later. But the conspiracists persist. "Although there would have been copies in London of the Churchill-Mussolini exchanges," wrote Clive Irving, "none has ever turned up and in April 1945, somebody in London was very anxious that Mussolini's copies should never see the light of day."[14]

The idea is simply irresistible. Churchill wanted Mussolini dead "to prevent the letters ... coming to light," speculated newspaper correspondent Henry Samuel, who then destroyed his credibility by saying they were written *before* the war.[15] An Italian writer speculated that Clara Petacci, Mussolini's mistress, was really a British spy, sent to steal the Churchill letters to protect the prime minister; and/or that one "Captain John" was

CHARTWELL WESTERHAM, KENT

WESTERHAM 93

22nd April, 1940

Your Excellency,

your letter of the 16th instant is in my possession. The various proposals placed before you by His Majesty's Government, cover a very large field and if accepted, I feel sure that the final issue will bring mutual rewards.

May I express my deep gratitude for the concern you have shown towards my country.

Your counter proposals, however, were placed before the Privy Council and broadly accepted.

From the text I note that a mutual understanding between your Country and Britain is possibl

Attached herewith is a copy of the agreement wich I beseech Your Excellency to place before His Majesty's approval, and return it at your earliest opportunity.

Cordially yours

Winston S. Churchill

His Excellency Signor Benito Mussolini,

Rome.

Forged Mussolini Letters (this page and the following two): The alleged letter of 22 April 1940, is headed Chartwell, which was closed during the war. Churchill, not then prime minister, would not have written formally to a foreign head of government. The text mentions Italian "proposals" which the Privy Council (not the War Cabinet?) has "broadly accepted." The signature is blotchy and uneven, as if copied and pasted in place; two words are misspelled; and the type is not the large font used in Churchill's official letters (Patrizio Giangreco).

ON HIS MAJESTY'S SERVICE

London, 15 May, 1940.

Your Excellency,

        now that I have taken up my office as Prime
Minister and Minister of Defence I look back to our meetings
in Rome and feel a desire to speak words of goodwill to you
as Chief of the Italian nation across what seems to be a
swiftly-widening gulf.

        Is it too late to stop a river of blood from
flowing between the British and Italian peoples? We can no
doubt inflict grievous injuries upon one another and maul
each other cruelly, and darken the Mediterranean with our
strife.
        If you so decree, it must be so; but I declare
that I have never been the enemy of Italian greatness, nor
ever at heart the foe of the Italian lawgiver.

        Down the ages above all other calls comes the
cry that the joint heirs of Latin and Christian civilisation
must not be ranged against one another in mortal strife.

        Hearken to it, I beseech you in all honour
and respect, before the dread signal is given.

        It will never be given by us. May God give
you wisdom in this solemn appeal.

                        Yours

                        Winston S. Churchill.

His Excellency Signor Benito Mussolini,
Duce of Fascism and Chief of the Italian Government,

                                    Rome.

The letter of 15 May 1940, contains some words Churchill actually *did* write, in his one and
only letter to Mussolini (16 May, described herein). But the letterhead is OHMS (On His
Majesty's Service), rather than 10 Downing Street, and is uses a salutation Churchill would
have choked over: "Duce of Fascism" (Patrizio Giangreco).

10. Downing Street,
Whitehall.

London, 31st March, 1945

Your Excellency,

I have only recently returned to Britain.

I am happy to state on behalf of His Majesty's
Government that your suggestion are accepted in thei entirety.

Your wishes therefore will be carried out
on the understanding that my requests are accorded as outlined
in my letters, particularly in my ultimo, the latter contents,
however, must be fully adhered to.

I feel sure that my personal admiration for
you warrants an affirmative and urgent reply.

Let me reassure Your Excellency that I have
taken all the necessary steps concerning your security and
safe conduct.

Your appeal safeguarding the interests
of your family and relatives is being dealt with by
Head Quarters.

Yours

Winston S. Churchill

His Excellency Signor Benito Mussolini,
Chief of the Italian Social Republic,

Milan.

The 31 March 1945, letter, supposedly offering support, gets the letterhead right, though the sender seems obliged to add "London." In it Churchill confesses "personal admiration" for the man he has vilified since 1940. He acknowledges Mussolini's "suggestion" (which "are accepted"), as if the Duce was then in any position to make any. The Churchill signature is suspect, the syntax is off, another word is misspelled, and the large type font absent (Patrizio Giangreco).

sent by Churchill to recover the file, which was captured from Mussolini—a scenario Italian historians dubbed *la pista inglese* (the English trail).[16]

In September 1945, the story continues, Churchill himself joined the quest. He traveled to Lake Como, an area that had been controlled by Mussolini's rump Republic of Salò, staying at the "Villa Aprexin," where a photograph was taken and published on page 210 of R.G. Grant's *Churchill: An Illustrated Biography*. Ostensibly on a painting holiday, Churchill's real purpose was to retrieve the letters. With so many people out to steal this correspondence, it's a wonder that none of them succeeded.

The problem with all this, as Giangreco noted, is that Churchill's villa, where he stayed from 2 to 19 September, was "La Rosa," and the photograph of him painting nearby is the one in Grant's book. From La Rosa Churchill went to Villa Pirelli near Genoa, and from there to Monte Carlo and the French Riviera.[17]

Still the beat goes on, Clive Irving fanning it in 2015: En route to Lake Como, he wrote, Churchill stopped in Milan to stand bareheaded at Mussolini's unmarked grave. No evidence is offered, nor is there any: Churchill flew from London 2 September and arrived in Como the same day.[18] Irving claimed Churchill flew to Milan under the cover name "Colonel Warden," which he says was his pilot's name. In fact it was Churchill's codename for himself throughout the war, probably taken from his honorary title of Lord Warden of the Cinque Ports.[19]

Churchill's villa at Como, Irving continued, was "owned by none other than Guido Donegani … an industrialist and Fascist collaborator," who was "interrogated by British intelligence and later released." Donegani apparently handed him the incriminating letters, papers or diaries—they are variously described. Irving claims that official biographer Martin Gilbert "concluded that the correspondence had been retrieved and handed over to Churchill but it never turned up in the Churchill archives and was never seen again."[20] This is passing strange, since Martin Gilbert dismissed the very idea of secret Mussolini correspondence, and his account does not mention Donegani. If Donegani *did* exist, and if he did own Churchill's villa, there is no evidence they ever met. Writing his wife the day after he arrived, Churchill said Villa La Rosa belonged to "one of Mussolini's rich *commerçants* who had fled, whither is not known."[21]

Churchill admitted in his memoirs that he had once expressed admiration for Il Duce as a bulwark against Bolshevism. He also distinguished between different types of fascism. He was unequivocally opposed to Nazism and its methods, and thoroughly anti-fascist in British affairs. He was favorable to fascism in Italy—until Mussolini turned into Hitler's poodle and declared war on the Allies in June 1940. The Prime Minister who would have "no truce or parley" with Hitler and his "grizzly gang" would never have offered support for the man he considered an opportunist, "frisking up at the side of the German tiger."[22]

Perhaps the best rejoinder to all this is by the historian Andrew Roberts: "Leaving aside the fact that Churchill would not at that stage have wanted or needed peace with Mussolini, one charge goes that the relevant documents are in a waterproof bag at the bottom of Lake Como. So, when one takes issue with them, the conspiracy theorists say 'go and look.' Of course, if you don't find anything, they just say, 'you haven't looked hard enough.'"[23]

21

Hitler as a "Great Contemporary"

The Myth: Churchill Praised and Admired Hitler

Churchill's critics have used his words to argue that he was "for Hitler before he was against him." As a politician Churchill did appreciate Hitler's skill and nerve. With his innate optimism he even hoped briefly that Hitler might mellow. But in his fundamental understanding, Churchill never wavered. He was right all along: dead right.

There is no evidence that Churchill read *Mein Kampf* until 1933,[1] but he was aware of Hitler earlier. Sir Ian Hamilton furnished the first reference to Hitler in Churchill's official biography, when he informed Churchill of remarks by the German shipping magnate and onetime chancellor, Wilhelm Cuno, in October 1930.

What Hamilton described as Hitler's "scoop" in the 1930 German elections was, according to Cuno, natural and hopeful: "The whole question … was whether the change would be to the right or to the left…. They had got their swing to the right and he hoped that responsibility of power would make this new Government more moderate in action than it had been in words."[2] The worst that can be said of Churchill regarding Hitler was that he too hoped for moderation, but that like many others, he misgauged the depth of Hitler's prejudice and hate.

Somber Forebodings

Churchill had served in Stanley Baldwin's 1924–29 Conservative government as Chancellor of the Exchequer, but had fallen out with the Tories later, when his principled resistance over self-government for India effectively barred him from their inner councils. It is often argued that he would have been more effective over Germany had he been less defiant over India. To Churchill, the government was making the same mistake in both cases: taking the easy, popular courses rather than risk being punished at the polls.

"The German situation is increasingly sombre," Churchill wrote his wife in March 1935.[3] When, later that year, Parliament voted a modest increase of £10 million in armaments, an enraged Hitler refused to receive British Foreign Secretary John Simon—"a measure," Churchill wrote, "of the conviction which Hitler has of the German Air Force and Army." Churchill was by now receiving detailed information on the enormous sums Hitler was spending on rearmament, figures that "would stagger us."[4]

The government maintained that Britain had not lost air superiority. Some of the figures Churchill cited proved later to be exaggerations, but his alarm was justified. Germany was fast catching up, particularly in the air. Two years after Hitler had come to power, Britain's Air Ministry had estimated 850 German first-line and reserve aircraft, against the most optimistic figure of 453 for Britain.[5] On 25 March 1935, Hitler announced German "parity" with Britain in air power. It wasn't yet true, but Churchill saw it as vindication of everything he had been saying.[6]

It is important to understand how accurately Churchill viewed Hitler, and how early.

In May 1935 the Führer wrote a revealing letter to the newspaper magnate Lord Rothermere, one of his British admirers, appealing for Anglo-German understanding. He had worked for rapport with "England" for fifteen years, Hitler said. Together, Britain and Germany could ensure peace for a generation. Except for his references to Aryan supremacy, a reader might think his letter was written by the Pope.

Britain and Germany had gained nothing by the late war, Hitler told Rothermere. Until 1914, the "two Germanic peoples" had spent 500 years without conflict: Britain had "opened a great part of the world to the white race." Germany's "cultural and economic activities for the welfare and the greatness of this old Continent are difficult to estimate." Their mutual enemy was Bolshevism, which "tears away a mighty slice of European-Asiatic breathing-space ['Lebensraum'] from the only possible international world economy." As a result the British Empire was "weakened rather than strengthened."

Hitler then spoke of his desire for peace. Never had he regarded World War I as anything "but a desperate, Niebelung-like war of annihilation, rising to frenzy, between the Germanic peoples.... I have preached unswervingly the necessity of both nations burying the hatchet forever.... I believe, my dear Lord Rothermere, [in restoring] a good and enduring understanding between both great Germanic peoples." Anglo-German understanding would combine "the unique colonial ability and sea-power of England" with "one of the greatest soldier-races of the world."[7]

Rothermere forwarded Hitler's letter to Churchill, whose reply was definitive: If Hitler was suggesting an Anglo-German agreement for Germany to dominate the continent, it would be counter to history, which had always arrayed Britain on the side of Europe's second strongest power: "Thus Elizabeth resisted Philip II of Spain. Thus William III and Marlborough resisted Louis XIV. Thus Pitt resisted Napoleon, and thus we all resisted William II of Germany." Anglo-German understanding would be agreeable, Churchill added, only if they "included France and gave fair consideration to Italy."[8]

Rothermere did not accept Churchill's arguments. Britain was defenseless, he said; France undone by socialism and communism, Italy preoccupied with invading Ethiopia: "Once Hitler feels strong enough, I believe he will challenge all three Powers, and from what one knows of their respective armaments Hitler will have an easy win.... Unless we can steer clear some way or another, the blow, in my opinion, will inevitably fall before the end of next year."[9] He was right about the blow. Churchill was right about Hitler.

"Hitler and His Choice"

During his exchange with Rothermere, Churchill was asked by *The Strand* magazine to write about Hitler. "I should like you to be as outspoken as you possibly can," wrote editor Reeves Shaw, "and absolutely frank in your judgment of his methods."[10]

Churchill's November 1935 article, "The Truth About Hitler," had a long life. Two years later, Churchill published a revision, "Hitler and His Choice," in *Great Contemporaries*, his book of character sketches.[11] Reviewing the draft, the Foreign Office thought it harsh.[12] Churchill toned it down; they still didn't like it.

Similar in tone was a Churchill article on Hitler published the week after release of *Great Contemporaries*. Most it was from "Hitler and His Choice," but Churchill—perhaps vexed at the Foreign Office's critique of his book—redeployed two sentences from his 1935 *Strand* article: "It is on this mystery of the future that history will pronounce Hitler either a monster or a hero. It is this which will determine whether he will rank in Valhalla with Pericles, with Augustus and with Washington, or welter in the inferno of human scorn with Attila and Tamerlane."[13] Yet none of this materially changes Churchill's doubts about Hitler as expressed to Rothermere.

Ah, say the critics, but what about this, from yet another article in September 1937? "If our country were defeated, I hope we should find a champion as indomitable to restore our courage and lead us back to our place among the nations."[14] That sentence has been used for years to prove that Churchill was pro–Hitler. Quoting it, the political commentator Patrick Buchanan wrote: "Thus did even the Great Man believe about Hitler…."[15]

Culled from Churchill's article without context, "a champion as indomitable" certainly seems like a testimonial. But Churchill had preceded that sentence by saying, "One may dislike Hitler's system and yet admire his patriotic achievement." He then stated his hope that Hitler's success would lead him to a more "mellow, genial air … and consolidate in tolerance and goodwill what has been gained by conflict."[16]

Churchill was simply expressing a hope. He was no enemy of Germany, but it was his duty to warn Britain. Churchill was never a poll-watcher. He said not what people wanted to hear, but what he thought they *should* hear. So he bluntly declared that Britain would never accept the "brutal intolerances of Nazidom" and "the paganism on which they are based." Britain would happily to coexist with Germany, but would never accept "a gigantic middle–Europe bloc. It would certainly not be in our interest to connive at such policies of aggression."[17]

Today, knowing precisely what Hitler was, it is possible to scoff at Churchill for tempering his writings in 1935–37, influenced by demands for moderation by the Foreign Office, or his own characteristic optimism. Yet Churchill had told "The Truth about Hitler" from the start. As Martin Gilbert wrote: "neither the toned-down essay [in *Great Contemporaries*] nor the conciliatory article in the *Evening Standard* marked any change in Churchill's attitude…."[18]

The Anglo-German Naval Agreement

On 18 June 1935 Britain and Germany agreed to set German navy tonnage at 35 percent of the Royal Navy's, much larger than allowed by the Versailles Treaty. Signed without French approval, it was hotly debated in the Commons. The government was accused of hypocrisy, claiming to stand by Versailles and the League of Nations while making its own deals with Germany. A complication was the League's demand for sanctions against Italy for its invasion of Ethiopia, which Churchill considered a side issue that could, and did, alienate Italy. (See previous chapter.)

Churchill was silent on Naval Agreement until July 11th. When he did speak, some contend he supported it, stating: "We have made a separate agreement for ourselves, of a perfectly innocent character...." In the round, however, his speech hardly minced words. The Agreement had weakened the principle of collective security, dissipating Britain's "moral position, or at any rate our logical position.... You could not have had a more complete and perfect example of how not to do it."[19]

Despite this, Churchill voted with the government, and was accused of misleading readers of his war memoirs by implying more opposition to Hitler than he actually expressed at the time. The reader may decide whether voting against the Naval Agreement, a singular act of rebellion, would have advanced his agenda or hampered it. He was in a box, not wishing to become an enemy of old colleagues, hoping for office, yet in turmoil over Hitler's remorseless rearmament. Against this backdrop, Churchill's unpolitic admission of 1936 places him on a high level indeed:

> I would endure with patience the roar of exultation that would go up when I was proved wrong, because it would lift a load off my heart and off the hearts of many Members. What does it matter who gets exposed or discomfited? If the country is safe, who cares for individual politicians, in or out of office?[20]

Not many politicians stand on such principle, then or now.

After Munich

The aftermath of the October 1938 Munich agreement, by which Prime Minister Chamberlain and the French agreed to Hitler's occupation of the Czech Sudetenland and cleared the path for Germany to absorb the rest of that country, would seem an odd time for Churchill to be caught praising Hitler. But some say he did—again.

In the Reichstag in November, Hitler attacked Churchill and others who opposed Munich by name, describing them as "warmongers." Replying in Parliament on 6 November, Churchill expressed surprise "that the head of a great State" should deign to attack private Members of Parliament who held no office. He then reprised his remark in the *Evening Standard* a year before: "I have always said that if Great Britain were defeated in war I hoped we should find a Hitler to lead us back to our rightful position among the nations."[21] Again, quoted alone, this seems a pro–Hitler sentiment. But now it was 1938, and Churchill added:

> I am sorry, however, that he has not been mellowed by the great success that has attended him." Everyone would rejoice, he added, see in Hitler "acts of magnanimity and of mercy and of pity to the forlorn and friendless, to the weak and poor." Unfortunately, Hitler was "unduly sensitive that there may be other opinions in Germany besides his own.... That he has the power, and, alas! the will, to suppress all inconvenient opinions is no doubt true. [But] let this great man search his own heart and conscience before he accuses anyone of being a warmonger."[22]

Saying Something Nice About the Führer

It is remarkable how often Churchill's final view of world figures ended on a generous note, even towards those he had excoriated. There may be only two or three about whom he was ultimately censorious. Churchill knew or wrote about an amazing array of characters: U.S. presidents from McKinley to Eisenhower, historical figures from Caesar to Napoleon, magnificoes, potentates, heroes, villains, dictators and democrats. Reading the sensitive appraisals in *Great Contemporaries,* one is hard-pressed to find shafts of pure hatred. About Hitler he extended the benefit of the doubt at times, but was famously vituperative during the war. Yet even then there were traces of a stubborn willingness to try to find something worthwhile, somewhere.

When on 1 May 1945 the German radio announced that Hitler had died "fighting with his last breath against Bolshevism," Churchill murmured: "Well, I must say I think he was perfectly right to die like that."[23] Years later his former private secretary Sir John Colville said, "I had the impression that somehow he grudgingly approved."[24]

Churchill did not know when he said this that Hitler had committed ignominious suicide in his underground bunker, surrounded by the Red Army, as Churchill might say "like a rat in a hole." After all, Churchill too had expected to die "fighting with his last breath," had the Germans invaded Britain and hewn their way to Downing Street. It would not likely have been so private a death.

22

The Voice They Heard

The Myth: Churchill's War Speeches
Were Delivered by an Actor

For nearly half a century it has been part of Churchill mythology that an actor, Norman Shelley—famed for BBC's *The Children's Hour* and for playing Watson to Carleton Hobbs's Sherlock Holmes—broadcast up to three of Churchill's immortal 1940 speeches over the BBC. As a result, goes the story, Britons were "tricked" into believing they were actually hearing their prime minister in those fateful hours.

The three speeches are prominent among those that inspired the nation: 13 May ("Blood, Toil, Tears and Sweat"), 4 June ("Never Surrender"), and 18 June, the greatest of them all, which had ended memorably: "If the British Empire and its Commonwealth last for a thousand years, men will still say, 'This was their Finest Hour.'"[1]

Origins of a Canard

Norman Shelley's first published claim to having stood in for Churchill appeared in *Those Vintage Years of Radio,* published in 1972.[2] Shelley maintained the assertion until he died eight years later. David Irving, who offered Shelley as his only source, restated it in his malevolent 1987 biography, concerning the 4 June "Never Surrender" speech: "That evening the BBC broadcast his speech after the News. The whole nation thrilled, not knowing that Churchill had refused to repeat it before the microphone. A BBC actor—'Larry the Lamb' of the *Children's Hour*—had agreed to mimic the prime minister before the microphone, and nobody was any the wiser."[3]

It was a dramatic allegation, wrote Robert Rhodes James. It sounded believable. After all, why would Shelley make what seemed an easily disprovable claim? No one at the time thought to consult the BBC Archives. It entered the lexicon of fact, without ever being disproven, to be uttered unthinkingly from biographies to blogs ever since. No one noticed, Rhodes James wrote, that Irving claimed he had interviewed Shelley in December 1981, sixteen months after Shelley's death. "Also, although a minor point, Shelley had not been 'Larry the Lamb' in 'Toytown,' but 'Dennis the Dachshund,' as those of my generation could have told Irving."[4]

The legend persisted, even involving the technical community. In 1991 Sensimetrics, a firm of communications analysts in Cambridge, Massachusetts, announced that computerized analysis "based on frequencies in the vocal tract formed by tongue, lips and jaws" (called "formants") had compared the three speeches to other verified speeches of Churchill, concluding that the speaker was different. The three speeches contained a "grossly artificial echo which was apparently added to make people believe they were listening to a live recording made in Parliament, when in fact they are hearing only a heavily edited anthology assembled years later in a room at Chartwell." Sensimetrics demanded that Decca and EMI, who produced recordings of the speeches during and after the war, "acknowledge Shelley's involvement."[5]

Peter Orr of Argo, publishers of the audiocassette version, rejected Sensimetrics' demand, replying that the analysis took no account of slight variations in recording speed and changes in a human voice over the years. The speeches could not be attributed to Shelley, Orr said, without putting his voice through similar tests. Years before, Orr said, he found that "a 33 rpm recording by Bing Crosby, played back at 45 rpm, sound exactly like Eartha Kitt." So he could he could "very well claim that Eartha Kitt records were actually made by Bing Crosby!"[6]

That the "formants" on the 13 May and 4 June speeches did not match those of the other Churchill speeches analyzed by Sensimetrics is not surprising, since they dated not to 1940, but to 1949. They were indeed recorded at Chartwell—by Churchill, though heavily abridged from the originals. First published as 78 rpm records, they were reissued

Churchill making his first wartime broadcast, 1 October 1939, after the defeat of Poland and its partition between Germany and Russia (Author's collection).

as long-playing records by Decca in 1964, as audiocassettes by Argo, and later as compact disks. Although they were recorded by Churchill himself, his voice pattern had certainly changed between 1940 and 1949. Those who had heard Churchill give them in the House of Commons, said the recordings lacked the fire of the originals.

It is however possible to sort out what British people actually heard from Churchill, over the wireless, in the crucial weeks of May and June 1940. We should note first that none of Churchill's perorations in Parliament were ever recorded: the first live radio broadcasts began in 1978. Television cameras did not enter the Lords until 1985, the Commons until 1989.

"Blood, Toil, Tears and Sweat," 13 May 1940

Churchill's first speech as prime minister, delivered to the House of Commons, was *not* repeated in the evening BBC broadcast. Tracking Shelley's claims, Robert Rhodes James cited C.H. Rolph, whose wife had been a script-writer in the BBC's Features and Drama Department. Rolph and his wife knew Shelley well, Rhodes James wrote; Shelley had even been best man at their 1947 wedding: "Shelley, whom Rolph regarded, but with some affection, as something of a mountebank, fancied his Churchill impersonation, although Rolph thought it compared poorly with the real thing."

According to Rolph, a commercial company had wanted a recording of the "Blood, Toil, Tears and Sweat" speech, and asked Shelley to do it. Churchill "wasn't much interested," Rolph said, "but said he would raise no objection." Apparently the BBC bought the Shelley spoof. To Rolph's astonishment, the BBC's Robin Day chose it for one of his Desert Island Discs—recordings celebrities would take with them to a desert island. "I heard that," Rolph wrote, "and I know it was Norman Shelley's voice. His Churchill impersonation was never quite as good as he thought it was, and I recognised (for the umpteenth time) the spots where he failed. This is the true version about the Shelley-Churchill thing. Not very important, I suppose, but it could well go down as yet another bogus little version unexposed."[7]

"Never Surrender," 4 June 1940

In his first broadcast as Prime Minister, on 19 May 1940, Churchill voiced the Biblical injunction, "Arm yourselves, and be ye men of valour."[8] This was not based on a speech in Parliament and was not claimed by Shelley. The next speech Shelley said he had rebroadcast was that of 4 June. Here Churchill had memorably promised to fight the Germans every step of their way: in France, at sea, in the air, on the beaches and landing grounds, in the fields, hills and streets: "We shall never surrender." Shelley's claim to the broadcast version was picked up by newspapers, wrote D.J. Wenden: "Sally Hine of the BBC Sound Archive states that Shelley did make a recording of the speech at the Transcription Service Studios near Regent's Park." (This proved to be on a later date; as noted below.)

Transcripts of Home News Broadcasts in the BBC Written Archives contain no broadcast by the Prime Minister on 4 June. Instead, Wenden learned, "They indicate that in the 6 p.m. and 9 p.m. news broadcasts, the newsreader quoted verbatim several passages…. The newsreader is unlikely to have been Shelley, since the BBC's policy was to establish a team of regular newsreaders whose voices could be readily identified by the public in case the Germans attempted to transmit false news at the time of an invasion."[9]

Preposterously, Irving continued to assert Shelley's claim to the 4 June broadcast and others in a letter to the *Guardian* in 1991, asserting that the public was blatantly fooled: "…several times in 1940 millions of radio listeners were tricked into believing that they were hearing Churchill's voice."[10] Yet all the BBC produced that evening were excerpts by newscasters. To her husband, Harold Nicolson, Vita Sackville-West wrote on the morning of the 5th: "I wish I had heard Winston making that magnificent speech! Even repeated by the announcer it sent shivers (not of fear) down my spine."[11]

"Their Finest Hour," 18 June 1940

As France fell, Churchill broadcast briefly on the 17th, assuring his country that "all will come right."[12] The next day saw his greatest fighting speech, preceded by an announcer saying: "Ladies and gentlemen, the Prime Minister." The first of five speeches actually rebroadcast on the radio, it is the most famous, and contentious, of the so-called actor presentations.[13]

Churchill's official biographer, Martin Gilbert, was frequently asked who the speaker was: "Quite why Churchill had not done it himself was never explained," Gilbert wrote; "after all, broadcasting was his strength and a main method of maintaining national morale."[14] Gilbert checked with Sir John Martin, Churchill's principal private secretary in 1940. He found that Martin himself had written about the PM's performance in a letter home three days later. Churchill's "halting delivery at the start," Martin wrote, "seems to have struck people and we had e.g. a telegram from someone saying that he evidently had something wrong with his heart and ought to work in a recumbent position. The fact was, I gather, that he spoke with a cigar in his mouth."[15]

Another witness to the radio rebroadcast was Harold Nicolson, who wrote his wife that the Prime Minister should "not talk on the wireless unless he is feeling in good form. He hates the microphone, and when we bullied him into speaking last night, he just sulked and read his House of Commons speech over again. Now, as delivered in the House of Commons, that speech was magnificent, especially the concluding sentences. But it sounded ghastly on the wireless. All the great vigour he put into it seemed to evaporate."[16] Clive Ponting, another biographer who claimed Shelley had rebroadcast that speech, quoted Nicolson's last three sentences, ignoring the first two, which make it clear that Churchill was the speaker.[17]

The Real Shelley

C.J. Rolph's report of a later Shelley recording of the 4 June "Beaches" speech had substance, though the press muddled the story. In 2000, *The Observer* noted that Shelley's son had uncovered a 78 rpm BBC recording of his father delivering the speech as Churchill. The recording bore a homemade label dated 7 September 1942—but this did not prevent the *Observer* from stating: "Proof that some of Winston Churchill's most famous radio speeches of the war were delivered by a stand-in has emerged...."[18] Why they would say that, given the date, was not explained.

Allen Packwood of the Churchill Archives Centre wondered why Shelley had recorded the "Never Surrender" speech on 7 September 1942. It was by then over two years old. There was no longer a threat of German invasion, when it might be useful to rebroadcast Churchill's defiant words. Perhaps, Packwood suggested, it was intended to for a propaganda film: "But it is a huge leap to say that, just because there is evidence he recorded this Churchill speech in 1942, that he delivered BBC broadcasts in the summer of 1940."[19]

Packwood kept digging, and finally heard the subject recording. To his surprise, it was not the "Never Surrender" speech at all; it was concerned with events in North Africa. Consulting the BBC and National Sound Archives, Packwood confirmed what Rolph had earlier reported:

> Churchill was asked by the British Council later in the war to make a recording for the United States.... Having rather a lot on his plate, he suggested they use an actor instead. Shelley did the recording, Churchill heard it, was much amused and gave his approval. Shelley told the story in a BBC radio interview in 1978. It is not known for sure when, if at all, his recording was used.[20]

C.J. Rolph was wrong in thinking the Shelley story was "not very important," said Robert Rhodes James, "because it has become part of the ugly tapestry of denigration of Churchill, of which Irving was the first practitioner, his lead followed by others who also claim to be reputable historians. Some of this so-called 'revisionism' is subtle, much of it less so, like the malicious and ludicrous exaggeration of his drinking, which ignores all the testimony to the contrary by those who worked closely with him."[21]

Based on contemporary accounts by such eyewitnesses as Martin and Nicolson, the Prime Minister was far less sanguine about rebroadcasting his speeches than delivering the originals. He had to be "bullied," Nicolson wrote; according to Martin, he chewed a cigar during at least one of them. Churchill was a showman, and loved an audience—provided it was live (as in the House of Commons). Speaking to a microphone in a drab BBC studio, he was less inspired. Those broadcasts inevitably came late in the day, after a drumfire of earth-shaking events. It expects too much of anyone to maintain the fire he had displayed to his political colleagues across the floor of the House of Commons. Nevertheless, there is no doubt that Churchill delivered those radio broadcasts himself, and nobody ever delivered one for him.

23

"Collar the lot"

The Myth: Churchill Wanted to Intern Refugees

"Shocked by anti–Muslim Hysteria? Churchill Wanted to 'Collar the Lot,'" headlined the *Huffington Post* in November 2015. Attempting to cite a historical precedent to Donald Trump's views on aliens who claim refugee status, the *Post* said that "Churchill went even farther. He ordered the internment of tens of thousands of Jewish refugees in England, labeling them dangerous enemy aliens."[1]

Just as we now fear that among refugees from the Middle East there could be deliberately planted terrorists, so there was a fear in 1940 that the Nazis might have agents among the refugees who had fled Germany. The internment of aliens was carried out under pre-war peacetime legislation. The imprisonment of suspects was a wartime measure under Regulation 18B of the 1939 Emergency Powers Act.

When war began in September 1939, Germans and Austrians in Britain were grouped according to threat level, the *Post* stated. This much is true: 600 "high security risks" were immediately interned. The vast majority, over 55,000, were deemed "no risk" and were left alone until May 1940, when Churchill became prime minister. But then the *Post* adds:

> Unwilling to consider which of those foreigners might actually be dangerous, Churchill commanded "Collar them all." Brushed aside were objections that huge numbers of those ordered interned were Jews who had fled for their lives from the Nazis. The irrational fear was that they might still somehow become a dangerous Fifth Column.[2]

"I don't know where to begin," a historian colleague wrote. "Whether Churchill is charged with philo-Semitism or anti–Semitism seems to depend on whether it is an odd or even day of the month. He's in good company; the same applies to Franklin Roosevelt. Stories like this are based on such epic levels of distortion and ignorance that a reasoned riposte would far exceed whatever space the *Huffington Post* allows for response."[3]

It would—and fortunately, we have enough space here.

Churchill had more pressing things to think of in May 1940 than which people to incarcerate. But those who write such things have no concept of what it was like to live in 1940 Britain, under bombardment and threat of invasion. Unless we were there, we cannot presume to know. That does not prevent us from separating truth from manufactured history.

The number "rounded up"—by MI5, Britain's domestic security agency—was more than 55,000. Historian Norman Rose put it at 70,000—Germans, Austrians and Czechs. They were not interned because they were Jews, a distinction that hardly occurred to the authorities in the initial wave of panic over the Fifth Column, but because of their nationality. The fears proved to be groundless, but it is understandable that they existed at the time.

Moreover, "collar the lot" or "collar them all" (expressions I have not found in Churchill's archive but do not dispute the possibility of him saying) had a more benign meaning than alleged. Churchill, Rose wrote, was "convinced that he was protecting them from 'outraged public opinion.'" It is true that many were appalled at their treatment. "Some committed suicide rather than be confined in British camps. Others were deported. This unhappy affair reached a horrible climax on 2 July when the *Arandora Star*, carrying 1200 aliens, was torpedoed in the Atlantic, 720 of whom were lost."[4]

The round-up, Rose wrote, was "a most unsavoury episode." That is also true. But consider the situation in Britain then. The intelligence historian David Stafford recalled Churchill's "ruthless determination to fight on against Hitler. Many of the detained aliens "were passionate enemies of Hitler. But things were so critical that distinctions between friends and enemies could not be drawn."[5] Churchill had no second thoughts, telling the House of Commons on 4 June:

I feel not the slightest sympathy. Parliament has given us the powers to put down Fifth Column activities with a strong hand, and we shall use those powers, subject to the supervision and correction of the House, without the slightest hesitation until we are satisfied, and more than satisfied, that this malignancy in our midst has been effectively stamped out.[6]

Contemporary documents show that Churchill quickly reconsidered his initial attitude. At the Cabinet meeting of 21 June 1940,

the Prime Minister asked that the War Office should again consider raising a Foreign Legion. Many enemy aliens had a great hatred of the Nazi regime, and it was unjust to treat our friends as foes. Equipment might not be available for such a force immediately, but it could be found in due course. It would be as well to have these men under discipline in the meantime. Their services might be used in, for example, Iceland.[7]

By August 1940 Churchill and the authorities had recognized their mistakes and reversed the policy. Now the policy was to release as many as possible, and by 1943, nine out of ten of employable enemy aliens were at work. The policy of mass deportation was a blot on the record, but that too was reversed by August. Instead, wrote the historian Paul Addison, "aliens were interned instead in hotels on the Isle of Man, where they led a relatively civilized life, setting up their own university and founding the celebrated Amadeus String Quartet."[8]

As the war progressed, Churchill increasingly deplored the internment powers of MI5, and scotched attempts to broaden its powers. "Every Department which has waxed during the war is now considering how it can quarter its officials on the public indefinitely," he said in 1943. "The less we encourage these illusions the better." Shortly after this, David Stafford wrote, "the Cabinet Secretary commissioned a report which condemned the security service for a lack of proper ministerial control, abuse of its powers and 'injustices to the public'—especially in the treatment of aliens."[9] Kevin Theakston added: "Although in 1920 [Churchill] had favoured the creation of a single intelligence service, he now rejected this idea, believing that the increased powers of the spy chiefs might be a threat to ministerial control and to parliamentary democracy."[10]

"Look what has happened to the liberties of this country during the war," Churchill lamented to the editor of the *Manchester Guardian* in October 1943. "Men of position are seized and kept in prison for years without trial and no 'have your carcase' [habeas corpus] rights … a frightful thing to anyone concerned about British liberties."[11] He was particularly incensed over the handling of Sir Oswald Mosley, the fascist leader, who had been interned without trial since 1940. Churchill had long been friends with Mosley, a fellow member of The Other Club, but was entirely sincere in his antipathy to imprisonment without trial.

Mosley was released in November 1943. "Was Churchill showing favouritism for a man of his own class, as so many alleged and is hinted at in his complaint about the fate of 'men and position?'" Stafford asked. "Perhaps. But Churchill also evoked a matter of principle. By now he was personally eager to see the repeal of Regulation 18B, the order permitting such detentions, but his hands were tied by the political realities of his coalition with Labour."[12] Again Churchill was unequivocal:

> The power of the Executive to cast a man into prison without formulating any charge known to the law, and particularly to deny him judgement by his peers for an indefinite period, is in the highest degree odious, and is the foundation of all totalitarian Governments, whether Nazi or Communist…. Nothing can be more abhorrent to democracy than to imprison a person or keep him in prison because he is unpopular. This is really the test of civilisation.[13]

Churchill was even determined to exempt communists from unlawful internment. In May 1943, Moscow dissolved the Comintern," Stafford added, but this "had done nothing to shake his anti–Bolshevism. Yet distinct from anti–Communism was the matter of riding roughshod over constitutional proprieties." When MI5 produced a list of suspected Communists in sensitive positions, and recommended their removal, "Churchill concurred, but he insisted that MI5's word alone on the guilt of suspects should not be accepted." He warned that "MI5 tends to see dangerous men too freely and to lack [a] knowledge of the world and sense of perspective." Thus Churchill arranged for a secret panel to review MI5's recommendations: "The final say on the employment of suspects would rest with departments and ministers concerned, not MI5."[14]

"The charge that WSC ordered Jews detained, as Jews, is absurd," says David Stafford. "He wanted to detain enemy aliens, i.e., mostly people of German and Austrian nationality. Many were Jews, for obvious reasons. But that's very different. Certainly too, he quickly began to reverse course. This all happened following the shocking and cataclysmic collapse of France and the Dunkirk evacuation, when invasion and Fifth Column fears were rampant."[15]

The myth of a Churchill eager and even anxious to infringe the rights of aliens and refugees reminds us once again of the error critics make when they consider Churchill's first reaction to a situation, while ignoring his final, considered verdict. In the classic words of William Manchester, he

> always had second thoughts, and they usually improved as he went along. It was part of his pattern of response to any political issue that while his early reactions were often emotional, and even unworthy of him, they were usually succeeded by reason and generosity. Given time, he could devise imaginative solutions.[16]

It was not worth remonstrating with the *Huffington Post* for its drive-by misrepresentation—hardly the first—of Churchill's views on alien refugees. It was mainly looking for another way to skewer the eminently skewerable Mr. Trump. Still, it is necessary to reflect on Churchill's consistent and decisive support of liberty against the depredations of the state, even in wartime, and his anxiety—excluding no reasonable proposal—to bring them to an end as quickly as possible.

Churchill's actions stand in worthy contrast to those of his allies. After Pearl Harbor, Roosevelt endorsed the forcible relocation and internment of over 125,000 ethnic Japanese, mostly on the west coast. In Canada under Prime Minister MacKenzie King, nearly 21,000 Japanese-Canadians in British Columbia were similarly treated. Three quarters of both groups were native-born citizens.[17] Anti-Asian policies had long been routine in Western North America. (In Hawaii, where 40 percent of citizens were of Japanese ancestry, very few were interned, though a few agents had sent information to Japan by wireless.) Historians have broadly blamed Canadian and American actions on racism, while in Britain the affected parties were primarily foreign nationals.

24

Torturous Topics

The Myth: Churchill Said, "We don't torture."

In a press conference on 29 April 2009, the recently inaugurated President Obama was asked to comment on "enhanced interrogation techniques" against terrorists—which, some claimed, had prevented further attacks of the 9/11 variety. "I was struck by an article that I was reading the other day," he replied,

> about the fact that the British during World War II, when London was being bombed to smithereens, had 200 or so detainees. And Churchill said, "We don't torture," when the entire British—all of the British people—were being subjected to unimaginable risk and threat.... The reason was that Churchill understood [that if] you start taking shortcuts, over time, that corrodes what's best in a people. It corrodes the character of a country. I am absolutely convinced that ... we could have gotten this information in other ways—in ways that were consistent with our values, in ways that were consistent with who we are.[1]

While it is always nice to hear a U.S. president invoke Sir Winston, the quotation, including paraphrases and key sections of it, is unattributed and almost certainly incorrect. It is true that Churchill expressed similar sentiments with regard to prison inmates, when he was a young Home Secretary with responsibility for prisons, in 1910–11. But he said no such thing about prisoners of war, enemy combatants or terrorists—who *were* in fact tortured by the British during World War II.

Camp 020

The president was referring to an article by journalist Andrew Sullivan in *The Atlantic*, "Churchill vs. Cheney," which calmly urged that former Vice President Cheney be prosecuted for war crimes committed through "enhanced interrogation." The British in World War II, he asserted,

> captured over 500 enemy spies operating in Britain and elsewhere. Most went through Camp 020, a Victorian pile crammed with interrogators. As Britain's survival hung in the balance—as women and children were being killed on a daily basis and London turned into rubble, Churchill nonetheless knew that embracing torture was the equivalent of surrender to the barbarism he was fighting.[2]

"Churchill nonetheless knew" appears suddenly and with no evidence to back it up. Sullivan made no other reference to Churchill, or to how he divined the Prime Minister's views on torture. His story, however, can be tracked to a 2006 article, by Ben Macintyre, about Camp 020's chief interrogator, Col. Robin "Tin Eye" Stephens—a swashbuckling figure remindful of a James Bond novel.

Stephens, an intelligence officer who extracted confessions from captured Nazi spies, was "a bristling, xenophobic martinet; in appearance, with his glinting monocle and cigarette holder, he looked exactly like the caricature Gestapo interrogator who has 'vays of making you talk.'" Stephens was terrifying, Macintyre wrote: "In the course of the war, some 500 enemy spies from 44 countries passed through Camp 020; most were interrogated, at some point, by Stephens; all but a tiny handful crumbled."[3]

"A breaker is born and not made," Stephens allegedly declared; his method was "psychological intimidation." Macintyre describes how he combined "personality, tone, and rapidity of questions, a driving attack in the nature of a blast which will scare a man out of his wits." Suspects were often grilled all night long. An amateur psychologist, Stephens used "every trick, lie and bullying tactic to get what he needed; he deployed threats, drugs, drink and deceit." But Stephens "never resorted to violence." A colleague wrote that he "obtained results without recourse to assault and battery. It was the very basis of Camp 020 procedure that nobody raised a hand against a prisoner." Stephens was

no squishy liberal: the eye was made of tin, and the rest of him out of tungsten. (Indeed, he was disappointed that only sixteen spies were executed during the war.) His motives were strictly practical. "Never strike a man. It is unintelligent, for the spy will give an answer to please, an answer to escape punishment. And having given a false answer, all else depends upon the false premise."

After the war, when Stephens applied to rejoin his former employers at MI5, he had to be cleared of a charge of "disgraceful conduct of a cruel kind."[4]

Nowhere in his article did Macintyre mention or quote Churchill. Yet in World War II, with his interest in secret intelligence and his plenary authority, it is hard to imagine Churchill being unaware of the activities at places like the "London Cage." Sir Winston's daughter, Lady Soames, was adamant that her father would pay any price, bear any burden for victory, which was always his first goal in any war.[5]

"The Cage"

"Tin Eye's" story may very well be true, but it is not a complete picture of British methods. According to *The Guardian,* tactics were much rougher in the "London Cage," a POW camp at 6–7–8 Kensington Palace Gardens, today one of London's most exclusive neighborhoods.

The Cage was run by MI 19, a section of the War Office responsible for gleaning information from enemy prisoners of war, and few outside this organisation knew exactly what went on beyond the single barbed-wire fence that separated the three houses from the busy streets and grand parks of west London. Here SS and Gestapo captives were subject to "beatings, sleep deprivation and starvation.[6]

Examining thousands of documents in the National Archives and International Committee of the Red Cross in Geneva, the *Guardian* disclosed The Cage's function, in part, as a torture center. Here large numbers of German officers and soldiers were subjected to systematic ill-treatment. SS Captain Fritz Knoechlein said he was stripped, beaten with a cudgel, forced to stand beside a blazing gas stove, showered with very cold water, then made to run in circles while carrying heavy logs. Admittedly, Knoechlein

The London Cage, scene of nefarious wartime interrogations, is now the home of the Russian ambassador (kbthompson, Wikimedia Commons).

was facing a death sentence at the time, having been convicted of murdering 124 British soldiers captured during the evacuation from Dunkirk.[7]

In June 1950 former Cage Commandant Lt. Col. Alexander Scotland submitted his memoirs to be censored by the War Office. Pandemonium ensued. Scotland was asked not to publish, threatened with prosecution, and his home was raided by detectives. The Foreign Office said his book would aid persons "agitating on behalf of war criminals."

Scotland had revealed breaches of the Geneva convention, reporting that "prisoners had been forced to kneel while being beaten about the head; forced to stand to attention for up to twenty-six hours; threatened with execution; or threatened with 'an unnecessary operation.'" A highly edited text was finally published seven years later.[8]

The Guardian article again does not mention Churchill, but to believe Churchill wasn't aware of such activity would be expecting much. Torture was something on which he spoke frequently, though it mostly involved enemy treatment of civilians. In his memoirs of World War I he wrote: "When all was over, Torture and Cannibalism were the only two expedients that the civilized, scientific, Christian States had been able to deny themselves: and these were of doubtful utility."[9] His general sentiment is clear enough, though combined with "cannibalism," he seems to be referring to practices of invading armies. And by World War II, sensibilities were not so noble.

If Churchill is on record specifically about "enhanced interrogation," his words have yet to surface. The nearest I can come to his view on such techniques refers not to terrorists or enemy combatants but to prison inmates. "Among the many hundreds of letters which Churchill received from his constituents in 1938," wrote Martin Gilbert, was "a request from Hilary A. Howe of Snaresbrook to help end the use of the 'cat' [o' nine tails] in prisons ('the use of instruments of torture can never be regarded by any decent person as synonymous with justice.')"[10] If that line appeals to President Obama, he can certainly use it with confidence. But it cannot be stated that Churchill ever said, "We don't torture."

Wisdom After the Fact

We must look at history in terms of what was going on and what was known *at the time*—and not through our modern perspective after many decades. It is worth mentioning, for example, that around the time of the activities at the London Cage, news was reaching London of the mass murder in specially-designed gas chambers of more than two and a half million Jews at Auschwitz, which had hitherto been identified only as a slave-labor camp. Here was a massive horror Churchill would try to alleviate (Chapter 31). Pondering the balance between morality and winning the war, he said: "Clearly, I cannot make headway against the parsons and the warriors at the same time."[11]

25

The Bombing of Coventry

*The Myth: Churchill Let Coventry
Be Bombed to Protect Secret Intelligence*

On the night of 14–15 November 1940, the story goes, Churchill left the city of Coventry undefended against a devastating German air raid. He did so, it is claimed, because defending it would have tipped off the Germans to "Ultra"—his decrypts of secret German codes being read by government cypher center at Bletchley Park. The so-called "Ultra Secret," the most closely guarded in the war, had to be protected, no matter the consequences.[1] The tale still circulates, sometimes by his admirers, who think it underscores his determination for victory at all costs.

The center of Britain's motor industry, Coventry was attacked by the Luftwaffe with 500 tons of explosives, 33,000 incendiary bombs and dozens of parachute mines. In one night over 500 civilians were killed and 420 seriously injured. The deaths almost equaled the number killed in the Coventry-Birmingham area the previous month, though this was but a fraction of the 5000 killed in the London Blitz.[2]

Rumor and Indictment

Searching for the source of the Coventry rumor, historian Peter McIver identified three authors who published books between 1974 and 1982. The first was former RAF Group Captain F.W. Winterbotham, writing entirely from memory, in 1974. Winterbotham was also first to break the news, hitherto a closely guarded secret, that Britain had cracked the German codes. According to Winterbotham, the name "Coventry" was spotted in a decrypted German communication on the afternoon of 14 November, and telephoned immediately to Downing Street. Thus Churchill must have known Coventry was the target long before darkness gathered.[3]

Two years later, Anthony Cave Brown not only agreed with Winterbotham, but said Churchill knew Coventry was the target two days earlier, on 12 November. The city, he wrote, was part of a three-target raid on the industrial Midlands, codenamed *Einheitopreis* (Unit price). The targets were the code words "umbrella" (for Birmingham), "all one price" for Wolverhampton, and "corn" for Coventry. "Umbrella" referred to the accessory always carried by Neville Chamberlain, a former mayor of Birmingham; "all one price" was said to derive from the slogan of Woolworth's, thus Wolverhampton. There was no connection of "corn" with Coventry. The raid, Cave Brown added, was Hitler's revenge for an RAF attack on Munich on 10 November.[4]

In 1982, William Stevenson repeated the Coventry story in *A Man Called Intrepid,* a spurious biography of Churchill's New York spymaster, Sir William Stephenson. (It appears Stephenson didn't apply that code name to himself until after the war.) Like Winterbotham, Stevenson claimed the word "Coventry" was sent *en clair,* not in code. Further elaborating on the account, Stevenson stated that Sir William himself advised Churchill to take no defensive measures, nor to evacuate Coventry, lest the Germans realize that their codes were being read. Melodramatically, Stevenson concluded, Churchill grimly took his advice, leaving the citizens of Coventry to their fate.[5]

David Irving, whose attacks on Churchill over the years were relentless, took up the theme with embellishments in 1987. Churchill, he wrote, had been advised that the German raid would be on London—so he had planned to "clear out of town as soon as he had cleared his appointments." Churchill summoned his Humber limousine and headed for Ditchley, Oxford. This was the country house (Irving spells it "Dytchley") where the Prime Minister spent weekends during the full moon, when Chequers, his official country residence, was considered too easily identifiable by enemy bombers.[6]

No sooner was Churchill off, Irving continues, than "The Humber had returned to Downing Street. The buff envelope in Churchill's hands had told him that the London raid was off, and that the beams had been found intersecting over Coventry ... he explained to his staff with perhaps less than utter candour that 'the beams' [Luftwaffe radio direction signals] indicated a colossal air raid on London that night, and he was 'not going to spend the night peacefully in the country while the Metropolis was under heavy attack'.... He felt little anxiety about Coventry."[7]

What Did Churchill Know, and When Did He Know It?

In the words of a 19th century cleric, "If you want truth to go round the world you must hire an express train to pull it; but if you want a lie to go round the world, it will fly...."[8] The Coventry story has since been fanned by the Internet. A 2008 play by Alan Pollock revived it for audiences in Coventry itself.[9] The problem is that it is not true, and the untruths begin with the considerable differences between the claimants.

When did Churchill know the raid would be on Coventry? Stevenson says he learned it from "Intrepid," but that book was dismissed as a combination of invention and the ramblings of an aging and infirm Sir William Stephenson. Cave Brown says Churchill knew on the 12th, while Winterbotham claims the news was only given the afternoon of the 14th. In fact, Coventry was *never* named as the target.

A German raid codenamed "Moonlight Sonata" was discovered in decrypts by the Air Ministry on 11 November. It included the first appearance of the codeword "corn." Dr. R.V. Jones, one of the Air Ministry scientists, believed "corn" referred not to a target but to the appearance of jammed radar screens.[10] The Air Ministry believed the raid would occur under a full moon, in three waves: incendiaries followed by two bombing attacks.

No one expected the Midlands to be the target of "Moonlight Sonata." Based on the decrypts and other intelligence—including a captured German target map—the Air Intelligence report cited five likely targets: Central London, Greater London, the Thames Valley, or the Kent or Essex coasts. The most likely area, it concluded, would be "probably in the vicinity of London."[11] The likely date was not stated. Also on 12 November, wrote McIver,

> Dr. Jones received a decrypt of a German message which indicated that there was to be a raid against Coventry, Wolverhampton and Birmingham. But there was nothing in this second message to connect it with "Moonlight Sonata." As early as the morning before the raid the connection had not been made and the Ministry were still expecting a raid on the capital. But what of Winterbotham's signal at three that afternoon? Dr. Jones, who was given copies of all "Ultra" decrypts at the same time as Winterbotham, states that there was no such message. In fact in his book he recalled traveling home that night and wondering where the raid was actually going to end up.[12]

"A German pilot who had been shot down on November 9th had, under interrogation, said that two cities—Coventry and Birmingham—would be attacked in a 'colossal raid' between 15 and 20 November," wrote Martin Gilbert … but the senior Air Intelligence Liaison officer at Bletchley, Squadron Leader Humphreys, noted, in contrast to this, that there was "pretty definite information that the attack is to be against London and the Home Counties." Bletchley thought the pilot's information doubtful, wrote Gilbert, "as it was earlier than the information available to Squadron Leader Humphreys."[13]

Churchill received these reports on the morning of 14 November, just after returning from the funeral of Neville Chamberlain. They informed him, Gilbert wrote,

> that whatever the target, the usual counter-measures had been prepared since early that morning, and would be activated as soon as the precise target was known. If, however, "further information were to indicate Coventry, Birmingham or elsewhere," it was hoped that the standard "Cold Water" instructions for counter-measures could be got out in time. These were instructions to rush fire engines and civil defence personnel to the area indicated from all the surrounding towns in a wide arc.[14]

Churchill's Movements

Churchill was scheduled to spend this full-moon weekend at Ditchley, and boarded his limousine that afternoon. As he was leaving, his principal private secretary, John Martin, handed him a lock-box containing a top secret message from Brigadier Menzies ("C"), head of the Secret Intelligence Service. Churchill read it as the car was passing the Albert Memorial. It stated that the raid was expected over London.

"On reading the document," wrote Peter McIver, "he ordered his driver to turn around and go back to Downing Street, explaining to his aide that the Air Ministry expected a major German raid on the capital that night." He explained to John Martin that he was not going to spend the night peacefully in the country while the capital was "under heavy attack."[15] A junior private secretary, Jock Colville, wrote in his diary that the raid "is known from the contents of those mysterious buff boxes which the PM alone opens, sent every day by Brigadier Menzies," but added, "its exact destination the Air Ministry say they find it difficult to determine."[16]

Back at Downing Street, Gilbert continues, Churchill sent

> the two duty private secretaries that evening, John Colville and John Peck, to the underground shelter at the disused Down Street underground railway station on the Piccadilly Line, telling them: "You are too young to die." He also gave instructions for the "Garden Room Girls"—the typists at 10 Downing

Churchill visiting the ruins of Coventry Cathedral, 15 November 1940, flanked by the Bishop (left) and Lord Mayor of Coventry. Behind and to the right of the Lord Mayor is the Prime Minister's bodyguard, inspector Walter Thompson, hat in hand (Wikimedia Commons).

Street—to be sent home. Churchill then went to the underground Central War Rooms (now known as the Cabinet War Rooms), but, as Colville noted in his diary that night, "became so impatient that he spent most of the time on the Air Ministry roof waiting for Moonlight Sonata to begin. Over London, it never did begin."[17]

Acting to Defend Coventry

"Proof enough that no one left Coventry to burn for reasons of high strategy is the fact that on the afternoon before the raid Bomber Command attacked 27 enemy airfields and even Berlin," wrote Peter McIver.[18] Martin Gilbert was even more precise:

The moment that German radio beams made it clear that Coventry was the target, the Air Ministry ordered eight British bombers to bomb the aerodromes—south of Cherbourg—from which the attackers were expected to take off. A continuous fighter patrol was maintained over Coventry itself, and the "Cold Water" defence preparations were activated…. [During the raid there were] five times as many anti-aircraft guns per head of the population as there were around London, and one hundred British fighters were airborne. But that could not save the city from the firestorm created by the incendiary bombs.[19]

Historians Hugh Trevor-Roper and Ronald Lewin firmly resisted fanning of the legend that Churchill sacrificed Coventry to save Ultra—a "monstrous distortion," Lewin wrote. The city was "twice-crucified," first by the Germans and second by the rumor mongers. Indeed it was doomed in any case, because air defenses were so rudimentary, and aircraft tracking still in its infancy, in 1940: "The initial errors of the Air Staff were irrelevant, for the Cold Water counter-measures could not have been very different even if the target of the raid had been known exactly," Lewin added:

> One hundred nineteen fighter sorties went up: uselessly, for the aircraft were without radar and the pilots untrained for night work. The anti-aircraft guns could only achieve a hit by extreme luck. A trivial raid over Berlin was an empty gesture…. Britain was not ready for a Blitz. But the real disaster was the clear moonlight night.[20]

Once the incendiaries had been dropped, the way for the bombers was clearly marked.

The Coventry story makes dramatic reading and offers melodramatic appeal to conspiracy theorists. But, like so many Churchill myths, it has no truth in reality. Of course, official silence over "Ultra" and other World War II intelligence—still unacknowledged when Winterbotham's book appeared—lent credence to his speculations. They seemed authoritative, since there were no records to check them against—and prompted numerous exciting news stories and elaborations on the Churchill-did-it theme. They were all wrong.

26

The Second Front Fracas

The Myth: Churchill Opposed the Invasion of France

Claims of Churchill's opposition to the "Second Front"—the capital letters denoting what Stalin, Roosevelt and Churchill continually referred to as a large-scale opposed invasion of France across the English Channel—began while World War II was still raging. Reports circulated and rumors leaked following each meeting of military and political leaders. Churchill, conscious of the noise, defended himself in his war memoirs:

> In view of the many accounts which are extant and multiplying of my supposed aversion [to the French landings] it may be convenient if I make it clear that from the very beginning I provided a great deal of the impulse and authority for creating the immense apparatus and armada for the landing of armour on beaches, without which it is now universally recognised that all such major operations would have been impossible.[1]

Churchill was not convinced that Germany could be defeated only by a cross-channel landing. While he was "always willing" to join a cross-channel assault, he "was not certain this was the only way of winning the war."[2] He was certainly influenced by the horrors of World War I's static trench warfare; but as the Germans had demonstrated in their invasion of France, warfare had changed since 1918. Churchill also remembered the losses in Britain's previous opposed landing—at Gallipoli in 1915 (Chapter 12). He expressed this concern to U.S. Secretary of War Henry Stimson in July 1943: "I see the Channel being full of corpses of defeated allies."[3] Even on the eve of D-Day, after laboring for months to make a success, he asked his wife: "Do you realise that by the time you wake up in the morning, "20,000 men may have been killed?"[4]

Churchill's interest in regaining what he called "a lodgment on the continent" began long before the Russians or Americans were in the war. A few weeks after Dunkirk, he asked his defense staff for methods of transporting and landing tanks on French beaches, and favored a corps of 5000 paratroopers.[5] The Special Operations Executive, designed to encourage cross-Channel raids and establish local resistance, was Churchill's idea. Of course this was nothing like a serious Second Front; but it did indicate his intent.

"Second Front Now"

After Hitler invaded Russia in June 1941 and Churchill declared all-out British aid to the USSR, Stalin began demanding an allied attack on Hitler from the west. He was

The Teheran Conference, 1943, saw the height of disagreements over Overlord. Stalin (left) wanted the Second Front immediately, if not sooner. Roosevelt (center) seemed to back Stalin, but knew it would not come until spring 1944. Churchill is on the right (Wikimedia Commons).

echoed by supporters in Britain, who argued noisily for a "Second Front Now." Churchill did wish to grapple with the enemy in Europe. After Japan attacked Pearl Harbor in December, he traveled hastily to Washington, anxious that the newly belligerent Americans adopt a policy of "Germany first," as agreed by their military staffs during the Anglo-American ABC-1 talks in March 1941.

It is widely thought that Churchill persuaded Roosevelt and the Americans to prioritize Germany. In fact, he was only partly successful. America had been grievously injured at Pearl Harbor. The Pacific had become a Japanese lake, and Roosevelt—understandably—could not ignore it. In March, the President informed Churchill that the Pacific war severely limited U.S. troop transports necessary for landing in France in the near future: "The present shipbuilding program seems to be about the maximum ... until after June, 1944." U.S. shipping could presently provide only 130,000 troops to England.[6]

Disappointed but still anxious to prepare for possible European action in 1942, Churchill advanced the concept of "Mulberry Harbors": floating piers, assembled in England, to be towed to the French coast: "They must float up and down with the tide," he directed in May. "Let me have the best solution worked out. Don't argue the matter.

The difficulties will argue for themselves."[7] Churchill also promoted "Pluto," (the pipe-line-under-the-ocean), to ensure a steady supply of fuel for tanks and army vehicles once the invasion was underway.[8]

If a cross–Channel invasion should prove impossible in 1942, Churchill looked for another area where the Anglo-Americans might strike to take pressure off the Russians. North Africa, where the British and Germans had engaged in a see-saw battle since June 1940, was the obvious place. Roosevelt who, shortly after Pearl Harbor, had also thought about such a campaign, agreed. Launched in November 1942, Operation Torch, the invasion of North Africa, opened what Churchill called a "Third Front," reserving the term "Second Front" for the cross-Channel invasion, Operation Round-Up. Meeting with Stalin in Moscow in 1942, Churchill said he expected that the Americans would have twenty-seven divisions in England by Spring 1943.[9]

The U.S. divisions did not materialize. Warren Kimball explained: "As American military planners reluctantly began to accept the idea that a cross-channel invasion was not feasible until the spring of 1944, they naturally began to look to other theatres … the Pacific forces seemed ready for more supplies and troops in order to take the offensive against Japan."[10] In late 1942 Churchill was told that the U.S. troop build-up in England would be delayed. Essential landing craft were also problematic. In January 1943, Lord Louis Mountbatten, Chief of Combined Operations, reported that contrary to an agreement, "the Americans were putting the good engines into their own [Pacific] landing craft and fitting ours with the unsatisfactory type."[11]

Churchill's frustration was palpable. "We had been preparing for 1,100,000 men," he wrote the President. "We had no knowledge that you had decided to abandon forever Round-Up … a most grievous decision." Churchill implored the President to think again: "Even in 1943 a chance may come."[12] FDR replied that he had "no intention of abandoning Round-Up…. It is my present thought that we should build up as rapidly as present active operations permit a growing striking force in the U.K. to be used quickly in event of German collapse or a very large force later if Germany remains intact and assumes a defensive position" (underline in original).[13] Given that the U.S. military was still pushing for Round-Up in 1943, this was an oddly confusing comment. Perhaps Roosevelt was following his practice of never telling one hand what the other was doing; but his words could reasonably be interpreted to mean that the Second Front was off until further notice by the Americans.

The shortage of U.S. troops continued to rankle. On 9 February 1943 Churchill informed Soviet Ambassador Ivan Maisky that only one American division had arrived in England. Instead of the promised twenty-seven divisions by spring, Washington forecast only four or five by August. Maisky asked what would happen if the Americans did not deliver. Churchill replied: "I'll carry out this operation whatever happens."[14] While this was certainly intended to assure the Russians of his resolve, it also sounds like a man frustrated over the delays in the cross-Channel invasion.

North Africa and Italy

As Churchill and Roosevelt had hoped, Operation Torch helped the hard-pressed Red Army, diverting Axis forces to North Africa, where they were destroyed. In February 1943 General Alexander, his Middle East commander, phlegmatically informed Churchill:

"Sir: The Orders you gave me on August 15, 1942, have been fulfilled. His Majesty's ene-mies, together with their impedimenta, have been completely eliminated from Egypt, Cyrenaica, Libya, and Tripolitania. I now await your further instructions." Churchill replied: "Well, obviously, we shall have to think of something else...."[15]

The "something else" was an extension of Churchill's "Third Front," with the inva-sions of Sicily (10 July) and Italy (3 September—the same day the Italian government sued for an armistice). But Mussolini's fascists resisted, the Germans rushed in troops, and the Italian campaign would chew up soldiers and resources well into 1944. It was over this campaign, and the competitive needs for the 1944 invasion of France—now named Operation Overlord—that the British, Americans and Soviets engaged in steady debate for over a year.

Churchill had always been drawn to peripheral strategies, some of which, notably the Dardanelles in 1915, had ended badly. With North Africa and Sicily secure, Italy invaded, and Overlord off until 1944, his questing mind envisioned opportunities to strike at the Germans from the south. Continuously over the next eighteen months he deprecated and fought the removal of troops and landing craft from Italy to England.

Churchill's more impractical ideas (like an attack on the Greek Dodecanese Islands or advancing through the narrow, vulnerable Ljubljana Gap between Venice and Vienna), were withdrawn when opposed by his own or the American military. Because he envi-sioned such strategies—and presciently realized it was preferable to "shake hands with the Russians as far to the east as possible"[16]—does not mean he wished to abandon Over-lord. The argument was more about how far in Italy the Allies should go, and whether Overlord should be the only Anglo-American drive against the Germans.

In the weeks preceding the Big Three Teheran Conference, in late November and early December 1943—Churchill found himself pressed hard on Italy by his Chief of Imperial General Staff, General (later Field Marshal) Alan Brooke. "It is becoming more and more evident that our operations in Italy are coming to a standstill," Brooke wrote in his diary for 25 October. "We shall have an almighty row with the Americans who have put us in this position with their insistence to abandon the Mediterranean operations for the very problematical cross Channel operations.... It is quite heartbreaking when we see what we might have done this year if our strategy had not been distorted by the Americans."[17]

Churchill often disagreed with Brooke, but never ignored his views. On this occasion they seemed to agree. On 29 October, Churchill's doctor found him "glum, his jaw set, misgivings filled his mind." Stalin, Churchill said, was "obsessed by this bloody Second Front. Damn the fellow." Italy, he declared, must be fought until victory. Overlord, planned for May 1944, was "subject to the exigencies" of Italy.[18] He clung stubbornly to this approach at the Teheran Conference, and only grudgingly conceded transfers of resources for D-Day. At Teheran Stalin needled him, asking if he really believed in Overlord. Churchill replied that, provided the conditions were right, "it will be our stern duty to hurl across the Channel against the Germans every sinew of our strength."[19] The reader may judge if this was bombast or sincerity.

Churchill always insisted there was no question of abandoning Overlord. However, he told Eden, retaining enough troops and equipment "in order not to lose the battle of Rome may cause a slight delay...."[20] Rome fell on 4 June 1944, two days before D-Day. Seven crack divisions were then pulled out of Italy to participate in an invasion of South-ern France—a "Fourth Front"—which Churchill viewed as a pointless sideshow. Churchill never gave up, even against the odds. He continued to argue his various schemes for pressing Germany from the south. In Italy the Allies advanced northward, capturing Florence and closing on the Gothic Line, the last German defensive position, in August 1944. Fighting in Italy continued until the German surrender on 29 April 1945.

Though gravely disappointed with his allies' low enthusiasm for Italian operations, and frustrated over his inability to sell his southern strategies, Churchill remained focused on Overlord. In January 1944 he sent a military delegation to Moscow, who secured Stalin's approval of deceptions to confuse the Germans: bogus Soviet landings in Romania and Norway.

More ambitious, Martin Gilbert wrote, was the "totally spurious First U.S. Army Group based in East Anglia, commanded by General Patton … supposedly planning to land in the Calais region, or on the Belgian and Dutch coasts, up to 200 miles from Normandy." The plan was the work of British Intelligence with Churchill's approval. Juan Pujol Garcia, whom the Germans thought was their agent, "kept sending them details about the FUSAG plans. He was in fact working for Britain, his reports to Berlin being the inventive creations of British Intelligence." The Germans, with their vast respect for Patton, were misled, and Hitler convinced that the main attack would be on Calais. At the same time Churchill met regularly with Eisenhower and his chief of staff, Bedell Smith, going over every aspect of the Normandy landings. He even enlisted the London Fire Brigade, which provided pumping resources to raise one of the Mulberry Harbors.[21]

"Nukes for Normandy"

Given all of the above, it was astonishing to read in 2016 yet another twist on the old story of Churchill's reluctance. On 12–13 August 1943, between sessions of the Quebec Conference, the prime minister stayed with Roosevelt at Hyde Park. There, according to *Commander-in-Chief,* a book by Nigel Hamilton, Roosevelt threatened to withhold U.S. atom bomb secrets from Britain unless Churchill supported invading France in 1944— the very year Roosevelt and Churchill had selected, after rejecting (for sound reasons) 1942 and 1943. Hamilton wrote that this was a "bitter pill" for the Prime Minister: "Churchill was not happy with the outcome—indeed he woke up in the night 'unable to sleep and hardly able to breathe.'"[22]

No evidence was offered for FDR's Nukes-for-Overlord demand other than the Churchill quote, which was far out of context. Churchill's complaint was not about FDR but the weather. "It was so hot," he wrote, "that I got up one night because I was unable to sleep and hardly to breathe, and went outside to sit on a bluff overlooking the Hudson River."[23] The thesis thus collapses on its face—another myth with no basis in reality.

Hamilton correctly cited Roosevelt's decision to invade France in 1944, rather than 1943—which, he rightly argues, would have been "mass slaughter." But he concludes that FDR's chief of staff George Marshall and Churchill, in their initial push for 1943, were dangerously naïve. Only Roosevelt was "determined to stop his top military staff from insisting upon a suicidal assault in the wrong place, at the wrong time."[24] Promotion for the book stated: "Roosevelt knew that the Allies should take Sicily but then stop, building experience but saving strength to invade France in early 1944. Churchill seemed to agree at Casablanca—only to undermine his own generals and the Allied command, testing Roosevelt's patience to the limit."[25]

This is hyperbole. "In wanting to attack everywhere," wrote Paul Reid,

Churchill manifested two abiding traits: impatience and flexibility in the face of changing fortunes. His belief in an opportunistic strategic approach—attack the weaker of two enemies if the stronger could not be engaged—had not diminished since the 1941 Greek debacle, nor since 1915 and the Dardanelles, for that matter. Now Italy was weak, and getting weaker.[26]

In all his proposals, practical and fanciful, Churchill was characteristically reacting to the situation as it had developed. He observed the slow build-up of U.S. troops for Overlord, and the opportunities offered in Italy—which, after all, had been invaded with Roosevelt's approval. Roosevelt did resist more easterly operations, and had good reason for doing so. He was sure that in the end, victory required crossing the Channel.

There is no doubt that Franklin Roosevelt was against invading France in 1943 because he knew it wouldn't succeed. By contrast, Churchill, *had* wanted to invade that year (and in 1942, originally). When he realized that circumstances had changed he gave those dates up, and when Mediterranean opportunities arose he pursued them. Both leaders wanted to win the war. Churchill challenged the assumption that Normandy was the only way; but he worked to ensure Overlord's success, right to the moment when the invasion fleet sailed on 6 June 1944.

Like the later decision to use the atomic bomb, the decision to postpone the cross-Channel invasion until June 1944 was officially that of the President and Prime Minister. But it was Roosevelt who was calling the shots. By 1943 Britain was very much the junior partner; the allocation of American troops and equipment governed every decision. Roosevelt acted as he did for sound and sensible military reasons. And Churchill was intrinsic to Overlord's success.

27

Mad Bomber

The Myth: Churchill Endorsed
Carpet-Bombing German Cities

Churchill was no enthusiast for what he called the "hideous process of bombing open cities [as opposed to military targets] from the air."[1] He sanctioned it at various times for three reasons: the Germans began it, over Warsaw and Rotterdam in 1939–40; his military chiefs, particularly Air Marshal Arthur "Bomber" Harris, held bombing the best way to attack Germany; and for a long time it was the only substitute for the "Second Front" Stalin demanded (previous chapter). Nevertheless, Churchill frequently challenged indiscriminate bombing—particularly "carpet bombing" of civilians—on the grounds both of morality and effectiveness—and he was the only one of the "Big Three" to do so.

There were exceptions, as there always are, especially in the heat of the moment. En route for America in December 1941, in a long series of policy papers for Roosevelt, Churchill mentioned "The burning of Japanese cities by incendiary bombs…."[2] That was ten days after the devastating Japanese attacks on Pearl Harbor and British East Asia. It reminds us again of William Manchester's comment that Churchill's early reactions were sometimes unworthy of him, but were usually succeeded by reason.[3]

The facts have not prevented Churchill from being cast as a bloodthirsty bomber. In 2015 a reader of my article on the Paris concert atrocities suggested that the West must do to ISIS what Churchill did to Berlin: "make the rubble dance." But Churchill never said that about Berlin. On the bombing of Barcelona during the Spanish Civil War, he had written that after awhile, more bombs would only "make the rubble jump."[4] During the London Blitz, he again used the expression. He was expressing disapproval, not approval.

In the Cold War, historian Michael Kramer noted, "the Soviet Union was highly interested in producing propaganda to alter memories and give people the impression that western-capitalist forces committed overly barbaric, immoral and unethical acts on innocent civilians."[5] The Soviets frequently denounced the bombing of Dresden, "the Florence on the Elbe," as an Anglo-American war crime—ironic, since they requested it, as we shall see.

Civilian vs. Military Objectives

Churchill certainly had no qualms about bombing "strictly military objectives," such as German synthetic gasoline plants, which he proposed on 14 September 1939, eleven days after Britain had declared war. Chamberlain's Air Minister, Sir Kingsley Wood, said that couldn't be done by Britain's "small and inferior air force"—the size of which, as Martin Gilbert has reminded us, Churchill had vainly lamented for the past six years.[6]

Churchill's attitude abruptly changed after he became prime minister. On 12 May 1940, the German air force wantonly attacked Rotterdam. "The War Cabinet discussed whether it was right 'on moral grounds' to bomb targets in Germany," Gilbert wrote:

> Summing up the general tenor of the discussion, Churchill told his colleagues: "…we were no longer bound by our previously held scruples…. The enemy had already given us ample justification for retaliation on his country." But the balance of opinion was against him the following day, when Neville Chamberlain—a member of his War Cabinet—opposed bombing military targets in the Ruhr, as it might lead to German retaliation in Britain.

A month later Churchill declared that victory required a "devastating, exterminating attack" by bombers. Air Marshal Harris, who would come to head Bomber Command in 1942, told Gilbert: "It was the origin of the idea of bombing the enemy out of the war. I should have been proud of it. But it originated with Winston." President Roosevelt echoed Harris' advice, urging a member of the British mission in Washington to "bomb Germany everywhere."[7]

As over chemical warfare (Chapter 15), Churchill adopted the policy of "Give it 'em back"—a phrase Cockneys shouted to him when he toured Blitz damage in London's East End. On 25 August 1940 the first German bombs fell on central London. Churchill immediately dispatched eighty bombers to Berlin. Little damage was done in either raid, but the precedent was set, and Britons were demanding it. In September, Churchill diverted bombers to the landing barges Hitler was amassing on the French coast for an invasion of England. The War Cabinet cautioned that this might cause the public to think he wasn't "hitting back hard enough at Germany…."[8]

Clearly, Churchill was under tremendous pressure to do what the Cockneys wanted, and their wishes were echoed by Stalin and Roosevelt. Yet he resisted targeting civilians and mainly stuck to industrial areas and railroad centers. Harris and Chief of Air Staff Sir Charles Portal argued that entire cities and towns should be obliterated. Churchill expressed doubt in their "cut and dried calculations."[9] He explained to Portal that even bombing military targets was "not decisive, but better than doing nothing."[10]

The bombing of Germany had an effect. As Gilbert recorded: "By June 1942, British bombing efforts were keeping one half of all German fighter strength away from the Eastern Front. Between July and September 1942 the Royal Air Force dropped 11,500 tons of bombs on Germany; 2500 tons were on the Ruhr industrial city of Duisburg." In early 1943, on two nights, "1050 tons of bombs were dropped on Berlin in fifty minutes, by 395 heavy bombers, for the loss of nine [aircraft; and] 900 tons of bombs were dropped on the Krupp Essen works."[11] Two months later, Harris objected to Churchill's order to bomb landing sites on Pantelleria Island in the Mediterranean, arguing that it diverted attacks on German cities.

Urgings from Stalin

In August 1942, Churchill flew to Moscow on a difficult mission: to inform Stalin that owing to military reality, there would be no Second Front in France in 1942 (previous chapter). "Stalin took issue at every point with bluntness, almost to the point of insult," Averell Harriman, Roosevelt's representative at the meeting, reported to the President. "You can't win wars if you aren't willing to take risks," Stalin said. To Churchill's fury he added: "You must not be so afraid of the Germans." Stalin admitted that he could not force a Second Front in 1942 but refused to accept Churchill's arguments. He even doubted the Anglo-Americans would invade in 1943—rightly, as it turned out. "So far," wrote Harriman, "there had been no agreement on any point and the atmosphere was tense."

Anxious to assuage the Soviet dictator, Churchill turned to British strategic bombing, quoting the latest statistics on damage to the Reich. "Here came the first agreement between the two men," Harriman reported:

> Stalin took over the argument himself and said that homes as well as factories should be destroyed. The Prime Minister agreed that civil morale was a military objective, but the bombing of working men's houses came as a by-product of near-misses on factories. The tension began to ease and a certain understanding of common purpose began to grow.[12]

Churchill had succeeded somewhat in placating his Russian ally without budging on his stance against specifically targeting civil populations. Stalin even became genial (for him), praising the effectiveness of British bombing. He told Churchill that his foreign minister, Molotov, had been in Berlin in 1940, negotiating with his opposite number. Von Ribbentrop had declared, "the British Empire is finished." Suddenly the bombers arrived. "Ribbentrop decided to continue the discussion in the dugout. When safely established underground Ribbentrop continued saying that, as he had already mentioned, the British Empire need no longer be taken account of. Molotov interrupted at this point with the awkward question: 'Then why are we down here now?'"[13]

Public Expressions, Private Regrets

Bombing intensity over Germany continued to mount. "The moral burdens of these lethal attacks on the largely unarmed were accepted by Mr. Churchill as a grim necessity of a just war," wrote Christopher Harmon. "To many, the weight would have been crushing. In Churchill's case the shoulders dipped only in private, and remarkably few occasions."[14] One of these was at Chequers, the night of 27 June 1943, as Churchill watched films of raids on the Ruhr. Richard Casey, Australian representative to the War Cabinet, was present. Suddenly, Casey reported, Churchill "sat bolt upright and said to me, 'Are we beasts? Are we taking this too far?' [It was] a momentary reaction from the very graphic presentation. I said that we hadn't started it, and that it was them or us."[15]

Churchill's stark question was uttered in private, and we wouldn't have it but for Casey. His public actions supported his private misgivings. Only two weeks before that signal remark, Martin Gilbert noted,

> the Point-Blank Directive of 10 June 1943 had been issued. This amended the Casablanca Directive in order to give first emphasis to the attack on German fighter forces and the German aircraft industry. The Point Blank targets included, from 29 June 1943, the Peenemunde rocket bomb experimental

station on the Baltic, which was bombed with 571 heavy bombers on 17 August 1943, setting back German progress.[16]

In preparation for D-Day, the invasion of France on 6 June 1944, Churchill continued to fret over civilian bombing casualties. In April, as Allied bombers began striking French railroad yards to impede enemy transportation, Churchill was told that up to 40,000 French civilians might be killed. "You are piling up an awful load of hatred," he wrote Portal.[17] To Eisenhower he urged that raids be limited by a cap on estimated casualties. President Roosevelt interceded:

> However regrettable the attendant loss of civilian lives is, I am not prepared to impose from this distance any restriction on military action by the responsible commanders that in their opinion might militate against the success of Overlord or cause additional loss of life to our Allied forces of invasion.[18]

Actual casualties from the bombing of French railways proved to be only ten percent of the number feared, and Churchill accepted that the action had been essential. In July, Churchill was confronted with the reality of Auschwitz, and faced with the question of bombing the camp, killing many inhabitants—another decision with no happy alternatives (see Chapter 31).

Dresden

Between 13 and 15 February 1945, 1247 British-American bombers dropped nearly 4000 tons of high-explosives and incendiaries on Germany, including the cities of Chemnitz and Magdeburg. Two-thirds of those aircraft attacked the historic medieval city of Dresden. The ensuing firestorm destroyed 1600 acres in the city center and killed between 23,000 and 25,000 people. Three later air raids by U.S. forces in March and April bombed railroad yards and industrial centers. Yet, as a military center, wrote RAF historian John Terraine, Dresden had "no outstanding significance."[19] Christopher Harmon added: "Dresden was without the explosives factories of a Hamburg, or the submarine engine factories of a Cologne; it had virtually no militarily important industries."[20]

In retrospect, bombing Dresden was a bloodthirsty and almost certainly unnecessary measure of war, and Churchill has received most of the blame. "Kurt Vonnegut's *Slaughterhouse-Five* (1969), with its nightmare evocation of the bombing of Dresden, remains one of the most popular American war novels."[21] Churchill has been regularly excoriated in print and on the Internet for indiscriminately and inhumanely murdering civilians.

Typical of the critics was Clive Ponting who, as so often in his book, was careful to quote only material that bolstered his case. The raid on Dresden, he wrote, was a direct result of Churchill's 26 January 1945 query to Air Minister Sir Archibald Sinclair "whether Berlin, and no doubt other large cities in East Germany, should not be considered especially attractive targets."[22] Ponting omits Sinclair's reply: The Air Staff would carry out attacks on "Berlin, Dresden, Chemnitz and Leipzig or against other cities where severe bombing would not only destroy communications vital to the evacuation from the East but would also hamper the movement of troops from the West," subject to not detracting "from our offensive on oil targets, which is now in a critical phase."[23] This is hardly a call for raining hellfire on civilian population centers.

The fairer-minded Harmon offered several reasons for the attack: "...it cannot be denied that one reason, the weakest reason, for fire-bombing Dresden was that it had a place on the list of fifty-eight cities through which 'Bomber' Harris was grinding his way. Even in 1945, he was convinced that he was shortening the war." More valid was the "conventional military reason," by then "a commonplace in the language of Royal Air Force directives: support for Soviet armies."

Dresden had become a center for German rail and road communications. "Stalin had pressed for attacks on German cities behind the whole front…. A Soviet intelligence report later proven erroneous stated that one or two German armored divisions were in Dresden on their way to reinforce the Eastern Front."[24] Thus the Soviets—who would later denounce the Dresden attack as an Anglo-American war crime—made the request that led to Dresden's destruction.

Ironically, Churchill had already left London for the Yalta Conference when the Soviet request came in. He wasn't even there to give the order. Yet it was clearly an urgent request. The task fell to Deputy Prime Minister Clement Attlee. Churchill did not learn of the Soviet request until he arrived in Yalta on 4 February. Stalin's first question to him was, 'Why haven't you bombed Dresden?'" Forty years later, Martin Gilbert revealed these facts in a Moscow lecture to an assembly of high-ranking Soviet officers. Of course it went against decades of official Soviet historiography. "It was greeted with disbelief," Sir Martin remembered. "Then to my rescue arose an old general bedizened with medals. During the war he had been General Antonov's deputy. He came to the microphone and said with a thick Russian accent: 'Everything Professor Gilbert says is true.' You could have heard a pin drop."[25]

When Gilbert repeated this story at his Washington, D.C. Churchill lecture in 2004, moderator Juan Williams of Fox News, asked: "Why do you think the controversy over Dresden specifically has never ceased? Isn't it a horrible fact that cannot be erased from the record?" Sir Martin replied:

> Who can say why one out of thousands of historical events creates interest while the others do not? The fire-bombing of Tokyo was far more devastating, and yet we never hear Tokyo discussed. To bomb Dresden, at the request of the Soviets, was but one small part in a broad campaign. It was not even ordered by Churchill … yet there is no reason to suppose Churchill would have reacted any differently.[26]

Dresden Aftermath

Churchill learned of the Dresden raid results by telegram on 14 February. After he returned home, he again questioned the rationale of bombing open cities. The moment had come, he wrote, to question bombing "simply for the sake of increasing the terror…. The destruction of Dresden remains a serous query against the conduct of Allied bombing. I am of the opinion that military objectives must henceforward be more strictly studied." Priority, he added, should go "upon military objectives, such as oil and communications," rather than "mere acts of terror and wanton destruction, however impressive."[27]

Air Marshal Portal "persuaded Churchill to withdraw the minute as originally phrased," wrote John Grigg:

> Two days later it was sent in revised form, with the query about Dresden removed and no mention of terror—only of the inexpediency of area bombing "from the point of view of our own interests," since

there would be "a great shortage of accommodation for ourselves and our Allies" if Germany, when conquered, were to be "an entirely ruined land."[28]

Clive Ponting put the worst spin on this. Portal, he wrote, was "incensed by Churchill's suddenly discovered aversion to area bombing" and "rewrote the minute himself."[29]

Gilbert's explanation was more prosaic and logical: "Portal pointed out 'that it had always been the aim of our bombing of large cities to destroy the industries and transportation services centred in those cities and not to terrorise the civilian population of Germany.' Churchill agreed to withdraw his 'rough' minute, and instructed Portal to redraft it in 'less rough terms.'"[30] The reader may decide if, as Ponting charged, Churchill's draft was written in shame, "with more than half an eye on history," or whether it represented Churchill's true view of terror bombing as expressed throughout the war.

There was no doubt that bombing exacted a fearful toll on the nation that had brought upon World War II. Churchill had also watched the powerful advances of the Red Army in the east, with ominous portents for the future. One evening at Chequers, Air Marshal Harris arrived with his charts showing the latest destruction of German cities, something of which Harris was rather proud, wrote Martin Gilbert:

> Instead of Churchill being excited and impressed by the charts, as he often was, he looked sombre. Then addressing Harris in the third person, something quite unusual, he said: "What I want to know is this: when Air Marshal Harris has finished the destruction of every German city, what will then lie between the white snows of Russia, and the white cliffs of Dover?"[31]

"Churchill did not think well of area bombing," Harmon concluded,

> but began to believe it could be a grim necessity after he watched devastating German air attacks on Warsaw, Rotterdam, and other places full of noncombatants; and he could see precious few ideas for hitting back. In the ever-lengthening build-up to Normandy, the bomber offensive was about the best he had to hurt the Germans and their industrial war effort. Later, when he saw France liberated, Germany's defensive lines being pierced, and the war being won, he quickly lost taste for it. Churchill's head of Bomber Command, Air Marshal Harris, seemed to think German morale might still be broken by bombing, but Churchill rebuked him after Dresden, and again, just as strongly for bombing Potsdam shortly thereafter. His mind had already turned to how the Allies would govern and occupy Germany; the time for destroying it was passing.[32]

New and perhaps even more formidable challenges were soon to face Britain and the West.

28

Starving the Indians

The Myth: Churchill Was Responsible
for the 1943 Bengal Famine

A reviewer of *The Churchill Factor*, by former London Mayor Boris Johnson, chased a familiar red herring. When famine threatened Bengal, India in 1943–44, he wrote,

Churchill announced that the Indians "must learn to look after themselves as we have done ... there is no reason why all parts of the British Empire should not feel the pinch in the same way as the mother country has done." Still more disgracefully, he said in a jocular way that "the starvation of anyhow under-fed Bengalis is less serious than that of sturdy Greeks." This is more than amusingly politically incorrect language: it had real consequences. Three million Bengalis died of starvation.[1]

Churchill once remarked, "I should think it was hardly possible to state the opposite of the truth with more precision."[2] The reason Boris Johnson omitted this common accusation is that it is not true. That has not prevented it from being repeatedly leveled. Most writers derive the charges from *Churchill's Secret War,* a 2010 book on the Bengal famine, accusing Churchill of committing what amounts to a war crime.[3] In reality, the Prime Minister did everything he could, in the midst of total war, to ease the plight of Bengalis—and without him the famine would have been worse. Australia, Canada and other parts of the British Empire also deserve credit for their selfless aid to India.

As so often in such cases, the incriminating quotations do not support the argument. "They must learn to look after themselves as we have done" is from a Churchill minute on 10 March 1943, six months before the famine, when "the Indian Ocean area" was requesting small amounts of cereals—"negligible additions to the crops in those countries." Left out is Churchill's following sentence: "The grave situation of the United Kingdom import programme imperils the whole war effort, and we cannot afford to send ships merely as a symbol of goodwill."[4]

The statement about "all parts of Empire" having to "feel the pinch" came even earlier, in November 1942. Churchill said this shortly after the Battle of Alamein had reduced threats to the Middle East sufficiently "that the British army could cut back substantially on reserves and supplies in this theatre."[5] Clearly Churchill was referring to *all parts,* not India alone—and a year before famine broke out in Bengal.

Most appallingly, the words "under-fed Bengalis" and "sturdy Greeks" (November 1943) were not by Churchill but by Secretary of State for India Leopold Amery, paraphrasing Churchill's attitude in his diary. Amery did not say Churchill was "jocular."

149

(Greeks at that time were indeed "sturdy," since Greece was experiencing a famine under Nazi occupation.) Left out of the quote is Amery's preceding comment: "Winston may be right." Amery did feel there was an "Empire responsibility" in Bengal but "we must not shift blame to that honorable man, who was as concerned about the famine as anyone."[6]

Orders to Amery and Wavell

Churchill had appointed Amery Secretary of State for India after becoming prime minister in May 1940. By October 1943, a crucial time in the war, with Indian food shortages spreading, Churchill told Amery his first duty was "to make sure that India was a safe base for the great operations against Japan which were now pending, and that the war was pressed to a successful conclusion, *and that famine and food difficulties were dealt with*" (emphasis added). Churchill also urged Amery to "assuage the strife between the Hindus and Moslems and to induce them to work together for the common good."[7]

A day later, Churchill sent virtually the same orders to Lord Wavell, the newly appointed Viceroy of India, adding:

> Peace, order and a high condition of war-time well-being among the masses of the people constitute the essential foundation of the forward thrust against the enemy. The material and cultural conditions of the many peoples of India will naturally engage your earnest attention. The hard pressures of world-war have for the first time for many years brought conditions of scarcity, verging in some localities into actual famine, upon India. Every effort must be made, even by the diversion of shipping urgently needed for war purposes, to deal with local shortages.[8]

This does not seem like one determined that the "under-fed Bengalis" should "feel the pinch." Indeed, as the historian Arthur Herman wrote, "We might even say that Churchill indirectly broke the Bengal famine by appointing as Viceroy Field Marshal Wavell, who mobilized the military to transport food and aid to the stricken regions (something that hadn't occurred to anyone, apparently)."[9]

Help from the Empire

Next Churchill turned to aiding Bengal through the Dominions. Canada had offered shipments of wheat, but in thanking Prime Minister MacKenzie King, Churchill noted a practical problem: "Even if you could make the wheat available in Eastern Canada, I should still be faced with a serious shipping question. If our strategic plans are not to suffer undue interference we must continue to scrutinise all demands for shipping with the utmost rigour." Churchill explained that he hoped to provide India with wheat from a much nearer source: "Wheat from Canada would take at least two months to reach India whereas it could be carried from Australia in 3 to 4 weeks." He asked King not to publicize Canada's offer because Britain would "have to say that no shipping was available. This would cause disappointment in India...."[10] He might have regretted that reasonable request had he lived to read books claiming he wanted the Bengalis to starve.

Instead Churchill turned to Australia, which promised 250,000 tons of wheat. MacKenzie King still wanted to help, but Churchill feared a resultant loss of war shipments between Canada and Australia. King assured him there would be no shortfall, and that Canada's contribution would pay "dividends in humanitarian aspects" and "intra-imperial relations."[11] Churchill responded by getting another 100,000 tons from Australia. Wavell noted, "all the Dominion Governments are doing their best to help."[12]

The famine continued into 1944, causing Amery to increase his grain request to one million tons. Churchill, who had been studying consumption statistics, believed India was now receiving more than she would need. Burdened by the food shortages everywhere, he remained concerned about the shipping problem, "given the effect of its diversion alike on operations and on our imports of food into this country, which could be further reduced only at the cost of much suffering." To Wavell Churchill telegraphed: "I will certainly help you all I can, but you must not ask the impossible."[13]

The Cabinet cited causes of the Bengal famine never mentioned in recent critiques of Churchill. The shortages were "partly political in character, caused by Marwari [Hindu] supporters of Congress [Gandhi's party] in an effort to embarrass the existing Muslim Government of Bengal."[14] So much for Churchill's hope that Hindus and Muslims would "work together for the common good."

Two other causes the Cabinet cited were corrupt local officials—"The Government of India were unduly tender with speculators and hoarders"—and Japan's control of Burma, which cut off India's main supply of rice imports when domestic sources fell in 1942. "With Burma in enemy hands," the Cabinet noted, "the situation could be exploited for either political or economic reasons." Amery told Wavell that Churchill "was not unsympathetic" to the terrible situation, but that no one had ships to spare given current military operations.[15]

Strained Resources

Amery and Wavell continued to press for wheat, and in the Cabinet of February 14th Churchill and his colleagues tried to accommodate them further. While shipping difficulties were "very real," they were "most anxious that we should do everything possible to ease the Viceroy's position." Churchill said their caution "was not due to our underrating India's needs, but because we could not take operational risks by cutting down the shipping required for vital operations." Unfortunately Lord Leathers, Minister of War Transport, determined that it was "out of the question" to maintain wheat shipments to India at 50,000 tons monthly; he offered instead 25,000 tons a month of Iraqi barley, achieved by cutting the UK's import program below the latest estimated needs. "It was," Leathers reported, "clearly quite impossible to provide shipping to meet the full demand of 1½ million tons made by the Government of India."[16]

Meanwhile the war pressed Churchill on all sides. At the same time as he was trying to meet, or at least approach, India's needs, he was distracted by other demands: "I have been much concerned at the apparently excessive quantities of grain demanded by Allied HQ for civilians in Italy, which impose a great strain on our shipping and finances," he wrote War Secretary Sir James Grigg in early 1944. He demanded reports on "rationing, grain collecting, milling, black markets and agricultural production … at the earliest possible moment."[17]

Churchill and his Cabinet continued to struggle to meet India's needs through February and March 1944. While certain that shipping on the scale Amery wanted was impossible without a "dangerous inroad into the British import programme or a serious inter-ference with operational plans," they considered every possibility. The 21st of February found them recommending diverting up to 50,000 tons of grain destined for the Balkan stockpile, and loading bagged wheat onto cargo ships bound for India from the U.S. or Australia, if space was available. Leathers reported that the Indians didn't want the Iraqi barley, but that he had found another 50,000 tons of wheat.[18]

Appeal to Roosevelt

A month later Churchill thought Bengal had turned the corner when Leathers announced "statistically a surplus of food grains in India." Still, Leathers emphasized "the need for imported wheat on psychological grounds." Amery explained that "the peasant in 750,000 villages" might hold back "his small parcel of grain" if no outside aid was in sight. Leathers said he could now ship from various sources 200,000 tons, "pro-vided that the twenty-five ships required were surplus to the Army's needs." Amery wanted double that quantity. Churchill, approving the 200,000, told Amery to get another 150,000 tons from Ceylon; thus, counting the 50,000 tons previously, committed, Amery would have the 400,000 he was asking for.[19]

The Cabinet's relief that it had met India's needs lasted only a month. On 24 April the Viceroy, Lord Wavell, who had been scrambling for supplies at his end, increased the request for imported wheat from 400,000 to 724,000 tons. Added problems were unsea-sonable weather and an explosion on a loaded grain ship in Bombay harbor. Peasants were still hoarding their rice crops, he said. Wavell then queried rumors "that London had refused to ask America for help." The exasperated Cabinet retorted: "If we now approached the United States and they were unable to help, it would at least dispel that allegation."[20]

One can sense Churchill's frustration. Whatever they did, however they wriggled, they seemed unable to appease the increasing demands from India. Churchill agreed to write President Roosevelt for help, and to replace the 45,000 tons lost in the Bombay explosion. But he "could only provide further relief for the Indian situation at the cost of incurring grave difficulties in other directions."[21]

As good as his word, and despite preoccupation with the imminent invasion of Nor-mandy, Churchill wrote FDR. No one, reading his words, can be in doubt about his sym-pathies:

> I am seriously concerned about the food situation in India.... Last year we had a grievous famine in Bengal through which at least 700,000 people died. This year there is a good crop of rice, but we are faced with an acute shortage of wheat, aggravated by unprecedented storms.... I have had much hesi-tation in asking you to add to the great assistance you are giving us with shipping but a satisfactory situation in India is of such vital importance to the success of our joint plans against the Japanese that I am impelled to ask you to consider a special allocation of ships to carry wheat to India from Australia.... We have the wheat (in Australia) but we lack the ships.[22]

Churchill had hesitated to ask, he said, because Wavell was "doing all he can"—but "I am no longer justified in not asking for your help." Roosevelt was unhelpful. He replied that while India had his "utmost sympathy," his Joint Chiefs had said they were "unable on military grounds to consent to the diversion of shipping.... Needless to say, I regret exceedingly the necessity of giving you this unfavorable reply."[23]

In September 1944, Churchill sent Sir Henry French, permanent secretary of the Ministry of Food, to India to investigate the food situation and make arrangements to prevent another famine. French reported back on 10 October. While he had been able to foster "some improvements in food administration," the effect would not be seen for another year or two. "The use of compulsion to obtain supplies of foodgrains from the Provinces which produce large surpluses must be ruled out as impracticable," French wrote. India would not be self-sufficient in foodgrains for the next four or five years. It was therefore "desirable that His Majesty's Government in the United Kingdom should make at an early date a comprehensive announcement as to its intentions respecting the import of wheat into India from overseas, which, at present, are not understood in India."[24]

Priority: Win the War

In September 1943, when the Churchill and the Cabinet learned the worst about the Bengal famine, the U-boat war was still raging in the Atlantic, threatening Britain's lifeline. The Russians had defeated the Germans at Kursk and the Americans had vanquished the Japanese at Guadalcanal, Arthur Herman noted,

> but both remained deadly opponents. Japan was still poised on the border of India, where a massive uprising instigated by Gandhi against British rule had just been suppressed. Meanwhile, America and Britain were bracing for their impending landings in Italy [Chapter 26]. How likely was it that Churchill would respond to the news of the Bengal famine—the seriousness of which was yet unrealized … as anything more than an unwelcome distraction? Leo Amery ultimately understood this. In a note to Wavell after D-Day, he wrote: "Winston, in his position, will naturally run any risk rather than one which immediately affects the great military stakes to which we are committed."[25]

Remarkably, and despite his reputation as a humanitarian, Gandhi expressed little interest in the Bengal famine. "The issue barely comes up in his letters, except as another grievance against the Raj—which, in peacetime, had always handled famines with efficiency," wrote Arthur Herman. "In February 1944 Gandhi wrote Wavell: 'I know that millions outside are starving for want of food. But I should feel utterly helpless if I went out and missed the food [i.e., independence] by which alone living becomes worthwhile.'"[26]

Gandhi's admirers would say, rightly, that his genius was his ability to focus on his main goal to the exclusion of everything else. May we not say the same of Churchill? Her father would do "anything" to win the war, Mary Soames mused—"and at the time, nobody knew if we were going to win."[27] Yet despite all his concerns about winning the war, Churchill repeatedly took measures, appointed people, and issued instructions to alleviate as best he could the famine in Bengal.

There is no doubt in those fraught months Churchill said things off the record about India and Indians that were unworthy of him. In the debates over what to do in November 1943, for example, he supposedly said Indians "breed like rabbits." Again, the facts are somewhat different. That comment was by Amery in his diary: "Winston, after a preliminary flourish on Indians breeding like rabbits and being paid a million a day by us for doing nothing about the war, asked Leathers for his view."[28] So, after spouting about the Indians, he asked his transport minister how they could be sent food.

Churchill probably did say something like this. He often sounded off privately, about all his allies at one time or another, when he was exhausted, frustrated or unhappy. Unfortunately for him, Amery wrote down every angry word—and the revisionists have made Churchill pay. But there is *no* evidence that Churchill wished any Indian to starve; and manifold evidence that, on the contrary, amidst a war to the death, he did his best to help them.

29

The Brain in Spain
Was Absent from the Plane

**The Myth: Churchill Sent Leslie Howard
to Keep Franco Out of the War**

In 2008 the *Daily Telegraph* (London) reported that British actor Leslie Howard, whose aircraft was shot down returning to Britain from Spain on 5 June 1943, was on a secret mission for Churchill. Howard (famous through *Gone with the Wind, Berkeley Square* and *The Scarlet Pimpernel*) had allegedly been sent to Spain by the Prime Minister to prevent Spain's dictator Francisco Franco from joining the Axis powers.[1]

The *Telegraph* was describing a concurrent conspiracy theory by Madrid journalist José Rey-Ximena,[2] claiming that Howard, with the help of his former lover, Conchita Montenegro, secretly met with Franco on Churchill's behalf. Montenegro told the story in an interview before she died in 2007 at the age of 96. She claimed she had had an affair with Howard after the pair had starred together in *Never the Twain Shall Meet* (1931).

As the story goes, Montenegro later married a senior member of the far-right Falangist Party and, using her husband's influence, arranged the meeting with Howard. But Howard was unable to report the results to Churchill because his plane, a BOAC DC-3, was shot down by the Luftwaffe, en route to Plymouth from Lisbon. "He has never been recognised as either a spy or as a hero," said Rey-Ximena.[3]

This story is remindful of Churchill's "secret peace offers to Mussolini" (Chapter 20) which alas are at the bottom of Lake Como where nobody can read them. But new legends and stories are always worth following up, with the help of capable authorities. One has only to ask.

David Stafford, a leading scholar of Churchill and Secret Intelligence, replied:

> I myself would never trust an ageing "luvvie," however glamorous and seductive a past she enjoyed, as an independent historical source. Besides, by 1943 Franco needed *no* persuading not to join Hitler; the Allies had landed in North Africa in November 1942 and the wily Franco could see the way the pendulum was swinging. I think this is complete fantasy.[4]

Churchill's official biographer, Martin Gilbert, replied:

> It sounds absurd to me. It is the year that is wrong. In *The Churchill Documents* I identify Juan March, in a note from Churchill to Admirals Phillips and Godfrey, as capable of playing an important role "in bringing about friendly relations with Spain…." The note anticipated Churchill's meeting

with Juan March at 5 p.m. that afternoon. But the date was 26 September 1939! And Churchill's main man in Spain was Hillgarth.[5]

Captain Alan Hillgarth, Naval Attaché in Madrid (1939–43) and Chief of British Naval Intelligence, Eastern Theatre (1944–46), has several entries in *The Churchill Documents*. On 29 April 1941 Churchill minuted Eden: "The basis of Captain Hillgarth's policy is of the most secret character, and cannot possibly be mentioned." Gilbert explains that "Hillgarth had been personally charged by Churchill, at the end of May 1940, with the task of keeping Spain out of the war. To this end Churchill had allocated $10 million (to be held in the United States) for the necessary payments to Spanish officials, primarily senior army officers."[6] The Hillgarth references clearly show that Churchill's concern about Spain joining Hitler peaked in 1939–41. Although Franco continued to worry the Americans, concern about him among the British was virtually non-existent by 1943. Rey-Ximena's theory doesn't even pass the logic test. Given the ongoing role of Hillgarth, if Churchill wanted someone to pry Franco loose from an unexpected lurch to the Axis in 1943, why would he send a film actor?

Mistaken Identities Not

A parallel and contemporary conspiracy theory arose out of Churchill's movements at the time. The Prime Minister was in Algiers on 4 June, planning to return to England the next day. In 2006 a British television production, "Churchill's Bodyguard," based on Tom Hickman's book by the same title, speculated that the Germans thought the plane they were shooting at contained Churchill and his bodyguard, Walter Thompson.[7]

According to the documentary, Howard had a business manager, Alfred Chenhalls, who closely resembled Churchill and affected similar clothing, including a Homburg hat. German spies believed Churchill was returning from North Africa in a flying boat, refueling in Lisbon and flying home to Plymouth—the route chosen, to their misfortune, by Howard and Chenhalls. Linda Stokes, Thompson's great-niece, even asserted that Howard and Chenhalls were "doubles," purposely used to throw the Germans off Churchill's trail. (Churchill had actually flown to Gibraltar in his Lancaster bomber; since the weather was bad, he continued on to England in that aircraft, rather than the flying boat he had intended to use.)[8]

Churchill himself wrote of the incident: "The brutality of the Germans was only matched by the stupidity of their agents. It is difficult to understand how anyone could imagine that with all the resources of Great Britain at my disposal I should have booked a passage in an unarmed and unescorted plane from Lisbon and flown home in broad daylight." Churchill had arrived in England without incident; he described the fate of Howard and his companions as a "painful shock," but blamed it only on "the inscrutable workings of Fate."[9]

Conspiracists maintained that Churchill was trying hard to cover his tracks in his memoirs—that Howard and his companions had been "sacrificed" to protect the Prime Minister. But Sir Laurence Olivier, a friend of Leslie Howard's, had replied to that notion years earlier: "Whatever [Churchill's] faults may have been, he was anything but a moral coward; he would never have condoned the killing of another person to save his own skin."[10]

Professor M.R.D. Foot, the Oxford scholar who wrote the official history of the Special Operations Executive in France, offered "a more banal but more plausible" reason for the destruction of Leslie Howard's aircraft:

> Another of the passengers in Howard's plane, also killed, was Wilfred Israel, the Jewish owner of a large department store in prewar Berlin, who happened to have a British as well as a German passport, and had so escaped from Germany. He had been in Lisbon, pursuing work to rescue Jewish children from the Nazis' clutches. He had long been on the Gestapo's black list. German secret service officers watched all departures from Lisbon airport from the airport cafe, which overlooked the boarding point. It is not hard to assume that one of them recognised Israel and rang up a friend in the Luftwaffe.[11]

Professor Foot's theory is logical, but the real explanation may be even more prosaic. *Oberleutnant* Herbert Hintze, leader of the Bordeaux-based *14 Staffeln*, said his fighter group shot down the DC-3 because it was "an enemy aircraft"—that the plane was civilian seemed to make no difference. Hintze did add that his pilots "were angry that the Luftwaffe had not informed them of a scheduled flight between Lisbon and the UK. Had they known, they could easily have escorted the DC-3 to Bordeaux and captured it and all aboard."[12] If they really expected Churchill to be aboard, surely this would have been the order. Another *Staffel* pilot was more categorical: "Whatever crossed our path was shot down."[13]

Franco and the Axis

The time Churchill worried about Franco joining the Axis was 1940, not 1943. He summarized that earlier concern in a speech to Parliament on 24 May 1944. In 1940, he said, it seemed almost certain that Spain would follow Italy and join the Germans. Hitler had proposed "triumphal marches" of Wehrmacht troops in Spanish cities, and Churchill had "no doubt" they had planned to seize Gibraltar, "which would then be handed back to a Germanized Spain."

If Spain had yielded to German blandishments, Churchill said, "our burden would have been much heavier." Access to the Mediterranean, Malta and Suez would have been cut off; German U-boats would have new bases along the Spanish coasts. Churchill credited his ambassador to Madrid, Sir Samuel Hoare, for influencing Franco to remain neutral. But the main reason, he averred, was owed to Spain's resolve to avoid hostilities: "They had had enough of war, and they wished to keep out of it."[14]

30

The Destruction of Monte Cassino

The Myth: Churchill Said Nothing
About Destroying the Historic Abbey

In 2013 an Italian journalist wrote me to ask why Churchill was silent about the bombing of Italy's historic Monte Cassino Abbey on 15 February 1944. "Churchill said nothing," he stated, although Roosevelt "tried to explain it in a White House press conference by revealing an Eisenhower letter about Italian historical monuments and military necessity." Churchill said nothing of the Abbey in his speech in Parliament on 22 February, "although he went into great detail about the Italian military and political situation.[1] As far as I know," he continued:

> Churchill described the Monte Cassino bombing only after the war, in his memoirs, *The Second World War*: "The monastery dominated the whole battlefield, and naturally General Freyberg, the Corps Commander concerned, wished to have it heavily bombarded from the air before he launched the infantry attack. The Army Commander, General Mark Clark, unwillingly sought and obtained permission from General Alexander, who accepted the responsibility."[2] This is very different from what Mark Clark claimed in his book, *Calculated Risk*. Clark wrote that the bombing was a "tragic mistake." This was echoed in the U.S. Army official history by Martin Blumenson, whose account was based on the diary of Gen. Alfred Gruenther, Clark's chief of staff.[3]

As Chapter 27 established, Churchill was the only wartime leader on either side to question the morality of bombing non-military targets—and even some military ones. During attacks on French railway marshaling yards in advance of D-Day he wrote to Eden: "Terrible things are being done." To Air Chief Marshal Tedder he said, "You are piling up an awful load of hatred."[4] Churchill's discomfort over bombing is the starting point in considering how he felt about Monte Cassino Abbey. He did not question its bombing on moral grounds—it was hardly an example of mass civilian slaughter, like Dresden—because he considered it a military target. He was not, however, silent, and he did question the necessity.

The Obstacle

In October 1943, with the U.S. Fifth Army threatening their Gustav Line, the Germans evacuated most of Monte Cassino's monks and art treasures. Turning over crates of artworks to the Vatican, they assured the Pope that the abbey would not be fortified or used for military purposes. The Americans promised that it would not be attacked from the air. In retrospect, though an obstacle to allied progress, it was not itself of strategic importance, surrounded as it was by even higher peaks.

By early 1944, however, reports circulated that the Germans were making military use of Monte Cassino after all. The British and American press wrote of observation posts and artillery positions inside the abbey—information, it now appears, that was considerably embellished.[5] Lieutenant General Ira Eaker, Commander of Allied Air Forces Mediterranean, after a personal fly-over, reported "a radio mast [and] German uniforms hanging on a clothesline in the abbey courtyard; [and] machine gun emplacements fifty yards from the abbey walls."[6] It is likely that Eaker saw one of the many lightning rods with which the old building was equipped; he would have had to fly very close indeed to identify German uniforms. Maj. Gen. Geoffrey Keyes of the U.S. II Corps, who also flew over the monastery, saw no Germans, and caustically remarked of rival reports, "They've been looking so long they're seeing things."[7]

Hindsight moralizing is easy to do. In the fog of war, decisions are more haphazard, based less on certainty. What the Germans had at the abbey at any given time was irrelevant, said New Zealand General Howard Kippenberger:

> If not occupied today, it might be tomorrow and it did not appear it would be difficult for the enemy to bring reserves into it during an attack, or for troops to take shelter there if driven from positions outside…. Smashed by bombing, it was a jagged heap of broken masonry and debris, open to effective fire from guns, mortars and strafing planes, as well as being a death trap if bombed again. On the whole I thought it would be more useful to the Germans if we left it unbombed.[8]

Whether the evidence, Kippenberger's reasoning prevailed. "The allied command declared that the abbey would no longer be spared," wrote Peter Calvocoressi and Guy Wint, "and although American, British and French generals opposed its bombardment it was attacked on 15 February by 142 Flying Fortresses and destroyed."[9]

Conspiracy of Silence?

Churchill was in touch with Roosevelt during the bombing of the monastery, but interest was focused elsewhere. At Anzio on the Italian west coast, where Allies had landed in January, the Germans had launched a counterattack. On 18 February, Churchill was grilled over Anzio during Question Time in the House of Commons. He was not happy. Despite American claims that they were doing all the fighting in Italy, he said, over 50,000 British and Commonwealth troops were engaged. Private secretary John Colville reflected his off-the-record view: "Actually it is the unenterprising behaviour of the American Command at Anzio that has lost us our great opportunity there."[10]

German propaganda made the most of the Monte Cassino's destruction, mentioning the art treasures the Germans had "saved" the previous October. Parliament took up the question of the moral implications. Given what most members, including Churchill said, we have a clear picture of how the British regarded the issues *at the time*—which may differ from how we regard it in hindsight.

The day after the bombing, in the House of Lords, Viscount Simon quoted Churchill directly. While admitting that there was "no excuse" for thinking that works of art didn't matter, Churchill had said,

> it is universally accepted and everywhere understood that the necessities of war must be put far in front of any consideration of special historical or cultural value at all ... the necessity of getting victory—victory as complete and as quickly as possible—make it ridiculous to compare the needs of that claimant with any artistic or cultural matter whatever.[11]

Simon then quoted Eisenhower's order for troops in the Italian Campaign (undoubtedly the same one quoted by Roosevelt at his Washington press conference): "If we have to choose between destroying a famous building and sacrificing our own men, then our men's lives count infinitely more and the buildings must go."[12]

Four days later in Parliament, Churchill himself said: "The bitterness and fierceness of the fighting now going on both in the bridgehead and at the Cassino front surpass all previous experience."[13] If that was the case—and it was—it seems logical that he would not want to wade into the bombing debate, a relative side issue.

Another MP spoke for the majority by saying that day:

> We ought not to have thought about ancient monuments or anything like that. If it is a matter of military tactics to get our men through, then warn the people to get out and get on with the job....
> When our men are fighting and sacrificing everything and then we say, "We cannot attack a certain place because of its historical value," and we sacrifice men's lives because of that, I claim that that is wrong to the men we are asking to give so much to the nation.[14]

The giving continued. On 7 March the Secretary of State for War Sir Percy Grigg was asked if the Abbey was yet occupied by Allied troops. Grigg replied, "No, Sir."[15]

Churchill questioned the targeting of Monte Cassino on March 20th, when he telegraphed General Alexander, the Allied commander in Italy: "I wish you would explain to me why this passage by Cassino Monastery Hill, all on a front of two or three miles, is the only place which you must keep butting at.... It seems very hard to understand why this most strongly defended point is the only passage forward." Alexander's reply, Churchill wrote, was "lucid and convincing": Along the whole Italian battle front, there was

> only Liri Valley leading direct to Rome which is suitable terrain for deployment of our superiority in artillery and armour. The main highway known as route six is [the] only road except cart-tracks which lead from the mountains where we are into Liri valley over Rapido river and this exit into plain is blocked and dominated by Monte Cassino on which stands the Monastery.[16]

We may choose to reject Alexander's conclusions—but this was what he believed *at the time.*

Monte Cassino was again on Churchill's mind in April. On the 12th he told Marshall: "Although the fighting at [Anzio] and the Cassino front has brought many disappointments," Hitler had admitted that it had tied down thirty-five German divisions.[17] When the Abbey was finally occupied, on 18 May, Churchill told Stalin it was "a trophy." Always ready to have his little dig, he informed the Soviet leader, who often disparaged the Poles and French, that they had fought outstandingly.[18]

The Real Sacrilege

At Question Time on 6 June, an MP asked whether the Prime Minister "will consider the complete restoration of the Abbey of Monte Cassino as a memorial to the heroes who fell in storming it, and at the expense of Germany, as a necessary part of her reparations after this war." In Churchill's absence, Deputy Prime Minister Attlee replied that it was "premature to consider such proposals."[19] (The rebuilt Abbey was consecrated by Pope Paul VI in 1964, and is surrounded by war graves. Memorials to the fallen also stand in Rome and Warsaw.)

The question tells us how Britons felt about the bombing in its immediate aftermath. They felt even worse in October, when War Minister Grigg announced that German soldiers had looted churches and art treasures throughout Italy virtually at will. While they had claimed to have moved Monte Cassino's treasures out of harm's way, they had actually engaged in systematic looting.

Before the battle, Grigg explained, the Germans had proudly described

the handing-over of so much treasure to the keeping of the Vatican authorities…. [But] of the 187 crates removed from Monte Cassino, only 172 were delivered to the Vatican; fifteen were retained by the Germans. And of the 172 crates, some had been opened (and opened by people who had the inventories at their disposal and knew very well what they were doing) and the best of their contents removed, generally to be replaced by something that the experts did not consider worth taking.[20]

A long list of treasures followed.

Retrospective

The disappointments of Monte Cassino added to the burdens of war. "PM this morning confessed he was tired," Alexander Cadogan noted in his diary on 21 March 1944: "He's almost done in." Harold Nicolson wrote on the 27th: "I am sickened by the absence of gratitude towards him. The fact is that the country is terribly war-weary, and the ill-success of Anzio and Cassino is for them a sad augury of what will happen when the Second Front begins."[21]

The story of Monte Cassino was revived in Parliament in 2001, in a debate over the bombing of civilians and bridges in Kosovo. The abbey, exclaimed Lord Howell, "was believed to contain munitions; instead it contained priceless books and frightened monks. That was a direct and intentional attack on a civilian objective." Lord Archer interjected: "It was thought to be a military objective." Well, replied Howell, "one person's military objective is another person's precious civilian site or institution. It is inevitable that there will be a difference of view."[22]

There is always a difference in view, except when you are trying to win a bloody war. Lord Howell had not read his history. There were few monks left when the abbey was bombed; if the Germans left any priceless books when they ransacked the place, they must have been interested in larger treasures; all responsible commanders in 1944 thought the monastery was a military objective.

It is fair to consider Monte Cassino as a sorry milestone in a major campaign that helped to end a terrible war. Perhaps there was another way around it, by which the fine old building might not have been destroyed. Postwar investigations ultimately concluded that at the time of the bombing, the abbey was probably unoccupied by the Germans.[23] That does not obviate General Kippenberger's argument that it could have easily been reoccupied and used offensively any time, or that commanders *at the time* thought there was no other way to move the campaign forward.

The leveling of this historic and religious symbol was regrettable. So was the destruction of Coventry Cathedral by the Luftwaffe in November 1940. War is hell, which is why we try so hard to avoid it. But it is wrong to say Churchill was silent over the fate of Monte Cassino.

31

What to Do About Auschwitz?

The Myth: Churchill Did Nothing to Stop the Holocaust

"War is mainly a catalogue of blunders," Churchill wrote.[1] Once the signal is given, a war leader is "no longer the master of policy but the slave of unforeseeable and uncontrollable events. Antiquated War Offices, weak, incompetent or arrogant Commanders, untrustworthy allies, hostile neutrals, malignant Fortune, ugly surprises, awful miscalculations—all take their seat at the Council Board...."[2] The failure to act, when action would seem in hindsight imperative, is often laid at the feet of statesman, and Churchill is no exception, particularly when he led Britain in World War II.

Churchill's most heinous inaction, according to many critics, was failing to bomb Auschwitz, the notorious Nazi death camp—or at least the rail lines leading to it from Hungary, where Jews were being shipped by the thousands. Serious opinion on both sides of the issue agrees that Churchill received confirmation of the full extent of the Holocaust too late to halt most of the exterminations. The controversy is over what he did or did not do when he learned of it, particularly concerning Auschwitz.

The Sum of All Fears

Rumors of what was happening in German concentration camps had circulated from early in the war. But it was not until mid–June 1944 that five escapees from Auschwitz brought concrete evidence which transformed Allied awareness of the nature of Nazi atrocities. Churchill received the details on 27 June 1944, through a telegram from Richard Lichtheim, a German Zionist in Switzerland, forwarded to the War Cabinet by the British legation in Berne. Lichtheim reported that nearly half of the 800,000 Jews in Hungary had been deported "to the death camp of Birkenau," where in the past year over 1.5 million European Jews had been killed. He offered detailed reports on four crematoriums which, in the event, were shown to be gassing and burning 12,000 Jews per day.[3] The same week, this news was reported by the *Manchester Guardian*.

Churchill immediately minuted Foreign Secretary Anthony Eden: "What can be done? What can be said?"[4] Amid the horrific facts, confusion reigned. The Jewish Agency in London even pondered an offer from Adolf Eichmann, a leading organizer of the "Final Solution," who had proposed to trade surviving Jews for military equipment: "I

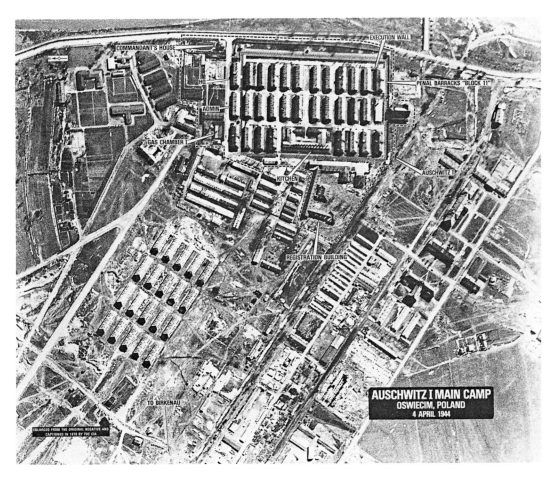

COMMANDANT'S HOUSE · EXECUTION WALL · HQ · PENAL BARRACKS "BLOCK 11" · ADMIN · GAS CHAMBER I · KITCHEN · AUSCHWITZ I · REGISTRATION BUILDING · TO BIRKENAU · ENLARGED FROM THE ORIGINAL NEGATIVE AND CAPTIONED IN 1978 BY THE CIA

AUSCHWITZ I MAIN CAMP
OSWIECIM, POLAND
4 APRIL 1944

Auschwitz: what Allied reconnaissance saw. Overflight photo from 1944 (U.S. Army Air Corps).

am prepared to sell you all the Jews. I am also prepared to have them all annihilated." Eichmann expressed himself indifferent: "It is as you wish."[5]

Even by then, Churchill had incomplete information about the extent of the killings. But his reaction was unequivocal:

> There is no doubt that this is probably the greatest and most horrible crime ever committed in the whole history of the world, and it has been done by scientific machinery by nominally civilised men in the name of a great State and one of the leading races in Europe. It is quite clear that all concerned in this crime who may fall into our hands, including the people who only obeyed orders by carrying out the butcheries, should be put to death after their association with the murders has been proved.[6]

A week after the Lichtheim telegram, Churchill and Eden received a report from the five escapees themselves. Their concern and that of the Jewish Agency was that deportations of Hungarian Jews were still going on. Two days later Chaim Weizmann and Moshe Shertok, the two senior Zionists in Britain, made five urgent requests. The first four were: (1) an Allied declaration of readiness to admit Jewish refugees; (2) issuance of protective documents for Budapest Jews by nations with embassies there; (3) an Anglo-American warning that any Hungarians involved in deporting Jews would be considered war criminals; (4) a similar warning by Stalin. The British government acceded immediately. Churchill himself drafted a declaration for Stalin to issue.

The fifth and key request by Weizmann and Shertok was that the railway lines leading from Budapest to Birkenau, and perhaps even the death camp itself, should be bombed. When Churchill read this, said Martin Gilbert,

> he did something I've not seen on any other document submitted to Churchill for his approval: He wrote on it what he wanted done. Normally, he would have said, "Bring this up to War Cabinet on Wednesday," or, "Let us discuss this with the Air Ministry." Instead, he wrote to Eden on the morning of 7 July: "Is there any reason to raise this matter with the Cabinet? Get anything out of the Air Force you can, and invoke me if necessary." I have never seen a minute of Churchill's giving that sort of immediate authority to carry out a request.[7]

Eden immediately conveyed Churchill's order to Minister of Air Archibald Sinclair, asking him what would be done. On 15 July—with a lack of celerity we may regret and even deplore—Sinclair replied. Destroying the railways, he wrote, was "out of our power"; it had been accomplished in Normandy only by "enormous concentration" of bombers, and at much shorter range from airbases. Bombing Auschwitz by night (the RAF's usual mission) was similarly impossible. Daytime bombing (the U.S. Army Air Force's usual mission) would be "costly and hazardous." But Sinclair would be happy to pass the query to Americans. "A characteristically unhelpful letter," Eden noted. "He wasn't asked his opinion of this; he was asked to act."[8]

U.S. Undersecretary of War John J. McCloy, the American to whom the request was then passed, had actually been approached earlier by Jewish leaders who asked him authorize bombing the railway lines from Hungary. He had refused. He would again. In all, five separate requests to bomb Auschwitz or its rail lines reached McCloy's desk. Each was denied. After the fifth request, in August, McCloy explained that bombing could only be done by diverting essential air support from current operations. Even then it would be of "doubtful efficacy." It might provoke "even more vindictive action by the Germans."[9] It is hard to conceive of more vindictive action.

A frequent argument against bombing Auschwitz itself was made by Jews themselves. One was Leon Kubowitzki, head of the Rescue Department of the World Jewish Congress. Unbeknown to McCloy, Kubowtzki argued that destruction from the air meant that "the first victims would be the Jews who are gathered in these camps."[10]

Kubowitzki's alternative was to despatch paratroopers to seize the camps and liberate the inmates. But where would they go? This was not clear, nor were the available resources at hand. Bombing Auschwitz would certainly mean death for most inmates, which had to be juxtaposed with saving future victims who had not yet arrived. There was also the question of whether the Germans would simply rebuild the death camp, or transport Jews to another one. The options were difficult to measure, the available information sparse and vague, the choices appalling.

The Mythology of Auschwitz

The evidence of Churchill's concern and urge to act seems plain, but he has his critics. The most eloquent of these, Michael J. Cohen, leveled several charges against Churchill and his biographer.[11] Cohen quoted Churchill's striking July 7th order as "get what you can out of the RAF," omitting Churchill's two imprecations: invoke his name, and bypass the War Cabinet. Discounting Churchill's description of "the greatest and most horrible crime in the whole history of the world," Cohen said those words were simply retreaded from something Churchill said about Turkish massacres of Armenians. No such earlier quotation can be found anywhere among Churchill's writings or papers.

Cohen did not credit Churchill for granting the Jewish Agency's first four requests, which certainly influenced the Hungarians and unquestionably saved Jewish lives. He rightly pointed out that Auschwitz continued to murder people for months after deportations from Hungary ended. In August, for example, thousands of Jews from the Lodz ghetto were deported to Auschwitz, where more than half were immediately gassed. According to Gilbert, nothing was known of these Lodz deportations, nor of trainloads from Rhodes and other places, until weeks later. But enough was known about further deportations to Auschwitz, Gilbert adds, "to stimulate a further Jewish request for the bombing of he camps ... on August 8, when the World Jewish Congress appealed to the War Refugee Board in Washington...."[12] This was the fifth and final request that John McCloy denied, as noted above.

The day after the Jewish Agency's five requests, July 8th Churchill was prodding Eden for a "tripartite declaration" by the Allies: "I am entirely in accord with making the biggest outcry possible." Two days later, he was pressing for a Jewish Brigade Group, something he campaigned for and finally saw accomplished in October.[13] Cohen ignored these evidences of Churchill's continued concern and claimed instead that he actually "turned down the bombing project" in letters to the Archbishop of Canterbury and Lord Melchett on 13 July.

The facts are very different, as one may learn by reviewing the actual letters. There is nothing in either letter about "turning down" the bombing. Churchill wrote Melchett and the Archbishop "that the most earnest consideration has been given by my colleagues and myself to this matter and to the question whether any action is open that might stay the criminals." He added, correctly, that the "principal hope" of Jews and other victims of Nazism was "the speedy victory of the Allied Nations."[14] This cannot be interpreted as a point-blank refusal to bomb Auschwitz or its rail lines—particularly since Churchill would not have the Air Ministry's appraisal for another four days.

While Professor Cohen agreed that deportations of Jews from Hungary ceased on 9 July, he alleged that the deportations from elsewhere, which cost 150,000 lives between July and November, "never occurred to Churchill." Yet in October 1944, when reports of continued murders reached him, Churchill wrote to Eden: "Surely publicity given about this might have a chance of saving the multitudes concerned."[15] The Soviets had demurred, furious over charges of Red Army massacres of Poles in the Katyn Forest. Anglo-American joint warnings were again issued, and to everyone's surprise, Berlin responded: "These reports are false from beginning to end." (If you're going to lie, lie big.)

Six months later, the extent of the Holocaust was being discovered by advancing Allied troops. Churchill wrote to his wife, who was in Moscow, of "the horrible revelations of German cruelty in the concentration camps." Eisenhower had asked for a visit by a Parliamentary delegation, he wrote: "They will go to the spot and see the horrors for themselves—a gruesome duty."[16]

The crucial days of June and July 1944, when news of the Holocaust was brought to London, were certainly replete with Churchill's descriptions of war: unforeseeable and uncontrollable events, untrustworthy allies, hostile neutrals, malignant fortune, ugly surprises and awful miscalculation. Whatever we may think of the decision not to bomb

Auschwitz or its rail lines, it was *not* based on Allied attitudes toward the Jews, but on military priorities and resources.

When Churchill first heard of the massacres, the most pressing Allied challenge was not Auschwitz. It was the break-out from the Normandy beachhead, where invading armies had been tied down, having not yet reached Caen and St. Lô. It would be ten more days before St. Lô fell and the armies could begin their advance across France. At home, Churchill faced another massacre, of British civilians from Hitler's flying bombs. No one at the time knew whether these were a feeble, last-ditch effort or the harbinger of a new form of mass destruction from the air. Churchill was not, as some of his supporters like to believe, all-prescient and all-knowing. But it is unfair to believe that he did not do all he could in response to the horror of Auschwitz.

32

Feeding the Oppressed

The Myth: Churchill Wished to Starve Occupied Europe

It is sometimes suggested that Churchill wanted to withhold food and medical aid to Nazi-occupied countries in order to spark revolts against the Germans, while President Roosevelt insisted on shipping aid to the needy. This claim emerged during the war, as Americans debated sending food to the oppressed, and learned that it was neither American nor British policy to do so. But it is an inaccurate interpretation of Churchill's and Roosevelt's views.[1]

From the Fall of France, Churchill wanted food shipments prioritized for countries still actively fighting Germany, ahead of countries already occupied by the Germans. By late 1940, the only Europeans still in the fight were the British and Greeks. Churchill did favor an exception for Spain, suggesting to Roosevelt in late 1940: "An offer by you to dole out food month by month so long as they keep out of the war might be decisive."[2]

In his reply Roosevelt added Vichy France to the possible food recipients, "for humanitarian and also political reasons," proposing to send "limited quantities of milk and vitamin concentrates for children" through the Red Cross to "unoccupied France and likewise, of course to Spain." Roosevelt assured Churchill that he had "not the slightest intention of undertaking any policy which would weaken or militate against the efficacy of the British blockade. It is Germany's responsibility to feed those in territories occupied by German forces...."[3] He admitted that distinguishing between occupied and unoccupied France would be difficult, though it was his hope—forlorn, as it proved—to try to pry "neutral" Vichy away from its German masters.

Churchill cautiously agreed to humanitarian relief shipments to Vichy, but asked for strict adherence to the conditions and assurances from FDR, and Vichy, acknowledging "the cooperation of His Majesty's Government...." He had no objection to saying the food relief was a U.S. initiative, Churchill wrote; but "we would like it stated that the relief goods are available only by good will of His Majesty's Government."[4]

Thereafter, relief became caught in the politics of Vichy neutrality. I could find no documents wherein Churchill argued that humanitarian relief should be withheld from unoccupied France. In 1940–41, Roosevelt and Churchill rejected food shipments to *occupied lands*—as the Belgians quickly learned when Paul-Henri Spaak, foreign minister in the exiled Belgian government, pleaded with Roosevelt for food aid to Belgium:

Spaak "exerted all my powers of persuasion to interest him in the fate of my compatriots." Roosevelt, he said, reacted coldly, without "warmth or compassion." Belgium's trials were not so tragic, FDR said. After all, Germany had gone through much the same food shortages after World War I, "and had yet produced a generation that was physically fit; the proof of this could be seen in the way the Germans were now fighting."[5]

As the Battle of the Atlantic took its toll on Britain's food shipments and strained the Royal Navy's resources, Churchill worried about the President's desire to aid Vichy. "We fear very much prolongation of the war and its miseries which would result from breakdown of blockade of Germany, and there are immense difficulties in preventing Germany from profiting directly or indirectly from anything imported into unoccupied France," he wrote Roosevelt in March 1941.

> Dealing with [Admiral] Darlan is dealing with Germany, for he will not be allowed to agree to anything they know about which does not suit their book. Also there is the danger of rationing spreading to occupied France, Belgium, Holland, and Norway.... It would be easier for you to talk to Vichy, with whom you are in regular diplomatic relations, than for us to negotiate via Madrid or by making speeches on broadcast. Besides this, Darlan has old scores to pay out against us in the dire action we were forced to take against his ships.[6]

In November 1942, U.S. Secretary of State Cordell Hull asked Churchill for assurance, which he gave, that Britain was in agreement with the U.S. on maintaining a strict blockade of enemy territory. "The single exception is Greece," Churchill reminded the President, where "the enemy allowed wholesale starvation conditions to develop."[7]

Roosevelt suggested that food aid to be extended to occupied Norway. Churchill resisted, reminding FDR of his policy toward Belgium:

> Conditions in Belgium are worse than in Norway and in our judgment it would not be right to make a concession to Norway and not to Belgium.... We have resisted extremely strong pressure from the Belgian Government and others to depart from [your policy]. To abandon the principle that the enemy is responsible for the territories he has conquered will lead very quickly to our having the whole lot on our backs, a burden far beyond our strength. In our view the plan you propose might therefore have the eventual effect of reversing our whole joint food blockade policy, and this, I am sure you will agree, we should not contemplate.[8]

Churchill did offer Roosevelt an idea to aid "our Norwegian friends without dangerous repercussions." In agreement with the Norwegian exiled government, the British would surreptitiously supply Norway limited quantities of supplies disguised as imports from Gothenburg, [Göteborg], to be distributed secretly in Norway: "We are also anxious to proceed with plans for the evacuation of Norwegian, Belgian, and other children to Sweden and Switzerland respectively, where they could be maintained by extra imports through the blockade."[9]

With the ring tightening on Nazi Germany in late 1943, Churchill again raised his concern over Allied food supplies, particularly with the ongoing famines in Greece and India (Chapter 28). In September, when the Bengal famine began, he wrote to Minister of Food Lord Woolton and Hugh Dalton at the Board of Trade: "It seems clear that there may be a world shortage of many important foodstuffs." It was critical, Churchill said, to avoid commitments to "any estimates of relief requirements, which might prejudice our own supplies, before the Cabinet has had an opportunity of discussing the whole question."[10]

As the Anglo-Americans prepared for D-Day in June 1944, Roosevelt decided the time had come for a more liberal policy: "limited feeding programs for children and nursing and expectant mothers in the German-occupied countries of Europe ... initially in Belgium, France, the Netherlands, and Norway. I bespeak your most earnest consideration of this proposal," he wrote Churchill. "I am convinced that the time has arrived when the continued withholding of food from these categories of the populations of the occupied countries is likely to hurt our friends more than our enemies...."[11]

In a letter which critics say displays his inhuman nature, Churchill rejected the President's proposal. While he shared FDR's desire to ease the burden on the peoples of occupied Europe, Churchill said it was "difficult to accept the view that the maintenance of our blockade policy is likely to hurt our friends more than our enemies." Less widely quoted than this part of his message was his explanation: "Our experience of the working of the Greek relief scheme has conclusively shown that it causes considerable difficulties for, and imposes restrictions on, our naval and air forces." Opening the necessary channels of transportation into Europe with D-Day pending would, Churchill added, "be wholly incompatible with the naval and military situation." Keeping the necessary ports and railways open, given the ongoing invasion, "would clearly be impossible."[12]

Roosevelt accepted Churchill's veto: "While I remain of the opinion that it would be humane and wise.... I am in complete agreement with you that nothing should be done that will interfere with or hamper forthcoming operations."[13] It is important to note that intelligence reports available to both leaders indicated that short rations did not damage enemy morale, and that the embargo and blockade on relief to occupied countries was, by 1944, of little strategic value. It has been said that Churchill, by holding back relief to countries like Belgium, hoped to create conditions so bad that the Belgians would revolt. There no indication in the documents that Churchill ever mentioned this, or that he incited the Belgians to rebel. Churchill was not that jaded, but he also knew that such a revolt, unlikely as it was, would be crushed like an eggshell by Nazi and Gestapo enforcers. Nor was there any indication that the Belgians had the stomach for it.

The charges leveled at Churchill, and to a lesser degree Roosevelt, for failing to send food aid to occupied Europe, is remindful of the "Auschwitz argument" (Chapter 31), that liberation would be quicker and more effective than dealing with the immediate situation: a permanent solution is better than a short-term prophylactic. This was no comfort, of course, to the inmates of Auschwitz, or the starving mothers of Belgium.

To the extent that Franklin Roosevelt comes out of this episode looking more humane than Churchill, it is because he did, in one instance in 1944, support food shipments to Belgium, the Netherlands and Norway, while Churchill, following the advice of his military, did not. The blockade of Nazi-occupied Europe was part of the war effort. Churchill objected in principle to sending food to countries occupied by the enemy, which were, he rightly maintained, the enemy's responsibility. An overt starvation campaign was not part of his strategy.

33

Spheres of Influence

The Myth: Churchill Sold Out Eastern Europe

At the Tolstoy conference in Moscow in October 1944, Churchill said to the Soviet dictator Josef Stalin, "Let us settle about our affairs in the Balkans." He then produced what he called a "naughty document," listing five Balkan countries and "percentages of interest" or spheres of influence by the great powers: Romania, Russia 90 percent, the others 10 percent; Greece, Great Britain in accord with USA 90 percent, Russia 10 percent; Yugoslavia and Hungary, 50–50 percent; Bulgaria, Russia 75 percent, the others 25 percent.[1]

As his words were translated, the Prime Minister pushed the paper across to Stalin who, without comment, "took his blue pencil and made a large tick upon it, and passed it back to us. It was all settled in no more time than it takes to set down." It might be thought cynical thus to have settled the fate of millions, Churchill thought: "Let us burn the paper." No, Stalin replied, "You keep it."[2] It exists today in Britain's National Archives.

The story sparks visions of fiefdom trade-offs between medieval potentates. To this day Westerners are shocked that Churchill would actually admit to such a bare-faced power scheme—but he did, in exquisite detail, in his war memoirs. He did not, however, tell all. The day after their meeting, he sent a draft of their discussion to Stalin, who struck out all references to the spheres of influence.[3] Stalin's "tick," of course, could have meant anything; certainly it did not signify formal agreement, and the Soviet leader might not have wanted to acknowledge the arrangement.

The "naughty paper" was taken seriously enough by their two foreign ministers. Eden and Molotov haggled over the percentages "as though they were bargaining over a rug in a bazaar, with Molotov trying, eventually successfully, to trim Britain's figures."[4] But Eden never spoke of spheres of influence, considering the paper a mere "practical agreement on how problems would be worked out in each country ... general rather than precise."[5]

Three Dominant Facts

From this stark display of power politics a vast subtext has grown to support the idea of Churchill (and Roosevelt at Yalta), selling out the Balkans and eastern Europe

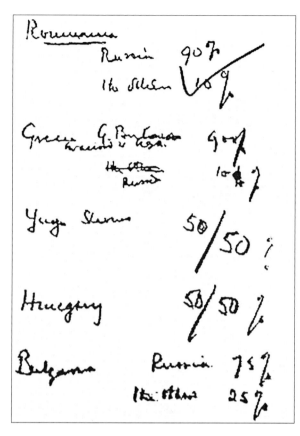

The "naughty paper": Churchill's handwriting, Stalin's checkmark (National Archives, PREM 3/66/7 [169]).

generally, leaving its peoples to a communized future. "Eastern Europeans do not look admiringly at Mr. Churchill," a descendant of one wrote me in 2015, "like my father, who fought with the British in his Polish uniform."[6] Being part-Latvian, I well understand that attitude, and have struggled with the same questions.

This is not the place for a detailed account of Churchill's and Roosevelt's actions over postwar Europe at the wartime summits ending in Yalta. Let us consider only the reasons for Churchill's outwardly shocking proposal, and what motivated it. The reader may judge whether or not Churchill did all he could have done on behalf of eastern Europe.

The Churchill scholar Larry Arnn lists three main facts about the Second World War which dominate our thinking in these matters, the first two unambiguous, the third deeply ambiguous. The first two were the emergence of an all-conquering Nazi Germany ("a bad fact") and the new relationship between Britain and the United States ("clearly, in Churchill's mind, a good fact … which would transform the world and ensure its security.")[7]

Arnn's third, ambiguous fact was cooperation with the Soviet Union, about which there are two important things to know: first, that the Soviet Union had been, until the very day of Hitler's attack on it, "one of the worst nations ever born"; second, and conversely, "it was the enemy of the Allies' enemy. Since that enemy was strong and fought well, Soviet participation in the war was fundamental to Allied strategy—the only strategy it was possible to conduct." Cooperation was necessary, "whether one likes it or not."[8]

Churchill was an eternal optimist. During the war, Arnn related, he observed Stalin celebrating Russian Orthodox clerics who had hitherto been proscribed, and touring the country making speeches about "Mother Russia." Churchill watched such developments and hoped they augured change: "It was not possible to know for sure what was going to happen in the Soviet Union after the war—no matter what Stalin said, or what Stalin had done in the past. One could only hope for the best. That was Churchill's attitude." We know also that World War II meant "a massive redefinition of world power. And there was not really very much that Churchill could do about those facts, except the best he could."[9]

The Outcome

In Bulgaria and Romania, ineffectual and unpopular monarchies were swept aside and those countries fell quickly behind what Churchill would later call the "iron curtain"; Britain didn't even have 10 percent influence. Bulgaria had been an Axis member early in the war, though it did not join Hitler's invasion of Russia and saved most of its Jews from annihilation. Czar Boris III abdicated after uprisings in mid–1943, leaving a power vacuum. When Bulgaria failed to expel the Germans in late 1944, Stalin declared war. The communist-dominated Fatherland Front expelled the Germans and made peace, and a one-party people's republic under Georgi Dimitrov was installed in 1946.[10]

In Romania, where he obtained a majority in fraudulent elections, Moscow-picked Gheorghe Gheorghiu-Dej forced the abdication of King Michael I in 1947, and proclaimed a people's republic.[11] Hungary, where Churchill had hoped for equal influence with Russia, was occupied by the Red Army in 1945. Stalin sent Mátyás Rákosi to head the Hungarian Communist Party, later the Hungarian Working People's Party; he remained the de facto ruler from 1949 to 1956.[12]

The percentages agreement did have some positive effects. Yugoslavia, one of the "50–50" countries, never aligned with Moscow. Under Tito, it was feisty and independent, and actually broke with Stalin over Greece. When civil war broke out in Greece, Tito joined Albania and Bulgaria in supporting the leftist National Liberation Front (EAM), and its military branch, the Greek People's Liberation Army (ELAS).[13] But Stalin stuck to his agreement with Churchill, who traveled personally to Athens to negotiate a truce at Christmas, 1944.

It is interesting that at this time Churchill's sense of betrayal was more toward Tito than Stalin. "Tito has turned very nasty," he wrote, and was thinking "of grabbing Trieste, Istria, Fiume, etc."[14] Churchill referred to the "naughty document" itself when he told Tito of an agreed Anglo-Soviet policy, "that our influence [in Yugoslavia] should be held on equal balance. But you seem to be treating us in an increasingly invidious fashion." "When you think what we have done for him," Churchill pouted to Eden.[15]

Greece

The Prime Minister's arrival in Athens to mediate the civil war was a tableau worthy of a Gilbert and Sullivan operetta, with all the Churchillian flourishes. Flying in on Christmas Day, he made his way to HMS *Ajax,* flagship of the British Mediterranean fleet, moored in Piraeus harbor and sporadically under fire from ELAS mortars. Dictating to his secretary during a near miss he shouted gaily, "There—you bloody well missed us! Come on—try again!"[16] He interviewed Georgios Papandreou, who had offered to form a unity government, and Archbishop Damaskinos, a hero of the Greek resistance, who had kept Jews out of Nazi clutches during the German occupation.

Arriving aboard *Ajax,* the towering Archbishop, even taller wearing his miter, was mistaken by sailors as a fellow celebrant of their fancy-dress Christmas party, and narrowly avoided being ritually tossed into the harbor. With a grin, Churchill described the Archbishop as a "scheming medieval prelate" and "pestilent priest from the Middle Ages"[17] He was just the man to serve as regent pending return of the King, whom the monarchist Churchill was sure would unify the country.

Later Churchill chaired a lantern-lit conference with the warring sides in Athens, with gunfire exploding all round, pounding home the need for a truce. He got one—only to return to face enormous criticism by left-wing Members of Parliament for reinstalling the King, and several raised eyebrows from Roosevelt. Stalin, true to the percentages agreement, said nothing.

Papandreou resigned in January, replaced by stolid General Plastiras, whom Churchill called "Plasterass." It was a rocky few years, with several failed peace treaties. In the end, ELAS gave up, demoralized by the split between their mentors, Tito and Stalin. Thus the ultimate effect of Churchill's "naughty paper" was a non-communist Greece, and an at least non-aligned Yugoslavia. Sometimes dirty deals actually work out for the best. In 1948 a communist uprising again threatened Greece—evidently Stalin had abrogated the "naughty paper" by then. President Truman invoked the Truman Doctrine, which saved Greece a second time.

Poland

Neither in the Balkans nor part of the percentages agreement, Poland was a special case. Britain had gone to war over Poland, and through 1944, Churchill accepted Stalin's promise to allow free elections there after the war. So hopeful was he that he accepted Stalin's demand to shift Poland west to encompass Silesia, leaving the eastern portion in Soviet hands—much to the outrage of the Polish exile government in London. Churchill thought this was a good trade: Britain had declared war and fought for the Poles to have "a proper land to live in," he told Eden, "but we have never undertaken to defend existing Polish frontiers."

After all, Churchill continued, Russia had undergone two wars costing 20–30 million Russian lives. The border shift left Poland "a fine seaboard and better territory than she had before. If she does not accept this, Britain has discharged to the full her obligations and the Poles can make their own arrangements with the Soviets."[18] Sir Owen O'Malley, British ambassador to the Polish exile government, called the new borders "morally indefensible." Churchill disagreed: "They are in my opinion no more than what is right and just for Russia, without whose prodigious exertions no vestige of Poland would remain free from German annihilation or subjugation."[19]

Demonstrably Churchill went as far as he could to appease Stalin and sell the border scheme to the Poles, but trouble rose quickly. In their Moscow meeting, and again at Yalta in February 1945, Stalin insisted on forming a provisional Polish government in Moscow, ignoring the exile government in London. Still, Stalin promised that the new Poland would be sovereign, with democratic elections. Churchill and Roosevelt returned from Yalta "whistling in the dark, trumpeting optimistic predictions that it heralded a new era."[20]

Two weeks after Yalta, Churchill said to his Cabinet: "Poor Neville Chamberlain believed he could trust Hitler. He was wrong, but I don't think I'm wrong about Stalin."[21] The Prime Minister was less certain than he sounded. A month earlier—two weeks *before* Yalta—he had said privately: "Make no mistake, all the Balkans, except Greece, are going to be Bolshevised; and there is nothing I can do to prevent it. There is nothing I can do for poor Poland either."[22]

His premonition proved sadly accurate. With the Red Army in absolute control of most of eastern Europe, there was nothing to be done. "Mr. Churchill had struggled to diminish totalitarian rule in Europe," said William Buckley, "which, however, increased."[23] That is a sad but incontrovertible fact. Churchill had done what he could, with the situation as it existed.

"Us" versus "Them"

It is possible to argue—and some have—that Churchill, with his cynical deal over Greece, was no better than the Russians over Poland: that after all, Churchill's main concern was British interests in Greece, just as Stalin's was Russian interests in Poland. But that there was a critical difference, Larry Arnn argued:

> Stop and consider. What were British interests in Greece? Greece is located on the sea, and Britain is a sea power, with an interest in the security of the eastern Mediterranean. Britain wants elections, in which governments are produced that protect the rights of minorities. It wants stability, trade and peace.
>
> Now ask yourself: what are Russian interests in Poland. The answer is: all the property in Poland. Whatever the Poles had or may produce, the Soviets set up a system for extracting it. What Churchill and Roosevelt asked for were free elections and free governments, able to do what they wanted to do, including (as Greece soon did) levying tariffs on British goods. The point is that British interests in Greece were considerably different from the interests Stalin had in Poland.[24]

There *is* a difference between "Us" and "Them."

The blanket charge that Churchill (and Roosevelt) consciously and intentionally assigned eastern Europe to the Soviet sphere of influence is defied by the military facts, in place since the turnaround of Russian forces at Stalingrad in 1942. From that point the war was destined to end with the USSR in military command of eastern Europe. The only way to prevent that would have been to stand aside when Russia was attacked by Hitler in June 1941—a subject worth a debate by fans of alternative history. It was, however, agreed Anglo-American policy to aim for a good working relationship with the USSR after the war, and scholarly studies have been written about the efforts, ultimately unsuccessful, to achieve it.[25]

Condemning Hungary, et al. to fifty years of enslavement was not the Anglo-American intent. But facts are stubborn things. Churchill did not write in his memoirs that the percentages agreement was a temporary wartime expedient, although he thought it was. That Churchill's skullduggery (as it is sometimes defined) led to a democratic Greece, and rendered Yugoslavia at least unabsorbed, is to his credit. The "naughty paper" may not have been prudent, considering the criticism Churchill would take for it. But however imperfectly, it worked.

34

Nuking Moscow

At the Potsdam conference on 22 July 1945, Churchill was briefed on results of the atomic bomb test in Alamogordo, New Mexico. The landscape had been obliterated for one mile around the detonation.[1] Churchill was then summoned by Truman. Until that moment, he wrote, the Allies had expected to face an invasion of Japan "by terrific air bombing and by the invasion of vary large armies…. The desperate resistance of the Japanese fighting to the death with Samurai devotion, not only in pitched battles, but in every cave and dug-out." He estimated the loss of a million American soldiers and half a million British—"or more if we could get them there: for we were resolved to share the agony."[2]

Hiroshima and Nagasaki

The news from New Mexico changed everything. In its place was the vision—"fair and bright," Churchill wrote, of the war ending "in one or two violent shocks." The Japanese, whose courage he had admired, might find in this "almost supernatural weapon" a plausible excuse to surrender honorably, preventing a bloodbath in an invasion of the home islands and a million or more American, British and Commonwealth lives. Moreover, Churchill added—a line of thought not lost on his American ally—"we should not need the Russians."[3]

"Churchill did not discuss the decision with his Cabinet or chiefs of staff," wrote Warren Kimball,

> writing in his war memoirs that "there was never a moment's discussion as to whether the atomic bomb should be used or not." Yet, amidst their concern over Soviet intentions in Europe, not needing the Russians must have counted with Truman and Churchill in their decision to use the bomb. After Roosevelt's death, Churchill casually initialed a minute telling British officials to go along with what the Americans decided.[4]

Historians have long since debated whether the bomb was necessary—or at least whether Nagasaki, bombed only three days after Hiroshima, should have been spared. Wasn't Japan nearing surrender? The debate is relevant here only as background to Churchill's thinking on a more contentious charge levied against him (below). It is worth

The first nuclear bomb dropped in anger, Hiroshima, 5 August 1945 (U.S. Army Air Corps).

mentioning, however, that even after Nagasaki, Emperor Hirohito's intervention was required to accept surrender. A military coup came close to succeeding. The argument that the bombs were unnecessary, wrote one observer, "seems based more on dislike of nuclear weapons than on the situation at the time. Churchill in 1940 said, 'We shall fight in the fields and in the streets, we shall fight in the hills ... we shall never surrender.' Why should anyone have expected the Japanese in 1945 to be any less resolute?"[5]

Churchill realized that the atomic bomb was a quantum advance in warfare, not just a "bigger bang." On 18 August 1946, a year after Hiroshima and Nagasaki, he wrote to George Bernard Shaw, the pacifist, who had sent him a remarkably complimentary letter: "You have never been a real Tory ... [you are] a phenomenon that the Blimps and Philistines and Stick-in-the-muds have never understood and always dreaded." Churchill waxed mellow under the praise of Shaw, his longtime nemesis. In his reply he voiced his growing misgivings about nuclear weapons: "Do you think that the atomic bomb means that the Architect of the universe has got tired of writing His non-stop scenario. There was a lot to be said for His stopping with the Panda. The release of the bomb seems to be His next turning point."[6]

Churchill's portent of disaster widened as the years passed. During and after the war he was anxious that American-British atomic secrets not be shared with any other country. At Fulton in 1946 he warned that the bomb might "possibly disintegrate the globe itself." By 1952, and the development of thermonuclear devices—when he began to advocate a "settlement" of the Cold War with the Soviets—he feared the world might otherwise enter "a preliminary stage of measureless agony from which neither side could at present protect itself." On the eve of retirement in 1955, observing children playing, he wondered "what would lie before them if God wearied of mankind." Listening to the news during the 1962 Cuban missile crisis, he muttered, "we are all going to be blown up."[7]

Nuking Moscow

Given the above, and what I know of Churchill's views, I was surprised to receive a call in 2014 from the London *Daily Mail,* which wanted to know what I thought of a shocking fact about Churchill. (shocking fact #22,385, by my count.) It had appeared in a new book on the Churchills and the Kennedys, by Thomas Maier.

During a visit to London in summer 1947, Maier wrote, New Hampshire Senator Stiles Bridges, a conservative active in foreign affairs, met with Churchill and reported their conversation—as politicians were then wont to do—to the FBI. According to Bridges, Churchill said "that if an atomic bomb could be dropped on the Kremlin wiping it out, it would be a very easy problem to handle the balance of Russia, which would be without direction." Bridges said Churchill believed that this was "the only salvation for the civilization of the world." If it wasn't done, Bridges had Churchill saying, "Russia will attack the United States in the next two or three years when she gets the atomic bomb and civilization will be wiped out or set back many years."[8]

The *Daily Mail* proposed to cover this a remarkable exposé. Their question for me was: "Did you know Churchill wanted the Americans to nuke Russia?"

I had to advise that such private asides by Churchill had been known for half a century. His momentary thought of nuking the Soviets were first revealed in his doctor's diaries in 1966, where his alleged sentiments are even colder: "America knows that fifty-two percent of Russia's motor industry is in Moscow and could be wiped out by a single bomb. It might mean wiping out three million people, but they would think nothing of that…. They think more of erasing an historical building like the Kremlin."[9]

Churchill's doctor, Lord Moran, dates this remark 8 August 1946. While it has been noticed since that not all of his "diaries" were contemporaneous, Churchill apparently said something similar at that time to Canadian Prime Minister MacKenzie King. As King remembered, Churchill believed "the West should make it clear that the Soviet Union must not extend its regime any further in Western Europe … that if the Soviets did not accept the ultimatum, a Western leader should tell them straight 'We will attack Moscow and your other cities and destroy them with atomic bombs from the air.'"[10]

Churchill occasionally voiced apocalyptic notions in private conversations, to see what the reaction would be. The historian Anthony Seldon, in a commendable book on Churchill's 1951–55 premiership, has an apposite comment on Moran. Churchill always treated his doctor in a polite and friendly fashion, Seldon wrote. But "he never regarded Moran as an intimate, nor is there any evidence that on matters of major importance, he let himself be influenced by him."[11] Churchill took Moran on trips abroad, "not just because it was a comfort to have his doctor on call, but also, one feels, because Moran would have been hurt not to have been included. Churchill's style of tossing ideas around with his companions, often to test their effect, mistakenly inclined Moran to give these half-formed thoughts and suggestions the status of hard fact."[12] (And, given his reported conversation with Bridges, not just Moran.)

As Leader of the Opposition, which he was in the early postwar years, Churchill never proposed to bomb Moscow, to Parliament, to President Truman, or to the State Department. Senator Bridges was a hard-liner on the Soviets, and it is impossible to know how much he embellished Churchill's private conservation to support his own leanings. Neither did Mackenzie King express any shock at the version he heard.

On the record, Churchill was more discerning, as Graham Farmelo recorded: "This was the zenith of Churchill's nuclear bellicosity. He soon softened his line."[13] Well *before* the Soviets had the bomb, Churchill was against challenging Russia militarily. Martin Gilbert said he was looking, rather,

for some policy which would enable war to be avoided. The "best chance of avoiding war," he felt, was, "in accord with the other Western democracies, to bring matters to a head with the Soviet Government, and, by formal diplomatic processes, with all their privacy and gravity, to arrive at a lasting settlement." Even this method would not guarantee that war would not come. "But I believe it would give the best chance of preventing it, and that, if it came, we should have the best chance of coming out of it alive."[14]

I sent all this material and more to the *Daily Mail's* reporter, adding: "I trust you are not going to say, as you did on the phone, that Churchill wanted to nuke Moscow. What he contemplated in private conversations, which never developed into any plan and was never formally proposed, can hardly be construed as something he 'wanted.'"

Alas, for populist newspapers shocking facts are mother's milk, and urging reason is like shouting into the wind. Forty-eight hours later the *Daily Mail* announced: "Winston Churchill's 'bid to nuke Russia' to win Cold War—uncovered…. Winston Churchill urged the United States to launch a nuclear attack on the Soviet Union to win the Cold War, a newly released document reveals. Read the full story."[15]

"Woman of the Streets"

After Stalin died and Churchill returned as prime minister, he attended a summit conference in Bermuda with newly elected President Eisenhower and Prime Minister Joseph Laniel of France. Churchill was intent on arranging Anglo-American summit with Stalin's successors; Eisenhower and John Foster Dulles, his secretary of State, were not.

Jock Colville recorded the end of their first plenary meeting on 4 December 1953:

> Ike followed with a short, very violent statement, in the coarsest terms. He [Eisenhower] said that as regards the P.M.'s belief that there was a New Look in Soviet Policy, Russia was a woman of the streets and whether her dress was new, or just the old one patched, it was certainly the same whore underneath.... I doubt if such language has ever before been heard at an international conference. Pained looks all round ... when Eden asked when the next meeting should be, the President replied, "I don't know. Mine is with a whisky and soda"—and got up to leave the room.[16]

Here is another scandalous story for the *Daily Mail* to uncover. Eisenhower's outburst has been little remarked over the years. That Churchill died despairing of his final goal of world peace tends not interest the populist media—which much prefers Shocking Facts, even if they are half a century old.

35

Trouble 'n' Strife

The Myth: Winston and Clementine
Had an Unhappy Marriage

One of the few times I ever saw Sir Martin Gilbert upset was when an author "discovered" that Churchill employed a ghost writer to draft a few articles—a fact Sir Martin himself had revealed thirty years earlier. I felt the same during the media kerfuffle over a recent biography of Clementine Churchill, which "revealed" that Lady Churchill destroyed the infamous Graham Sutherland painting of her husband.[1] The burning of the portrait, which had been presented by Parliament on Churchill's 80th birthday in 1954—was reported in 1979 by Lady Soames in her biography, *Clementine Churchill*—a true picture of a great woman.

Clementine's action symbolized her devotion to her husband. As their daughter explained, her father had not seen the finished painting until a fortnight before its presentation. When he did, he was deeply offended, though Sutherland was an artist he liked and trusted. It was "a cruel and gross travesty of Winston, showing all the ravages of time, and revealing nothing of the warmth and humanity of his nature. Quickly, Clementine threw her influence into calming his wounded sensibilities."[2] Without confiding in him, she told their family "it would never see the light of day." Consulting no one, "some time in 1955 or 1956, she gave instructions for the picture to be destroyed." Their loyal secretary, Grace Hamblin, and her brother carted it to a field in the dead of night and burned it to ashes. Within a month of Clementine's death her daughter revealed the portrait's fate to the public. Kindly she notified Sutherland in advance, so he wouldn't be taken unawares; he was mortified that the painting had so troubled her father.[3]

The significance of this story is that it belies the picture given by the later biography of a dysfunctional marriage.[4] No marriage survives without bumps, but Clementine and Winston were deeply in love throughout their fifty-seven years together. Theirs was rightly regarded "one of the strongest unions in politics."[5] It remained steadfast into old age, as Clementine's action over the portrait demonstrated.

Models of Loyalty

They were loyal to one another: Despite all that has been written about them both, only two rumors ever surfaced of affairs. Clementine was said to have fallen for a young

Winston and Clementine at the time of their wedding, 1908 (Philco postcards).

adventurer, Terence Philip, who accompanied her on her 1935 voyage to the South Seas; upon her return he quickly vanished from her life. Lady Soames said she did not know how far that shipboard romance had gone.[6] Around the same time, Winston was said to have romanced Maxine Elliott, their American-born actress friend, whom he visited occasionally in the South of France; but this rumor had only one source, and was never confirmed by any correspondence or testimony.[7]

I read the recent Clementine biography expecting something new, since its author wrote off Soames's work as "the family's viewpoint, with conspicuous gaps." But when a book covers the last twenty years of the Churchills' lives in thirty pages, missing almost every event of significance, it can hardly be deemed comprehensive. I was hard-pressed to find significant new material—aside from a very good account of Lady Churchill's important work and influence during World War II—unless we include its investigations into loves and lovers, with implications backed by hearsay. The book offers little understanding of how the upper classes regarded love and sex in the Twenties and Thirties— a necessary context, because it was quite different than ours today.

One cannot write about the Churchills without an understanding of military and political history, but the book's analyses repeatedly betrayed unfamiliarity with facts. Early in his career Young Winston supports Free Trade because "it would keep food prices low." In World War I, he rallies the defense of Antwerp because he "could not resist the call of romantic heroism." The 1915 Dardanelles and Gallipoli operations, which so gravely affected Clementine and Winston, are an unfathomable soup. We are told the landings at Gallipoli were repulsed because the Turks had ammunition left over from the Dardanelles.[8] (See chapters 11 and 12 herein.)

Churchill's reaction to the 1936 death of Ralph Wigram, his key informant on German rearmament, is "single-minded," leaving Clementine to comfort "a brave man's griev-

ing widow" In reality they both mourned Wigram all their lives, and were forever solicitous toward his wife Ava. Also in 1936, we are told, Clementine wanted a divorce—the
only source for which is one of the most scurrilous books ever published on the
Churchills, described as "a grim diet of ghoulishness and tittle-tattle."[9] "Perhaps," Clementine "came back" to him in 1938.[10] Whenever someone would say "perhaps," Sir Martin
Gilbert would always reply: *Perhaps not!*" No such rule applies here. Churchill's December 1944 flight to Athens is treated as spoiling Christmas for his family. Off he goes,
taking "his two most attractive typists"—this means what, exactly?—yet he earns "supportive cables from Clementine," her composure "rapidly restored."[11] True, Clementine
had taken great pains to plan Christmas at Chequers—and the war interfered, as it had
for five years. Mary Soames wrote: "It was so rare for Clementine to give way; she was
accustomed to sudden changes of plan, and had, in these last years especially, developed
a strict sense of priorities. Somehow this sudden departure of Winston laid her low; but
not for long."[12]

Matters of Reality

What are the facts? Clementine was fragile and high-strung. She had the fate of
falling for a whirlwind; she lived and breathed for Winston and his politics. Mary Soames
made frequent references to Clementine's need to "get away" for breaks lasting from a
few days to a month or more. Yet their bond was manifest in their constant letters to
each other, even when they were under the same roof—for Clementine found it more
useful to influence Winston in a handwritten note than in conversation when he was distracted. She was protective of him, and wary of his friends, notably Max Beaverbrook,
F.E. Smith (Lord Birkenhead) and Brendan Bracken—whom she referred to as the "three
terrible B's." In the end she came to appreciate them for their friendship to Winston.
Field Marshal Montgomery, whom she regularly upbraided, took her criticisms with
grace. The only crony who met with her full approval was "The Prof" (Professor Lindemann), who never patronized her. He also played her favorite game—they were both
accomplished tennis players.

From early on in their marriage she fought for Winston with vigor. In 1915, when
he was about to be dismissed from the Admiralty over the Dardanelles fiasco, she wrote
personally to Prime Minister Asquith: "Winston may in your eyes & in those with whom
he has to work have faults, but he has the supreme quality which I venture to say very
few of your present or future Cabinet possess—the power, the imagination, the deadliness,
to fight Germany." Asquith dismissed it as "the letter of a mad-woman."[13] She also served
as Winston's "life-coach," a term they would not have understood, though popular today.
In 1943 as he traveled to Cairo, to meet Roosevelt before their Teheran conference with
Stalin, she wrote him: "Never forget that when History looks back, your vision and your
piercing energy, coupled with your patience and your magnanimity, will all be part of
your greatness. So don't allow yourself to be made angry—I often think of your saying
that the only worse thing than Allies is not having Allies!"[14]

Withal, Clementine remained her own woman, a lifetime Liberal, a potent influence
her husband respected and (sometimes) listened to. John Colville recalled the "astonishment" in 1958, when the aging Sir Winston said he hoped that Churchill College, founded
as a national memorial to him, would admit women on equal terms with men. "No college

Visit to Holland 1946. Left to right: Prince Bernhard, Winston Churchill, Princesses Beatrix, Margriet and Irene, Princess Juliana (standing behind the princesses), Clementine and Mary Churchill (Author's collection).

at Oxford or Cambridge had ever done any such thing," Colville wrote. "I asked him afterwards if this had been Clementine's idea. 'Yes,' he replied, 'and I support it.'"[15]

Churchill's Views

Churchill for his part repaid her devotion. "What it has been to me to live all these years in your heart and companionship no phrases can convey," he wrote her in 1935. "Time passes swiftly, but is it not joyous to see how great and growing is the treasure we have gathered together, amid the storms and stresses of so many eventful and to millions tragic and terrible years?"[16] His marriage, he said, was "the most fortunate and joyous event which happened to me in the whole of my life, for what can be more glorious than to be united in one's walk through life with a being incapable of an ignoble thought."[17] Persuading her to marry him was "quite my most brilliant achievement."[18]

Sir Robert Rhodes James, with his usual acuity, identified the key to their relationship: exactly the words that summarized their union. It was Winston's letter "to be opened in the event of my death," sealed in an envelope as he was about to depart for the trenches in late 1915:

Do not grieve for me too much. I am a spirit confident of my rights. Death is only an incident, and not the most important wh[ich] happens to us in this state of being. On the whole, especially since I met you my darling one I have been happy, & you have taught me how noble a woman's heart can be. If there is anywhere else I shall be on the look-out for you. Meanwhile look forward, feel free, rejoice in life, cherish the children, guard my memory. God bless you. Good-bye.[19]

Latterday biographers will need to understand that letter, Sir Robert wrote.[20] I am astonished that they did not. It captures the unifying bond, the secret to success, of their long marriage: it was based on simple and abiding mutual respect. Without that, most marriages falter.

Lady Soames's *Clementine Churchill* is a complete and personal record of how the two of them came to feel about a marriage which endured the worst storms that have rocked civilization. Amid these storms, it lasted nearly six decades, when often the press of events weighed heavily on them both. Mary Soames liked to quote her father to describe the sheet anchor of his life: "Here firm, though all be drifting."[21] Whenever she read long-established facts republished as new revelations, the elevation of trivia over substance, and insensitive portrayals of her parents, Mary would just sadly shake her head. Perhaps we should, too.

36

On European Union

The Myth: Churchill Would Have Voted to Remain in the EU

We should not construe, from anything Churchill did in his time, how he would react to today's issues. But the temptation for conjecture was irresistible in the debate surrounding Britain's June 2016 referendum resulting in the decision to leave the European Union ("Brexit"). Proponents of both the "Leave" and "Remain" campaigns alluded repeatedly to Churchill's statements, particularly in the early postwar years, as if to convey his approval or rejection of today's European Union—an entity of which Churchill never conceived.

We cannot declare with certainty how Sir Winston would have reacted to Brexit, though he was ardently in favor of British sovereignty. What we *can* do at this distance is to consider his thoughts about European unity and cooperation as early as 1938—and, perhaps, learn something along the way.

Pan-European Awakening, 1918–1945

After the horrors of World War I, a movement arose for European unity. By the late 1930s, with Germany acquiring more and more territories to which she was not entitled, it found a parallel in what Churchill and others termed "collective security." Democratic Europe, went the argument, must form closer ties—how close was debatable. The Austrian-Japanese politician-philosopher Count Richard Coudenhove-Kalergi, founder-president of the Paneuropean Union, went so far as to advocate a federal state resembling today's European Union. He peppered Churchill with his ideas, and the Englishman said they "had much to recommend them."[1]

In 1938 Churchill penned an article, "The United States of Europe," citing some of Coudenhove-Kalergi's arguments. Any step that would make Europe more prosperous, peaceful and free was, he wrote, "conducive to British interests." Nothing but good lay in diminution of tariffs and armaments. Britain would certainly support such developments. He did however add a critical qualification with respect to his own country, its transatlantic relations and global responsibilities:

> But we have our own dream and our own task. We are with Europe, but not of it. We are linked, but not comprised. We are interested and associated, but not absorbed. And should European statesmen

address us in the words which were used of old, "Wouldest thou be spoken for to the king, or the captain of the host?," we should reply, with the Shunammite woman: "I dwell among mine own people."[2]

His broad knowledge of the Bible notwithstanding, Churchill insisted he was "not a pillar of the church but a buttress—I support it from the outside."[3] Such was his view toward European unity. Early in World War II he expressed his hope that when peace returned "there would be a United States of Europe, and this Island would be the link connecting this Federation with the new world and able to hold the balance between the two."[4]

In a May 1943 conversation with U.S. Vice-President Henry Wallace, Churchill imagined a postwar Europe of a dozen "states or confederations," which might form a "European Council." France, a key power, would stand by herself, but there might be Danubian and Balkan federations of smaller states, and Belgium and Holland might group the Low Countries with Denmark. "Each of the dozen or so European countries should appoint a representative to the European Regional Council," he told Wallace, "thus creating a form of United States of Europe."[5]

It is significant that Churchill here spoke of sovereign states and small federations as members of a "council," which he never described in detail. Nor did he include Britain, except as an outside supporter. During the Brexit campaign the pro–Leave campaign widely circulated a wartime remark of Churchill to de Gaulle: "...each time we must choose between Europe and the open sea, we shall always choose the open sea."

The quote was accurate, but incomplete. In the very next sentence Churchill said: "Each time I must choose between you and Roosevelt, I shall always choose Roosevelt."[6] Clearly he was referring not to European unity but to French intransigence over Allied war strategy. The proof lies in Churchill's letter to the President at that time, June 1944, about the stubborn attitude of de Gaulle: "I think it would be a great pity if you and he did not meet," Churchill wrote FDR. "I do not see why I have all the luck." Historian Warren Kimball noted: "Someone on the American side underlined the final three words of Churchill's message to Roosevelt: 'all the luck' ... that phrase was the sort of sarcasm which appealed to his sense of humor and fit his annoyance with de Gaulle."[7]

"Europe Unite," 1945–1950

In his 1930 autobiography, Churchill had declared that he'd always urged fighting wars "with might and main" till victory was won, and then offering the hand of friendship to the vanquished: "Thus, I have always been against the Pacifists during the quarrel, and against the Jingoes at its close."[8] After World War II, welcomed as a hero across the continent, the leader who had saved them from a new Dark Age urged Europeans to adopt his maxim: in victory, magnanimity. Expressing his lifelong preference for coalitions and alliances, Churchill called for a new spirit of unity and cooperation. Speaking at Zurich University in September 1946, he went further, with words he said would "astonish" his listeners, and probably did:

> ... the first step in the re-creation of the European family must be a partnership between France and Germany.... There can be no revival of Europe without a spiritually great France and a spiritually great Germany. The structure of the United States of Europe, if well and truly built, will be such as to make the material strength of a single state less important. Small nations will count as much as large ones and gain their honour by their contribution to the common cause.[9]

By 1948 there was a Congress of Europe, and in May Churchill addressed it at The Hague: "A high and a solemn responsibility rests upon us here this afternoon in this Congress of a Europe striving to be reborn."[10] His speech at Fulton, Missouri, in March 1946, was mainly remembered for ringing down the "Iron Curtain." Yet there too, in middle America, he had reminded listeners: "The safety of the world requires a new unity in Europe, from which no nation should be permanently outcast."[11]

During the Brexit debate, the *Daily Telegraph* declared that a European Union had been a CIA project from the start, and Churchill's pro–Europe speeches were part of America's plan to create a united Europe that would stand up to the Soviets.[12] While the U.S. traditionally favored what became the EU, there is no solid evidence to make such a claim. It is true that Churchill entitled one of his postwar speech volumes *Europe Unite,* and his speeches at Zurich and The Hague lend credence to the idea that he looked kindly on the European project. But any fair-minded person is obliged to consider: Why, after such speeches supporting European unity (never fully defined) as Britain's postwar Leader of the Opposition, did Churchill forestall British involvement in the movement after returning as Prime Minister in 1951?

"We are not merged," 1951–1953

In 1951, the Treaty of Paris united Belgium, France, West Germany, Italy, the Netherlands and Luxembourg in the European Coal and Steel Community. First proposed in 1950 by French foreign minister Robert Schuman, ECSC was an international authority designed to control production of steel and coal, which Britain was invited to join. A revealing clue as to what Churchill thought about a federal Europe—which is where the ECSC would ultimately lead—was his message his Cabinet about this "Schuman Plan." Britain's attitude, Churchill explained,

> resembles that which we adopt about the European Army. We help, we dedicate, we play a part, but we are not merged with and do not forfeit our insular or commonwealth character. Our first object is the unity and consolidation of the British Commonwealth. Our second, "the fraternal association" of the English-speaking world. And third, United Europe, to which we are a separate closely-and specially-related ally and friend…. It is only when plans for uniting Europe take a federal form that we ourselves cannot take part, because we cannot subordinate ourselves or the control of British policy to federal authorities.[13]

If that statement does not firmly array Churchill against Britain joining a federal system, consider what he replied to a question in Parliament seven months later: "I do not myself conceive that federalism is immediately possible within the Commonwealth. I have never been in favor of it in Europe…."[14] Then there were his remarks to the Commons in May 1953, reprising words from his 1938 article:

> We are not members of the European Defence Community, nor do we intend to be merged in a Federal European system. We feel we have a special relation to both. This can be expressed by prepositions, by the preposition "with" but not "of"—we are with them, but not of them. We have our own Commonwealth and Empire.[15]

While these statements were definitive at the time, the concepts and forms of the 1950s are not those of today. It may be tempting to suggest that they prove Churchill would be pro–Brexit, but too much has changed to be certain. Neither Europe nor the British Commonwealth are what they were then. (Churchill *did* foresee a single currency—as early as 1933. It was what he called the sterling/dollar or dollar/sterling. Nothing like the euro ever occurred to him—or was then proposed.)

Last Thoughts, 1962

It is necessary to clear up a story bandied about by "Leave" side of the Brexit debate, from Field Marshal Montgomery, who wrote that Churchill in 1962 was "protesting against Britain's proposed entry into the Common Market" (the European Economic Community, a free-trade zone that preceded the European Union). Montgomery's statement not only took advantage of a private conversation with an old and ailing friend; it may have misrepresented Churchill's views. Sir Winston's daughter wrote: "What I remember clearly is that not only my father, but all of us—particularly my mother—were outraged by Monty's behaviour, and he was roundly rebuked."[16]

Sir Winston's last private secretary, Sir Anthony Montague Browne, believed that Montgomery, while not entirely inventing Churchill's remark, had seriously misinterpreted his opinion. Consulting no one, Montague Browne released to the press a statement of Churchill's views on the subject from a previously unpublished letter to his Woodford constituency chairman, Mrs. Moss, in August 1961:

> For many years, I have believed that measures to promote European unity were ultimately essential to the well-being of the West. In a speech at Zurich in 1946, I urged the creation of the European Family, and I am sometimes given credit for stimulating the ideals of European unity which led to the formation of the economic and the other two communities. In the aftermath of the Second World War, the key to these endeavours lay in partnership between France and Germany. At that time this happy outcome seemed a fantasy, but it is now accomplished, and France and West Germany are more intimately linked than they have ever been before in their history. They, together with Italy, Belgium, Holland and Luxembourg, are welding themselves into an organic whole, stronger and more dynamic than the sum of its parts. We might well play a great part in these developments to the profit not only of ourselves, but of our European friends also…. I think that the Government are right to apply to join the European Economic Community, not because I am yet convinced that we shall be able to join, but because there appears to be no other way by which we can find out exactly whether the conditions of membership are acceptable.[17]

Sir Anthony admitted that this was "a fence-sitting letter" with mild opinions, but it "took the heat off" and pacified both the Euro-skeptics and the Euro-enthusiasts.[18]

In fairness, it is possible that Montgomery was telling the truth—and that, by putting Churchill's thoughts into what was effectively a press release, Montague Browne was behaving no differently than Monty. But Churchill's remarks were about the Economic Community, not today's far more amalgamated EU, or anything like it. Thus, as regards the Brexit debate, they are non-sequitur.

Montague Browne did believe that if Churchill had been able "with all his old fire and eloquence to lead Britain into Europe," the outcome might have been different. But Churchill was too tired, and the opportunity was lost:

> Some old friends and associates, notably Violet Bonham Carter and Count Coudenhove-Kalergi, one of the founding notables of the European Movement, urged the Prime Minister to espouse a more positive role towards Europe. They were treated civilly, but no more…. People find it very hard to recognise that a Prime Minister, especially an old man, has to ration his time with the utmost strictness and conserve his energies with a reasonable amount of relaxation.[19]

I quote these passages at length to record what is known regarding Churchill's views on European Unity. What was in 1962 a free trade agreement, providing practical and beneficent commercial arrangements for member nations, has morphed into something entirely different—which the British electorate chose in 2016 to reject.

It is impossible to know how the choices before Great Britain vis-à-vis the European Union would be viewed by Churchill, Sir Anthony wrote, and "improper use should not be made of him."[20] Churchill's repeated vision was a sovereign Britain linked first to the Commonwealth, second to the Atlantic community (including North America), and third to Europe. But Churchill never had to contemplate anything like the EU of 2016. And improper use should not be made of him now.

37

The Common Touch

In an excellent book about the opening months of World War I, the historian Max Hastings suggested that Winston Churchill disdained the common folk. Citing the wartime Prime Minister H.H. Asquith as providing a tow for a broken-down motorist and giving two children a lift in his car, Hastings wrote: "It is hard to imagine Winston Churchill behaving in such a fashion."[1]

It is not hard at all. Even good writers fall for this stereotype picture, having heard it for decades. In reality, Churchill performed frequent kindnesses for ordinary people he encountered, privately and without fanfare. We know about them mainly through private correspondence, the official biography, and contemporary observers.

Westerham Characters

A prominent example is the gypsy couple Churchill befriended in Westerham. Grace Hamblin, longtime secretary and first administrator of Chartwell, said he had a romantic view of the free-spirited Romany culture. He called them "Mr. and Mrs. Donkey Jack" because they had a donkey and a cart, and lived life their way. Hamblin's father, a farmer, "called them parasites because they subsisted on stolen potatoes, strawberries and apples." Sir Winston strongly demurred: "He thought it was wonderful."[2]

When Jack died, she explained, his donkey had to be destroyed, and there was nowhere for poor Mrs. Donkey Jack to go: "Sir Winston allowed her to live in his wood, in a little gazebo which had been there for years, full of earwigs and that sort of thing, but she loved it. It would have been stupid to offer her a house because she wouldn't have understood it. He knew just what would give her pleasure."[3]

In 1935 Mrs. Donkey Jack suffered a fractured ankle. Churchill sent her to the nearest hospital, directing that the bills be sent to him. Realizing that her woodland camp and two dogs would be unattended, he asked his gardener Arnold to look after them. "Should the worst be realized I shall try and get her into a decent home," Churchill wrote his absent wife:

> Meanwhile her savage dog (the little one) still stands a faithful sentry over her belongings. He allows
> Arnold to bring food at a respectable distance and consents to eat it, but otherwise he remains like

the seraph Abdiel in *Paradise Lost*: "Among innumerable false, unmoved; Unshaken, unseduced, unterrified; His loyalty he kept, his love, his zeal."[4]

Those lines could be applied alike to Grace Hamblin, and almost everyone who worked for Churchill over the years.

Two other Westerham villagers who benefited from the boss's characteristic kindliness were Tom and Alice Bateman, brother and sister farmers who scratched out a living near Chartwell. Percy Reid, a stringer for a London newspaper, who kept an eye on Chartwell doings after World War II, wrote charmingly of a cattle sale, where the Batemans had put up one of their heifers. Churchill had given it to them as a calf when he heard they had been out of luck in their farming. "Pedigree?" repeated Alice, with a touch of rural common sense: "I suppose we could have had the pedigree if we'd liked but then—we don't farm their way. The paper wouldn't make much difference to whether it was a good cow or not."[5]

Alice Bateman had lots of time for the great man, her neighbor: "Got more in his little finger than most of us have in our whole bodies," she said. For a year years she worked at Chartwell. "Not to sleep in," she added quickly. "Always has a word for you, has Winston. So has Mary, his daughter."[6]

Phil Johnson, a Westerham car mechanic and sometime driver, told a delightful story showing another side to Alice. Churchill, being driven up the hill to Chartwell from Westerham village, spotted her trudging along the road and stopped his Humber limousine. His impulse was to offer her a lift, but realizing she would be too proud to accept one, he shouted encouragement: "Come on Alice, you can do better than that!"

"G'wan, yer fat old man, you get out of that car and walk yourself, you'll live longer!" Alice retorted. "I'll outlive you, Alice!" chuckled Churchill, who liked to claim (inaccurately) that he took exercise only as a pallbearer for friends who had exercised all their lives. "Yer will not!" Alice shot back. "And he didn't," Phil Johnson added: "Alice survived him by six or eight years."[7]

"Kent folk don't make friends easily," wrote Percy Reid:

> Theirs is a sturdy independence which is readily mistaken for surly insularity. Once won over, however, Kentish people will remain your sincere if somewhat over-frank friends for good. It was somewhat on these lines that the unusual relationship, which finally developed between Westerham folk and Churchill and his family, grew up.[8]

Churchill and His Staff

Churchill was a Victorian, with most of the attitudes of his class and time toward what they sometimes called the lower orders. "Servants exist to save one trouble," he told his wife in 1928, "and should never be allowed to disturb one's inner peace."[9] In the 1930s he arrived one night in a violent rainstorm at his friend Maxine Elliott's Chateau d'Horizon in the south of France. "My dear Maxine," he said as she ushered him in, "do you realise I have come all the way from London without my man?" Never lost for words, Elliott replied: "Winston, how terribly brave of you."[10]

That attitude was ingrained, but atypical of his generation was how Churchill handled servants. To him, said a former bodyguard, the staff was part of the family:

> We all know how plainly we speak to one's spouse or children: no discourtesy is intended but there are no frills. This is how Churchill treated his staff. He just told them what he expected. His plain

speaking ruffled some, but he was not being rude. It was just his way of getting the maximum done in the minimum of time. He worked his staff to the limit of endurance. When they reached the breaking point he became sympathetic and solicitous. They were gratified, and so continued *beyond* the limit of endurance![11]

Staffers who knew him briefly and not well, like Phyllis Moir, an American secretary on his 1932 U.S. lecture tour who had the chutzpah to write a book about it,[12] complained of his gruff manner. They were mistaking his single-minded intensity for the job at hand, whether it was compiling a thank-you letter to a host or a major speech on Anglo-American relations.

William Manchester said Churchill's first reactions were often emotional and unworthy, but he usually had second thoughts full of "reason and generosity."[13] This extended to servants and staffers. When Churchill finally realized he was being too hard on someone, he would find a way to express his regret. Elizabeth Layton Nel, a wartime secretary, recalled how she once had a bad cold and was sniveling when he sent for her, his manner curt and demanding. Noticing her quietly blowing her nose, he thought she was crying. "Good heavens," he said, "you mustn't mind me. We're all toads beneath the harrow, you know." Dictating a brief message he took it from her and added: "Oh, very good indeed, very well typed, how quick you were."[14]

At his London home at Hyde Park Gate, visiting dignitaries arrived one day in 1947 to present one of Churchill's many Freedoms of Cities. After the ceremony, a glass of sherry and speeches, Churchill exclaimed, "Greenshields, bring the cigars." The butler went away and came back with a cigar box, handing them round. Host and visitors lit up. Churchill took one puff, hesitated, then fixed a stony stare at Greenshields: "Not these, you damn fool!" he said in a stage whisper. "Poor Greenshields," said a witness. "The butler had made the mistake of handing round Mr. Churchill's best cigars, the ones he smoked himself. Later, Churchill complimented Greenshields on the elegance of his manner!"[15] Mary Soames wrote: "'Let not the sun go down upon your wrath' was a Biblical precept which Winston often quoted, and which he practised in all his relationships."[16]

"I think being shouted at was one of the worst things to get over," said Grace Hamblin, secretary to Winston and later Clementine for over thirty years, typical of the Kentish country folk who served and loved them. "I'd come from a very quiet family and I'd never been shouted at in my life. But I had to learn it, in time."[17] She recalled an occasion early in her career when Churchill commanded Kathleen Hill, a secretary who had worked with him on *Marlborough:* "Fetch me Klop." Miss Hill disappeared for awhile, then proudly struggled back under the weight of Onno Klopp's fourteen giant volumes, *Der Fall des Hauses Stuart.* "Christ Almighty!" Churchill roared.[18] What he meant was his hole punch, invariably called "Klop." (He despised staples and paper clips: piles of papers had to be "klopped" and then fastened together with a "treasury tag," a bit of thread with metal "Ts" at each end.)

At first Grace Hamblin found it all very daunting:

the strangeness of a large house, getting used not only to him, but to his family, his staff and friends who came and went. It was all quite difficult. I went through many, many doubtful periods and was always comforted by the thought that I would only be there for a few months, and then go back to my old job.

She wound up staying over thirty years, until he died in 1965, and then remained as the first administrator, helping to turn Chartwell into a National Trust property.

The boss reviewing proofs, held together with "Treasury tags," in his Chartwell study, 1947. "Klop," his hole-punch, is close at hand, along with his weak whisky-and-water (N.R. Farbman publicity photo for Houghton Mifflin's first edition of *The Gathering Storm*, 1949).

I found myself trying hard to please him, to help instead of to hinder. He had a charisma: a way of making one feel wanted, making the most mundane task feel important.... He worked day in and day out and most terribly hard himself, and I think he drove us. He had a way of almost shaming one into overcoming a problem. His well-worn expression was, "Find Out." He would say, for example: "Do you know where Lord Beaverbrook is this weekend?" No, I'm afraid I don't. *"Well, find out!"* So one got into the habit of saying, "No, I'm afraid I don't but I'll find out," which was a much better answer. Another thing he often said, if you looked a little bit doubtful about anything: "But surely *you* don't find that difficult?"[19]

Churchill went out of his way to be kind to newcomers. Lettice Marston, fair-haired and blue-eyed "like a fairy," was a secretary who went to him when she was 19. Apparently he said to his wife when she first appeared, "Oh dear, she's very young. I mustn't frighten her!" Miss Hamblin added, "I can well imagine him saying it. On her first dictation, he said something to her that he never said to me: 'Don't worry if you don't get it all—I always remember what I've said.'"[20]

Lunchtime Visitors

The secretaries at Chartwell worked on the ground floor, which Churchill called his "factory," and which he liked to visit. He loved dropping by unannounced, plunking himself on a chair, or welcoming a guest for lunch: "Do come in and see my factory." On one such occasion Hamblin was alone when he arrived: "This is my factory, and this is my secretary…. She's quite uneducated…. And to think I once commanded the Fleet." The visitors (and Grace) stirred in embarrassment, until Churchill winked and added, "But she arranges flowers beautifully."[21]

Chartwell lunches were elaborate occasions, but the host was sometimes less tolerant of guests than his own staff. He had a reputation for brusqueness, Ronald Golding remembered, summing people up after two sentences of conversation:

> They were classified, it seemed to me, in either the "interesting" or "uninteresting" class. With the former, conversation ensued; with the latter, Churchill would ignore them. On such occasions Mrs. Churchill frequently came to the rescue, engaging the luckless in conversation. If they were tongue-tied she would do most of the talking until it was time for them to leave. Mrs. Churchill was a charming woman, who rescued many social and civic events because of the inability of her husband to engage in small talk.[22]

On Trust and Loyalty

"He taught us all there is to know about trust and loyalty," said Grace Hamblin, and Elizabeth Nel added: "Once accepted as a member of his staff … one's errors might be pointed out with vehemence, but they would soon be forgiven; one's efforts on his behalf were appreciated, in the long run. Indeed I think he became attached to his staff, and in general he greatly disliked changes."

Nel remembered an emotional moment at Downing Street: Victory in Europe Day, 8 May 1945, the height of Churchill's victory. Pandemonium had broken out in the delirium of triumph after seven terrible years. Full of the moment, Churchill was about to leave with his ministers to acclaim the King, when there arrived his devoted cook, Georgina Landemare, who had been unable to leave her kitchen sooner, and had battled her way through the corridors to see the fun.

> On seeing her he broke away from them, came and shook her hand and thanked her for having looked after him so well through those years. When he had gone she turned to me almost in tears, and said that being spoken to like that meant much more to her than just seeing the crowds. In thinking of him nowadays in a general way, I remember particularly how he endeared himself to those around him—and how funny he always was. As long as one could "take it," one loved him with a deep devotion. Difficult to work for? Yes, mostly. Lovable? Always. Amusing? Without fail.[23]

Ends come, as ends must—as this book has. At the end, Grace Hamblin went along with the family to Bladon, to the boss's burial near his birthplace at Blenheim:

To me that quiet, humble service in the country churchyard was much more moving than had been the tremendous pomp and glory of the state ceremony in London. As the train made its slow journey through the snow-covered countryside on that bitterly cold day, men and women were standing in their little gardens behind their cottages, out in the fields or in the stations we passed, the men with their heads bared, saying a silent farewell to their hero.

She quoted one of the many letters Lady Churchill had received on his death, from a distinguished American, whom she did not reveal: "That he died is unimportant, for we must all pass away. That he lived is momentous to the destiny of decent men. He is not gone. He lives wherever men are free."[24]

Appendix 1:
Minor Myths, Fables
and Things That Go Bump
in the Night

A variety of lesser Churchill fables circulate repeatedly in the digital age, most of them long exposed by writers considerably more expert than I on the subjects. Those authors are identified in the first endnote under each topic, which also contains the location of their work in print or on the web. The final category, "Things That Go Bump in the Night," is so named because the myths are so blatantly absurd. Perhaps I dignify them with a mention, but since Churchill is spared nothing by the rumor mills, why not? If nothing else, they provide amusement. Any reader requiring further information, or with questions on these or any subject in this book, is welcome to contact me at cbh-rml@sneak email.com.

1874–1965: Churchill Was Mentally Ill

Google "churchill and depression" and you'll find endless arguments that the man suffered from everything from severe depression to bipolar disorder. "Churchill would be surprised to know that his many references to his innocent childhood phrase 'Black Dog' would be used after his death to declare him mentally ill," wrote Carol Breckenridge. Hers is the best treatment of the topic I have read. I warmly recommend it to readers who wish to understand the truth.[1]

In 1966, Churchill's doctor Lord Moran published a controversial account of Churchill's last twenty years of active life (1940–60), which many of Sir Winston's colleagues considered privileged doctor-patient information. In an alleged 1944 conversation with Churchill, Moran referred to "Your troubles—I mean the Black Dog business."[2] This implied that Churchill himself used the term—and he did. Moran also quoted Brendan Bracken: "Winston has always been moody; he used to call his fits of depression the 'Black Dog.'"[3]

Jock Colville, Churchill's longtime private secretary, maintained that "Black Dog" was an expression of Victorian nannies (like Churchill's Mrs. Everest) to connote bleak moods among their charges. To Sir Winston, the phrase meant no more than worry or sadness, Colville said; but he predicted that Moran's "hypothetical depression" would become "accepted dogma." Indeed it did. In 1969 Anthony Storr, a psychiatrist who had never met Churchill, argued that he was afflicted with melancholia, the severest form of depression, possibly inherited from his forebears; nowadays this is described as bipolar disorder.[4]

Breckenridge found claims of Churchill's mental illness arose from two sources: those qualified to make a diagnosis but with superficial knowledge of Churchill; and those who knew something of Churchill but little or nothing about mental illness. An art therapist long interested in Churchill, she understood both the clinical definitions and Churchill's behavior patterns. She cited three distinguished psychiatrists who, presented with anonymous descriptions of Churchill's personality, symptoms and a general account of his achievements, agreed that no one who accomplished so much could possibly have suffered from bipolar disorder or major depression.

According to *The Diagnostic and Statistical Manual of Mental Disorders*, wrote Breckenridge, a patient must exhibit at least five out of nine symptoms for a "major depressive episode" within any two-week period (omitting those stemming from medical conditions such as stroke): depressed mood, diminished interest or pleasure, significant weight change, insomnia or hypersomnia, psychomotor agitation or retardation, fatigue, feelings of worthlessness or guilt, diminished concentration, and recurrent thoughts of death. None of these were significantly present for such periods, Breckenridge concludes, except depressed moods after such episodes like the Dardanelles-Gallipoli debacle, or the 1945 election. Concerning these, his daughter Lady Soames said: "Some of the things he went through would depress anybody."[5] While one can argue that some of the *DSM* symptoms may have occurred at one time or another, it is not possible to find five of them together in any two-week period in Churchill's life.

The Manic Episode, Breckenridge continued, "must last at least seven days" (or less if the patient were hospitalized). The *DSM* lists seven symptoms of Hypomanic and Manic Depression, three of which would quality a patient for a "Manic Episode." The symptoms are: inflated self-esteem (hardly), decreased need for sleep (his energizing nap was a lifetime habit), increased talking (never a problem with Churchill), racing thoughts with difficulty to focus, diminished concentration, psychomotor agitation, and excessive pleasurable or dangerous activity. Breckenridge found it impossible to ascribe three of these to Churchill within the space of a week. Excessive activity, while often part of his life, was "focused but not pathological. He had no fear of anything, and some of the adventures he indulged in were indeed risky—but was this involvement 'excessive'? Clearly he took life as it came."[6]

His daughter, the last living person who knew Churchill intimately, summed up her belief that her father was mentally normal:

> A lot has been made of the depressive side of his character by psychiatrists who were never in the same room with him. He himself talks of his black dog, and he did have times of depression, but marriage to my mother very largely kennelled the black dog. Of course, if you have a black dog it lurks somewhere in your nature and you never quite banish it; but I never saw him disarmed by depression. I'm not talking about the depression of his much later years, because surely that is a sad feature of old age which afflicts a great many people who have led a very active life.[7]

Periods of sadness are inherent aspects of the human experience, Breckenridge concluded:

This was certainly true of Churchill, who lived a life that was quite human and profoundly inspirational. He was a man with a huge personality who enjoyed life, family and the fulfillment of destiny, without the hobble of a debilitating mental illness. The myth of the "Black Dog" as Churchill's metaphor for severe clinical mood disorder is just that—a myth.[8]

1880s/1943: Alexander Fleming Twice Saved Churchill's Life

The story that Sir Alexander Fleming saved Churchill's life on two occasions over six decades apart has roared around the Internet for years. Charming as it is, it is certainly fiction. In 2009 a researcher, Ken Hirsch, used Google Book Search to track what is likely the first appearance of this tale: a 1944 article by Arthur Keeney (1893–1955).[9] Keeney was a Florida and Washington, D.C., newsman who had served during World War II in the Office of War Information. "Since Keeney's story was published only a year after Churchill was stricken with pneumonia," Hirsch wrote, "I think it may be the first appearance of the myth."[10]

According to legend, a very young Winston is saved from drowning in a Scottish loch by a farm boy named Alex (or his father; accounts vary), who was plowing a nearby field. Some time later Lord Randolph Churchill tells Alex that in gratitude, he will sponsor Alex's otherwise unaffordable medical school education. Alex graduates with honors and in 1928 discovers that certain bacteria cannot grow in certain vegetable molds. In 1943, when Churchill becomes ill in the Middle East, Alex's creation, penicillin, is flown out to effect his cure. Thus once again Alexander Fleming saves the life of Winston Churchill.

"A fundamental problem with the story is that Churchill was treated for this serious strain of pneumonia not with penicillin but with 'M&B,' a short name for sulfadiazine produced by May and Baker Pharmaceuticals," wrote Dr. John Mather.

> Since he was so ill, it was probably a bacterial rather than a viral infection, and the M&B was successful. (Churchill often humorously referred to his doctors, Lord Moran and Dr. Bedford, as "M&B." When discovered taking the drug with whisky or brandy, Churchill is alleged to have remarked: "Pray remember that man cannot live by M&B alone.") But there is no evidence that he received penicillin for any of his wartime pneumonias. He did have infections in later life, and I suspect he was given penicillin or some other antibiotic that would have by then become available, such as ampicillin. And Churchill did consult with Sir Alexander Fleming on 27 June 1946 about a staphylococcal infection which had apparently resisted penicillin.[11]

Official biographer Martin Gilbert added that the ages of Churchill and Fleming do not support the various accounts. Alexander Fleming was seven years younger than Churchill. If he was plowing a field at say age 13, Churchill would have been 20. One account of the story has young Winston's savior as Fleming's father—in which case Alex would not have saved him twice. But there is no record of Churchill nearly drowning in Scotland at any age; or of Lord Randolph paying for Fleming's education. Sir Martin also noted that Lord Moran's diaries, while mentioning "M&B," say nothing about penicillin, or the need to fly it out to Churchill in the Middle East in 1943.[12]

1907: Churchill Considered Becoming a Muslim

"The idea that Winston Churchill wanted to convert to Islam is utter tripe," wrote the historian Andrew Roberts.[13] This has not prevented one writer from claiming that he did—a recent addition to the never-ending Churchill myths.

Churchill, wrote Patrick Sawyer,

> was a strong admirer of Islam and the culture of the Orient—such was his regard for the Muslim faith
> that relatives feared he might convert.[14] The revelation comes with the discovery of a letter to
> Churchill from his future sister-in-law, Lady Gwendoline Bertie, written in August 1907, in which she
> urges him to rein in his enthusiasm.

Discovery? Lady Gwendoline's letter was first published by Martin Gilbert in 1969!

Churchill certainly *was* a strong admirer of certain aspects of Islam, such as military prowess. Prowling the stricken field at Omdurman after British mechanized firepower had destroyed the Dervish army of Sudan in 1898, he wrote that there was nothing "dulce et decorum" about the fallen; yet those Muslim warriors were "as brave men as ever walked the earth … their claim beyond the grave in respect of a valiant death was as good as that which any of our countrymen could make."[15]

But Sawyer misconstrued Lady Gwendoline's letter, which was clearly written in a light-hearted vein. As Undersecretary of State for the Colonies, Churchill was about to depart on an inspection tour of British East Africa, and Lady Gwendoline was wishing him a joshing farewell:

> I must content myself by wishing you from here a very pleasant, happy and delightful journey, which
> I feel sure it will be, it will be wildly interesting, and you will be wildly interested, but please don't
> become converted to Islam; I have noticed in your disposition a tendency to orientalism, pasha-like
> tendencies I really have; you are not cross with my writing this, so if you come in contact with Islam,
> your conversion might be effected with greater ease than you might have supposed, call of the blood,
> don't you know what I mean, do fight against it![16]

Anyone who knew Churchill could appreciate his taste for luxury, his "pasha-like tendencies." But anyone who thinks this a serious warning not to become a Muslim has too much time on their hands (and probably doesn't know that Churchill was not notably attached to any religion, including the one he was born to).

Lady Gwendoline's relating him to a pasha must have amused Churchill, who repeated it in a letter a month later, which Sawyers also quoted:

> First I am going at 10.30 to row about in a gondola with Gladys D. [Deacon, later Duchess of Marl-
> borough] all the morning and then climb the tower of San Giorgio Maggiore. Then lunch with Helen
> [Vincent]: and afterwards gondola with that other person! Such a dream of fair women. You will
> think me a pasha. I wish I were.[17]

Churchill was writing from Venice, to his former fiancée and lifetime friend Pamela Lytton (née Plowden). But neither is this an expression of desire to follow the Prophet. Writing as he was to Pamela, it is clearly a jocular remark of self-evaluation.

1910–1913: Churchill Was an Unrepentant Eugenicist

"The unnatural and increasingly rapid growth of the Feeble-Minded and Insane classes, coupled as it is with a steady restriction among all the thrifty, energetic and superior stocks, constitutes a national and race danger which it is impossible to exaggerate," Churchill wrote in 1910. That statement, and others like it, easily found on the Internet, where he is condemned for disdaining civil liberties. His biographer Martin Gilbert, in one of his last major articles, put the matter in context in 2011. This should be considered by anyone interested in the facts about Churchill and Eugenics.[18]

As a young man Churchill wrote that "the improvement of the British breed is my political aim in life."[19] There is no getting around the fact that he, like many other educated people in the early 1900s, was briefly taken in by Eugenics. A 1908 Royal Commission "on the Care and Control of the Feeble-Minded" actually recommended to the Liberal government, of which Churchill was a member, that Britain's 120,000 "mental deficients" be incarcerated, or even sterilized to prevent the spread of "undesirable traits."[20]

As Home Secretary (February 1910–October 1911) Churchill asked his officials to consider an Indiana law mandating sterilization and refusing the right of marriage to "mentally unfit" individuals in state custody. His prisons medical adviser, Dr. Horatio Donkin, told him Indiana's law was "an arrogation of scientific knowledge by those who had no claim to it…. It is a monument of ignorance and hopeless mental confusion."[21] Churchill nevertheless continued to believe in state action to improve the British breed, saying he preferred sterilization to confinement.

No such laws were passed while Churchill was at the Home Office, but Eugenics remained a popular theory. In 1912, a London international Eugenics conference spurred public support, and in 1913 Parliament passed the Mental Deficiency Bill with only three dissenting votes. Rejecting sterilization, as occurred in Canada and the United States during the early 20th century, the British bill authorized confinement in institutions. The Bill was not repealed until the Macmillan government in 1959.[22]

Churchill's interest in Eugenics vanished after 1913, as the so-called science began to be rejected by thoughtful Britons who favored a more humane approach to mental illness. But his fling with the idea left him open to criticism. "It is rare to discover in the archives the reflections of a politician on the nature of man," wrote Paul Addison:

> Churchill's belief in the innate virtue of the great majority of human beings was part and parcel of an optimism he often expressed before the First World War … in his view, sterilisation was a libertarian measure intended to free the unfortunate from incarceration. But Churchill's optimism was tempered, it seems, by a fear of national decline…. Churchill's intentions were benign, but he was blundering into sensitive areas of civil liberty….[23]

To brand Churchill as an unrepentant Eugenicist is an exaggeration. He was attracted to the theory when it was a popular view in most industrial societies. But advances in medical science and ethics, Martin Gilbert wrote, left

> fewer and fewer categories of "mental deficients…." Causes such as food and nutritional deficiency, poverty and deprivation, abuse and neglect were identified as among the reasons—and early diagnosis, medication, therapy, community care and family support systems as the methods of treatment— of what was considered, at the time of Churchill's support for eugenics before the First World War, as hereditary "feeble-mindedness" without a cure.[24]

1940, 1941: Churchill Quoted the Revolutionist Claude McKay

In 2012, Jamaica celebrated its 50th anniversary of independence, and an old story circulated that Churchill quoted the Jamaican revolutionary Claude McKay's famous poem "If We Must Die" to the House of Commons in 1940 and the United States Congress in 1941. Asked to confirm this by the *New York Times* and BBC, I reported that Churchill did not repeat McKay's poem, though in my opinion he shared the sentiments:

> If we must die, let it not be like hogs
> Hunted and penned in an inglorious spot,

While round us bark the mad and hungry dogs,
Making their mock at our accursed lot.
If we must die, O let us nobly die,
So that our precious blood may not be shed
In vain; then even the monsters we defy
Shall be constrained to honor us though dead!
O kinsmen! we must meet the common foe!
Though far outnumbered let us show us brave,
And for their thousand blows deal one death blow!
What though before us lies the open grave?
Like men we'll face the murderous cowardly pack,
Pressed to the wall, dying, but fighting back!

The Jamaica Observer, which had asserted the connection during the celebrations, kindly published my correction.[25] This referred to an earlier piece by Professor David Freeman. McKay first published "If We Must Die" in *The Liberator* of July 1919, Freeman wrote, "inspired in reaction to the race riots that took place in the United States during the 1919 'Red Scare.'" Born in Jamaica, McKay emigrated to the U.S. in 1912 and become active in radical politics. After World War II it was alleged that Churchill had quoted all or part of McKay's poem to Parliament and/or the United States Congress: a famous white leader citing a black poet. But there is no evidence in Hansard or the Congressional Record.

"The confusion stems perhaps from the fact that the poem sounds like something Churchill might have said," Freeman added. "Perhaps the more egregious appropriation of McKay was carried out by those who seek to restrict the poet to a black studies paradigm that distorts the emphatically international contours of a remarkable career."[26]

1941: Churchill [and/or FDR] Knew in Advance of the Attack on Pearl Harbor

Discussing the myth of Churchill's conspiring to sink the *Lusitania* (Chapter 13), Harry Jaffa was reminded

of the widespread belief—sedulously cultivated by Mr. Roosevelt's most vehement political enemies—that the Pacific fleet at Pearl Harbor had been deliberately betrayed in 1941 in order to get the United States into World War II…. Yet the most exhaustive inquests, both by the American Congress under Republican leadership and by professional scholars, have revealed nothing but extraordinary coincidence and extraordinary bungling in that tremendous event. The moral seems to be that intelligence, whether secret or open, has almost no impact upon unwilling minds.[27]

An offshoot of "Roosevelt Knew" is "Churchill Knew"—but refrained from warning Roosevelt of the approaching Japanese fleet in order to inflict maximum damage on the U.S. and get America into World War II. Typical of this theory was a 1998 Documentary by the History Channel,[28] almost immediately "sent to the bottom" by Ron Helgemo, formerly with the CIA.[29]

Methodically, Helgemo punctured testimony of the infamous "Seaman Z" (Robert Ogg), whose story (which varies) is that he heard "queer signals" from the Japanese fleet in San Francisco which were somehow not picked up in Hawaii—itself odd, since the Japanese claimed they had dismantled telegraph devices to ensure radio silence. The History Channel interviewed Eric Nave, a British cryptologist who co-authored *Betrayal at*

Pearl Harbor, claiming Churchill hid what he knew from Roosevelt. Nave had left his station at Singapore in February 1940, Helgemo wrote. He "had no further involvement with the JN-25 [the Japanese code] and could not have known of the Japanese change to the JN-25B code in December 1940," which no one could read at the time of Pearl Harbor. Helgemo quotes a cryptologist who *was* there, Duane Whitlock, stationed on Corregidor: "I can attest from first-hand experience that as of 1 December 1941 the recovery of JN-25B had not progressed to the point that it was productive of any appreciable intelligence."[30]

There is much more to Helgemo's account, including the nonsense about the supposed attack signal ("Winds Code"), supposedly heard in Maryland but nowhere else. He punctures the notion that U.S. Secretary of State Cordell Hull knew, or that General Marshall purpose went horseback riding the morning of December 7th so he would not be available to answer questions about the attack.

The imminence of war was obvious to any reasonably intelligent person, Helgemo wrote. But to understand why the Pacific did not get the attention it needed, we must put ourselves in the shoes of contemporary leaders. The British were fighting for life with Germany; the Americans were engaged an undeclared war with the Germans in the North Atlantic. Navy cryptologists had decrypted 2413 pre–Pearl Harbor intercepts; they might have had some inkling of the attack if they had read *all 26,581*—provided they could discern anything from "all that noise." Finally, Helgemo quoted Professor Warren Kimball: "…to brand WSC and/or FDR as conspirators requires that they be seen as evil geniuses. But for them to allow the U.S. Fleet to be clobbered means they were stupid. That doesn't compute."[31]

Alas, lamented Helgemo (and this was in 1998):

> The reason such garbage passes for history [is because] standards for evidence have virtually disappeared … remnant evidence is better than tradition-creating evidence; corroborated testimony is better than uncorroborated testimony; forensic evidence is better than hearsay. Our inability to be skeptical, to think critically, to ask questions, to compare and contrast, leads to the perpetuation of one urban legend after another.[32]

1945: Churchill Refused to Attend Roosevelt's Funeral

The notion that Churchill reneged from attending Franklin Roosevelt's funeral is a minor but long-running fiction. Even the admirable Jon Meacham, in a fine book about the two leaders, suggested it. Churchill's decision, to stay home, he wrote,

> was partly political and partly emotional, the product of a prideful moment in which Churchill, after playing the suitor to Roosevelt, wanted to himself be courted…. Was Churchill, tired of dancing to another man's tune, relieved Roosevelt was dead? Had it all been an act? … Everything in him would have pressed him to make the trip. The prime minister's letter to George VI does not suggest that the king had taken a stand either way.[33]

Meacham was echoed by later writers. A biographer of Clementine Churchill thought her husband refused to go because of "all that he had endured at Roosevelt's hands."[34]

Former London Mayor Boris Johnson, author of a popular Churchill biography, suggested that the Prime Minister was "miffed" at the President: "…astonishing when you consider how integral their relationship had been to Allied success; not so astonishing when you think of the gradual estrangement that had begun between them … the fundamental divergence was on the matter of Stalin, Russia and the postwar world."[35]

Let us chop away at this underbrush of misinformation. Immediately upon hearing of Roosevelt's death, Churchill telegraphed Lord Halifax, his ambassador in Washington, to ask if it would be suitable to attend the funeral. Halifax spoke to Harry Hopkins and Secretary of State Stettinius, who were "much moved by your thought of possibly coming over and who both warmly agree with my judgment of the immense effect for good that would be produced."[36] Churchill prepared to fly at 8:30 on 13 April, and Halifax looked forward to the PM having "two of three days talk" with President Truman.

At the last minute, Churchill cancelled. "It would have been a solace to me to be present at Franklin's funeral," he telegraphed to Hopkins, "but everyone here thought my duty next week lay at home."[37] To his absent wife Churchill telegraphed: "I decided not to fly to Roosevelt's funeral on account of much that was going on here."[38]

Contrary to Meacham, "everyone here" included the King, who had objected through his private secretary, Sir Alan Lascelles: "Winston toyed with the idea—and came back to it in the evening—of flying over to the funeral. I opposed this firmly on the King's behalf, and I'm glad to say that it has now been decided that Eden should go."[39] Eden's undersecretary, Alexander Cadogan wrote in his diary: "P.M. of course wanted to go. A[nthony Eden] thought they oughtn't both to be away together.... P.M. says he'll go and A. can stay. I told A. that, if P.M. goes, he must.... Churchill regretted in after years that he allowed himself to be persuaded not to go."[40]

It is always useful to consider the context of the time. When Roosevelt died, Germany was nearing surrender, in a war that had taxed Churchill and Britain for seven years. The surrender actually would not come until May, after Hitler's death on 30 April. But this of course was not then known.

A sub-text of this story involves Churchill's own funeral in 1965, in which it is sometimes suggested that President Lyndon Johnson refused to attend as "payback" for Churchill missing FDR's funeral. The President was suffering from a severe cold. In his place he sent Chief Justice Earl Warren and Secretary of State Dean Rusk. President Eisenhower joined them and gave a moving eulogy on the BBC. Johnson's statement was anything but spiteful: "When there was darkness in the world … a generous Providence gave us Winston Churchill.... He is history's child, and what he said and what he did will never die."[41]

Things That Go Bump in the Night

1929: Churchill Helped Cause the Wall Street Crash

Pat Riott's *The Greatest Story Never Told* (1994) takes my award for the most absurd Churchill conspiracy theory to date. Stringing together a series of coincidences during Churchill's 1929 tour of North America, Riott suggested that Churchill and his financier brother helped engineer the Wall Street stock market crash as part of a larger plot involving world trade.[42] "While the book looks documented, in fact it isn't," wrote Christopher Sterling, "making wild accusations that are impossible to pin down."[43]

It's not hard to write such things if you feel no responsibility toward facts. Churchill's visit—mainly a holiday trip with his brother Jack and two of their sons—was aided by the generosity of wealthy friends, from Bernard Baruch to William Randolph Hearst. Most of these magnificoes survived the crash and subsequent Depression; therefore they and Churchill must have been responsible for it. The trip coincided with a visit to the U.S. by Ramsay MacDonald (the first serving British prime minister to visit America), who met many of the same high-rollers; therefore the Tory Churchill must have been in collusion with the socialist MacDonald. The Dow Jones Average remained buoyant during the early, Canadian portion of Churchill's trip, but steadily dived immediately after he entered the U.S.; therefore his influence in the Wall Street debacle is obvious.

In 1925, Churchill (then Chancellor of the Exchequer) took Britain back to the gold standard which, Riott says, "plunged England's economy into ruins. By 1931 Churchill took Great Britain *off* the gold standard to boost British exports." (Churchill hadn't been chancellor since 1929, but never mind.) "In 1933 another one of Bernard Baruch's closest friends and admirers, Franklin Roosevelt, did the exact same thing in the United States. While the USA suffered during the 1930s, Great Britain did fantastically well...."[44] We are in fantasy-land here. In the 1930s Britain lost half its world trade, a third of its heavy industry, nearly four million jobs. If leaving gold enabled Britain to do "fantastically well," why didn't it work for the USA?

On "Black Tuesday," 29 October 1929, after the market had lost $14 billion of wealth in eight hours, Riott portrays Churchill as "guest of honor at a bizarre 'celebration' attended by over forty 'bankers and master plungers' of Wall Street at the Fifth Avenue mansion of Bernard Baruch."[45] It is true that Baruch had gathered leading bankers and financiers. But Churchill remembered "that when one of them proposed my health he addressed the company as 'Friends and former millionaires.'"[46] Riott insists that "the mood was jubilant and ecstatic."[47]

Churchill's bank manager was not so jubilant. His client's personal losses were more than $75,000 (about $1 million today). It's quite true that Baruch, that canny investor, made almost $2 million in 1929, but that doesn't make him a conspiracist. Bradley Tolppanen, who studied Churchill's 1929 travels, wrote that "Baruch felt some blame for Churchill's misfortune and paid his friend $7200 to compensate for losses incurred using Baruch's brokers.... Despite the beating he had taken, Churchill continued to play the stock market and sought Baruch's advice on investments."[48] For the most part, Tolppanen says, the advice was sound, and Churchill's portfolio slowly recovered.

Riott cited Baruch's November 1929 cable to Churchill, "financial storm definitely passed," as "precisely on target." The Dow climbed back to nearly 300 by April 1930: "Don't you just wish that your broker had the remarkable inside knowledge that Bernard Baruch had? Sorry, that insight is reserved for the makers and shakers of the markets ... the plungers." Riott describes Churchill's return to America on a lecture tour in 1931–32 as "Return of the Vampire!"[49] Actually, Churchill made that trip hoping to recoup some of what the Depression had cost him.

In Baruch's autobiography, Riott adds, "the fact that neither of Churchill's visits in 1929 or 1931–32 are described provide further evidence of the dirty secret he took with him at his cremation in 1965."[50] I combed this book diligently, looking for some document or conversation to substantiate just one Riott's charges; I found none. I must fall back on a serviceable line by a fellow reviewer: "I read this book so you don't have to."

1941: Churchill Tricked Hitler into Invading Russia

It's barely a footnote after *The Greatest Story Never Told,* but runner-up in the silliness sweepstakes is another 1994 book, *Churchill's Deception,* which claimed that Churchill secretly tricked Hitler to attacking the Soviet Union in June 1941.[51] Author Louis Kilzer hangs his case on Rudolf Hess's bizarre flight to Scotland in May 1941. Conspiracy theories about the Hess flight would fill a book of their own. But in this case Hess arrives to reveal Hitler's plan to attack Russia to British peace activists, dismissing Churchill, and fixing a truce with Hitler while the Germans knocked out the evil Bolsheviks. Churchill's trick was apparently convincing Hitler that this was feasible.

William Partin reviewed this book in 1994. Kilzer, he wrote, even suggested that the Hess imprisoned at Spandau Prison through his death in 1987 was an imposter. The implication is

> that Churchill wanted no witnesses to his deception. Yet Kilzer offers no clear explanation as to how or why an impostor was put in Hess's place…. The author's arguments about Churchill's great conspiracy to deceive Hitler and his alleged responsibility for the Holocaust and the Cold War are often so difficult to follow that (to use Kilzer's own words) that "the conspiracy theory gets very complicated and at times borders on the absurd."[52]

I think I can accept that.

Appendix 2:
Red Herrings:
Mythological Churchill Quotes

Along with lies, myths and rumors, false Churchill quotes are a problem. He is persistently credited with remarks he never made, often put in his mouth to make them more interesting. In a few cases he was actually queried about them, and denied authorship. Some of his quips were not coined by him: often he would preface them with phrases like "as has been said…" He sometimes deployed famous maxims without quote marks, because he assumed his listeners would recognize them. In April 1941, responding to Roosevelt's message quoting Longfellow ("Sail On, O Ship of State") Churchill broadcast his reply, which quoted the poet Arthur Hugh Clough: "Westward, look, the land is bright!" His listeners listened with understanding, for most of them had recited Clough's "Say Not the Struggle Naught Availeth," in school. In Churchill's time people were simply better read than they are today.

Ribald quotations are also often ascribed to Churchill, but are so far out of character as to be undeserving of notice. One example will suffice: a curvaceous female admirer who meets him at the unveiling of his sculpture says: "I got up at dawn and drove a hundred miles for the unveiling of your bust"; Churchill supposedly replies, "Madam, I would happily reciprocate the honour." In reality, Churchill simply was not given to salacious remarks, and nearly always treated the opposite sex with Victorian courtesy.

Listed below are over eighty common misquotes, some of which (as the notes indicate), sound very much like him. For example, "The heaviest cross I have to bear is the Cross of Lorraine" is so well established that I was surprised to learn that someone else said it.

Entries are sorted by key phrases. In cases of quotes long thought to be Churchill's, I provide explanatory notes. "No attribution" means that the quote, variations and segments of it are not found in the fifty million words by and about Churchill to which I have access. Books cited are in the Bibliography.

America and World War I

"America should have minded her own business and stayed out of the World War. If you hadn't entered the war the Allies would have made peace with Germany in the Spring of 1917. Had we made peace then there would have been no collapse in Russia followed by Communism, no breakdown in Italy followed by Fascism, and

Germany would not have signed the Versailles Treaty, which has enthroned Nazism in Germany. If America had stayed out of the war, all these 'isms' wouldn't today be sweeping the continent of Europe"—1936, quoted in the *New York Times, 22 October 1942.*

In 1942 a lawsuit was brought against Churchill (who had denounced the quotation as fiction) by publisher William Griffin of the *New York Enquirer.* It was dismissed for lack of evidence. See Chapter 14.

Amusing and Serious

"You cannot deal with the most serious things in the world unless you also understand the most amusing."—no attribution

Arboricide

"You are guilty of arboricide!"—ca. 1935

Alleged remark to Clementine Churchill when she cut down a favorite tree. Although he once accused her of "arboricidal mania," he did not originate "arboricide." The *Oxford English Dictionary* tracks it to H.G. Graham's *Social Life of Scotland* (1899): "the crime of arboricide was distressingly frequent."

Attlee, Clement

"An empty car drew up and Clement Attlee got out."—ca. 1950

"That sheep in sheep's clothing!"—ca. 1950

The Quote Verifier editor Ralph Keyes wrote to the author: "When asked, Churchill said this was based on a more pointed remark he'd once made about someone else." Churchill had high respect for Attlee and on several occasions strongly denied making disparaging statements about his wartime colleague.

Balfour, Arthur

"If you wanted nothing done, Arthur Balfour was the best man for the task. There was no one equal to him."

Supposedly WSC made this wry remark when Lloyd George said he heard that Balfour was "dominating the League of Nations." The quote has been ascribed to *Lord Riddell's War Diary,* but no such words appear there.

Beer Bottles, Hit Them With

"…we shall fight in the fields and in the streets, we shall fight in the hills…. And we will hit them over the heads with beer bottles, which is about all we have got to work with."—alleged aside, 18 June 1940 BBC broadcast)

The only published reference to this offhand remark (with Churchill allegedly covering the BBC microphone during his rebroadcast of the speech), was by Robert Lewis Taylor, who wrote that it was heard by "one of England's highest clergymen, who was present at the studio…." Sir John Colville, who was present, told the author he did not hear it. Wonderful as it is, it must be regarded as unproven.

Birth

"Although present on that occasion I have no clear recollection of the events leading up to it."—Manchester, *Last Lion* I, 107

This famous and oft-quoted expression cannot be tracked. In the canon it is not among Churchill's own words, and it appears only in Manchester, whose notes do not lead the reader to its origin.

Botswana

"What is Botswana worth?"—ca. 1960

Allegedly posed by Churchill in Parliament ("£40,000" was the supposed answer). But he said nothing in Parliament after retiring as Prime Minister in 1955, and Bechuanaland did not adopt the name Botswana until 1966.

Bring a Friend, If You Have One

[Bernard Shaw: "Am reserving two tickets for you for my premiere. Come and bring a friend—if you have one."] WSC: "Impossible to be present for the first performance. Will attend the second—if there is one."—ca. 1924

The play was "Saint Joan," but according to the Churchill Archives Centre, the exchange was forcefully denied in 1949 letters by both Churchill and Shaw, replying to a correspondent who asked them specifically to verify it.

Cigars and Women

"Smoking cigars is like falling in love; first you are attracted to its shape; you stay for its flavour; and you must always remember never, never let the flame go out."—*The American Spectator*, July-August 2005; no attribution

Common Language

"Britain and America are two nations divided by a common language."—no attribution

Also credited to Bernard Shaw and Dylan Thomas, also without attribution. Ralph Keyes's *The Quote Verifier* suggests it originated in Oscar Wilde's "The Canterville Ghost" (1887): "We have really everything in common with America nowadays, except, of course, language." Verdict: adapted Wilde.

Courage

"Courage is what it takes to stand up and speak; courage is also what it takes to sit down and listen."—no attribution

Cross of Lorraine

"The heaviest cross I have to bear is the Cross of Lorraine."—1943

Allegedly in reference to de Gaulle and the Free French, this was actually said by General Edward Louis Spears, WSC's military representative to the French government in 1939–40.

Defenders of the Peace

> "People sleep peaceably in their beds at night only because rough men stand ready to do violence on their behalf."

> "We sleep safely at night because rough men stand ready to visit violence on those who would harm us."

Though occasionally attributed to Churchill, it is more often assigned to George Orwell. Wikiquotes reports: "There is no evidence that Orwell ever wrote or uttered either of these…. They do bear some similarity to comments made in an essay that Orwell wrote on Rudyard Kipling."

Democracy

> "The best argument against Democracy is a five-minute conversation with the average voter."

Commonly quoted, never with attribution. Though he sometimes despaired of democracy's slowness to act for its own preservation, Churchill had a much more positive attitude towards the average voter.

> "Many forms of Government have been tried, and will be tried in this world of sin and woe. No one pretends that democracy is perfect or all-wise. Indeed it has been said that democracy is the worst form of Government except for all those other forms that have been tried from time to time…."—House of Commons, 11 November 1947

Although these are Churchill's words, he clearly did not originate the famous remark about Democracy. Credit Churchill as publicist for an unsourced aphorism.

Dignity

> "I know of no case where a man added to his dignity by standing on it."—Manchester, *Last Lion II*, 25

Rather than reply to Labour Party attacks, Churchill's colleagues supposedly urged him to "stand on his dignity." Unconfirmed and without attribution.

Dinner, Wine and Women

> "Well, dinner would have been splendid if the wine had been as cold as the soup, the beef as rare as the service, the brandy as old as the fish, and the maid as willing as the Duchess."

Sometimes we know intuitively that such quotations are manufactured. WSC would not have stayed for the second course of such a meal, and his remarks about women were, with rare exceptions, gallant.

Dog Days

> "Every dog has his day."—1944; Churchill, *Triumph and Tragedy,* 611

An old saying, not Churchill's, in his memo to chief of staff General Ismay regarding the shipping of World War I–era long-range heavy guns to bolster the invasion of Germany.

Drugs

> "Dear nurse, pray remember that man cannot live by M&B alone."—Carthage, 1943

Not found in Churchill's canon, though it sounds like him. WSC delighted in the sulfa drug M&B, and referred to his doctors, Lord Moran and Dr. Bedford.

Dukes

> "…a fully equipped duke costs as much to keep as two dreadnoughts; and dukes are just as great a terror and they last longer."—Newcastle, 9 October 1909

Sometimes attributed to Churchill, this was uttered by David Lloyd George, his ally in the campaign to reform the House of Lords. *Dreadnought* was the first of a new class of fast, powerful battleships developed by the Royal Navy.

Enemies

> "You have enemies? Good. That means you've stood up for something, sometime in your life."—no attribution

Fanatic

> "A fanatic is someone who won't change his mind, and won't change the subject."

Often attributed to Churchill or President Truman. "It's a quotation I see often, but without a source. I doubt that it's Truman; if he ever said it, it did not originate with him" (Ralph Keyes, editor, *The Quote Verifier*).

Feet-First

> "Not feet-first, please!"—Monte Carlo, 1962

Supposedly said to the stretcher-bearer after breaking his leg at Monte Carlo, but no attribution can be tracked.

First Thoughts

> "Distrust first thoughts—they are usually honest."—Commons, 15 July 1948

Churchill uttered these words, within quote marks, preceding them by saying, "As the cynic has said…"

France

> "The destiny of a great nation has never yet been settled by the temporary condition of its technical apparatus."—Commons, 2 August 1944

Not Churchill though quoted by him; WSC himself attributed it to Leon Trotsky.

Free Lunch

> "There ain't no free lunch."

Churchill is alleged to have uttered these five words at a university commencement ceremony, and then resumed his seat. Ralph Keyes in *The Quote Verifier* tracks the phrase to various people from Milton Friedman to Merrill Rukeyser. It can also be found in

Rudyard Kipling's *American Notes* (1891), which states that it was the custom of San Francisco bars to provide food to customers who ordered at least one drink.

Gandhi

"[Gandhi] ought to be laid, bound hand and foot, at the gates of Delhi and then trampled on by an enormous elephant with the new Viceroy seated on its back."—4 November 1940, Alfred Duff Cooper, *Old Men Forget*, 103

An example of how hearsay becomes enshrined. This recollection reappeared as a direct quotation in the highly unreliable *Private Lives of Winston Churchill,* and was repeated by Sarvepalli Gopal in "Churchill and India" (Blake & Louis, *Major New Assessment,* 459). For genuine Gandhi quotations see Chapter 19.

Genius

"True genius resides in the capacity for evaluation of uncertain, hazardous, and conflicting information."—no attribution

German Resistance

"...in Germany there lived an opposition which was weakened by their losses and an enervating international policy, but which belongs to the noblest and greatest that the political history of any nation has ever produced. These men fought without help from within or from abroad—driven forward only by the restlessness of their conscience. As long as they lived they were invisible and unrecognisable to us, because they had to camouflage themselves. But their death made the resistance visible."—1946; Lamb, *Churchill as War Leader,* 292, 363

This is the only appearance in English. Lamb quotes a letter from Churchill to Walter Hammer of Hamburg, 19 November 1946: "I have had a search made through my speeches … but so far no record can be found of any such pronouncement by me. But I might quite well have used the words you quote as they represent my feelings on this aspect of German affairs."

Golf

"A curious sport whose object is to put a very small ball in a very small hole with implements ill-designed for the purpose."—ca. 1915. Manchester, *Last Lion* I, 213

Manchester's footnote is unhelpful. The remark is not, as he states, in the Official Biography's Document Volumes, nor in a work by General Sir Hubert Gough. It is likely to have been uttered by any golfer at one time or another.

Harlot's Prerogative

"Power without responsibility … the prerogative of the harlot through the ages."

Not Churchill but Rudyard Kipling. Subsequently used by Baldwin in 1931 without reference to Kipling (his cousin).

Health

"Half the world's work is done by people who don't feel well."

Another recent entry on the Internet; no attribution.

Hell

> "If you're going through hell, keep going."—no attribution

Horses

> "The outside of a horse is good for the inside of a man."

Repeatedly attributed to everyone from Woodrow Wilson's physician and Ronald Reagan to Henry Ward Beecher and Oliver Wendell Holmes. "Long-time male equestrian wisdom" (Ralph Keyes, *The Quote Verifier*, 91).

Ingratitude

> "Ingratitude towards their great men is the mark of strong peoples."—Churchill, *Gathering Storm*, 10

Although often ascribed to him, Churchill credited Plutarch with this remark. He was commenting on the discarding of French war leader Georges Clemenceau after the victory of World War I.

Italians

> [German Ambassador von Ribbentrop: "Remember, Mr. Churchill, if there is a war, we will have the Italians on our side this time."] WSC: "My dear Ambassador, it's only fair. We had them last time."—1937

An alleged aside during Churchill's famous meeting with the "Londonderry Herr," German Ambassador to Britain. No attribution.

Jaw, Jaw; War, War

> "Jaw, jaw is better than war, war."—Washington, 1954

Sir Martin Gilbert noted that Churchill actually said, "Meeting jaw to jaw is better than war." Four years later, during a visit to Australia, Harold Macmillan said the words wrongly, attributed to Churchill: "Jaw, jaw is better than war, war."

Kiss a Girl, Climb a Wall

> "The most difficult things for a man to do are to climb a wall leaning towards you, and to kiss a girl leaning away from you." [Sometimes added: "…and to make an after-dinner speech"].

Commonly ascribed, but nowhere in Churchill's canon. Recently claimed by religion columnist Marion de Velder, but probably a much older expression.

Liberal and Conservative

> "If a man is not liberal in youth he has no heart. If he is not conservative when older he has no brain."

> "When I was a young liberal I thought with my heart; when I grew wiser and conservative I thought with my brain."

All over the internet, but without attribution in Churchill's canon.

Liberty

"They who can give up essential liberty to obtain a little temporary safety deserve neither liberty nor safety."—ca. 1920

This remark dates back at least to 1776 and Benjamin Franklin, though it may be as old as 1755. If Churchill used it, which I cannot verify, he was quoting Franklin.

Lies

"There are a terrible lot of lies going about the world, and the worst of it is that half of them are true."—22 February 1906

Churchill did use these words, but explained that they were the remark of a "witty Irishman."

"A lie will gallop halfway round the world before the truth has time to pull its breeches on."—ca. 1940s

Commonly ascribed to Churchill (who would have said "trousers" not "breeches"), this appeared in the *Memoirs Cordell Hull*, I 220.

Living and Life

"You make a living by what you get; you make a life by what you give."

Reiterated many times, including a 2005 TV ad by Lockheed Martin. An old saw put in Churchill's mouth.

Living Dog, Dead Lion

"A living dog is better than a dead lion."—Churchill, *English-Speaking Peoples* II, 95

Churchill was quoting John Dudley, First Duke of Northumberland, before being executed by Mary Tudor (Mary I) upon her ascent to the throne in 1553.

Looking Ahead

"It is always wise to look ahead—but difficult to look further than you can see."—no attribution

Looking Backward

"The further backward you look, the further forward you can see."

"The farther backward you can look, the farther forward you can see."—ca. 1944

Often ascribed to Churchill, even by HM The Queen (Christmas Message, 1999). What Churchill actually said was "The longer you can look back, the farther you can look forward."

MacDonald, Ramsay

"After the usual compliments, the Prime Minister said: "We have never been colleagues, we have never been friends—at least, not what you would call holiday friends—but we have both been prime minister, and dog doesn't eat dog."—31 January 1931; Kay Halle, *Irrepressible Churchill*, 114

According to Halle, this was "an imaginary conversation dreamed by WSC between Prime Minister Ramsay MacDonald and Lloyd George."

Marx Brothers

> "You are my fifth favourite actor. The first four are the Marx Brothers."

Reported in at least one Churchill quotations book. No sign of this comment appears in the literature.

Montgomery, Field Marshal Bernard

> "In defeat, indomitable; in victory, insufferable."

> "Indomitable in retreat, invincible in advance, insufferable in victory."

Widely bruited about, but without attribution. Likely adapted from "Indomitable in victory, insufferable in defeat," by American football coach Woody Hayes.

> "The Field Marshal lived up to the finest tradition of Englishmen. He sold his life dearly."—1958

Churchill allegedly said this when advised that Monty's memoirs were earning more than his *History of the English Speaking Peoples*.

Naval Tradition

> "Don't talk to me about naval tradition. It's nothing but rum, buggery [sometimes "sodomy"] and the lash."—Admiralty, ca. 1914–15

Churchill denied saying this in a 1955 conversation with Anthony Montague Browne. Harold Nicolson's diary quotes him secondhand on 17 August 1950: "Naval tradition? Monstrous. Nothing but rum, sodomy, prayers and the lash." But the *Oxford Dictionary of Quotations* lists "Rum, bum, and bacca" and "Ashore it's wine women and song, aboard it's rum, bum and concertina" as 19th century naval catchphrases.

Never Give In

> "Never give in" [or: "Never give up"].—Harrow School, 29 October 1941

Often represented as a three-word speech which Churchill allegedly delivered, and then sat down. "Never give in" simply occurs in a speech to the boys at Harrow: "…never give in, never, never, never, never—in nothing, great or small, large or petty—never give in except to convictions of honour and good sense."

Never Quit

> "Never, never, never quit! [Also sometimes quoted as "Never, never, never give up!"]

Misquotations from the 1941 Harrow speech.

Nuisenza

> "It is a nuisenza to have the fluenza."—25 October 1943, Churchill, *Closing the Ring*, 279

Represented sometimes as a Churchillism, this was actually Roosevelt writing to Churchill.

Oats and Sage

> "The young sow wild oats, the old grow sage."

Constantly ascribed to Churchill but not among his published words. Henry James Byron in "An Adage" wrote: "The gardener's rule applies to youth and age; When young 'sow wild oats,' but when old, grow sage."

Opportunity

> "To each there comes in their lifetime a special moment when they are figuratively tapped on the shoulder and offered the chance to do a very special thing, unique to them and fitted to their talents. What a tragedy if that moment finds them unprepared or unqualified for that which could have been their finest hour."

Commonly attributed, but no part of the quotation can be found. That it is made up is suggested by its use of "finest hour," from WSC's famous speech of 18 June 1940, which he would have been unlikely to repeat in so offhand a context. It is also too wordy to escape Churchill's deft editorial pen.

People Will Put You Out

> [Lord Shawcross: "We are the masters at the moment, and not only at the moment, but for a very long time to come."] WSC: "Oh no you're not. The people put you there and the people will put you out again."—Commons, 1946

Labour peer Lord Shawcross is often misquoted as having said, "We are the masters now." He always maintained that he spoke as quoted above. However, Churchill's supposed retort is not established and is likely apocryphal.

Pessimist and Optimist

> "A pessimist sees the difficulty in every opportunity; an optimist sees the opportunity in every difficulty."—no attribution

Poison in Your Coffee

> [Nancy Astor: "If I were married to you, I'd put poison in your coffee."] WSC: "If I were married to you, I'd drink it."—Blenheim Palace, ca. 1912

Martin Gilbert (*In Search of Churchill*, 232) suggested the author was F. E. Smith, Lord Birkenhead, "a much heavier drinker than Churchill, and a notorious acerbic wit." But Fred Shapiro (editor, *Yale Book of Quotations*) says the riposte dates back even farther, to a joke line in the *Chicago Tribune* of 3 January 1900: "'If I had a husband like you,' she said with concentrated scorn, 'I'd give him poison!' 'Mad'm,' he rejoined, looking her over with a feeble sort of smile, 'If I had a wife like you I'd take it.'" Verdict: F. E. Smith, giving new life to an old wisecrack.

Prepositions

> "This is the kind of tedious nonsense up with which I will not put." [Sometimes rendered as "pedantic nonsense" or "tedious nuisance."]—27 February 1944

Originally attributed to WSC in cable reports in the *New York Times* and *Chicago Tribune*, 28 February 1944. "The Times … made one change that seems to undercut Churchill's humor completely: they 'fixed' the quote so that there are no fronted prepositions," writes Fred Shapiro, editor, *Yale Book of Quotations*. "*The Wall Street Journal*, 30 September 1942, quotes an undated article in *Strand Magazine*. When a memorandum passed round a certain Government department, one young pedant scribbled a postscript drawing attention to the fact that the sentence ended with a preposition, which caused the original writer to circulate another memorandum complaining that the anonymous postscript was 'offensive impertinence, up with which I will not put.'"

Prisoners of War

"A prisoner of war is a man who tries to kill you and fails, and then asks you not to kill him."—no attribution

Risk, Care and Dream

"Risk more than others think is safe. Care more than others think is wise. Dream more than others think is practical. Expect more than others think is possible."

Inspirational prose ascribed to Churchill to make it more interesting. Quoteworld.org ascribes this to Claude Thomas Bissell, Canadian author and educator.

Sex

"It gives me great pleasure."

In a supposed after-dinner activity of The Other Club, a member drawn at random would chalk a word on a blackboard, and a second member, also chosen by lot, had to make an impromptu speech about it. Churchill drew the response when a member chalked "sex" on the blackboard. If actually delivered, this would be Churchill's shortest speech. No attribution is found.

Shy a Stone

"You will never get to the end of the journey if you stop to shy a stone at every dog that barks."—Shepherd's Bush Empire, London, 3 December 1923

Churchill was quoting someone else. He preceded this by stating, "As someone said…"

Simple Tastes

"I am a man of simple tastes—I am quite easily satisfied with the best of every-thing."—ca. 1930s

According to Sir John Colville, WSC's close friend F. E. Smith, Lord Birkenhead, said, "Mr. Churchill is easily satisfied with the best." Churchill with his great memory could easily have repeated and embroidered Birkenhead's remark when he visited the Plaza Hotel in New York, shortly after Birkenhead's death in 1931, as is sometimes stated. Credit: F. E. Smith.

Speeches, Long vs. Short

"I am going to make a long speech today; I haven't had time to prepare a short one."

If he said this (there is no evidence), WSC borrowed the idea from Blaise Pascal who, in

1656, wrote to a friend: "I have only made this letter rather long because I have not had time to make it shorter." ("*Je n'ai fait celle-ci plus longue que parceque je n'ai pas eu le loisir de la faire plus courte.*")

Stalin and Russia

"In the course of three decades, however, the face of the Soviet Union has become transformed. The core of Stalin's historic achievements consists in this, that he had found Russia working with wooden ploughs and is leaving her equipped with atomic piles. He has raised Russia to the level of the second industrial Power of the world. This was not a matter of mere material progress and organisation. No such achievement would have been possible without a vast cultural revolution, in the course of which a whole nation was sent to school to undergo a most intensive education."

Supposedly a tribute by Churchill after Stalin's death or later, this has no relation to any known statement.

Strategy and Results

"However beautiful the strategy, you should occasionally look at the results."—no attribution

Success

"Success is not final, failure is not fatal: it is the courage to continue that counts."

"Success is going from failure to failure without losing your enthusiasm."

Broadly attributed but nowhere in Churchill's canon. An almost equal number of sources credit the second version to Abraham Lincoln; but none provides attribution.

Taking Office

"Take office only when it suits you, but put the government in a minority whenever you decently can."—Churchill, *Lord Randolph Churchill,* 188

WSC put this maxim in quotations because he did not claim it, but ascribed it to his father.

Trees and the Sky

"The trees do not grow up to the sky."—*News of the World,* 25 September 1938

Described by Churchill as an "old German saying" following his expressed concerns about dramatic falls in future birth rates. Also deployed with slightly different wording over bombing London.

Troubles

"Most of the things I have worried about never ended up happening."

Inaccurate version of a phrase Churchill himself quoted. Fred Shapiro, editor, *Yale Book of Quotations,* believes the originator was Mark Twain or Thomas Jefferson. Twain: "I am an old man and have known a great many troubles, but most of them never happened." Jefferson: "How much pain have cost us the evils which have never happened!" (to John Adams, 8 April 1816).

Virtues and Vices

> "He has all the virtues I dislike and none of the vices I admire."

> "He was possessed of all the virtues I despise and none of the sins I admire."

Prominently quoted with respect to Stafford Cripps and Churchill's longtime election opponent in Dundee, Edwin Scrymgeour; no evidence of this or variations on it in the canon.

While England Slept

The American edition of *Arms and the Covenant*, whose title inspired young John Kennedy's subsequent *Why England Slept*, was not Churchill's title. His cable suggesting *The Locust Years*, to his American publisher Putnam, was garbled to read *The Lotus Years*. Baffled, Putnam's looked up "lotus," which was described as a plant inducing dreaminess. An editor suggested *While England Slept*. Churchill was delighted.

White Meat

> "I would be much obliged if you would pin this to your white meat."—1946, no attribution

After asking for a chicken breast at a Virginia buffet, Churchill was informed by his genteel hostess that Southern ladies preferred the term "white meat." The next day he supposedly sent her a corsage, with a card stating the above.

Winston Is Back!

> "I therefore sent word to the Admiralty that I would take charge forthwith and arrive at 6 o'clock. On this the Board were kind enough to signal the fleet, 'Winston is back.'"—Churchill, *Gathering Storm*, 320

Although quoted by WSC and some admirers, Sir Martin Gilbert and other biographers have never found a record of such a signal being sent to the fleet when Churchill returned to the Admiralty in September 1939.

Words

> "We are the masters of the unsaid words, but slaves of those we let slip out."

> "It has been said words are the only things which last forever."—10 June 1909

Used by Churchill several times in his writings and speeches, but as the second version indicates, he admitted it did not originate with him.

Yale and MIT

> "An after-dinner speaker was giving the audience at least fifteen minutes for each of the four letters that spell Yale ... 'Y is for Youth.... A is for Achievement.... L is for Loyalty.... E is for Enterprise.' Halfway through 'Enterprise' a voice was heard: 'Thank God he didn't go to the Massachusetts Institute of Technology.'"

Occasionally attributed to Churchill but no instance has been found, though members of his family use the joke frequently (not attributing it to him).

Ypres, Belgium

> "I should like us to acquire the ruins of Ypres … a more sacred place for the British race does not exist in the world."—1918

Widely attributed to Churchill, but no reliable source can be found, although these were certainly his sentiments, according to his private secretary Eddie Marsh's diary of 29 October 1918: "Winston wants to turn that group of buildings into a cemetery, with lawns and flowers among the ruins, and the names of innumerable dead."

Appendix 3:
The Hillsdale College
Churchill Project

Hillsdale College launched the Churchill Project in 2006 to propagate a right understanding of Churchill's record, and to "teach statesmanship" through its distinguished academic resources at all levels from undergraduate to online education programs.

Since 2006, Hillsdale College Press has been the publisher of *Winston S. Churchill*, the official biography, including its eight biographic and nineteen (to date) document volumes through 2016. The Churchill Project will complete the remaining volumes of *The Churchill Documents*, bringing to over thirty volumes what is already the longest biography in history.

The Churchill Project is also the archive for the papers of Sir Martin Gilbert, Churchill's official biographer from 1968 to 2012. And it will promote Churchill scholarship through national conferences, scholarships, online courses, and an endowed faculty chair. Through these endeavors, Hillsdale College will establish itself at the forefront of Churchill research, scholarship, and analysis.

For more information please visit The Churchill Project website, winstonchurchill. hillsdale.edu. There you may subscribe for frequent updates of articles and videos, and news of seminars and educational programs.

Chapter Notes

"**CBH**" refers to Richard M. Langworth, ed., *Churchill by Himself* (electronic edition, New York, Rosetta Books, 2015; Public Affairs, 2011); *Churchill in His Own Words* (revised print edition, London: Ebury Press, 2012). "**WSC**" refers to the official biography, *Winston S. Churchill*, by Randolph S. Churchill (vols. 1–2) and Martin Gilbert (vols. 3–8); "**WSC DV**" refers to the accompanying volumes of *The Churchill Documents*, edited by Randolph S. Churchill (1–5), Martin Gilbert (6–16), and Martin Gilbert and Larry P. Arnn (17–on), Hillsdale, Mich.: Hillsdale College Press). For individual titles and publishing data, see Bibliography.

Preface

1. Harry V. Jaffa, *Statesmanship* (1981), 273.
2. Winston S. Churchill, *The Gathering Storm* (1948), 571.
3. Martin Gilbert, "Churchill for Today," *Finest Hour* 73 (1991), 11.
4. Martin Gilbert, *Churchill: A Life* (1991), 208.
5. M.K. Gandhi (1935), *The Churchill Documents*, vol. 12, 1265.
6. Paul Addison, *Churchill on the Home Front* (1992), 125.
7. Gilbert, "Churchill for Today."
8. William F. Buckley, Jr., Intl. Churchill Conference, Boston, 27 October 1995.
9. Churchill, House of Commons, 5 May 1952.
10. Churchill, House of Commons, 12 May 1901.

Chapter 1

1. CBH, 122–23.
2. Robert Pilpel, *Churchill in America 1895–1961: An Affectionate Portrait* (New York: Harcourt, Brace, Jovanovich, 1976), 3.
3. Correspondence with the National Congress of American Indians and British Embassy, Washington, February–November 1963. Churchill Archives Centre, CHUR 2/540/75–105.
4. Roy Howells, *Simply Churchill* (London: Robert Hale, 1965), 119.
5. Ralph G. Martin, *Jennie*, vol. I, *The Romantic Years 1854–1895* (Englewood Cliffs, New Jersey: Prentice-Hall 1969), 340–41. Martin admitted there were "no genealogical facts to support any Indian ancestry," and ascribes the story to "Jerome family legend."
6. WSC1, 15–16.
7. Elizabeth Churchill Snell, "Urban Myths: Indian Forebears," *Finest Hour* 104, Autumn 1999, 31–32. Scott C. Steward, "Notable Kin," in *Nexus* (Journal of the New England Historic Genealogical Society) XIII: 5, 1997,

167. Bertha W. Clark typescript on the descendants of Francis Baker of Yarmouth; see Gary Boyd Roberts and Michael J. Wood, "Notable Kin," *Nexus* V:3, 1988, 94–95.
8. Steward, "Notable Kin," 171–72; *Nexus* V:3, 95.
9. Cf. Anita Leslie, *Lady Randolph Churchill: The Story of Jennie Jerome* (New York: Scribner 1969). *Nexus* V:3, 95. Snell, "Urban Myths," 32.
10. Snell, "Urban Myths," 32. *Nexus*, XIII:5, 172.
11. Shane Leslie, *Long Shadows* (London: Murray 1966), 19. Anita Leslie, *The Remarkable Mr. Jerome*, New York: Henry Holt 1954, 22.
12. Lady Soames, conversation with the author, 1995.
13. Richard M. Langworth, "Randolph Churchill 1911–1968," *Finest Hour* 79, International Churchill Society, Second Quarter 1993, 11.
14. Pilpel, *Churchill in America*, 3.
15. Winston S. Churchill, *The Great Republic: A Brief History of America*, edited by his grandson (New York: Random House, 1999), x.
16. Winston S. Churchill (grandson), conversation with the author, 1999.

Chapter 2

1. William Manchester, *The Last Lion: Winston Spencer Churchill*, vol. 1, *Visions of Glory 1874–1932* (Boston: Little Brown, 1982), 137.
2. Ralph G. Martin, *Jennie, The Dramatic Years 1895–1921* (Englewood Cliffs, New Jersey: Prentice-Hall 1971), 23–24.
3. William Manchester, *The Last Lion: Winston Spencer Churchill*, vol. 2, *Alone 1932–1940* (Boston: Little Brown, 1988), 15.
4. Norman Rose, *Churchill: The Unruly Giant* (New York: Free Press, 1995), 254 n.44. Frank Costigliola, *Roosevelt's Lost Alliances: How Personal Politics Helped Start the Cold War* (Princeton, N.J.: Princeton University Press, 2012), 31 n.36.
5. Richard Hough, *Winston and Clementine* (London: Bantam, 1990), 30.

6. Ralph Martin, *Jennie: The Romantic Years 1854–1895* (Englewood Cliffs, N.J.: 1969), 134. Following a lawsuit by Peregrine Churchill, the offending part of this text (through "prime of his vigour") was deleted from the English edition, and several thousand earlier editions containing it were destroyed.

7. Anita Leslie, *Edwardians in Love* (London: Hutchinson, 1972), 196.

8. Leslie, *Edwardians*, 197.

9. *Ibid.*

10. Peregrine S. Churchill to the author, 1989.

11. Leslie, *Edwardians*, 197. Anne Sebba, *American Jennie: The Remarkable Life of Lady Randolph Churchill* (New York: Norton, 2007), 203.

12. Leslie, *Edwardians*, 197.

13. Richard M. Langworth, "A New Gathering Storm?," *Finest Hour* 67, Second Quarter 1990, 29. Peregrine S. Churchill and Richard Hough, letters to the editor, *Sunday Telegraph*, London, 29 April 1990.

14. Peregrine Churchill to the author, 1989. Sir Robert Rhodes James to the author, 1992.

Chapter 3

1. Winston S. Churchill, *My Early Life* (London: Thornton Butterworth, 1930), 53, 15.

2. CBH, 526, E.D.W. Chaplin, *Winston Churchill at Harrow* (Harrow, Middlesex: The Harrow Bookshop, 1941), 45. Churchill returned to Harrow to lecture on his Boer War experiences in 1900; as chancellor of the exchequer in 1928; to judge the Bourchier Reading Prize in 1938; as prime minister in 1940 and 1941, and on many occasions after World War II. His last visit was in 1962.

3. Sir Cyril Norwood, former president of St. John's College, Oxford, in Chaplin, *Churchill at Harrow*, 3.

4. Churchill, *My Early Life*, 17.

5. WSC1, 47, 55–56.

6. Churchill, *My Early Life*, 26–27.

7. CBH, 451.

8. Robert Lewis Taylor, *Winston Churchill: An Informal Study of Greatness* (Garden City, N.Y.: Doubleday, 1952), 60.

9. Sir Gerald Woods Wollaston, "Churchill at Harrow," in Charles Eade, *Churchill by His Contemporaries* (London: Hutchinson, 1953), 1–6.

10. Celia and John Lee, *Winston and Jack: The Churchill Brothers* (London: Privately published, 2007), 77.

11. Geoffrey J. Fletcher, "Spencer-Churchill (p) at Harrow School 1888–1892," Part 1, *Finest Hour* 133, Winter 2006–07, 31–35.

12. CBH, 377.

13. A.W. Simmons, "Spencer Churchill, W.L.," in Chaplin, *Churchill at Harrow*, 11–12.

14. Taylor, *Informal Study*, 60–62.

15. Wollaston, "Churchill at Harrow," 3.

16. Wright Cooper in Chaplin, *Churchill at Harrow,"* 84.

17. Peregrine S. Churchill to the author, 1992. Jim Golland, *Not Winston, Just William? Winston Churchill at Harrow School* (Harrow: Herga Press, 1988), Wollaston, "Churchill at Harrow," 2.

18. Taylor, *Informal Study*, 62.

19. Geoffrey J. Fletcher, "Spencer-Churchill (p) at Harrow School 1888–1892," Part 2, *Finest Hour* 134, Spring 2007, 31–35. Fletcher quoted three: "*Ecce signum*" (Look at the proof); "*Fas est ab hoste doceri*" (It is right to be even taught by the enemy); and "*Eheu fugaces, Postume, Postume, labuntur anni*" (Alas Postumus, Postumus the flying years fall past us).

20. CBH, 195.

21. Pilpel, *Churchill in America*, ix.

22. CBH, 54. The exchange was with Hugh Gaitskell on 5 March 1953.

23. Fletcher, "Spencer Churchill," Part II, 35.

24. A.W. Simmons in Chaplin, *Churchill at Harrow*, 11–12.

25. Churchill, *My Early Life*, 39–40. Fletcher, Part II, 34.

26. CBH, 448. Churchill was awarded the Nobel Prize for Literature in 1953.

27. Periodical contributions G1-G6, in Ronald I. Cohen, *Bibliography of the Writings of Sir Winston Churchill*, 3 vols. (London: Continuum, 2006) III 1853–54. Young Winston had evidently been reading the anonymous "Letters of Junius," in the *Public Advertiser* between 1769 and 1822. They attacked the government of George III with merciless invective and influenced the style of English polemics.

28. Wollaston, "Churchill at Harrow," 5.

29. Douglas S. Russell, *Winston Churchill Soldier: The Military Life of a Gentleman at War* (London: Brassey's, 2005), 29.

30. CBH, 60.

31. Fletcher, "Spencer Churchill," Part II, *35*.

32. Churchill, *My Early Life*, 57.

Chapter 4

1. Paul Addison, *Churchill on the Home Front 1900–1955* (London: Jonathan Cape, 1992), 7.

2. WSC1, 86.

3. Anthony Montague Browne, *Long Sunset* (London: Cassell, 1995), 122. A recent work claiming syphilis, despite modern findings, is Andrew Norman, *Winston Churchill: Portrait of an Unquiet Mind* (London: Pen and Sword Books, 2012), 248.

4. Mary Soames, *A Churchill Family Album* (London: Allen Lane, 1982), 8.

5. Winston S. Churchill, *Lord Randolph Churchill* (London: Odhams, 1952), 50.

6. Arthur Herman, *Gandhi & Churchill* (New York: Bantam, 2007), 24. Cf. Lord Rosebery, *Lord Randolph Churchill* (London: Arthur Humphreys, 1906).

7. Martin Gilbert, remarks at the launch of *Churchill: A Life*, London, 18 March 1991.

8. John H. Mather MD, "Lord Randolph Churchill: Maladies et Mort," *Finest Hour* 93, Winter 1996–97, 23–28. This essay may be read online at http://bit.ly/1Todh1F.

9. Mather, "Maladies et Mort," 25.

10. Frank Harris, *My Life and Loves*, 5 vols. (privately published 1922–27), single volume edition (New York: Grove Press 1963), 482–85; Dr. Mather to the author, 30 January 2016. Harris' original was banned in America and Britain for forty years, then reappeared in print long after its targets (including the Brownings, Gladstone, Wilde, Lord Salisbury and Cecil Rhodes, among others) were long dead. Harris (1856–1931) made a career out of scandal, a fact that should have made his "diagnosis" of Lord Randolph problematic from the start.

11. *The People's Almanac, The Book of Lists* (New York: Bantam Doubleday Dell, 1978), 326. Manchester, *Last Lion*, I 96–97.

12. Ted Morgan, *Churchill: The Rise to Failure* (London: Cape, 1983), 25. Anita Leslie, *Lady Randolph Churchill*, 108. R.F. Foster, *Lord Randolph Churchill: A Political Life* (London: Oxford University Press, 1981), 389.

13. Mather, citing R.C. Mulholland, "Historical Perspective: Sir William Gowers, 1845–1915," *SPINE* 21:9, 1106–10. Thomas Buzzard, *Clinical Aspects of Syphilitic Nervous Affections* (Philadelphia: Lindsay and Blakiston, 1874), 11.

14. W.B. Bean, ed., *Sir William Osler: Aphorisms from His Bedside Teachings and Writings* (Springfield, Ill.: Charles C. Thomas, second edition), 133. Osler (1849–1919), often called "the father of modern medicine," created the first residency program for specialty training of physicians at Johns Hopkins Hospital.

15. Mather citing E.C. Robson Roose, *Remarks upon Some Diseases of the Nervous System* (Brighton: Curtis Bros. and Townes, 1875), 12. Roose to the Prince of Wales, December 1894, in WSC-DV1, 544.

16. WSC-DV1, 515.

17. Robert Rhodes James, *The British Revolution 1880–1939* (London: Random House, 1977), 113.

18. Mather, "Maladies et Mort," 28.

19. Sir Robert Rhodes James to the author, 1999.

20. Dr. John Mather to the author, 2016.

21. *Ibid.*

22. Peregrine Churchill to the author, 1989.

23. Peregrine Churchill to the author, 1989.

Chapter 5

1. "Person of the Century," *Time*, 26 December 1999. George F. Will, "A Stark Perspective on a Radical Century," *Jewish World Review*, 31 December 1999, http://bit.ly/1mgMPtp, accessed 4 February 2016.

2. Mark Thompson, "The Rise and Fall of a Female Captain Bligh," *Time*, 3 March 2010, http://ti.me/1PnLx8n. Daniel Knowles, "Time to scotch the myth of Winston Churchill's infallibility," *Telegraph Blogfeed*, 10 July 2012 http://xrl.us/bnge7y. Sources accessed 5 February 2016.

3. Winston S. Churchill, "Comments on [1874] *Annual Register*, 1897, in WSC-DV2, 765.

4. Kevin Theakston, *Winston Churchill and the British Constitution* (London: Politico's, 2004), 102. See also Addison, *Churchill on the Home Front*, 48.

5. Lady Randolph Churchill, *Reminiscences* (London: Arnold, 1908), 128–29.

6. Martin Pugh, *State and Society: A Social and Political History of Britain since 1870*, 4th ed. (London: Oxford University Press, 2012), 150–53.

7. Philip Guedalla, *Mr. Churchill: A Portrait* (London: Hodder and Stoughton, 1941), 135.

8. Clementine Churchill to *The Times*, 30 March 1912, in Mary Soames, *Clementine Churchill* (Boston: Houghton Mifflin, 1979), 79.

9. Rose, *Unruly Giant*, 66.

10. Addison, *Churchill on the Home Front*, 129.

11. Addison, *Churchill on the Home Front*, 49.

12. WSC2, 393–94. Taylor, *Churchill*, 236, 394.

13. Rose, *Unruly Giant*, 66. The "rather tepid" remarks were made by his friends Charles and Lucy Masterman.

14. Paul Addison, *Churchill: The Unexpected Hero* (Oxford: Oxford University Press, 2005), 48–49.

15. WSC2, 401.

16. Winston S. Churchill to the Master of Elibank, 18 December 1911, in CBH, 427.

17. Winston S. Churchill, "Women in War," *The Strand Magazine*, February 1938, republished in *The Collected Essays of Sir Winston Churchill*, 4 vols. (London: Library of Imperial History, 1975), I 380–87.

18. Robert Rhodes James, *Churchill: A Study in Fail-*

ure 1900–1939 (London: Weidenfeld and Nicolson, 1970) 302–03.

19. John Colville, *The Churchillians* (London: Weidenfeld and Nicolson, 1981), 123; CBH, 426–27.

20. Theakston, *Churchill and the British Constitution*, vii. CBH, 76.

21. Henry Durant, "Voting Behaviour in Britain," in Richard Rose, ed., *Studies in British Politics* (London: Macmillan, 1969), 162. Lady Soames to the author, 1995.

Chapter 6

1. Winston S. Churchill to his wife, 18 April 1912, in WSC-DV5, 1542–43.

2. Robert Strange, *Who Sank the Titanic? The Final Verdict* (London, Pen and Sword Books, 2012).

3. Anton Gill, *Titanic: The Real Story of the Construction of the World's Most Famous Ship* (London: Channel 4 Books, 2010), 104.

4. Katherine Felkins, H.P. Leighly and A. Jankovic, "The Royal Mail Ship *Titanic*: Did a Metallurgical Failure Cause a Night to Remember?" *JOM* (Minerals, Metals and Materials Society), 1998, 50 (1): 12–18.

5. WSC2, 254.

6. Michael Richards, "Who Sank the *Titanic*?," *Finest Hour* 156, Autumn 2012, 53.

7. Strange, *Titanic*, 20.

8. Strange, *Titanic*, 195.

Chapter 7

1. Donald Rumbelow, *The Siege of Sidney Street: The True Story of Winston Churchill and the Anarchist Rebellion of 1911* (London: St. Martin's Press, 1974).

2. Winston S. Churchill, "The Battle of Sidney Street," in *Thoughts and Adventures* (London: Leo Cooper, 1990), 43.

3. Christopher C. Harmon, "Churchill and the Terrorism of His Day," unpublished manuscript, 2009, courtesy of the author.

4. Churchill, "The Battle of Sidney Street," 44.

5. Stanley Smith, "The Siege of Sidney Street: A Bizarre Escapade of Churchill Derring-Do," *Finest Hour* 43, Spring 1984, 8–9.

6. A.L. Rowse, *The Later Churchills* (London: Macmillan, 1958), 390.

7. *Ibid.*

8. Winston S. Churchill, "The Vortex of Uncertainty," Shepherd's Bush Empire, London, 3 December 1923, in Robert Rhodes James, ed., *Winston S. Churchill: His Complete Speeches 1897–1963* (hereinafter *Speeches*), 8 vols. (New York: Bowker, 1974), IV 3425.

9. Violet Bonham-Carter, *Winston Churchill: An Intimate Portrait* (New York: Harcourt Brace and World, 1965), 236.

10. Harmon, "Churchill and the Terrorism of His Day."

Chapter 8

1. Harold Wilson, House of Commons, 25 January 1965, cited in *Life*, 5 February 1965, 68A.

2. WSC2, 373.

3. Bonham-Carter, *Intimate Portrait*, 233.

4. WSC2, 377–78.

5. WSC2, 377.

6. Addison, *Churchill on the Home Front*, 143.

7. Addison, *Churchill on the Home Front*, 143–44. Churchill to David Lloyd George, 3 March 1911, in WSC-DV2, 1248.

8. WSC-DV4, 1290.
9. WSC2, 386.
10. Addison, *Churchill on the Home Front*, 150–52, and correspondence with the author, 2015.
11. Morgan, *Rise to Failure*, 328.
12. Morgan, *Rise to Failure*, 307.
13. Addison, *Churchill on the Home Front*, 150.
14. Winston. S. Churchill, speech at Cardiff, 8 February 1950, *In the Balance* (London: Cassell, 1952), 181.
15. WSC2, 378.
16. W.H. Mainwaring in the BBC documentary "The Long Street: Road to Pandy Square" (1965), http://bit.ly/1LW5odn, accessed 2 March 2016.

Chapter 9

1. Cordell Hull, *Memoirs of Cordell Hull*, 2 vols. (New York: Macmillan, 1948), I 220. Hull was quoting a variation of proverbial wisdom that tracks back at least to 1820. See Ralph Keyes, *The Quote Verifier* (New York: St. Martin's, 2006), 121.
2. Addison, *Churchill on the Home Front*, 7.
3. WSC-DV2, 751.
4. Churchill to the president of North-West Manchester Liberal Association, 18 April 1904, in WSC-DV3, 337.
5. CBH, 166. House of Commons, 8 May 1904, and 20 February 1905.
6. Jeremy Havardi, *The Greatest Briton: Essays on Winston Churchill's Life and Political Philosophy* (London: Shepheard-Walwyn, 2009), 108.
7. CBH, 167, 15 February 1911, 30 April 1912.
8. CBH, 231, from Churchill in *The World Crisis 1911–1914* (London: Thornton Butterworth, 1923), 193.
9. Paul A. Cantor, "Churchill and the Irish Question in *The World Crisis*," American Political Science Convention Churchill Panel, September 1996, in *Churchill Proceedings 1996–1997* (Hopkinton, N.H.: Churchill Centre, 2000), 18. For Churchill's general tendency to view political problems in technical terms, see his essay "Parliamentary Government and the Economic Problem," in his *Amid These Storms* (New York: Scribner, 1932), 229–41.
10. Paul Addison, "The Search for Peace in Ireland," in James W. Muller, ed., *Churchill as Peacemaker* (Cambridge: Cambridge University Press, 2003), 199–200.
11. *Ibid.*
12. Havardi, *Greatest Briton*, 110–11.
13. Manchester, *Last Lion*, I 723–24.
14. WSC4, 745. For a full account see Winston S. Churchill, "How We Made the Irish Treaty" in his *Thoughts and Adventures* (Wilmington, Del.: Intercollegiate Studies Institute Press, 2009).
15. Winston S. Churchill, *The World Crisis*, vol. 4, *The Aftermath* (London: Thornton Butterworth, 1929), 317.
16. WSC4, 679.
17. Winston S. Churchill, *The Aftermath*, 308.
18. Paul Addison to the author, 2016.
19. Churchill, House of Commons, 28 October 1948, in CBH, 341.
20. WSC8, 368.

Chapter 10

1. H.H. Asquith to Venetia Stanley, 4 August 1914, in H.H. Asquith, *Memories and Reflections*, 2 vols. (Boston: Little Brown, 1928), II 21. WSC3, 30.
2. Winston S. Churchill to his wife, 28 July 1914, in WSC-DV6, 1989.

3. *Ibid.*
4. WSC3, 30. WSC-DV6, 18.
5. See reviews of Patrick J. Buchanan, *Churchill, Hitler and the Unnecessary War* and Nicholas Baker, *Human Smoke: The Beginnings of World War II, the End of Civilization* (both 2008), *Finest Hour* 138, Summer 2008, http://bit.ly/1YKByzF, accessed 12 March 2016.
6. Max Hastings, *Catastrophe 1914: Europe Goes to War* (New York: Random House, 2013, Vintage Books paperback 2014), 102. Portions of my comments were originally written for the Hillsdale College Churchill Project, http://bit.ly/1YKDAjo, accessed 12 March 2016.
7. Hastings, *Catastrophe 1914*, 85.
8. *Ibid.*, 37. For Churchill's memorandum contemplating the use of British ground forces see Winston S. Churchill, "Military Aspects of the Continental Problem," 13 August 1911, in *The World Crisis 1911–1914*, 60–64.
9. *Ibid.*, 88.
10. *Ibid.*, 72.
11. WSC-DV11, 560.
12. Hastings, *Catastrophe 1914*, 39.
13. Winston S. Churchill, *The World Crisis 1911–1914*, 72, 148.
14. For complete details see John H. Maurer, "Churchill's Naval Holiday: His Plan to Avert War," *Finest Hour* 163, Summer 2014, 10–19, available online at: http://bit.ly/1QUwOT0.
15. Winston S. Churchill to William Royle, 20 December 1911, in WSC-DV4, 1360–61. Winston S. Churchill, "Free Trade," speech of 4 August 1908, in *Speeches* II 1081–82.
16. Winston S. Churchill, "Navy Estimates," House of Commons, 18 March 1912, in *Speeches*, III 1925.
17. Lichnowsky to Bethmann Hollweg, 20 April 1913, in Maurer, "Naval Holiday," 11, 13.
18. Winston S. Churchill, "Navy Estimates," House of Commons, 26 March 1913, in *Speeches*, III 2077.
19. Maurer, "Naval Holiday," 13, 15.
20. *Ibid.*, 17.
21. Morgan, *Rise to Failure*, 422.
22. Michael and Eleanor Brock, eds., *H.H. Asquith Letters to Venetia Stanley* (New York: Oxford University Press, 1982), 129. David Dilks to the author, May 2015.
23. Brock, *Asquith Letters*, 130, n.2.
24. *Ibid.*, 130, n.3.
25. Winston S. Churchill to Clementine Churchill, 28 July 1914, in WSC-DV6, 1989–90.
26. Manfred Weidhorn, "Oh, the Pity of It," review of Richard M. Langworth, *Churchill and the Avoidable War*, *Finest Hour* 173, Summer 2015.

Chapter 11

1. Hastings, *Catastrophe 1914*, 446–55.
2. *Ibid.*
3. "The British Army 1914–1918," http://www.1914–1918.net/63div.htm, accessed 14 March 2016.
4. WSC3, 48.
5. See Winston S. Churchill, "Military Aspects of the Continental Problem," in *The World Crisis 1911–1914*, 60–64.
6. WSC3, 104.
7. *Ibid.*
8. Asquith, *Memories and Reflections*, II 41.
9. WSC3, 131.
10. CBH, 524.
11. Hough, *Winston and Clementine*, 288.
12. Henry Pelling, *Winston Churchill*, 1974. Revised

and extended softbound edition. (Ware, Herts.: Words-worth Editions, 1999), 184.

13. WSC3, 113–14.

14. J.E. Edmonds, *Military Operations France and Bel-gium, 1914: Mons, the Retreat to the Seine, the Marne and the Aisne August–October 1914*. History of the Great War Based on Official Documents by Direction of the His-torical Section of the Committee of Imperial Defence I, 2nd ed. (London: Macmillan, 1926), 46–48.

15. H.A. Gwynne, "The Antwerp Blunder," *Morning Post*, London, 13 October 1914, in WSC 3, 125–26.

16. WSC3, 125.

Chapter 12

1. WSC-DV6, 204. Mark Kerr (1864–1944), head of the British Naval Mission to Greece, 1913–14; invited by the Greeks, he commanded the newly formed Royal Hel-lenic Navy in 1914–16.

2. Churchill, *The World Crisis 1911–1914*, 489–90.

3. Martin Gilbert, "What About the Dardanelles?" *Finest Hour* 126, Spring 2005, 23–27.

4. H.H. Asquith to Venetia Stanley, 31 October 1914, in WSC3, 216.

5. Earl of Birkenhead, *Churchill 1874–1922* (London: Harrap, 1989), 341. Admiral Sir Sackville Carden (1857–1930), Commander-in-Chief, Mediterranean Expedi-tionary Force, 1914–15.

6. Gilbert, "What About the Dardanelles?," 23–27.

7. Manchester, *Last Lion* I 517.

8. WSC3, 222.

9. Stephen Roskill, *Churchill and the Admirals* (Lon-don: Collins, 1977), 42.

10. Allan Moorhead, *Gallipoli* (New York: Harper, 1956), 34.

11. Fisher to Churchill, 28 January 1915, in Gilbert, WSC-DV6, 460.

12. Maurice Hankey Memoirs, quoted in Gilbert, WSC3, 252.

13. Maurice Hankey minutes of the War Council, quoted in Churchill, *The World Crisis* vol. 2 *1915* (Lon-don: Thornton Butterworth, 1923), 111.

14. Martin Gilbert, *In Search of Churchill* (New York: Wiley, 1994), 55.

15. Gilbert, *In Search*, 57.

16. David Fromkin, *A Peace to End All Peace: The Fall of the Ottoman Empire and the Creation of the Modern Middle East*. (New York: Henry Holt, 1989), 135.

17. Roskill, *Admirals*, 48. Admiral of the Fleet Sir John de Robeck (1862–1928), Commander-in-Chief, Mediterranean Fleet, 1915–16.

18. Robert Rhodes James, *Gallipoli: A British Histo-rian's View* (Parkville, Victoria, Australia: Department of History, University of Melbourne, 1965), 61.

19. Harvey Broadbent, *Gallipoli: The Fatal Shore* (Camberwell, Victoria, Australia: Viking/Penguin, 2005), 35.

20. Edward Erickson, *Ordered to Die: A History of the Ottoman Army in the First World War* (Westport, Conn.: Greenwood Publishing, 2000), 45–46.

21. Gilbert, *In Search of Churchill*, 22, 64.

22. Winston S. Churchill, "Painting as a Pastime," *Strand Magazine*, 1921, revised and republished in *Thoughts and Adventures* (London: Leo Cooper, 1992), 223–24 (first published 1932).

23. Gilbert, WSC3, 473.

24. Lord Mountbatten, "Churchill the Warrior," re-marks to the Sir Winston S. Churchill Society of Ed-monton, Alberta, 1966.

25. Cf. Jeffrey D. Wallin, *By Ships Alone: Churchill and the Dardanelles: Politics and Strategy of a Decision* (Durham, N.C.: Carolina Academic Press), 1981.

26. Christopher C. Harmon, "Whose Disaster Was Gallipoli?," address to the 15th International Churchill Conference, San Diego, 5 November 2001, *Churchill Pro-ceedings 2001–2003* (Hopkinton, N.H.: Churchill Centre, 2006), 31.

27. Harmon, "Gallipoli," 32.

28. Pelling, *Winston Churchill*, 220.

29. Trumbull Higgins, *Winston Churchill and the Dardanelles: A Dialogue of Ends and Means* (London: Heinemann, 1963), 67.

30. Winston S. Churchill, *Their Finest Hour* (London: Cassell, 1949), 15.

31. For a striking example see Churchill's queries to General Brooke on the 1941 invasion exercise "Victor" in Eliot A. Cohen, "Churchill and His Military Com-manders," Part 2, "Method of Command," Hillsdale Col-lege Churchill Project, 2016, http://bit.ly/1pZ6u3Q, ac-cessed 29 March 2016: "How many ships and transports [were involved]? How many Armoured vehicles…. How many motor lorries, how many guns, how much ammu-nition, how many men, how many tons of stores, how far did they advance in the first forty-eight hours, how many men and vehicles were assumed to have landed in the first twelve hours, what percentage of loss were they debited with? [etc.]"

Chapter 13

1. John Updike, "Remember the Lusitania," in *The New Yorker*, 1 July 2002.

2. Churchill to Walter Runciman, 12 February 1915, in WSC-DV6, 501.

3. Colin Simpson, *The Lusitania* (Boston: Little Brown, 1972). Nigel Hamilton, *The Mantle of Command* (Boston: Houghton Mifflin, 2015).

4. I am indebted to my late friend Professor Harry V. Jaffa, for permission to quote extensively from his essay, "The Sinking of the *Lusitania*: Brutality, Bungling, or Betrayal?," in Jaffa, ed., *Statesmanship: Essays in Honor of Sir Winston Churchill* (Durham, N.C.: Carolina Aca-demic Press, 1981). Dr. Jaffa (1918–2015) was Professor Emeritus at Claremont McKenna College and a distin-guished fellow of the Claremont Institute, a leading scholar of Aristotle, Lincoln, Jefferson, Churchill, Amer-ican constitutionalism, and natural law.

5. Thomas A. Bailey, "The Sinking of the *Lusitania*," *American Historical Review* 41, October 1935, 54–73. Dr. Bailey (1902–1983) was a professor of history at Stanford University, noted for his witty lectures and monographs. He contended, rightly I think, that foreign policy is sig-nificantly affected by public opinion, and that current policymakers can learn from history.

6. Simpson, *Lusitania*, 151.

7. Bailey, "Sinking of the *Lusitania*," 58.

8. M.R. Dow, "Complete Fiction," Amazon reviews, 13 September 2014, http://amzn.to/1ROXM46, accessed 30 March 2016. Bailey, "*Lusitania*," 58.

9. *Ibid.*

10. Bailey, "*Lusitania*," 61.

11. Thomas A. Bailey and Captain Paul B. Ryan, *The Lusitania Disaster: An Episode in Modern Warfare and Diplomacy* (New York: Free Press, 1975).

12. Bailey, "Sinking of the *Lusitania*," 71.

13. Simpson, *Lusitania*, 183.

14. Bailey, "Sinking of the *Lusitania*," 70. Jaffa, *States-manship*, xxx.

15. Simpson, *Lusitania*, 130.
16. Jaffa, *Statesmanship*, xxx.
17. Simpson, *Lusitania*, 131.
18. Jaffa, *Statesmanship*, xxx.
19. David A. Ramsay, "The Dardanelles Strategy," *Churchill Proceedings 2001–2003*, 24. Sir Alexander Ludovic Duff (1862–1933) was at the time second in command of the 4th Battle Squadron. Ramsay's book, *Lusitania: Saga and Myth* (New York: Norton, 2002), confirms the views of Bailey, Jaffa and others. See Ramsay's letter, "*Lusitania* Not," Despatch Box, *Finest Hour* 114, Summer 2004, 4:
20. David A. Ramsay, "*Lusitania* Not," *Finest Hour* 114, Summer 2004, 4.

Chapter 14

1. Bob Ruggenberg, "Why America Should Have Stayed Out," *The Heritage of the Great War*, http://xrl.us/2s8z, quoting alleged Churchill statements first appearing in the *New York Enquirer*, August 1936.
2. Winston S. Churchill, *The World Crisis*, vol. III, Part 1 *1916–1918* (London: Thornton Butterworth, 1927), 226–27.
3. *Ibid.*
4. Churchill, *World Crisis* III, Part 1, 213–14.
5. *National Enquirer*, http://bit.ly/juAt0j, accessed 22 February 2013.
6. "The Press: Tactful William," *Time*, 8 May 1939, http:// ti.me/ilNXiY. (Henry Luce's *Time*, strongly interventionist, added that the isolationists "had hit on a new scheme to keep out of war: stir up bad feeling over the War debts, which nobody could do better than William Griffin."
7. "William Griffin," on Metapedia, "The Alternate Encyclopedia," http://bit.ly/lhCn2o. *New York Times* archives, researched by Michael McMenamin, accessed 23 February 2013.
8. John Roy Carlson, *Under Cover: My Four Years in the Nazi Underworld of America* (New York: Dutton, 1943), 246.
9. "The Record of Strange Associates of Hamilton Fish," *Putnam County Courier*, Carmel, New York, 15 October 1942, 11 (http://bit.ly/j7dKoi). Hamilton Fish III (1888–1991), New York Congressman 1920–45. An advocate of U.S. isolation. Prescott Dennett (1907–1992), secretary-treasurer, Make Europe Pay War Debts Committee; also ran the Columbia Press Service, a Nazi front. Together with Nazi propagandist George S. Viereck, he organized the Citizens Committee to Keep America Out of the War. Dennett was a defendant in the Great Sedition Trial of 1944. Viereck was imprisoned in 1942–47 for failing to register as a foreign agent.
10. Enquirer-Star Group, Inc. Company History, www.fundinguniverse.com, accessed 23 February 2013.
11. William Griffin, "When Churchill Said Keep Out!," *Scribner's Commentator*, February 1941, pp 25–28. Why Churchill, at Morpeth Mansions, would send a telegram to Griffin, at the Savoy, is unclear.
12. Churchill Private Office notes, Chartwell Papers (hereinafter "CHAR"), Churchill Archives Centre, CHAR 2/383/44–46.
13. Griffin, "Keep Out!," 26.
14. *Ibid.*
15. *Ibid.*, 27.
16. The phrase is from Winston S. Churchill, *The Gathering Storm* (London: Cassell, 1948), 62.
17. William N. Stokes, Jr. to Senator Robert Reynolds, enclosed in Stokes's letter to Churchill, 22 July 1939,

CHAR 2/383/12. The inference is that this allegation surfaced in the summer of 1939.
18. Stokes to Churchill, 27 September 1939, CHAR 2/383/11. *Time* (footnote 6) reported that Reynolds had "introduced a resolution to send William Griffin abroad as a special envoy to remind European nations of their debts." Reynolds remained a strident isolationist through 1941, when the Roosevelt Administration arranged for him to be shuffled aside by a pro-FDR Senator.
19. Correspondence, CHAR 2/383/12.
20. John Boland, Secretary, Catholic Truth Society, to Churchill, 11 October 1939, CHAR 2/383/15.
21. Alan C. Collins to Churchill, 19 September 1939, CHAR 2/383/1.
22. Churchill Archives cuttings file, CHAR 2/383/23.
23. William Griffin sworn deposition, CHAR 2/383/101.
24. Winston S. Churchill to J. Arthur Levy, 1 November 1939 CHAR 2/383/25–26.
25. Winston S. Churchill to Levy, 15 November 1939, CHAR 2/383/38.
26. *New York Enquirer*, 29 January 1940, CHAR 2/408/71.
27. Winston S. Churchill to Ambassador Lord Halifax, 14 February 1940, CHAR 2/408/77.
28. Griffin, "Keep Out!," 26–27.
29. "Scribner's," St. James Encyclopedia of Popular Culture, BookRags, 2005–06, http://bit.ly/m4mXfl, accessed 23 February 2013.
30. Winston S. Churchill to Halifax, 28 July 1942, T. 1050/2, CHAR 20/88.
31. *The New York Times*, 22 October 1942 and *New York Times* archival material researched by Michael McMenamin.
32. J.F.C. Fuller, *Decisive Battles of the Western World and Their Influence Upon History*, vol. 3 (London: Cassell, 1956), 271. Frank Johnson, *The Spectator*, 9 October 1999. At his birthday parade, reviewing a long line of armored vehicles, Hitler said to Fuller, "I hope you were pleased with your children?" Fuller replied, "Your Excellency, they have grown up so quickly that I no longer recognise them." From Max Boot, *War Made New: Technology, Warfare and the Course of History, 1500 to Today* (New York: Penguin, 2006), 224.
33. Winston S. Churchill, "The Truth About War Debts," *Answers*, 17 March 1934, reprinted in *Collected Essays* II 314–18.
34. Churchill, *Gathering Storm*, 3–15.
35. See for example Jonathan Petropoulos, *Royals and the Reich* (Oxford University Press, 2006), 170 et. seq. and Alan Palmer, *The Kaiser: Warlord of the Second Reich* (New York: Scribner, 1978), 226.

Chapter 15

1. Michael Duffy, "Weapons of War: Poison Gas" on firstworldwar.com, posted 2009, http://bit.ly/1RN15Wx, accessed 31 March 2016.
2. Churchill minute from the War Office, 12 May 1919, in WSC-DV8, 649. CBH, 189.
3. WSC-DV8, 661–62.
4. WSC-DV8, 662.
5. Martin Gilbert, "Churchill and Bombing Policy," Fifth Churchill Lecture, Washington, D.C., 18 October 2005, http://xrl.us/bgy3j2, accessed 31 March 2016.
6. Churchill to Sir Hugh Trenchard, 29 August 2910, in WSC-DV9, 1190.
7. "Chemical Weapons in World War I," on Wiki-

pedia, http://bit.ly/1RN3bpn, accessed 31 March 2016. See also "Sulphur Mustard," http://bit.ly/15pE8hL.

8. Giles Milton, "Winston Churchill's Shocking Use of Chemical Weapons," *The Guardian*, 1 September 2013, http://xrl.us/bprq4v.

9. *Ibid.*

10. Simon Jones, "'The right medicine for the Bolshevist': British air-dropped chemical weapons in north Russia, 1919," *Imperial War Museum Review* 12, 1999, 78–88.

11. War Office to General Officer in Charge Archangel, telegram, 7 February 1919, Public Record Office. Jones, "The right medicine," 80.

12. Jones, "The right medicine," 83.

13. King's College, London, "The Serving Soldier: Major General Charles Foulkes (1875–1969)," http://xrl.us/bprrmo, accessed 31 March 2016.

14. Winston S. Churchill to Chief of Imperial General Staff, 25 January 1919, supplied by Allen Packwood, Churchill Archives Centre, 4 September 2013.

15. "Disarmament Problems," House of Commons, 13 May 1932, in Winston S. Churchill, *Arms and the Covenant* (London: Harrap, 1938), 23–24. CBH, 190.

16. WSC7, 352–53. On 20 March 1942, Churchill had written Stalin: "His Majesty's Government will treat any use of this weapon of poison gas against Russia exactly as if it was directed against ourselves." See Winston S. Churchill, *The Hinge of Fate* (London: Cassell, 1950), 329.

17. Churchill, *Hinge of Fate*, 353.

18. Martin Gilbert, *Churchill: A Life* (London: Minerva, 1992), 783.

19. *Ibid.*

20. *Ibid.*

21. Sir Martin Gilbert to the author; private correspondence, 1993.

22. Winston S. Churchill, *The World Crisis, 1911–1914*, 382. I am grateful to Professor Antoine Capet for bringing this to my attention.

23. Lady Soames to the author; private correspondence, 2005.

Chapter 16

1. Warren F. Kimball, "The Alcohol Quotient," *Finest Hour* 134, Spring 2007, 31–32. The C.P. Snow remark is from Raymond O'Connor to Warren Kimball, 21 December 1987 (personal correspondence).

2. Churchill, *My Early Life*, 141.

3. CBH, 546.

4. David Lough, *No More Champagne: Churchill and His Money* (New York: Picador, 2015), 92. Peter Clarke, "Pounds, Shillings and Pence," *Finest Hour* 171, Winter 2016.

5. Mark 10:4 (Churchill would have quoted the King James version.) Rhodes James, *Study in Failure*, 306.

6. Christian Pol-Roger to the author, 1990.

7. Dalton Newfield, International Churchill Society President and Editor, 1970–75, *Finest Hour* 37, Autumn 1982, 4.

8. A.L. Rowse, "'There Was Once a Man': A Visit to Chartwell, 1955," Hillsdale College Churchill Project, http://bit.ly/1T4oraD, accessed 7 May 2016.

9. CBH, 536.

10. Jack Fishman, *My Darling Clementine* (New York: McKay, 1963), 341.

11. WSC7, 1225–27.

12. Ronald Golding to the author, 1985. Churchill was actually paraphrasing a W.C. Fields line from the film, *It's a Gift*: "…I'll be sober tomorrow and you'll be crazy the rest of your life." CBH, 550.

13. Danny Mander, Letter to the editor, *Finest Hour* 135, Summer 2007, 4. CBH, 374.

14. Barry Singer, *Churchill Style: The Art of Being Winston Churchill* (New York: Abrams, 2012), 156.

15. Churchill, *My Early Life*, 140–41.

16. Manchester, *Last Lion*, II 10. Singer, *Churchill Style*, 130.

17. Rhodes James, *Study in Failure*, 305–06.

18. He refused Rothermere's first bet of £2000 to go completely teetotal, because "life would not be worth living." Churchill to his wife from Morocco, 30 December 1935, in WSC-DV12, 1367.

19. Christian Pol-Roger to the author, CBH, 537. Richard M. Langworth, "Churchill on Champagne," *Finest Hour* 86, Spring 1995, 14.

20. Kay Halle, *Irrepressible Churchill* (Cleveland: World, 1966), 4.

21. CBH, 544.

22. *Ibid.*, 536.

23. *Ibid.*, 455.

24. Gilbert, *In Search of Churchill*, 199.

25. Abraham Lincoln on Ulysses S. Grant, 1864, Quoteworld.com, http://www.quoteworld.org/quotes/8323, accessed 9 May 2016. This is an alleged quote for which Quoteworld supplies no documentation.

Chapter 17

1. WSC IV, 270.

2. *Speeches* III, 2798.

3. Martin Gilbert, *Churchill's Political Philosophy* (London: British Academy, 1981), 75, quoting Churchill in the *Weekly Dispatch*, 22 June 1919.

4. WSC IV, 355.

5. National Press Club, Washington, 28 June 1954, in CBH, 381.

6. House of Commons, 26 January 1949. The interrupter was Labour MP Seymour Cocks. See CBH, 148; and *Speeches* VII 1774.

7. N.G.O. Pereira, "White Power during the Civil War in Siberia (1918–1920): Dilemmas of Kolchak's 'War Anti-Communism,'" *Canadian Slavonic Papers* (1987) I (29), 45–62.

8. M.I. Smirnov, "Admiral Kolchak," *The Slavonic and East European Review* (1933) 11 (32): 373–87.

9. Evan Mawdsley, *The Russian Civil War* (London: Pegasus, 2007), 3.

10. Winston S. Churchill, Mansion House, 19 February 1919, in *Speeches* III 2671.

11. Martin Gilbert, *Churchill: A Life* (London: Heinemann, 1991), 389.

12. Gilbert, *Churchill: A Life*, 426.

13. Churchill to John Colville, Chequers, 21 June 1941, in CBH, 276.

14. Ivan Mikhailovich Maisky (1884–1975). A Menshevik, he was exiled to Siberia by the Czar, escaped, took an economics degree in Germany and lived in London 1912–17. Returning to Russia during the revolution, he became a Bolshevik. Soviet Ambassador to Britain, 1932–43, Deputy Foreign Minister, 1943–45.

15. WSC-DV13, 403, 410 n.1; Churchill to Maisky, 14 November 1936, CHAR 2/260/93.

16. David Irving, *Churchill's War* (Bullsbrook, Australia: Veritas, 1987), 101. Though citations in this work are often doubtful, this one is consistent with Churchill's attitude toward reaching an understanding with the Soviets.

17. Maisky to Churchill, Memorandum of 4 October 1938, CHAR 9/130, in WSC-DV13, 1201. Harold Nicolson diary, 26 September 1938 in WSC-DV13, 1179.

18. Harold Nicolson: Diary, 3 April 1939 (Nicolson Papers), in WSC-DV13, 1429.

19. Antoine Capet, "'The Creeds of the Devil': Churchill between the Two Totalitarianisms, 1917–1945," 37–38. Paper based on "Britain and the Cold War," Institute of Historical Research, University of London, June 2009, http://bit.ly/1TyMgYx, accessed 22 May 2016.

20. Winston S. Churchill, "The Fourth Climacteric," world broadcast, 22 June 1941, in Churchill, *The Unrelenting Struggle* (London: Cassell, 1942), 178–79.

21. Capet, "'The Creeds of the Devil,'" 40–41.

Chapter 18

1. See for example Roger Cohen, "Jews in a Whisper," *The New York Times Sunday Review*, 21 August 2011, http://nyti.ms/p7QPGv, accessed 23 May 2016.

2. Cf. Winston S. Churchill, "Zionism vs. Bolshevism," *Illustrated Sunday Herald*, 8 February 1920, reprinted in *Collected Essays*, IV 26–30.

3. *Ibid.*

4. *Ibid.*

5. Martin Luther King, Jr., "I Have a Dream," Lincoln Memorial, Washington, 28 August 1963, http://bit.ly/25nULhT, accessed 25 May 2016.

6. Cohen, "Jews in a Whisper," note 1.

7. Churchill, "Zionism vs. Bolshevism," 29.

8. Eli Shealtiel comment in Lital Levin, "Ahead of Republican Primaries, Winston Churchill is Back in Style in U.S. and Israel," *Haaretz*, 10 January 2012.

9. Churchill to Chaim Weizmann, 17 November 1944, CBH, 442.

10. WSC2, 82. Churchill's letter to Laski was published in the *Manchester Guardian*, *The Times* and the *Jewish Chronicle*. See Ronald I. Cohen, *Bibliography of the Writings of Sir Winston Churchill*, entries G66a-66c.

11. Malcolm E. Yapp, *The Making of the Modern Near East 1792–1923* (London: Longman, 1988), 290.

12. WSC4, 650.

13. *Ibid.*, 653.

14. Paul Johnson, *Churchill* (New York: Viking, 2009), 63.

15. WSC8, 1329.16. Churchill, House of Commons, 12 November 1940, CBH, 53.

16. CBH, 53.

17. Michael J. Cohen, "Churchill and the Jews: The Facts," *The Jewish Star*, 16 December 2015, http://bit.ly/1U9pCDa, accessed 30 May 2016.

Chapter 19

1. Mohandas Gandhi to Rajkumari Amrit Kaur, May 1940, regarding the military situation between England and Germany quoted in Gandhi, *Collected Works*, 95 vols. (New Delhi: Ministry of Information and Broadcasting, New Delhi, 1979), LXXV 70.

2. Larry P. Arnn, "Churchill's Greatness (3): The Gandhi Factor," *Finest Hour* 108, Autumn 2000, 12, http://bit.ly/1Zmu7Ph, accessed 3 June 2016.

3. *Ibid.*

4. Winston S. Churchill, "Shall We Give Up on India?," *Answers*, 21 July 1934, reprinted in *Collected Essays* II 348–53.

5. *Ibid.*

6. Manfred Weidhorn, introduction to the new edition of Winston S. Churchill, *India* (Hopkinton, N.H.: Dragonwyck Publishing, 1991), vii.

7. Yogesh Chadha, *Rediscovering Gandhi* (London: Century Books, 1997), 436.

8. Weidhorn, *India*, xxxvi.

9. Churchill, *India*, 94; CBH, 342.

10. CBH, 343.

11. Herman, *Gandhi & Churchill*, 149.

12. Colonial Office correspondence, CO 291/103/39670, quoted in James D. Hunt, *Gandhi in London* (New Delhi: Promilla, 1993), 80.

13. Herman, *Gandhi & Churchill*, 152.

14. House of Commons, 8 July 1920, in CBH, 443.

15. Herman, *Gandhi & Churchill*, 399.

16. G.D. Birla to M.K. Gandhi, 25 August 1935 (Birla Papers), WSC-DV12, 1243.

17. WSC-DV12, 1244.

18. WSC-DV12, 1265.

19. Churchill to Evelyn Shuckburgh, Eden's private secretary, 18 February 1955, CBH 165.

20. William F. Buckley, Jr., "Let Us Now Praise Famous Men," Boston Churchill Conference, 27 October 1995, *Churchill Proceedings 1994–1995*, 82.

21. M.K. Gandhi to Churchill, 17 July 1944, in Herman, *Gandhi & Churchill*, 538.

22. Herman, *Gandhi & Churchill*, 539.

23. Arnn, "The Gandhi Factor," 12.

24. Richard M. Langworth, "'Welcome, Mr. Gandhi'—Winston Churchill," *The Weekly Standard*, 21 July 2014, http://bit.ly/1m2ltzX, accessed 3 June 2016. The Honourable Society of the Middle Temple is one of the four Inns of Court exclusively entitled to call their members to the English Bar as barristers, who litigate at the higher levels of the British court system.

25. In 1948, Smuts, a former segregationist, backed the Native Laws (Fagan) Commission, which urged easing of black segregation; he was defeated by the pro-Apartheid National Party. Though he had earlier opposed enfranchising South African Indians, Gandhi admired him. Smuts called Gandhi a "great man," and in 1939 contributed an essay to a commemorative book on Gandhi's 70th birthday. (*Sunday Times*, London, 30 April 2006.)

Chapter 20

1. WSC5, 456–57.

2. Clive Irving, "The Untold Story of Mussolini's Fake Diaries," *Daily Beast*, 12 April 2015 (http://thebea.st/1IW9HUS), accessed 11 June 2016. Note: Italy joined the Axis in 1936, not 1940; Churchill wrote, not "a series" of letters to Mussolini but one letter, which the Italian leader rejected in writing. The article concerns alleged letters, not "diaries."

3. WSC5, 142.

4. *Ibid.*, 226.

5. Churchill, *Their Finest Hour*, 106–07.

6. WSC5, 456–57.

7. *Ibid.*, 669, 676.

8. Churchill, *Their Finest Hour*, 107.

9. WSC5, 740.

10. Harold Nicolson: diary, 3 April 1939 (Nicolson Papers), in WSCDV-13, 1429.

11. Churchill, *Their Finest Hour*, 107–08.

12. CBH, 365.13. Cf. Arrigo Petacco, *dear Benito—caro Winston* (Rome, Mondadori, 1985).

13. Patrizio R. Giangreco, "Leading Myths: 'Churchill Offered Peace and Security to Mussolini,'" *Finest Hour* 149, Winter 2010–11, 52–53, 57.

14. Clive Irving, "Untold Story."

15. Henry Samuel, "Winston Churchill 'ordered assassination of Mussolini to protect compromising letters,'" *Daily Telegraph*, 2 September 2010, http://bit.ly/1UKdn00, accessed 11 June 2016.

16. Cf. Ubaldo Giuliani-Balestrino, *Il carteggio Churchill-Mussolini alla luce del processo Guareschi = The Churchill-Mussolini File in light of the Guareschi trial* (Rome: Edizioni Settimo Sigillo, 2010).

17. See R.G. Grant, *Churchill: An Illustrated Biography* (London: Bison Books, 1989), 210. For Churchill's travels at this time see WSC8, 134–51.

18. WSC7, 134.

19. Warren F. Kimball, *Churchill & Roosevelt: The Complete Correspondence* (hereinafter *C&R Correspondence*) 3 vols. (Princeton, N.J.: Princeton University Press, 1984), II 344. Lady Soames to the author, 2010.

20. Clive Irving, "The Untold Story."

21. WSC7, 344; Martin Gilbert, conversation with the author, 2010.

22. Broadcast, London, 27 April 1941, in CBH, 365.

23. Andrew Roberts, "Churchill's Reputation," remarks at the Cabinet War Rooms, London, 16 November 2005.

Chapter 21

1. Adolf Hitler, *Mein Kampf*, 2 vols. (Berlin: Eher Verlaf, 1925–26). An abridged English edition was first published by Hurst and Blackett, London, on 13 October 1933, though excerpts appeared in *The Times* during July

2. Ian Hamilton to Churchill, 24 October 1930, in WSC-DV12, 208–09 (Churchill papers: 8/269). In the 14 September German election the National Socialists received 6.4 million votes (18 percent), taking 107 seats, second highest in the Reichstag. The Social Democrats won 143 seats, the Communists 77, the Center Party 68.

3. Churchill to his wife, "Chartwell Bulletin No. 8," 8 March 1935, in WSC-DV12, 1107.

4. Churchill on Air Estimates, House of Commons, 19 March 1935, in CBH, 249.

5. WSC-DV12, 1145, note 1.

6. Churchill to his wife, "Chartwell Bulletin No. 10," 5 April 1935, in WSC-DV12, 1145.

7. Adolf Hitler to Rothermere, Berlin, 3 May 1935. Churchill Papers, CHAR 2/235/79–86.

8. Winston S. Churchill to Rothermere 12 May 1935, in WSC-DV 12, 1169–70.

9. Lord Rothermere to Churchill, 13 May 1935, in WSC-DV 12, 1171–72.

10. Reeves Shaw to Churchill, 15 May 1935, in WSC-DV12, 1175.

11. Winston S. Churchill, "Hitler and His Choice," in *Great Contemporaries* (London: Thornton Butterworth, 1937). Quoted from the 1990 edition (London: Leo Cooper), 165–72.

12. Martin Gilbert, *Churchill: A Life*, 580–81.

13. Winston S. Churchill, "This Age of Government by Great Dictators," in *Collected Essays*, IV 397.

14. Winston S. Churchill, "Friendship with Germany," *Evening Standard*, 17 September 1937, in *Step by Step* (London: Odhams, 1947), 156.

15. Patrick J. Buchanan, *Churchill, Hitler, and the "Unnecessary War"* (New York: Crown, 2008), 174.

16. Churchill, *Step by Step*, 156.

17. Churchill to Lord Londonderry, 23 October 1937, in Gilbert, *Churchill: A Life*, 581.

18. Gilbert, *Churchill: A Life*, 581.

19. *Speeches*, VI 5653–56. Richard Howard Powers, "Winston Churchill's Parliamentary Commentary on British Foreign Policy, 1935–1938," *The Journal of Modern History* 26:2, June 1954, 179.

20. Winston S. Churchill, 20 July 1936, in CBH, 493.

21. Winston S. Churchill, 6 November, 1936, in CBH, 346.

22. *Ibid.*

23. CBH, 348.

24. Sir John Colville, conversation with the author, 1985.

Chapter 22

1. CBH, 4–5.

2. D.J. Wenden, "Churchill, Radio and Cinema," in Robert Blake and Wm. Roger Louis, eds., *Churchill: A Major New Assessment of His Life in Peace and War* (New York: Oxford University Press, 1993), 237. John Snagge, *Those Vintage Years of Radio* (London: Pitman, 1972).

3. David Irving, *Churchill's War*, 313.

4. Robert Rhodes James, "An Actor Did Not Give Churchill's Speeches," *Finest Hour* 92, Autumn 1996, 24.

5. Richard M. Langworth, "Datelines," *Finest Hour* 72, Third Quarter 1991, 6.

6. Richard M. Langworth, "Datelines," *Finest Hour* 79, Second Quarter 1993, 8.

7. Robert Rhodes James, *Finest Hour* 92, 24.

8. CBH, 4.

9. Wenden, "Churchill, Radio and Cinema," 237.

10. *Ibid.*

11. Vita Sackville-West to Harold Nicolson, 5 June 1940, in *Harold Nicolson: Diaries and Letters 1939–45* (London: Collins, 1967), 93.

12. CBH, 273.

13. National Sound Archive, London, ref. 2488–91.

14. Gilbert, *In Search of Churchill*, 272.

15. *Ibid.*

16. Harold Nicolson to Vita Sackville-West, 19 June 1940, in *Nicolson Diaries 1939–45*, 97.

17. Clive Ponting, *1940: Myth and Reality* (London: Hamish Hamilton 1990), 158. Wenden, "Churchill, Radio and Cinema," 238.

18. "Datelines," *Finest Hour* 109, Winter 2000–01, 6–7.

19. *Ibid.*

20. Allen Packwood, *Finest Hour* 112, Autumn 2001, 27, n.6.

21. Rhodes James, *Finest Hour* 92, 24.

Chapter 23

1. Barry Lando, "Shocked by anti-Muslim Hysteria? Churchill Wanted to 'Collar The Lot,'" *Huffington Post*, 23 November 2015, http://huff.to/28KQfjR, accessed 21 June 2016.

2. *Ibid.*

3. David Freeman to the author, 24 November 2015.

4. Rose, *Unruly Giant*, 265–66. Peter and Leni Gillman, *Collar the Lot! How Britain Interned and Expelled Its Wartime Refugees* (London: Quartet Books, 1980), 115–29.

5. David Stafford, *Roosevelt and Churchill: Men of Secrets* (Woodstock, N.Y.: Overlook Press, 1999), 42.

6. Churchill, "The War Situation," House of Commons, 4 June 1940, WSC6, 467.

7. Cabinet Papers, 65/1, 21 June 1940, in WSC-DV15, 391.

8. Paul Addison to the author, 29 June 2016.

9. Stafford, *Roosevelt and Churchill*, 145.

10. Theakston, *Churchill and the British Constitution*, 10.

11. Stafford, *Churchill and Secret Service* (Toronto: Stoddardt, 1997), 255. W.P. Crozier, *Off the Record: Political Interviews 1933–1943* (London: Hutchinson, 1973), 138.

12. Stafford, *Churchill and Roosevelt*, 145.
13. CBH, 102.
14. Stafford, *Churchill and Secret Service*, 258.
15. David Stafford to the author, 22 June 2016.
16. Manchester, *Last Lion* I, 843–44.
17. Warren F. Kimball to the author, 2 July 2016. "Japanese American Internment," *U.S. History*, http://bit.ly/29ok1II. "Japanese Internment: Banished and Beyond Tears," *The Canadian Encyclopedia*, http://bit.ly/29ojBIu, accessed 3 July 2016.

Chapter 24

1. Steve Malzberg, "Obama's Torture Tactics," *Reflections* 1:4, May 2009, http://bit.ly/28MPDKo, accessed 22 June 2016.
2. Andrew Sullivan, "Churchill vs. Cheney," *The Atlantic*, 30 April 2009, http://theatln.tc/28MRa39, accessed 22 June 2016. Alex Spillius, "Obama Likes Winston Churchill After All," *Daily Telegraph*, 30 April 2009, and *Telegraph* readers responding to this article.
3. Ben Macintyre, "The Truth that Tin Eye Saw," *The Times* Online, 10 February 2006.
4. *Ibid.*
5. See also the end of Chapter 15, Chemical Warfare. Lady Soames to the author; private correspondence, 2005.
6. Ian Corbain, "The Secrets of the London Cage," *The Guardian*, 12 November 2005, http://bit.ly/28MZ9No, accessed 22 June 2016.
7. *Ibid.*
8. *Ibid.* Cf. Alexander P. Scotland, *The London Cage*, first published 1957; new edition (London: George Mann Books, 1973).
9. Churchill, *The World Crisis* I 11. Grateful thanks to Cdr. Larry Kryske USN (ret.) for this reference.
10. WSC-DV13, 1292, n.2.
11. Gilbert, *Churchill: A Life*, 783.

Chapter 25

1. I am indebted to two writers who long ago researched this story, with whose findings I felt every agreement: Martin Gilbert, "Coventry: What Really Happened," *Finest Hour* 141, Winter 2008–09, 32–33; and Peter J. McIver, "Winston Churchill and the Bombing of Coventry," *Finest Hour* 41, Autumn 1983, 10–11.
2. Gilbert, "Coventry," 32, citing Premier papers, 3/108, folios 39–43. Gilbert gives the death toll as 507, but a more recent source states 568; see WSC-DV17, 497.
3. F.W. Winterbotham, *The Ultra Secret* (New York: Harper and Row, 1974), 82–84.
4. Anthony Cave Brown, *Bodyguard of Lies* (New York: Bantam, 1976). 38–44. Cave Brown's book incorrectly used the code name "All One Piece."
5. William Stevenson, *A Man Called Intrepid* (New York: Ballantine, 1982). David Stafford, correspondence with the author, January 2016.
6. David Irving, *Churchill's War*, 462.
7. *Ibid.*, 464.
8. Charles Haddon Spurgeon, English clergyman, 1855, tracked by Keyes, *Quote Verifier*, 121. See also Chapter 9, n. 1.
9. "The Belgrade Theatre presents One Night in November by Alan Pollock," http://ind.pn/291JY6Y, accessed 26 June 2016.
10. R.V. Jones, *Most Secret War* (London: Coronet, 1979), 201.
11. Memorandum to Directorate of Home Operations, 12 November 1940, National Archives (formerly Public Records Office), Air Ministry papers, 2/5238.
12. McIver, "Bombing of Coventry," 11, citing National Archives, AIR 20/2419.
13. Gilbert, "Coventry," 32, citing National Archives, AIR 2/5238.
14. Gilbert, "Coventry," 32–33, citing Air Staff summary, 14 November 1940, National Archives, AIR 2/5238.
15. McIver, "Bombing of Coventry," 11. Sir John Martin, letter to *The Times*, 28 August 1976. Norman Longmate, *Air Raid: The Bombing of Coventry* (London: Hutchinson, 1976), 57–58.
16. WSC6, 912.
17. Gilbert, "Coventry," 33, citing Colville diary for 14 November 1940, and Sir John Martin, private letter, 24 February 1983.
18. McIver, "Bombing of Coventry," 11.
19. War Cabinet No. 289, 15 November 1940, Cabinet papers, 65/10. Sir Archibald Sinclair, Secretary of State for Air, to Churchill, 15 November 1940, Premier papers, 3/22/3, folio 199, cited in Gilbert, "Coventry," 33.
20. Ronald Lewin, *Ultra Goes to War* (New York: Mc-Graw Hill, 1978), 103.

Chapter 26

1. Churchill, *Their Finest Hour*, 224.
2. Winston S. Churchill, *Closing the Ring* (London: Cassell, 1952), 514.
3. Winston S. Churchill to Stimson, July 1943, in Richard Lamb, *Churchill as War Leader: Right or Wrong?* (London: Bloomsbury, 1991), 225.
4. Winston S. Churchill to his wife, 5 June 1944, in Soames, *Clementine Churchill*, 355.
5. Geoffrey Best, *Churchill: A Study in Greatness* (London: Hambledon and London, 2001), 232.
6. Franklin Roosevelt to Churchill, 7 March 1942, in Kimball, *C&R Correspondence*, I 392.
7. Prime Minister to Chief of Combined Operations, 30 May 1942, CBH, 284.
8. Lewis Broad, *Winston Churchill*, revised extended edition (London: Hutchinson, 1945), 481.
9. Gabriel Gorodetsky, ed., *The Maisky Diaries: Red Ambassador to the Court of St. James's, 1932–1943* (New Haven, Ct.: Yale University Press, 2015), 480. Churchill to Maisky, 9 February 1943: "When I was in Moscow, I proceeded from the assumption that by spring 1943, the Americans would have dispatched twenty-seven divisions to England, just as they had promised. This was my assumption during my conversations with Stalin."
10. Kimball, *C&R Correspondence*, II 38.
11. Lord Louis Mountbatten to Chiefs of Staff Committee, 8 January 1943, Cabinet papers 79/58; WSC7, 264.
12. Winston S. Churchill to Roosevelt, 24 November 1942, Kimball, *C&R Correspondence*, II 39.
13. Franklin D. Roosevelt to Churchill, 25 November 1942, Kimball, *C&R Corresondence*, II 41.
14. Gorodetsky, ed., *Maisky Diaries*, 480.
15. CBH, 281–82.
16. Winston S. Churchill, *Triumph and Tragedy* (London: Cassell, 1954), 409.
17. Alanbrooke Diary, 25 October 1943, in WSC-DV19 (forthcoming, 2016).
18. Lord Moran, *Churchill: Taken from the Diaries of Lord Moran. The Struggle for Survival 1940–1965.* Boston: Houghton Mifflin, 1966, 130.
19. WSC7, 579.
20. Winston S. Churchill to Eden, 29 October 1943, Churchill Papers 20/122, WSC-DV19.

21. Martin Gilbert, "Churchill and D-Day," *Finest Hour* 122, Spring 2004, 26.

22. Nigel Hamilton, *Commander-in-Chief: FDR's Battle with Churchill, 1943* (New York: Houghton Mifflin Harcourt, 2016), 314–15, 320.

23. Churchill, *Closing the Ring*, 73.

24. Hamilton, *Commander-in-Chief*, 36, 38, 93.

25. Publisher's promotion for Hamilton, *Commander in Chief*, http://amzn.to/29rhGDa accessed 4 July 2016.

26. Paul Reid and William Manchester, *The Last Lion: Winston Spencer Churchill*, vol. 3, *Defender of the Realm 1940–1965* (New York: Little Brown, 2012), 451, 602.

Chapter 27

1. Churchill, *Gathering Storm*, 14, http://bit.ly/29xg0Ih, accessed 6 January 2016.

2. Winston S. Churchill to Roosevelt, 17 December 1941, in Kimball, *C&R Correspondence*, I 307.

3. Manchester, *Last Lion*, I 843–44.

4. Comments on Richard M. Langworth, "Hollande's Churchill Moment," *The American Spectator*, 19 November 2015. Winston S. Churchill, "Let the Tyrant Criminals Bomb!" in *Colliers*, 14 January 1939, reprinted in *Collected Essays* I 426

5. Michael W. Kramer, "The WWII Bombing of Dresden," http://www.blex.org/research/dresden.html, accessed 6 July 2016.

6. Martin Gilbert, "Churchill and Bombing Policy," Fifth Churchill Lecture, Washington, D.C., 18 October 2005, *Finest Hour* 137, Winter 2007–08, 28.

7. *Ibid.*, 28–29.

8. War Cabinet, 15 October 1940, Cabinet Papers 65/9, in WSC6, 844.

9. Defence Committee (Operations) minutes, 13 January 1941, Cabinet papers, 69I/2.

10. Winston S. Churchill to Portal, 13 March 1942, Churchill Papers 20/67.

11. Gilbert, "Bombing Policy," 33.

12. Averell Harriman to Roosevelt, 12 August 1942, in *Special Envoy to Churchill and Stalin* (New York: Random House, 1975), 152–53.

13. Arthur Bryant, *The Turn of the Tide 1939–1943* (New York: Doubleday, 1957), 389.

14. Christopher C. Harmon, *"Are We Beasts?" Churchill and the Moral Question of World War II "Area Bombing,"* Newport: U.S. Naval War College, 1991), 3.

15. Lord Casey, *Personal Experience 1939–1946* (London: Constable, 1962), 166.

16. Gilbert, "Bombing Policy," 34.

17. WSC7, 784.

18. Franklin D. Roosevelt to Churchill, 11 May 1944, in Kimball, *C&R Correspondence*, III 496

19. WSC7, 1219. John Terraine, *A Time for Courage: The Royal Air Force in the European War 1939–1945* (New York: Macmillan, 1985), 677.

20. Harmon, *Moral Question*, 20.

21. Adam Kirsch, "Is World War II Still the Good War?," *New York Times Sunday Book Review*, 27 May 2011, http://nyti.ms/ltQtuk, accessed 8 July 2016.

22. Clive Ponting, *Churchill* (London: Sinclair Stevenson, 1994), 640.

23. Ian Hunter, ed., *Winston and Archie: The Letters of Sir Archibald Sinclair and Winston S. Churchill 1915–1960* (London: Politico's, 2005), 411.

24. Harmon, *Moral Question*, 20. The report was false in Peter Calvocoressi and Guy Wint, *Total War: Causes and Courses of the Second World War* (London: Penguin, 1974), 534, showed that the armor was a panzer division

being moved from the failed Ardennes offensive to Hungary.

25. Martin Gilbert to the author, 18 October 2005. Aleksei Antonov (1896–1962), deputy chief, Soviet General Staff, 1942–45, chief Soviet military spokesman at Yalta and Potsdam conferences.

26. Richard M. Langworth, "Fifth Churchill Lecture and Teacher Seminar," 18 October 2005, *Finest Hour* 130, Spring 2006, 28–33 (29).

27. Prime Minister's Personal Minute, D.83/5, WSC7, 1257.

28. John Grigg, *1943: The Victory that Never Was* (New York: Hill and Wang, 1980), 149.

29. Ponting, *Churchill*, 641.

30. WSC7, 1257, quoting Chiefs of Staff Committee minutes, 29 March 1945, Cabinet Papers 79/31.

31. Martin Gilbert, *Churchill's London: Spinning Top of Memories* (Hopkinton, N.H.: Churchill Literary Foundation, 1987), 25.

32. Christopher Harmon, "Datelines," *Finest Hour* 110, Spring 2001, 8.

Chapter 28

1. Philip Hensher, "Does Boris Johnson really expect us to believe he's Churchill?" A review of Boris Johnson, *The Churchill Factor: How One Man Made History*, *The Spectator*, London, 25 October 2014. See also note 6.

2. Churchill, House of Commons, 8 December 1944, in CBH, 176.

3. Cf. Madhusree Mukerjee, *Churchill's Secret War: The British Empire and the Ravaging of India during World War II* (New York, Basic Books, 2010).

4. Winston S. Churchill to Lord Leathers, 10 March 1943, Prime Minister's Personal Minute, M.150/3 (Churchill Papers, 4/397A), in WSC-DV18, 604.

5. Mukerjee, *Secret War*, 191. Christopher Bell, *Churchill and Sea Power* (New York: Oxford University Press, 2013), 274.

6. Amery Diary, 24 November 1943, in John Barnes and David Nicholson, eds., *The Empire at Bay: The Leo Amery Diaries, 1929–1945* (London: Hutchinson, 1987), 943. (Amery's reference to the Greeks was over a simultaneous Greek famine under Nazi occupation.)

7. War Cabinet, Confidential Record, 7 October 1943, in WSC-DV19 (forthcoming 2016; other Churchill and Cabinet Papers quoted are from the same source).

8. Winston S. Churchill to the War Cabinet, 8 October 1943 (Churchill Papers 23/11).

9. Arthur Herman, quoted in Richard M. Langworth, "Myth: 'Churchill Caused the 1943–45 Bengal Famine," *Finest Hour* 142, Spring 2009, 35.

10. Winston S. Churchill to William Lyon Mackenzie King, 4 November 1943. Prime Minister's Personal Telegram T.1842/3 (Churchill Papers, 20/123).

11. Winston S. Churchill to King, 11 November 1943. Prime Minister's Personal Telegram T.1942/3 (Churchill Papers, 20/124); King to Churchill, 13 November 1943, Prime Minister's Personal Telegram T.1961/3 (Churchill Papers, 20/124).

12. Arthur Herman, "Absent Churchill, India's 1943 Famine Would Have Been Worse," *Finest Hour* 149, Winter 2010–11, 51.

13. Winston S. Churchill to Wavell, 14 February 1944, in Arthur Herman, "Absent Churchill," 51.

14. War Cabinet: Conclusions, 7 February 1944 (Cabinet Papers, 65/41). Churchill stated that "for the four

years ending 1941/42 the average consumption was 52,331,000 tons, i.e., 2½ million tons less than the figure cited by the Secretary of State. This difference would, of course, more than make good the 1½ million tons calculated deficit."

15. War Cabinet: Conclusions, 7 February 1944; Herman, "Absent Churchill," 51.

16. War Cabinet: Conclusions, 14 February (Cabinet Papers, 65/41).

17. Winston S. Churchill to Sir James Grigg, 19 February 1944, Prime Minister's Personal Minute M.147/4 (Churchill papers, 20/152).

18. War Cabinet: Conclusions, 21 February 1944 (Cabinet Papers, 65/41).

19. War Cabinet: Conclusions, 20 March 1944 (Cabinet papers, 65/41).

20. War Cabinet: Conclusions, 24 April 1944 (Cabinet papers, 65/42).

21. *Ibid.*

22. Winston S. Churchill to Roosevelt, 29 April 1944, in Kimball, *C&R Correspondence,* III 117.

23. Franklin D. Roosevelt to Churchill, 1 June 1944, in Kimball, *C&R Correspondence,* III 155.

24. Sir Henry French, "Indian Food Situation," report to the Cabinet, 10 October 1944, in WSC-DV19.

25. Herman, "Absent Churchill," 51.

26. *Ibid.*

27. Lady Soames to the author, 2005.

28. Barnes and Nicholson, eds., *Amery Diaries,* 950.

Chapter 29

1. Fiona Govan, "Actor Leslie Howard kept Spain out of WWII, claims author," *Daily Telegraph,* 6 September 2008, http://xrl.us/ot49n, accessed 6 June 2016.

2. Cf. José Rey-Ximena, *El Vuelo de Ibis* (Madrid: Editions Facta, 2008).

3. José Rey-Ximena, quoted in Govan, "Actor Leslie Howard."

4. David Stafford to the author, 3 October 2008, quoted in Richard M. Langworth, "Leading Myths: Leslie Howard Kept Spain out of the War," *Finest Hour* 141, Winter 2008–09, 10–11.

5. WSC-DV14, 161, and Martin Gilbert, correspondence with the author, 4 October 2008.

6. WSC-DV16, 569.

7. Richard M. Langworth, "What Killed Leslie Howard?," *Finest Hour* 131, Summer 2006, 6. The book was Tom Hickman, *Churchill's Bodyguard* (London: Headline, 2005).

8. Martin Gilbert, *Churchill: A Life,* 747.

9. Churchill, *Hinge of Fate,* 742.

10. Sir Laurence Olivier, quoted in Carlos Thompson, *The Assassination of Winston Churchill* (Gerrard's Cross: Smythe, 1969), 82.

11. M.R.D. Foot, "Why Was Leslie Shot Down?," *Finest Hour* 133, Winter 2006–07, 4.

12. Chris Goss, *Bloody Biscay: The Story of the Luftwaffe's Only Long Range Maritime Fighter Unit, V Gruppe/ Kampfgeschwader 40, and Its Adversaries 1942–1944* (London: Crécy, 2001), 50–56.

13. Soenke Neitzel and Harald Welzer, *Soldaten: On Fighting, Killing, and Dying: the Secret WWII transcripts of German POWs* (Melbourne: Scribe, 2012), 67.

14. *Speeches,* VII 6935.

Chapter 30

1. Correspondence, Nando Tasciotti and the author,

27–30 May 2013. For Eisenhower's order on troops vs. famous buildings, see note 12.

2. Churchill, *Closing the Ring,* 442.

3. Nando Tasciotti to the author, 27 May 2013.

4. WSC7, 784.

5. David Hapgood and David Richardson, *Monte Cassino: The Story of the Most Controversial Battle of World War II* (Cambridge, Mass., Da Capo Press, 2004), 161.

6. *Ibid.,* 185.

7. *Ibid.,* 169.

8. Fred Majdalnay, *Cassino: Portrait of a Battle* (London: Longmans Green, 1957), 121–22.

9. Calvocoressi and Wint, *Total War,* 534–36.

10. WSC7, 681.

11. The Lord Chancellor (Viscount Simon), "Preservation of Historical and Art Treasures," 16 February 1944, *Hansard,* vol. 130, cc 813–62.

12. Gen. Dwight D. Eisenhower, "Historical Monuments," to All Commanders, 29 December 1943. AG 000.4–1, http://bit.ly/29TgRAe, accessed 13 February 2016.

13. Winston S. Churchill, *The Dawn of Liberation* (London: Cassell, 1945), 10.

14. Joe Tinker, MP for Leigh, 22 February 1944, *Hansard,* vol. 397, cc 725

15. Question by Mr. Ivor Thomas, 7 March 1944, *Hansard,* vol. 397, cc 1861.

16. Churchill, *Closing the Ring,* 448.

17. WSC7, 736–37.

18. *Ibid.,* 774.

19. Question by Capt. Alan Graham, 6 June 1944, *Hansard,* vol. 400, cc 1199–1200.

20. Sir Percy Grigg, "Italian Art Treasures (German Looting), 3 October 1944, *Hansard,* vol. 403, cc. 776–90.

21. WSC7, 714, 720–21.

22. "Jurisdiction of the Court," 8 March 2001, *Hansard,* vol. 623, cc 346–87.

23. Hapgood and Richardson, *Monte Cassino,* 237.

Chapter 31

1. CBH, 187.

2. CBH, 192.

3. Martin Gilbert, *Auschwitz and the Allies* (New York: Holt, Rinehart and Winston, 1981), 251. The initial estimate was 15,000, a slight exaggeration.

4. Gilbert, *Auschwitz,* 252; Premier Papers, 4/51/10.

5. Gilbert, *Auschwitz,* 201–02; Foreign Office Papers, 371/42811.

6. Churchill to Eden, 11 July 1944, Foreign Office papers, 371/42809.

7. Martin Gilbert, "Churchill and the Holocaust," Holocaust Museum, Washington, 8 November 1993, *Proceedings 1992–1993* (Hopkinton, N.H.: International Churchill Society, 1995), 57.

8. Gilbert, *Auschwitz and the Allies,* 285.

9. David S. Wyman, "Why Auschwitz Was Never Bombed, *Commentary,* May 1978 65(5): 40.

10. Leon Kubowitzki to War Refugee Board, 1 July 1944.

11. Michael J. Cohen, "The Churchill-Gilbert Symbiosis: Myth and Reality," review of Gilbert's Churchill and the Jews, *Modern Judaism,* 2008 28(2): 204–28. See also his book, *Churchill and the Jews* (London: Frank Cass, 1985; second edition, London: Routledge, 2008).

12. Gilbert, *Auschwitz and the Allies,* 302–03.

13. Prime Minister's Personal Minutes M 806/4 (8 July 1944) and C 45/4 (10 July 1944).

14. Winston S. Churchill to the Archbishop of Canterbury; Churchill to Lord Melchett, both 13 July 1944, Chartwell Papers CHAR 20/138A. Forthcoming in WSC-DV20, Hillsdale College Press, 2017.

15. Premier Papers, 3/352/4/ folio 70. Gilbert, *Auschwitz and the Allies*, 325.

16. Winston S. Churchill to his wife, 20 April 1945, in Mary Soames, ed., *Speaking for Themselves: The Personal Letters of Winston and Clementine Churchill* (New York: Doubleday, 1998), 527.

Chapter 32

1. See for example Lizzie Collingham, *Taste of War: World War II and the Battle for Food* (New York: Penguin, 2012), Part II, Sec. 8, "Greek Famine and Belgian Resilience." This chapter is derived from "Leading Churchill Myths: 'Churchill Tried to Starve Occupied Europe,'" by the author and Warren F. Kimball, *Finest Hour* 144, Autumn 2009, 35.

2. Winston S. Churchill to Roosevelt, 23 November 1940 in Kimball, *C&R Correspondence*, I 86.

3. Franklin D. Roosevelt to Churchill, 31 December 1940 *ibid.*, I 118.

4. Winston S. Churchill to Roosevelt, 3 January 1941 *ibid.*, I 126.

5. Paul-Henri Spaak, *The Continuing Battle: Memoirs of a European 1936-1966* (Boston: Littlehampton, 1971), quoted in "Spaak Memoir Recalls Presidential Meetings," *The Indianapolis Star*, publisher's extra edition, 3 September 1972, 149.

6. Winston S. Churchill to Roosevelt, 12 March 1941, in Kimball, *C&R Correspondence*, I 14. Admiral François Darlan (1881-1942), Vichy's prime minister, 1941-42, commanded the French Navy in July 1940, when the British destroyed four French battleships in North African ports, lest they fall into German hands. Darlan had stated that he might use the French fleet to prevent British interference with the importation of food and other supplies to occupied France.

7. Winston S. Churchill to Roosevelt, 1 January 1943, in Kimball, *C&R Correspondence*, II 105.

8. *Ibid.*

9. *Ibid.*

10. Winston S. Churchill to President of the Board of Trade Hugh Dalton and Minister of Food Lord Woolton, 30 September 1943, PM's Personal Minute M.618/3, Churchill Papers 20/104, in WSC-DV19 (forthcoming, 2016).

11. Franklin D. Roosevelt to Churchill, 15 March 1944, Kimball, *C&R Correspondence*, III 47.

12. Winston S. Churchill to Roosevelt, 8 April 1944, *ibid.*, III 85.

13. Franklin D. Roosevelt to Churchill, 8 April 1944, *ibid.*, III 86.

Chapter 33

1. WSC7, 993.

2. Churchill, *Triumph and Tragedy*, 198. The document is PREM 3/66/7 (169).

3. Gabriel Kolko, *The Politics of War: The World and United States Foreign Policy 1943-1945* (New York: Pantheon, 1990), 145.

4. Henry Butterfield Ryan, *The Vision of Anglo-America: The U.S.-UK Alliance and the Emerging Cold War 1943-1946* (Cambridge: Cambridge University Press, 1987), 137.

5. Kolko, *Politics of War*, 145.

6. Christine Marki to the author, via email, 10 December 2015.

7. Larry P. Arnn, "Principles and Compromise," in *Churchill Proceedings 1994-1995* (Washington: The Churchill Centre, 1998), 107.

8. *Ibid.*, 107-08.

9. *Ibid.*, 108.

10. R.J. Crampton, *A Concise History of Bulgaria* (Cambridge: Cambridge University Press, 2005), 271.

11. "Romania," in *CIA World Fact Book*, 2016.

12. "Hungary's 'Forgotten' War Victims," BBC News, 7 November 2009, http://bbc.in/2a4z0LK, accessed 4 February 2016.

13. Robert Service, *Comrades! A History of World Communism* (Cambridge, Mass.: Harvard University Press, 2007), 266-68.

14. Winston S. Churchill to Smuts, 3 December 1944 in WSC7, 1082.

15. Winston S. Churchill to Tito, 3 December 1944 (he copied Stalin, who confirmed their agreement "to pursue as far as possible a joint policy towards Yugoslavia). Churchill to Eden, 28 November 1944. WSC7, 1083-84.

16. WSC7, 1121.

17. CBH, 556

18. Winston S. Churchill to Eden, 7 January 1944, Churchill papers, 20/179, in WSC-DV19, forthcoming 2016.

19. Winston S. Churchill to Eden, 15 February 1944, Churchill papers, 20/152, *ibid.*

20. Warren F. Kimball, *Forged in War: Roosevelt, Churchill and the Second World War* (New York: Morrow, 1997), 317-18.

21. Diary of Hugh Dalton, 23 February 1945, Dalton Papers, in David Dilks, *The Great Dominion* (Toronto: Thomas Allen, 2005), 360.

22. John Colville, *The Fringes of Power: Downing Street Diaries 1940-1955*, 2 vols. (Sevenoaks, Kent: Sceptre, 1986-87), II 194.

23. William F. Buckley, Jr., "Let Us Now Praise Famous Men," *Churchill Proceedings 1994-1995*, 81.

24. Arnn, "Principles and Compromise," 109.

25. See for example Lloyd Gardner, *Spheres of Influence: The Great Powers Partition in Europe, from Munich to Yalta* (Lanham, Md., Ivan R. Dee, 1994); and Warren F. Kimball, *The Juggler: Franklin Roosevelt as Wartime Statesman* (Princeton, N.J.: Princeton University Press, 1991).

Chapter 34

1. Gilbert, *Churchill and Bombing Policy*, 36.

2. Churchill, *Triumph and Tragedy*, 552.

3. *Ibid.*, 552-53.

4. Warren F. Kimball, "The Bomb and the Special Relationship," *Finest Hour* 137, Winter 2007-08, 40.

5. Jonathan A. Hayes "Despatch Box," *Finest Hour* 141, Winter 2008-09, 4.

6. WSC6, 253.

7. CBH, 314. Lady Soames to the author, 1992.

8. D.M. Ladd to J. Edgar Hoover, FBI memorandum, 5 December 1947, in Thomas Maier, *When Lions Roar: The Churchills and the Kennedys* (New York: Crown, 2014), 433.

9. Moran, *Struggle for Survival*, 337-38.

10. Graham Farmelo, quoting *The MacKenzie King Record* (1970) in *Churchill's Bomb* (New York: Basic Books, 2013), 339.

11. Anthony Seldon, *Churchill's Indian Summer: The*

Conservative Government 1951–55 (London: Hodder and Stoughton, 1981), 32.

12. *Ibid.*
13. Farmelo, *Churchill's Bomb*, 339–40.
14. WSC8, 397.
15. Daniel Bates, "Winston Churchill's bid to nuke Russia," *Daily Mail*, 8 November 2014, http://dailym.ai/1IKaue5, accessed 15 February 2016.
16. Colville, *Fringes of Power*, II 348.

Chapter 35

1. Cf. Sonia Purnell, *First Lady: The Life and Wars of Clementine Churchill* (New York: Viking, 2015).
2. Mary Soames, *Clementine Churchill*, 446.
3. *Ibid.*, 663. Grace Hamblin to the author, 1987.
4. Purnell, *First Lady*, 26, 70, 73, 199.
5. Andrew Roberts to the author, 2015.
6. Lady Soames to the author, 1995.
7. Henry Thynne, Sixth Marques of Bath, to the author, 1985.
8. Purnell, *First Lady*, 23, 70, 73.
9. John Pearson, *Citadel of the Heart: The Private Lives of Winston Churchill* (New York: Simon and Schuster, 1991), reviewed by this author, *Finest Hour* 73, Fourth Quarter 1991, 20–21.
10. *Ibid.*, 194–99.
11. *Ibid.*, 307.
12. Soames, *Clementine Churchill*, 478–79.
13. *Ibid.*, 123.
14. Gilbert, *Churchill: A Life*, 759.
15. John Colville, *The Churchillians*, 123.
16. Churchill to his wife, 23 January 1935, WSC-DV12, 1042.
17. Winston S. Churchill, "My Life," Part 7, *News of the World*, 24 February 1935, reprinted in *Collected Essays* III, 176.
18. Peter de Mendelssohn, *The Age of Churchill: Heritage and Adventure 1874–1914* (New York: Alfred Knopf, 1961), 352.
19. WSC4, 512. Richard M. Langworth, "Winston and Clementine: A New Gathering Storm?," *Finest Hour* 67, Second Quarter 1990, 31.
20. Sir Robert Rhodes James to the author, 1991.
21. CBH, 511.

Chapter 36

1. Churchill, *Hinge of Fate*, 718. The Paneuropean Union still exists, rating politicians as to their advocacy of its principles. See http://www.paneuropa.org.
2. Winston S. Churchill, "The United States of Europe," in *News of the World*, 9 May 1938, reprinted in *Collected Essays*, II 185. WSC was quoting the King James Bible, II Kings 4:8, "Elisha passed to Shunem, where was a great [prominent] woman; and she constrained him to eat bread"; and II Kings 4:13, "[Elisha] said… Behold, thou hast been careful for us with all this care; what is to be done for thee?" Elisha received the reply Churchill quoted.
3. CBH, 465.
4. Churchill to John Colville, 10 August 1940, in Colville, *Fringes of Power*, I 253.
5. Churchill, *Hinge of Fate*, 717–18.
6. Charles de Gaulle, *Unity 1942–1944* (New York: Simon & Schuster, 1959), 153.
7. Kimball, *C&R Correspondence*, III 169.
8. Churchill, *My Early Life*, 346.
9. Churchill, *Speeches*, VII 7381.

10. Churchill, *Speeches*, VII 7640.
11. CBH, 434.
12. Ambrose Evans-Pritchard, "The European Union Always Was a CIA Project, as Brexiteers Discover," *Daily Telegraph*, 27 April 2016, http://bit.ly/2btDsE6, accessed 3 July 2016.
13. Churchill, 29 November 1951, National Archives, CAB 129/48C(51)32.
14. Churchill to Herbert Morrison MP, Question Time, 8 July 1952, in Hansard, Vol. 503: 1093.
15. Churchill, "Foreign Affairs," House of Commons, 11 May 1953, in *Speeches*, VIII 8481.
16. Lady Soames to the author, 2001. WSC8, 1337.
17. Montague Browne, *Long Sunset*, 273–74.
18. *Ibid.*, 275.
19. *Ibid.*, 138.
20. *Ibid.*, 274.

Chapter 37

1. Max Hastings, *Catastrophe 1914*, reviewed by Richard M. Langworth, Hillsdale College Churchill Project, 21 January 2016, http://bit.ly/2boqmrt.
2. Grace Hamblin, "Chartwell Memories," speech to the International Churchill Conference, 30 October 1987, *Proceedings of the International Churchill Society 1987*, 46.
3. *Ibid.*
4. WSC-DV12, 982.
5. Percy Reid, *Churchill: Townsman of Westerham* (Folkestone, Kent: Regency, 1969), 46.
6. *Ibid.*
7. Phil Johnson to the author, 1995.
8. Reid, *Townsman of Westerham*, 11.
9. WSC-DV11, 1349.
10. Sir John Colville to the author, 1987, CBH, 530.
11. Ronald Golding to the author, 1985.
12. Cf. Phyllis Moir, *I Was Winston Churchill's Private Secretary* (New York: Wilfred Funk, 1941).
13. Manchester, *Last Lion* I 843–44.
14. Elizabeth Nel, *Mr. Churchill's Secretary* (London: Hodder and Stoughton, 1958), 58. Again Churchill's elephantine memory served: "Toads beneath the harrow" is a line from the poem "Pagett, MP" by Rudyard Kipling, one of his favorite authors.
15. Ronald Golding, "WSC: The Memories," *Finest Hour* 35, Spring 1982, 10; CBH, 538.
16. Soames, *Clementine Churchill*, 92.
17. Hamblin, "Chartwell Memories," 39.
18. WSC8, 665. Grace Hamblin to the author, 1987.
19. Hamblin, "Chartwell Memories," 39.
20. *Ibid.*
21. *Ibid.*, 41.
22. Golding, "WSC: The Memories," 10–11.
23. Elizabeth Layton Nel, "Loyalty—A Churchillian Characteristic," *Finest Hour* 52, Summer 1986, 9.
24. Hamblin, "Chartwell Memories," 49.

Appendix 1

1. Carol Breckenridge, "The Myth of the Black Dog," *Finest Hour* 155, Summer 2012, 28–31, available online as a pdf at http://bit.ly/2boTn6v.
2. Moran, *Struggle for Survival*, 180.
3. *Ibid.*, 794.
4. Anthony Storr, "The Man," in A.J.P. Taylor, ed., *Churchill: Four Faces and the Man* (London: Allen Lane, The Penguin Press, 1969), 203–46.
5. Lady Soames to the author, 2005.

6. Breckenridge, "Myth of the Black Dog," 31.

7. Lady Soames, "Life with my Parents," an interview with Naim Attallah, *Finest Hour* 91, Summer 1996, 17.

8. Breckenridge, 31.

9. Arthur Gladstone Keeney, "Dr. Lifesaver," *Coronet*, December 1944, 17–18.

10. Ken Hirsch, quoted in Richard M. Langworth, "The Churchill-Fleming Non-Connection," *Finest Hour* 102, Spring 1999, 47.

11. John Mather, MD., *ibid.*; CBH, 573; Moran, *Struggle for Survival*, 335.

12. Sir Martin Gilbert to the author, November 1998.

13. Andrew Roberts, quoted in a post by the author on which this entry is based, Hillsdale College Churchill Project, 15 April 2015, http://bit.ly/2bqvJXt, accessed 13 March 2016.

14. Patrick Sawyer, "Winston Churchill quietly flirted with Islam," *Daily Telegraph*, 28 December 2014, republished by the *National Post*, http://bit.ly/2bqx54e, accessed 13 March 2016.

15. Winston S. Churchill, *The River War*, 2 vols. (London: Longmans Green, 1899), II 221.

16. Lady Gwendoline Bertie to Winston S. Churchill, 27 August 1907, in WSC-DV3, 672.

17. WSC to Lady Lytton, 19 September 1907, in WSC-DV4, 679–80.

18. Churchill to H.H. Asquith, 1910, in Martin Gilbert, "Churchill's Campaign Against the 'Feeble-Minded,'" *Finest Hour* 152, Autumn 2011, 44–48.

19. Churchill to Ivor Guest, 19 January 1899, in WSC-DV3, xxvii.

20. Report of the Royal Commission on the Care and Control of the Feeble-Minded, 1908. His Majesty's Stationery Office, Command Paper 4202, 1908.

21. National Archives, Home Office papers, 144/1098/197900.

22. Royal Assent, 29 July 1959. The 1959 Mental Health Act mandated treatment and care, but not incarceration, of mentally disordered people.

23. Addison, *Churchill on the Home Front*, 126.

24. Gilbert, "Churchill's Campaign," 48.

25. Richard M. Langworth, Letter to the *Jamaica Observer*, 25 September 2012, http://bit.ly/2aUtKhd, accessed 12 April 2016.

26. David Freeman, "Inside the Journals," *Finest Hour* 125, Winter 2004–05, 33.

27. Jaffa, *Statesmanship*, 259.

28. The History Channel, "Betrayal at Pearl Harbor," a television documentary, aired 7 December 1998.

29. Ron Helgemo, "Opium for the People," *Finest Hour* 101, Winter 1998–99, 37–39, http://bit.ly/2aUuJOF, accessed 14 April 2016.

30. *Ibid.*, 38.

31. *Ibid.*, 39.

32. *Ibid.*

33. Jon Meacham, *Franklin and Winston* (New York: Random House, 2003), 350.

34. Purnell, *First Lady*, 317

35. Boris Johnson, *The Churchill Factor* (London: Hodder and Stoughton, 2014), 280.

36. WSC7, 1291.

37. *Ibid.*, 1294.

38. Winston S. Churchill to his wife, 14 April 1945, in Soames, *Speaking for Themselves*, 526.

39. Alan Lascelles, *King's Counsellor: Abdication and War* (London: Weidenfeld and Nicolson, 2006) entry for Friday 13 April 1945, 313.

40. David Dilks, ed., *The Diaries of Sir Alexander Cadogan OM, 1938–1945* (London: Cassell, 1971), 727.

41. Lyndon B. Johnson, quoted in H.A. Grunwald, ed., *Churchill: The Life Triumphant* (New York: American Heritage, 1965), 140.

42. Cf. Pat Riott, *The Greatest Story Never Told: Winston Churchill and the Crash of 1929* (Oak Brook, Ill.: Nanoman, 1994).

43. Christopher H., Sterling, *Writing About Winston* (Washington: Self-published, 2013), 15.

44. Riott, *Greatest Story*, 87.

45. *Ibid.*, 127.

46. WSC5, 350.

47. Riott, *Greatest Story*, 127.

48. Bradley P. Tolppanen, "Great Contemporaries: Bernard Baruch," Hillsdale College Churchill Project, August 2016, https://winstonchurchill.hillsdale.edu. For a detailed and accurate account of Churchill's 1929 sojourn see Tolppanen's *Churchill in North America, 1929* (Jefferson, N.C.: McFarland, 2014).

49. Riott, *Greatest Story*, 142, 172.

50. *Ibid.*, 135.

51. Cf. Louis Kilzer, *Churchill's Deception: The Dark Secret that Destroyed Nazi Germany* (New York: Simon and Schuster 1994).

52. William Partin, "His Reach Has Exceeded His Grasp," *Finest Hour* 84, Third Quarter 1994, 22.

Bibliography

Interviews and Correspondence

Paul Addison; Peregrine S. Churchill; Randolph S. Churchill; Winston S. Churchill (grandson); Sir John Colville; David Dilks; Sir Martin Gilbert; Ronald Golding; Grace Hamblin; Warren F. Kimball; Phil Johnson; Danny Mander; Christine Marki; Sir Anthony Montague Browne; Elizabeth Nel; Allen Packwood; Christian Pol-Roger; Sir Robert Rhodes James; Andrew Roberts; Douglas Russell; The Lady Soames; David Stafford; Nando Tasciotti; Henry Thynne Sixth Marquess of Bath.

Archives

The Churchill and Chartwell Papers, Churchill Archives Centre, Cambridge; National Archives (formerly the Public Records Office), London; National Sound Archive, London; the Martin Gilbert Papers, Hillsdale College Churchill Project.

Official Biography

Winston S. Churchill, by Randolph S. Churchill (vols. 1–2) and Martin Gilbert (vols. 3–8), and accompanying volumes of The Churchill Documents, edited by Randolph S. Churchill (1–5), Martin Gilbert (6–16), and Martin Gilbert and Larry P. Arnn (17–19 of a projected 23 volumes) (Hillsdale, Mich.: Hillsdale College Press).

Winston S. Churchill: The Narrative Volumes (WSC 1–8)

Volume 1: Youth, 1874–1900 (2006) Volume 2: Young Statesman, 1901–1914 (2007) Volume 3: The Challenge of War, 1914–1916 (2008) Volume 4: World in Torment, 1916–1922 (2008) Volume 5: The Prophet of Truth, 1922–1939 (2009) Volume 6: Finest Hour, 1939–1941 (2011) Volume 7: Road to Victory, 1941–1945 (2013) Volume 8: Never Despair, 1945–1965 (2013)

Winston S. Churchill: The Churchill Documents (WSC-DV 1–19)

Volume 1: Youth, 1874–1896 (2006) Volume 2: Young Soldier, 1896–1901 (2006) Volume 3: Early Years in Politics, 1901–1907 (2007) Volume 4: Minister of the Crown, 1907–1911 (2007) Volume 5: At the Admiralty, 1911–1914 (2007) Volume 6: At the Admiralty, July 1914–April 1915 (2008) Volume 7: "The Escaped Scapegoat," May 1915–December 1916 (2008) Volume 8: War and Aftermath, December 1916–June 1919 (2008) Volume 9: Disruption and Chaos, July 1919–March 1921 (2008) Volume 10: Conciliation and Reconstruction, April 1921–November 1922 (2008) Volume 11: The Exchequer Years, 1922–1929 (2009) Volume 12: The Wilderness Years, 1929–1935 (2009) Volume 13: The Coming of War, 1936–1939 (2009) Volume 14: At the Admiralty, September 1939–May 1940 (2011) Volume 15: Never Surrender, May 1940–December 1940 (2011) Volume 16: The Ever-Widening War, 1941 (2011) Volume 17: Testing Times, 1942 (2013)

Volume 18: One Continent Redeemed, January–August 1943 (2015)

Volume 19: Fateful Questions, September 1943–April 1944 (HCP, 2017)

Works by Winston S. Churchill

Amid These Storms. New York: Scribner, 1932.
Arms and the Covenant. London: Harrap, 1938.
Great Contemporaries, 1937. New edition, London: Leo Cooper, 1990.
In the Balance. London: Cassell, 1952.
India, 1931. First U.S. edition, Hopkinton, N.H.: Dragonwyck Publishing, 1991.
Lord Randolph Churchill, 1906; new edition. London: Odhams, 1952.
My Early Life. London: Thornton Butterworth, 1930.
Painting as a Pastime, 1921, republished in Thoughts and Adventures, 1932.
The River War, 2 vols. London: Longmans Green, 1899.
The Second World War, 6 vols. London: Cassell, 1948–54.
Step by Step, 1939. New Edition, London: Odhams, 1947.
Thoughts and Adventures, 1932. New edition, London: Leo Cooper, 1990.
The Unrelenting Struggle. London: Cassell, 1942.
The World Crisis, 5 vols. in 6 parts. London: Thornton Butterworth, 1923–31.

Collected Works

Collected Essays of Sir Winston Churchill, 4 vols., Michael Wolff, ed., London: Library of Imperial History, 1975.

The Great Republic: A Brief History of America, Winston S. Churchill, ed., New York: Random House, 1999.

Winston S. Churchill: His Complete Speeches 1897–1963, 8 vols., Robert Rhodes James, ed., New York: Bowker, 1974.

Books by Other Authors

Addison, Paul. *Churchill on the Home Front 1900–1955*. London: Jonathan Cape, 1992.

_____. *Churchill: The Unexpected Hero*. Oxford: Oxford University Press, 2005.

Arnn, Larry P. *Churchill's Trial: Winston Churchill and the Salvation of Free Government*. Nashville, Tenn.: Thomas Nelson, 2015.

Asquith, H.H. *Memories and Reflections,* 2 vols. Boston: Little, Brown, 1928.

Bailey, Thomas A., and Captain Paul B. Ryan *The Lusitania Disaster: An Episode in Modern Warfare and Diplomacy.* New York: Free Press: 1975.

Bantam, eds. *The People's Almanac, The Book of Lists.* New York: Bantam Doubleday Dell, 1978.

Barnes, John, and David Nicholson, eds., *The Empire at Bay: The Leo Amery Diaries, 1929–1945*. London: Hutchinson, 1987.

Bean, W.B., ed. *Sir William Osler: Aphorisms from His Bedside Teachings and Writings*. Springfield, Ill.: Charles C. Thomas, second edition, 1933.

Bell, Christopher. *Churchill and Sea Power.* New York: Oxford University Press, 2013.

Best, Geoffrey. *Churchill: A Study in Greatness.* London: Hambledon & London, 2001.

Birkenhead, Earl of. *Churchill 1874–1922.* London: Harrap, 1989.

Blake, Robert, and Wm. Roger Louis, eds. *Churchill: A Major New Assessment of His Life in Peace and War.* New York: Oxford University Press, 1993.

Bonham-Carter, Violet. *Winston Churchill: An Intimate Portrait.* New York: Harcourt Brace & World, 1965.

Boot, Max. *War Made New: Technology, Warfare and the Course of History, 1500 to Today.* New York: Penguin, 2006.

Broad, Lewis. *Winston Churchill, 1941.* Revised extended edition, London: Hutchinson, 1945.

Broadbent, Harvey. *Gallipoli: The Fatal Shore.* Camberwell, Australia: Viking/Penguin, 2005.

Brock, Michael, and Eleanor Brock, eds. *H.H. Asquith Letters to Venetia Stanley.* New York: Oxford University Press, 1982.

Bryant, Arthur. *The Turn of the Tide 1939–1943.* New York: Doubleday, 1957.

Buchanan, Patrick J. *Churchill, Hitler, and the "Unnecessary War."* New York: Crown, 2008.

Buzzard, Thomas. *Clinical Aspects of Syphilitic Nervous Affections.* Philadelphia: Lindsay & Blakiston 1874.

Calvocoressi, Peter, and Guy Wint. *Total War: Causes and Courses of the Second World War.* London: Penguin, 1974.

Carlson, John Roy. *Under Cover: My Four Years in the Nazi Underworld of America.* New York: Dutton, 1943.

Casey, Lord. *Personal Experience 1939–1946.* London: Constable, 1962.

Cave Brown, Anthony. *Bodyguard of Lies.* New York: Bantam, 1976.

Chaplin, E.D.W. *Winston Churchill at Harrow.* Harrow, Middlesex: The Harrow Bookshop, 1941.

Churchill, Lady Randolph. *Reminiscences.* London: Arnold, 1908.

Cohen, Michael J. *Churchill and the Jews.* London: Frank Cass, 1985; 2nd ed., London: Routledge, 2008.

Cohen, Ronald I. *Bibliography of the Writings of Sir Winston Churchill,* 3 vols. London: Continuum, 2006.

Collingham, Lizzie. *Taste of War: World War II and the Battle for Food.* New York: Penguin, 2012.

Colville, John. *The Churchillians.* London: Weidenfeld and Nicholson, 1981.

_____. *The Fringes of Power: Downing Street Diaries 1940–1955,* 1985. Two-volume edition, Sevenoaks, Kent: Sceptre, 1986–87.

Costigliola, Frank. *Roosevelt's Lost Alliances: How Personal Politics Helped Start the Cold War.* Princeton, N.J.: Princeton University Press, 2012.

Crozier, W.P. *Off the Record: Political Interviews 1933–1943.* London: Hutchinson, 1973.

Crampton, R.J. *A Concise History of Bulgaria.* Cambridge: Cambridge University Press, 2005.

Danchev, Alex, and Daniel Todman, eds. *War Diaries 1939–1945 by Field Marshall Lord Alanbrooke.* Berkeley: University of California Press, 2001.

de Gaulle, Charles. *Unity 1942–1944.* New York: Simon & Schuster, 1959.

de Mendelssohn, Peter. *The Age of Churchill: Heritage and Adventure 1874–1914.* New York: Alfred Knopf, 1961.

Dilks, David. *The Great Dominion: Winston Churchill in Canada.* Toronto: Thomas Allen, 2005

_____, ed. *The Diaries of Sir Alexander Cadogan OM, 1938–1945.* London: Cassell, 1971, 727.

Duff Cooper, Alfred. *Old Men Forget: The Autobiography of Duff Cooper.* London: Rupert Hart-Davis, 1953.

Eade, Charles, ed. *Churchill by his Contemporaries.* London: Hutchinson, 1953.

Edmonds, J.E. *Military Operations France and Belgium, 1914: Mons, the Retreat to the Seine, the Marne and the Aisne August–October 1914.* Second ed. London: Macmillan, 1926.

Erickson, Edward. *Ordered to Die: A History of the Ottoman Army in the First World War.* Westport, Conn.: Greenwood Publishing, 2000.

Farmelo, Graham. *Churchill's Bomb.* New York: Basic Books, 2013.

Fishman, Jack. *My Darling Clementine.* New York: McKay, 1963.

Foster, R.F. *Lord Randolph Churchill: A Political Life.* London: Oxford University Press 1981.

Fromkin, David. *A Peace to End All Peace: The Fall of the Ottoman Empire and the Creation of the Modern Middle East.* New York: Henry Holt, 1989.

Fuller, J.F.C. *Decisive Battles of the Western World and*

Their Influence Upon History, vol. 3. London: Cassell, 1956.

Gandhi, Mohandas. *Collected Works*, 95 vols. New Delhi: Ministry of Information and Broadcasting, New Delhi, 1979.

Gardner, Lloyd. *Spheres of Influence: The Great Powers Partition in Europe, from Munich to Yalta.* Lanham, Md., Ivan R. Dee, 1994.

Gilbert, Martin. *Auschwitz and the Allies.* New York: Holt, Rinehart and Winston, 1981.

_____. *Churchill: A Life.* London: Minerva, 1992.

_____. *Churchill's London: Spinning Top of Memories.* Hopkinton, N.H.: Churchill Literary Foundation, 1987.

_____. *Churchill's Political Philosophy.* London: British Academy, 1981.

_____. *In Search of Churchill.* New York: Wiley, 1994.

Gill, Anton. *Titanic: The Real Story of the Construction of the World's Most Famous Ship.* London: Channel 4 Books, 2010.

Gillman, Peter, and Leni Gillman. *Collar the Lot! How Britain Interned & Expelled its Wartime Refugees.* London: Quartet Books, 1980.

Giuliani-Balestrino, Ubaldo. *Il carteggio Churchill-Mussolini alla luce del processo Guareschi.* Rome: Edizioni Settimo Sigillo, 2010.

Golland, Jim. *Not Winston, Just William? Winston Churchill at Harrow School.* Harrow: Herga Press, 1988.

Gorodetsky, Gabriel, ed. *The Maisky Diaries: Red Ambassador to the Court of St. James's, 1932–1943.* New Haven, Ct.: Yale University Press, 2015.

Goss, Chris. *Bloody Biscay: The Story of the Luftwaffe's Only Long Range Maritime Fighter Unit, V Gruppe/Kampfgeschwader 40, and its Adversaries 1942–1944.* London: Crécy, 2001.

Grant, R.G. *Churchill: An Illustrated Biography.* London: Bison Books, 1989.

Grigg, John. *1943: The Victory That Never Was.* New York: Hill and Wang, 1980.

Grunwald, Henry Anatole, ed. *Churchill: The Life Triumphant.* New York: American Heritage, 1965.

Guedalla, Philip. *Mr. Churchill: A Portrait.* London: Hodder & Stoughton, 1941.

Halle, Kay. *Irrepressible Churchill.* Cleveland: World, 1966.

Hamilton, Nigel. *Commander-in-Chief: FDR's Battle with Churchill, 1943.* New York: Houghton Mifflin Harcourt, 2016

_____. *The Mantle of Command.* Boston: Houghton Mifflin, 2015.

Hapgood, David, and David Richardson. *Monte Cassino: The Story of the Most Controversial Battle of World War II.* Cambridge, Mass., Da Capo Press, 2004.

Harmon, Christopher C. *"Are We Beasts?" Churchill and the Moral Question of World War II "Area Bombing."* Newport, R.I.: U.S. Naval War College, 1991.

_____. *"Churchill and the Terrorism of His Day,"* unpublished manuscript, 2009, courtesy of the author.

Harriman, Averell (Elie Abel, ed.). *Special Envoy to Churchill and Stalin.* New York: Random House, 1975.

Harris, Frank. *My Life and Loves,* 5 vols., 1922–27. One vol. edition, New York: Grove Press 1963.

Havardi, Jeremy. *The Greatest Briton: Essays on Winston Churchill's Life and Political Philosophy.* London: Shepheard-Walwyn, 2009.

Hastings, Max. *Catastrophe 1914: Europe Goes to War,* 2013. Paperback edition, New York: Vintage Books, 2014.

Herman, Arthur. *Gandhi & Churchill.* New York: Bantam, 2007.

Hickman, Tom. *Churchill's Bodyguard.* London: Headline, 2005.

Higgins, Trumbull. *Winston Churchill and the Dardanelles: A Dialogue of Ends and Means.* London: Heinemann, 1963.

Hitler, Adolf. *Mein Kampf,* 2 vols., 1925–26. Abridged English edition, London: Hurst & Blackett, 1933.

Hough, Richard. *Winston and Clementine.* London: Bantam, 1990.

Howells, Roy. *Simply Churchill.* London: Robert Hale, 1965.

Hull, Cordell. *Memoirs of Cordell Hull,* 2 vols. New York: Macmillan, 1948.

Hunt, James D. *Gandhi in London.* New Delhi: Promilla, 1993.

Hunter, Ian, ed. *Winston and Archie: The Letters of Sir Archibald Sinclair and Winston S. Churchill 1915–1960.* London: Politico's, 2005.

Irving, David. *Churchill's War.* Bullsbrook, Australia: Veritas, 1987.

Jaffa, Harry V., ed. *Statesmanship: Essays in Honor of Sir Winston Churchill.* Durham, N.C.: Carolina Academic Press, 1981.

Johnson, Boris. *The Churchill Factor.* London: Hodder & Stoughton, 2014.

Johnson, Paul. *Churchill.* New York: Viking, 2009.

Jones, R.V. *Most Secret War.* London: Coronet, 1979.

Keyes, Ralph. *The Quote Verifier.* New York: St. Martin's, 2006.

Kilzer, Louis. *Churchill's Deception: The Dark Secret that Destroyed Nazi Germany.* New York: Simon & Schuster 1994.

Kimball, Warren F. *Churchill & Roosevelt, The Complete Correspondence,* 3 vols. Princeton, N.J.: Princeton University Press, 1984.

_____. *Forged in War: Roosevelt, Churchill and the Second World War.* New York: Morrow, 1997.

_____. *The Juggler: Franklin Roosevelt as Wartime Statesman.* Princeton, N.J.: Princeton University Press, 1991.

Kolko, Gabriel. *The Politics of War: The World and United States Foreign Policy 1943–1945.* New York: Pantheon, 1990.

Lamb, Richard. *Churchill as War Leader: Right or Wrong?* London: Bloomsbury, 1991.

Langworth, Richard M., ed. *Churchill by Himself.* New York, Rosetta Books, 2015.

_____, ed. *Churchill in His Own Words.* London: Ebury Press, 2012; New York: Rosetta Books, 2015.

Lascelles, Alan. *King's Counsellor: Abdication and War.* London: Weidenfeld & Nicolson, 2006.

Lee, Celia, and John Lee. *Winston & Jack: The Churchill Brothers.* London: Privately published, 2007.

Leslie, Anita. *Edwardians in Love.* London: Hutchinson, 1972.

_____. *Lady Randolph Churchill: The Story of Jennie Jerome*. New York: Scribner 1969.

_____. *The Remarkable Mr. Jerome*. New York: Henry Holt 1954.

Leslie, Shane. *Long Shadows*. London: Murray 1966.

Lewin, Ronald. *Ultra Goes to War*. New York: McGraw-Hill, 1978.

Longmate, Norman. *Air Raid: The Bombing of Coventry*. London: Hutchinson, 1976.

Lough, David. *No More Champagne: Churchill and His Money*. New York: Picador, 2015.

Maier, Thomas. *When Lions Roar: The Churchills and the Kennedys*. New York: Crown, 2014.

Majdalnay, Fred. *Cassino: Portrait of a Battle*. London: Longmans Green, 1957.

Manchester, William. *The Last Lion: Winston Spencer Churchill,* vol. 1, *Visions of Glory 1874–1932*; vol. 2, *Alone 1932–1940*. Boston: Little Brown, 1982, 1988.

Manchester, William, and Paul Reid. *The Last Lion: Winston Spencer Churchill,* vol. 3, *Defender of the Realm 1940–1965*. New York: Little Brown, 2012.

Martin, Ralph G. *Jennie,* vol. 1, *The Romantic Years 1854–1895; Jennie, The Dramatic Years 1895–1921*. Englewood Cliffs, New Jersey: Prentice-Hall 1969, 1971.

Mawdsley, Evan. *The Russian Civil War*. London: Pegasus, 2007.

Meacham, Jon. *Franklin and Winston*. New York: Random House, 2003.

Moir, Phyllis. *I Was Winston Churchill's Private Secretary*. New York: Wilfred Funk, 1941.

Montague Browne, Anthony. *Long Sunset: Memoirs of Winston Churchill's Last Private Secretary*. London: Cassell, 1995.

Moorhead, Allan. *Gallipoli*. New York: Harper, 1956.

Moran, Lord. *Churchill: Taken from the Diaries of Lord Moran. The Struggle for Survival 1940–1965*. Boston: Houghton Mifflin, 1966.

Morgan, Ted. *Churchill: The Rise to Failure*. London: Jonathan Cape, 1983.

Mukerjee, Madhusree. *Churchill's Secret War: The British Empire and the Ravaging of India during World War II*. New York, Basic Books, 2010.

Muller, James W. ed. *Churchill as Peacemaker*. Cambridge: Cambridge University Press, 2003.

Neitzel, Soenke, and Harald Welzer. *Soldaten: On Fighting, Killing, and Dying: the Secret WWII transcripts of German POWs*. Melbourne: Scribe, 2012.

Nel, Elizabeth. *Mr. Churchill's Secretary*. London: Hodder & Stoughton, 1958.

Nicolson, Harold. *Diaries and Letters 1939–45*. London: Collins, 1967.

Norman, Andrew. *Winston Churchill: Portrait of an Unquiet Mind*. London: Pen & Sword Books 2012.

Palmer, Alan. *The Kaiser: Warlord of the Second Reich*. New York: Scribner, 1978.

Pearson, John. *Citadel of the Heart: The Private Lives of Winston Churchill*. New York: Simon & Schuster, 1991.

Pelling, Henry. *Winston Churchill*, 1974. Revised and extended edition, Ware, Herts.: Wordsworth Editions, 1999.

Petacco, Arrigo. *Dear Benito—caro Winston*. Rome, Mondadori, 1985

Petropoulos, Jonathan. *Royals and the Reich*. Oxford: Oxford University Press, 2006.

Pilpel, Robert. *Churchill in America 1895–1961: An Affectionate Portrait*. New York: Harcourt, Brace, Jovanovich, 1976.

Ponting, Clive. *Churchill*. London: Sinclair Stevenson, 1994.

_____. *1940: Myth and Reality*. London: Hamish Hamilton 1990.

Pugh, Martin. *State and Society: A Social and Political History of Britain since 1870*, 4th ed. London: Oxford University Press, 2012.

Purnell, Sonia. *First Lady: The Life and Wars of Clementine Churchill*. New York: Viking, 2015.

Ramsay, David A. *Lusitania: Saga and Myth*. New York: Norton, 2002.

Reid, Percy. *Churchill: Townsman of Westerham*. Folkestone, Kent: Regency, 1969.

Rey-Ximena, José. *El Vuelo de Ibis*. Madrid: Editions Facta, 2008.

Rhodes James, Robert. *The British Revolution 1880–1939*. London: Random House, 1977.

_____. *Churchill: A Study in Failure 1900–1939*. London: Weidenfeld & Nicolson, 1970.

_____. *Gallipoli: A British Historian's View*. Parkville, Victoria, Australia: Department of History, University of Melbourne, 1965.

_____, ed. *Winston S. Churchill: His Complete Speeches 1874–1965*, 8 vols. New York: Bowker, 1974.

Riott, Pat. *The Greatest Story Never Told: Winston Churchill and the Crash of 1929*. Oak Brook, Ill.: Nanoman, 1994.

Roose, Robson. *Remarks upon Some Diseases of the Nervous System*. Brighton: Curtis Bros. & Townes 1875.

Rose, Norman. *Churchill: The Unruly Giant*. New York: Free Press, 1995.

Rose, Richard, ed. *Studies in British Politics*. London: Macmillan, 1969.

Rosebery, Lord. *Lord Randolph Churchill*. London: Arthur Humphreys, 1906.

Roskill, Stephen. *Churchill and the Admirals*. London: Collins, 1977.

Rowse, A.L. *The Later Churchills*. London: Macmillan, 1958.

Rumbelow, Donald. *The Siege of Sidney Street: The True Story of Winston Churchill and the Anarchist Rebellion of 1911*. London: St. Martin's Press, 1974.

Russell, Douglas S. *Winston Churchill Soldier: The Military Life of a Gentleman at War*. London: Brassey's, 2005.

Ryan, Henry Butterfield. *The Vision of Anglo-America: The US–UK Alliance and the Emerging Cold War 1943–1946*. Cambridge: Cambridge University Press, 1987.

Scotland, Alexander P. *The London Cage*, 1957. New edition, London: George Mann Books, 1973.

Sebba, Anne. *American Jennie: The Remarkable Life of Lady Randolph Churchill*. New York: Norton, 2007.

Seldon, Anthony. *Churchill's Indian Summer: The Conservative Government 1951–55*. London: Hodder & Stoughton, 1981.

Service, Robert. *Comrades! A History of World Com-*

munism. Cambridge, Mass.: Harvard University Press, 2007.

Simpson, Colin. *The Lusitania*. Boston: Little Brown, 1972.

Singer, Barry. *Churchill Style: The Art of Being Winston Churchill*. New York: Abrams, 2012.

Snagge, John. *Those Vintage Years of Radio*. London: Pitman, 1972.

Soames, Mary. *A Churchill Family Album*. London: Allen Lane, 1982.

_____. *Clementine Churchill*. Boston: Houghton Mifflin, 1979.

_____, ed. *Speaking for Themselves: The Personal Letters of Winston and Clementine Churchill*. New York: Doubleday, 1998.

Spaak, Paul-Henri. *The Continuing Battle: Memoirs of a European 1936–1966*. Boston: Littlehampton, 1971.

Stafford, David. *Churchill and Secret Service*. Toronto: Stoddart, 1997.

_____. *Roosevelt and Churchill: Men of Secrets*. Woodstock, N.Y.: Overlook Press, 1999.

Sterling, Christopher H., *Writing about Winston*. Washington: Self-published, 2013.

Stevenson, William. *A Man Called Intrepid*. New York: Ballantine, 1982.

Strange, Robert. *Who Sank the Titanic? The Final Verdict*. London, Pen & Sword Books, 2012.

Taylor, A.J.P., ed. *Churchill: Four Faces and the Man*. London: Allen Lane, The Penguin Press, 1969.

Taylor, Robert Lewis. *Winston Churchill: An Informal Study of Greatness*. Garden City, N.Y.: Doubleday, 1952.

Terraine, John. *A Time for Courage: The Royal Air Force in the European War 1939–1945*. New York: Macmillan, 1985.

Theakston, Kevin. *Winston Churchill and the British Constitution*. London: Politico's, 2004.

Thompson, Carlos. *The Assassination of Winston Churchill*. Gerrard's Cross: Smythe, 1969.

Tolppanen, Bradley P. *Churchill in North America, 1929*. Jefferson, N.C.: McFarland, 2014.

Wallin, Jeffrey D. *By Ships Alone: Churchill and the Dardanelles, Politics and Strategy of a Decision*. Durham, N.C.: Carolina Academic Press, 1981.

Winterbotham, F.W. *The Ultra Secret*. New York: Harper & Row, 1974.

Yapp, Malcolm E. *The Making of the Modern Near East 1792–1923*. London: Longman, 1988.

Periodicals

American Historical Review 1933

The Atlantic, 2009

BookRags, 2005–06

Canadian Encyclopedia, 2012

Canadian Slavonic Papers, 1987

Churchill Proceedings, 1994–2000

CIA World Fact Book, 2016

Commentary, 1978

Coronet, 1944

Daily Beast, 2015

Daily Mail, 2014

Daily Telegraph, 2008–16

Finest Hour (Journal of the International Churchill Society), 1968–date

The Guardian, 2013

Haaretz, 2012

Hansard (Parliamentary Debates) 1944–2001

Huffington Post, 2015

Imperial War Museum Review, 1999

Indianapolis Star, 1972

Jamaica Observer, 2012

Jewish Star, 2015

Jewish World Review, 1999

JOM (International Minerals, Metals & Materials Society), 1998

Journal of Modern History, 1954

Morning Post, 1914

New York Times Sunday Book Review, 2011

Nexus (New England Historic Genealogical Society), 1988–1997

Proceedings of the International Churchill Society, 1987–1993

Scribners Commentator, 1941

Slavonic and East European Review, 1933

The Spectator, 1999–2014

Sunday Telegraph, 1990

Time, 1939–2010

The Times (London), 1976–2006

Index

Numbers in **_bold italics_** indicate pages with photographs.